ALSO BY NANCY SILVERTON

The Mozza Cookbook
(with Matt Molina and Carolynn Carreño)

A Twist of the Wrist
(with Carolynn Carreño)

Nancy Silverton's Sandwich Book
(with Teri Gelber)

Nancy Silverton's Pastries from the La Brea Bakery
(in collaboration with Teri Gelber)

The Food of Campanile
(with Mark Peel)

Nancy Silverton's Breads from the La Brea Bakery
(in collaboration with Laurie Ochoa)

Mark Peel and Nancy Silverton at Home:
Two Chefs Cook for Family and Friends

Desserts
(with Heidi Yorkshire)

MOZZA
AT HOME

MOZZA
AT HOME

More than 150 Crowd-Pleasing Recipes for Relaxed, Family-Style Entertaining

Nancy Silverton

WITH CAROLYNN CARREÑO

Photographs by Christopher Hirsheimer

ALFRED A. KNOPF   NEW YORK   2016

THIS IS A BORZOI BOOK
PUBLISHED BY ALFRED A. KNOPF

www.aaknopf.com

Knopf, Borzoi Books, and the colophon are registered trademarks of
Penguin Random House LLC.

Library of Congress Cataloging-in-Publication Data
Silverton, Nancy, author.
Mozza at home / by Nancy Silverton with Carolynn Carreño;
photographs by Christopher Hirsheimer.
pages   cm
Includes index.
ISBN 978-0-385-35432-5 (hardcover)—ISBN 978-0-385-35433-2 (ebook)
1. Cooking, Italian.   2. Entertaining.   3. Pizzeria Mozza.
I. Carreño, Carolynn, author.   II. Hirsheimer, Christopher, photographer.   III. Title.
TX723.S4838 2016   641.5945—dc23   2015029125

Jacket photographs by Christopher Hirsheimer
Jacket design by Abby Weintraub

Manufactured in China/Singapore
First Edition

To my parents, Doris and Larry
Thank you for our nightly family table,
the most beautiful experience a child can ever have.

Contents

6

7

MOZZA
AT HOME

Introduction

Owning four busy Mozza restaurants in Southern California and two in Singapore, it's surprisingly easy to forget how and why I started down the path that led me here so many years ago: because of the immense pleasure I get from cooking a meal and serving it to family and friends. For many years while running La Brea Bakery and the pastry kitchen at Campanile, my first restaurant, which I opened in 1989 with my then husband, I didn't cook at all—other than foods, such as pasta with butter, for my kids' dinner. But that changed about fifteen years ago, when I started spending time in Italy. From the very first summer that I rented an apartment in a small medieval hill town on the Umbria-Tuscany border where I now own a home, my being situated in Umbria and the bounty of the area turned out to be the perfect storm that blew me back into the kitchen.

With local ingredients including cherry tomatoes, red torpedo onions, and fragrant basil at the height of their season; regional specialties such as chickpeas, lentils, and sheep's milk cheese; long summer days when it stays light until almost ten o'clock; and an endless cast of hungry friends who arrived weekly from Los Angeles and rented apartments and houses in the same town, I started cooking again—more than I ever had. And despite the fact that I had rented a house with a tiny kitchen stocked with aluminum pots and pans and one dull knife, I was reminded of how much I love preparing food for family and friends—old and new.

My friend Suzanne Tracht, also a chef and restaurant owner, of the Los Angeles chophouse Jar, had rented an apartment right on the piazza, in the center of town. During the day, Suzanne and I and other friends would explore the surrounding areas, discovering cheese makers, farm stands, outdoor markets that popped up in different towns on different days, and little artisan shops that sold pastas, oils, vinegars, and other condiments. We were like kids in candy stores. We bought everything that delighted us, brought it home to our inadequate kitchens, and we cooked. And cooked and cooked.

While we were preparing the food, the guys and the kids would set up a long table outside, essentially *in* the piazza (in fact, an indoor/outdoor restaurant now exists in the very space where we once put our table). Suzanne and I would put out platters of food as they were done, preparations that showcased all the wonderful ingredients we found locally: balsamic-glazed onions with fresh bay leaves, slow-roasted tomatoes on the vine, radicchio salad, hand-sliced local prosciutto, and grilled bread—simple, rustic foods that could be prepared ahead of time, so we could sit down and enjoy the meal with everyone else. Soon, we discovered we loved our own private "restaurant" as much as going out, and we began to entertain in this way night after night and, after I bought a home in the town, year after year.

Meanwhile, back in Los Angeles, I had a patio built, including an outdoor fireplace to cook in and a wisteria-covered pergola under which I put a long dining table. And I began to entertain not just in Italy in the summertime, but on a year-round basis. Over the last fifteen years, I have found myself saying countless times, "Let's have it at my house." I've hosted regular weeknight get-togethers with close friends, baby showers for Mozza staff members, birthday parties, charity events, and even a couple of weddings.

This book is a collection of recipes that reflects the style I developed in cooking those meals. There are no intricately plated dishes here and nothing that needs to be served piping hot. Antipasti, whether Marinated Olives with Fresh Pecorino, Pickled Vegetables, or Pimento Cheese with Celery Sticks, can be put out while you're assembling the rest of the meal. Salads, built of sturdy lettuces such as radicchio and other chicories, Little Gem, and hearts of romaine that don't wilt quickly, are piled high in large, wide-mouthed bowls. The simple preparations of side dishes such as Slow-Roasted Roma Tomatoes with Garlic and Thyme, Corn on the Cob with Chile Butter, Roasted Carrots with Chickpeas and Cumin, and Roasted Asparagus with Herb Vinaigrette take advantage of the natural flavor of seasonal vegetables. And main dishes are kept simple, either marinated and grilled, as is the case with Grilled Lamb Shoulder Chops with Mint Yogurt Sauce and Sicilian Swordfish Spiedini, or as with Dave's Oven-Roasted Grouper with Spicy Tomato Marmalade and Tahini, and are cooked in the oven and served in the pans in which they were cooked.

I'm not saying these are thirty-minute meals, because they're not. Home cooking is often slow cooking. There is no shortcut to braising an oxtail, but it *can* be done in advance, and the oven does all the work for you while you're making side dishes or taking a shower. Eggplant Lasagne, made with store-bought noodles, can be assembled hours ahead and put in the oven just in time for dinner. And all of the desserts can be made many hours prior to serving time. Or maybe not at all. When I don't have time to prepare dessert, I pass ice cream bars around after dinner, or toss a selection of artisan candy bars into the center of the table. Friends break them up and share. It's like breaking bread—only sweeter. That, for me, is what entertaining is all about.

The book is organized by meals; for each, I give one main dish and a selection of antipasti, side dishes, and salads to choose from to go with the main dish. Additionally, I give suggestions under the heading "Other Menu Options" for recipes that appear elsewhere in the book but would complement the meal. My idea in building the book this way isn't that you make everything listed (which would be impossible or at least insane in some instances), but that you use the items listed as a guideline for what to serve with this main dish. These are flavors and textures that go well together and that wouldn't offend me if I saw them all on one plate. I'm not a fan of potlucks for that very reason: people bring all kinds of things that don't necessarily go with one another but that end up touching each other on guests' plates. I do understand the appeal of the potluck in terms of easing the load for the host or hostess. If you have a friend or family member who enjoys cooking or baking and really wants to contribute, have them choose from the recipes listed under the main dish you're making.

Desserts are in their own chapter. For each dessert I suggest what main dishes I would serve it with, and there are a few cases in which I am specific about which dessert I recommend, such as Mexican Wedding Cookies with Sal's Roasted Pork Shoulder. But with few exceptions, you could serve any dessert with any meal in the book.

Because I really just *love* feeding crowds of people, working on the recipes in this book challenged me to think about how to optimize the guests' experience. When I started out, my one requirement was that every dish should hold up on a buffet, which meant it had to taste good at room temperature, wouldn't wilt after an hour, and also wouldn't look terrible as guests started digging in. But as I got into the process of producing the book, all the while hosting dinners and parties offering the foods that I was including here, I went a step further: I began to think of creative ways that I could make the buffet table work to my advantage. I started putting a block of cheese and a grater alongside salads that called for grated cheese, such as the Whole Leaf Caesar Salad with Fried

Parsley Leaves and Anchovy Croutons, so that guests could grate a fresh dusting of cheese on their own servings. Having the cheese and grater also makes it easy for me to freshen up the serving bowl with a snowdrift of cheese when I walk by. I knew I couldn't put an arugula salad on my buffet table, because arugula wilts if you look at it sideways. But when I found myself wanting arugula alongside Prosciutto Mozzarella Parcels, I found a way to do it: I put out a bowl of arugula, along with bottles of olive oil and balsamic vinegar, and bowls of lemon and sea salt for guests to make their own arugula salads on their plates. In many instances, such as with Flattened Chicken Thighs with Charred Lemon Salsa Verde or Blistered Green Beans with Yogurt Dressing, I spoon or drizzle just enough sauce on the dish so guests understand where it goes, and serve the rest on the side. The desserts are left unsliced, presented with a knife so guests can cut the size serving they want. And the frostings for Spiced Carrot Cake with Molasses Cream Cheese Frosting and Devil's Food Rings with Spiced White Mountain Frosting are served on the side. I think personalizing your food adds to your guests' experience, and that's what I am after when I entertain. I want to offer my friends and family not just great food, but a great *experience*. Because I can't have all of you to my house, I hope you'll enjoy the experience of cooking from this book—and, of course, I hope you'll enjoy the food.

How to Pull It Off

I recently wrote a story for the *Los Angeles Times* revealing my biggest secret when it comes to entertaining: enlisting the help of your guests. When I have a party—whether it's a huge fund-raising event or a dozen friends on a weeknight—I can say without a doubt: I never do it alone. For one, I *couldn't* do it alone. The kind of food I cook involves some effort. There are vinaigrettes to whisk, vegetables to roast, salads to toss. Even the simplest appetizer, guacamole and chips, needs somebody to put those two things in bowls and carry them to the table. And that's just the food. Wine bottles need to be opened, bags of ice dumped into the beverage tub, the grill needs to be lit, the table needs to be set. Then there are the candles, the music, the sweeping of the patio . . . If I had to do it all myself, I probably wouldn't find myself saying, "Let's have it at my house," as often as I do. But the other, more important reason to enlist help is that it's so much more fun to prepare a meal with friends.

In my mother's day, the hostess would never have asked her friends to pitch in. My mother, for instance, despite the fact that she worked as a television writer while raising two children, would have wanted to take care of every last detail. When guests arrived, it wasn't, "Here, put this on the table," as I am known to do. My mother (and probably every other woman of her generation) wanted her guests to be impressed, to wonder how she did it. And these were her friends! Thankfully, times have changed. There is no illusion or façade, at least not in my world. My friends all know how much effort it takes to host a meal, large or small, and when we're not hosting, we want to help the one who is.

I do want to emphasize that I'm a nice "boss." When my volunteer help comes, I always offer them a glass of wine, and our own little party starts while we pile side dishes onto platters and look for just the right serving utensils to go with them.

Cooking from This Book

Each of these chapters is built around a main dish, with a list of side dishes and condiments to serve with it. In some chapters, the list includes more options than you may want to make. In addition to the items listed in the menus is a list of "Other Menu Options." These are dishes that exist elsewhere in the book but that go well with the main dish in the chapter. Pick from these lists to create a menu that works for you, based on what you feel like cooking and what is in season.

All of the recipes in this book make enough for six or more. I figure if you are cooking for others, the least number you could be is four. You're probably six, and if you're anything like me, the minute you decide to have people over, you start thinking of who you want to invite, and you're up to ten. The truth is that because these aren't plated dinners, guests take what they want. So the serving size of any one dish depends on how many total dishes you're serving. When I plan a menu, I always err on the side of more because I like to offer a variety. I also tend to get carried away creatively. Thankfully, I'm a big fan of leftovers.

A Note on Olive Oil

You'll notice I make three distinctions when I call for olive oil in the recipes in this book: olive oil, extra-virgin olive oil, and finishing-quality extra-virgin olive oil. Although this might seem like a lot of bottles of olive oil to buy or have on your counter, it might actually save you money because you won't be using your good olive oil where it doesn't make a difference. When I call for "olive oil," I'm referring to any decent olive oil. I use this when the oil isn't a component to a dish or a condiment—for instance, to sear or roast vegetables or meats. This olive oil doesn't even need to be extra virgin. It just needs to not be rancid; over time, you'll learn to recognize rancid oil by the smell. If you cook much at all, this oil won't go rancid because you'll use it more than any other oil. I call for "extra-virgin olive oil" when the oil is part of the finished product, such as a vinaigrette or salsa verde. For this, I use a slightly higher quality oil; I prefer those produced in Italy, Spain, or France. "Finishing-quality extra-virgin olive oil" is my way of referring to the special, costlier bottles of olive oil that you see in specialty food stores. I reach for one of these when I am using the oil as a condiment, whether to drizzle over a vegetable dish or grilled meats, or as an unexpected complement for the Bittersweet Chocolate Tartufo with Olive Oil Croutons and Sea Salt.

A Note on Anchovies

Alici di Cetara are a very special variety of anchovies from a seaside village called Cetara on Italy's Amalfi Coast; they have all the deliciousness of the fish with none of the hard-to-take, overly fishy qualities often associated with anchovies. Cetara anchovies are harvested from April to September and placed in large plastic drums, layered in salt, where they remain for twelve months. After that time, the anchovies are cleaned, dried, filleted by hand, and laid out on linen cloths to dry, a process that supposedly absorbs some of their briny flavor. The fish are packed standing up in either sunflower oil, olive oil, or a combination. I generally like salt-packed anchovies better than those packed in oil, but these are the exception. I use them anytime I am serving anchovies in their whole form (other than marinated white anchovies, which are a different thing altogether). You can find them at online outlets that specialize in Italian food exports.

What Kind of Yogurt to Use

I call for yogurt in several recipes in this book. In Los Angeles, we're lucky to have a specialty Greek grocery named Papa Cristo's, where we get fresh yogurt made that day. In these recipes, I specify the yogurt that I found was the closest in consistency to Papa Cristo's and also widely available, Straus Family Creamery Organic Greek Yogurt, which is thinner than other commercial Greek-style yogurts. If you can't find Straus (or a place like Papa Cristo's where you can buy homemade Greek yogurt), use regular whole-milk plain yogurt.

Washing Greens

You may notice that in these recipes I don't ask you to wash and dry lettuce or other greens. The reason is that I assume home cooks wash and dry all vegetables and fruits before cooking them. When making salads, it's important that the vegetables be completely dry before you dress them; I do this by using a salad spinner, or draining the vegetables in a colander and then spreading them out on a dry dish towel or paper towels to drain. I am a fan of prewashed lettuce and other greens that are now widely available at farmers' markets.

Color Is Flavor!

One of the things I'm known to say in the kitchen is "Color is flavor!" I say this when I want my cooks to achieve that beautiful, dark golden color that makes vegetables and meats look so appetizing. Whether it's Glazed Onions Agrodolce or the broccolini for Charred Broccolini with Salami and Burrata, the deep brown color, a result of direct, high-heat cooking, is part of both the visual appeal and the flavor of the finished dish. The challenge is to get that color without overcooking the vegetables or meat in the process. At Mozza, we are able to get that deep brown caramelization because our ovens are extremely powerful. At the Pizzeria specifically, to roast vegetables we use the pizza oven, which offers intense heat, and also a solid surface (as opposed to an oven rack) that conducts heat evenly. The pizza oven gave me the idea to try using the oven floor to imitate that solid surface, and it worked perfectly.

Thus, throughout these recipes, you will see that I often call for you to put the baking sheet on the oven floor. In some ovens, the heating mechanism is on the oven floor, so you don't have the option of putting a baking sheet on it. In that case, I offer an alternative of putting a rack as close to the floor as possible, and putting a pizza stone on the rack, if you have one.

To the same end, I often call for large baking sheets throughout these recipes. By "large," I'm referring specifically to a half sheet pan (so named because it mimics the pan used to make a half sheet cake), which is 12 x 16 inches and fits in every home oven I've ever encountered. It's important when you're roasting vegetables that they are spread out in a single layer. If they're too close together or on top of one another, the water released from the vegetables during cooking will cause the vegetables to steam rather than roast. Half sheet pans aren't expensive. I suggest you invest in two or even four, and make sure they're industrial-quality, thicker baking sheets, which are available anywhere cooking supplies are sold. The thicker baking sheets conduct heat better than thinner baking sheets do, which means they provide a hotter, more even cooking surface, and they don't buckle in the oven the way thin baking sheets do. Once you invest in them, if you're not already in the habit of doing so, you'll be amazed at how often you reach for baking sheets when you cook—to put seared vegetables or meats on when you take them out of the pan; to bring foods outside to grill; to chill grains, pasta, and vegetables after they're boiled or blanched; to put pie and tart dishes on, making them easier to slide into the oven and to catch juices that bubble over the dish, and, of course, to roast vegetables.

Buffet versus Sit Down

The majority of the meals in this book were designed to be served buffet style, but if you are serving a party of ten or fewer, serve family style, if you prefer. I'm a big fan of the buffet, for a lot of reasons. As a hostess, I like the abundant look of a buffet and the "water cooler" aspect, meaning that the buffet table is a great place for guests to interact with one another. Serving this way also ensures that guests won't be seated next to the same person for two hours the way they would be at a sit-down dinner, so each guest will get a chance to meet or visit with more guests. As an eater, I like a buffet because I like to eat standing up; I'm definitely of the school that food eaten standing up doesn't have calories in it. Also, I'm a picker. I'd much prefer to go back to the buffet repeatedly, for a bit of this and a bit of that, rather than commit to a big plate of food, and then sit down and eat it all at once.

That said, every once in a while I do like to serve a sit-down dinner. There's something nice about passing side dishes at the table, like a big family, and seeing the large serving platters of food that guests can dig in to for seconds and thirds throughout the meal. The Backyard Peel 'n' Eat Shrimp Boil is especially suited to a sit-down dinner. I put a giant bowl of shrimp on my outdoor table with dipping sauces alongside; guests sit around the table peeling and eating and making a fun, communal mess. The Braised Oxtails and the Saturday Night Chicken Thighs with Italian Sausage and Spicy Pickled Peppers are also conducive to serving family style. They both look so beautiful and dramatic, served in the dishes in which they were baked; it's nice to plunk the dishes down so guests can appreciate how pretty they are.

Presenting Food

For me, part of creating a beautiful party is how I present the food. Whether it's a buffet or sit-down, I want my table to look rustic, abundant, and with a balance of shapes, colors, sizes, and textures both in terms of the food and what it's presented on. Nothing has to match, but everything has to go together. I might have a tiny dish of braised garlic cloves, presented like delicious little jewels in a bowl I found at an Italian flea market. I'll lay out a selection of sliced meats on a cutting board made for me by my dad. I put side dishes in one of the many serving bowls I've collected or that people have given me as gifts over the years. And I pile a salad in a wooden bowl with natural edges, carved by an artisan out of a single piece of wood and that, when it isn't holding lettuce leaves, sits in my living room as an art piece.

In each of the recipes, I give suggestions for serving, including what type of vessel to present the food in. In general, when selecting a serving piece, choose a platter, cutting board, cake stand, or bowl that enhances the natural beauty of the food. Also, make sure the food looks abundant, which usually means, reach for something that is smaller than you think you will need. The one exception is salads, which are best in wide-mouthed bowls, so the leaves don't get crushed by their own weight.

If you like to host dinners or parties, whether for forty people or just four (which I assume you do if you're holding this book), I suggest you embark on the rewarding and entertaining project of collecting platters, plates, baking dishes, cutting boards, and serving utensils. They don't have to be expensive. You can find these at flea markets, thrift stores, and made by artisans when you travel. If you're like me, you'll enjoy pulling out these finds when the need arises, and remembering where they came from. And you'll get pleasure seeing the fruits of your kitchen labors looking so pretty, as they will when presented on just the right thing.

Platters Living in California, I'm a fan of Heath, an iconic ceramics producer from Sausalito, in Northern California. Over the years, I've collected Heath serving platters and bowls in every size and shape imaginable. I've stuck to a color palette of earth tones, so there aren't any two items in my cupboards that won't look good together. When you buy items that you like, you'll find they all work together, because even if they seem random, they're bound by one thing: your taste.

Serving Utensils What can I say except that no matter how many serving utensils I have, I always need more. There is invariably that one dish or condiment or cheese that begs for a specific type of tongs or spoon or a tiny ladle or a forked spoon or . . . Again, buy them when you see them. Scour flea markets when you're abroad. Buy what you love. You'll be so pleased when you open the drawer and find just the utensil you need.

Baking Dishes Throughout these recipes you'll see many foods that I suggest you serve in the same dish they're baked in. I love this style of cooking and serving. I like the look of the layers and cooked-on bits encrusted along the sides of the pan, which are like evidence of the long cooking it took to make it. I like the feeling of bringing this homemade creation to the table. And I also like the excuse to buy rustic cast-iron, enamel, or hand-forged copper pots when I find ones I love. In Italy they have a word for a baking dish that is pretty enough to be acceptable to take to the table: a *pirafola*. We all have our own standards as to what we'd be willing to present at our table and what we wouldn't, so go with what works for you. You could, of course, transfer the food to a serving platter, and in many recipes I've given you directions for both ways of presenting a dish, but for me, there's something wonderfully satisfying about going from start to finish in one pan. To me, transferring food to a clean platter is the equivalent of a woman who is all fixed up with plastic surgery compared with a beautifully aged woman whose beauty is enhanced by her gray hair, wrinkles, and other so-called imperfections.

Napkins These days I really don't see any reason to use paper napkins. Cloth napkins are so inexpensive. And it's really not that much work to use them. Unlike my mother, I do not iron my napkins. I wash, fold, and go. Come party time, there is invariably one friend who comes early to help but doesn't feel comfortable cooking, and I give him or her the task of rolling silverware in cloth napkins, often tying them with butcher's twine.

Who Is Liz?

Throughout this book, you'll hear me mention the name Liz—a lot. Liz is Liz Hong, the executive chef of Osteria and Pizzeria Mozza. Liz started with us in 2008, working with me behind the Mozzarella Bar on toast duty (which, at Osteria Mozza, is not the small job you might think). From there, Liz was promoted to the salad station, and she worked her way through the various stations and up the ranks until she became the chef at the Pizzeria. When I started thinking of this book and who I wanted to help me create the recipes, Liz leaped to mind. Not only did I know she had the cooking knowledge and talent to do it, but more important, Liz loves a project. Evidently, the fifty or sixty hours a week she works as a chef aren't enough. Whenever I want to play with creating a dish, to hunt down an unusual or hard-to-find ingredient, or to make something outside the Mozza repertoire for a special event, Liz is the first to volunteer. And Liz turned out to be the perfect choice for this book. For a year and a half, she worked tirelessly, implementing my vision for a recipe and often injecting her own to make it better. In fact, we worked so well together and I came to trust her work ethic and her cooking sensibility to such a degree that, when, recently, my partners and I were faced with the near-impossible challenge of filling the shoes of Matt Molina, our founding executive chef, Liz, again, was the obvious choice for the job. Talk about hard work paying off.

1

Umbrian Tavola 18

Other Menu Options

Umbrian Tavola

This meal is different from all the others in the book in that there is no main dish listed here. The focus of the meal is the collection of side dishes that I set out on the *tavola*, or, "table," at my house in Umbria. The tavola changes from one party to another, and my repertoire has expanded throughout the years to the point where about a third of the vegetable and legume dishes in this book have been on that table at one time or another. Although I don't give a meat recipe here, I do always serve meat and, in fact, my tavola is often an excuse to cook the meat that I've brought home after a day trip to Dario Cecchini's butcher shop in Tuscany. I usually favor *bistecca alla Fiorentina*, which is a thick-cut T-bone, grilled and sliced, and a selection of Italian pork sausages that are also cooked on the grill. If you don't want to fire up the grill, serve a selection of *affettati*, Italian sliced meats, and a variety of fresh cheeses, such as burrata, mozzarella di bufala, and fresh ricotta, as the centerpiece.

There are an extraordinary number of additional menu options listed here, and that's no coincidence: my original idea for this book was that it be a collection of recipes for what and how I cook in Italy. When planning which dishes to serve on your tavola, think about the balance of colors, flavors, and textures you will be serving, as well as the cooking methods that will be required. If you plan to fire up an outdoor grill, pick a few items that you can cook on it. Choose one or two easy items, and another two or three things that can be made well in advance of serving them.

Ella's Pinzimonio

Even though I've spent every summer since 2000 in the same town in Umbria, it wasn't until the summer of 2014 that I discovered, through Carolynn Carreño, my friend and coauthor of this book, a vegetable stand that sold beautiful produce, all grown right on the property, about a ten-minute drive from my house. Carolynn had shopped there a number of times over the years and assumed I had, too, but when she drove me there for the first time, I was stunned—both at how great it was and also that I didn't know about it. That same summer, I was hosting a party for my friend Phil Rosenthal, who was in town from Los Angeles filming me and "my Umbria" for his PBS television show, *I'll Have What Phil's Having.* Inspired by the beautiful produce at my newly discovered stand, I decided to serve *pinzimonio,* which is basically Italian crudites. The man who runs the stand told me to come back the next day so he could pick what I wanted for my party fresh that morning, and when I arrived the next day, he handed me a big wooden box loaded with gorgeous just-picked carrots, celery, cucumbers, onions, and radicchio.

Meanwhile, back at the house, Carolynn, along with a talented young Angeleno chef, Ella Freyinger, who was staying in my town for the summer with her husband, Ben, were helping me cook for the party. I handed the box over to Ella and Carolynn and left for a few hours to film with Phil. When I came back, I found that they had taken an enormous olive wood board that I had in my kitchen, lined it with fig leaves from the tree across the street, and arranged the most stunning pinzimonio I'd ever seen. The most memorable component was the spring onions, which Ella had cut into quarters and sliced very thin, with the roots still intact, so the layers stayed intact. Ella called them "eyelashes," and that's exactly what they looked like. Normally, the vegetables for pinzimonio are served unadorned, but Ella tossed the onion slices in Lemon Vinaigrette (page 125), which had the effect of softening and sweetening them as they sat out for guests. I have never seen people talk about raw onions the way they talked about these. One guest after another would approach the display of vegetables, grab a few things, and talk about how pretty and tasty everything was. But when they got around to eating an onion slice, they would just about fall over with excitement and surprise that an onion could be so delicious.

To make pinzimonio, go to a farmers' market or another source for beautiful produce and pick out the prettiest, freshest-looking vegetables you can find. Scrub
them clean and trim and cut them in a way that shows off their natural beauty.
Arrange the vegetables, grouped together, artfully on a cutting board, platter, or a
stone slab. Serve with a bowl of your best olive oil seasoned with salt and pepper,
and another bowl of lemon vinaigrette, Parmigiano Cream (page 298), or Bagna
Cauda (page 88).

Oven-Roasted Grapes on the Vine

This method of preparing and presenting grapes is a perfect example of the simple magic that happens when you put something in the oven. Of course, grapes are delicious just as they are, and you can eat or serve them without doing anything more than rinsing them. But roasting them transforms grapes into something unusual and eye-catching. Roasting intensifies the flavor of the grapes by drawing out the liquid, so they taste like a really fresh raisin. And it gives them a different kind of beauty, like the beautiful patina of old silver. These grapes could find their place on almost any table except that of a Mexican or chili-themed party, and they make a stunning and delicious accompaniment to fresh ricotta drizzled with honey, or on any cheese board.

This preparation will yield a delicious result using ordinary supermarket grapes, but it will be even better made with grapes found at farmers' markets, such as Thompson seedless, pale multicolored muscat, or super-sweet Concord grapes. Use this method to roast as many bunches of grapes as you want.

Adjust an oven rack to the middle position and preheat the oven to 350°F.

Put the grape bunches in a single layer on a baking sheet and roast them for 45 minutes to 1 hour 15 minutes, until the skins are blistered and the grapes look like they are one-third of their way to becoming raisins. The time varies depending on the size and variety of grapes you use. If you're roasting more than one variety of grapes, keep them separated on the baking sheet so you can remove each variety as it's done. Remove the grapes from the oven and carefully take the grapes from the baking sheet and lay them out on a pretty cutting board or platter. Serve on their own, with fresh ricotta, with honey, or with a selection of other cheeses as well.

Marinated Roasted Sweet Peppers

SERVES 10 OR MORE

8 large red bell peppers

½ cup extra-virgin olive oil

½ cup balsamic vinegar

4 anchovy fillets (preferably
salt-packed; rinsed and backbones
removed if salt-packed),
finely chopped and smashed
to a paste with the side of a knife

3 tablespoons capers
(preferably salt-packed; soaked for
15 minutes if salt-packed), rinsed,
drained, and finely chopped

1½ teaspoons kosher salt

6 to 7 large garlic cloves, peeled
and sliced ¹⁄₁₆ inch thick lengthwise,
preferably on a mandoline

20 to 25 small fresh basil leaves

I love roasted sweet peppers, and I'm always looking for new ways to prepare and serve them. In this recipe, I marinate roasted peppers in balsamic vinegar and layer them in a canning jar, which is both a convenient way to store them and also a pretty way to present them. When it's time to serve the peppers, I just take off the lid and plunk the jar on the table. Years ago, I visited a piquillo pepper farm in Spain. The people giving the tour informed me that it was sacrilegious to let the pepper meet the knife, ever. Now, I never cut any variety of roasted pepper, including these, because they can so easily be torn into the perfect size strip.

When choosing a balsamic vinegar to marinate the peppers in, choose a midlevel balsamic vinegar: not a hundred-dollar, thick, drizzling vinegar, but also not the three-dollar bottle you get at the supermarket. Find one in the twenty-dollar range; it will be slightly more viscous and will have better flavor. I call for red peppers because that's what I prefer to use for these, but you could also use orange or yellow if you wanted a mix of colors.

I give you methods to char the bell peppers on a grill, in a grill pan or cast-iron skillet; to roast them in the oven; or to char them directly over the flame of a gas stove.

If you have a mandoline, use it to make easy work of slicing the garlic for this recipe.

To char the peppers on a grill or in a grill pan or cast-iron skillet, preheat the grill until it is very hot or preheat the grill pan or skillet over high heat. Place the peppers on the grill or in the grill pan or skillet, and cook, turning them frequently, until they are blackened all over and softened, 10 to 20 minutes.

To char the peppers over an open flame, turn the burner on a gas range to the highest flame. Put the peppers on the burner grate and cook, turning them frequently, until they are blackened all over and softened, 10 to 20 minutes.

To char the peppers in the oven, adjust the oven rack to the middle position and preheat the oven to 500°F. Place the peppers on a baking sheet and put them in the oven until they are charred on all sides, about 20 to 35 minutes, turning them once or twice with tongs during the cooking time so they char evenly. Remove the peppers from the oven.

Put the peppers in a plastic bag or a large bowl. Close the bag or seal the bowl tightly with plastic wrap and set the peppers aside to steam until they collapse and are cool enough to touch.

Meanwhile, stir the olive oil, vinegar, anchovies, capers, and salt together in a large bowl.

Using a clean kitchen towel, rub the peppers to remove the charred skins and discard the skins. (Do not rinse the peppers under water to remove the skins; you will rinse away the char flavor you just went to great effort to achieve.) Remove and discard the core and seeds. Rip the peppers into thirds or fourths, depending on their size, and put them in the bowl with the marinade. Gently toss the peppers to coat them all over with the marinade.

Layer the peppers in a 1-quart canning jar (or another covered container), scattering the garlic slices and basil leaves between the layers of peppers and pouring a few tablespoons of the marinade between each layer. When you've put all the peppers into the jar, add enough marinade to fill the jar. Set the peppers aside to marinate for at least 20 minutes, or cover and refrigerate for up to 1 week. Bring the peppers to room temperature before serving.

Serve the peppers from the jar or layer the peppers, garlic slices, and basil leaves on a platter with a lip and drizzle the marinade over and around the peppers. Serve with tongs or a fork.

Glazed Onions Agrodolce

6 medium onions (such as torpedo onions, spring onions, Spanish yellow onions, or red onions), unpeeled

¼ cup plus 2 tablespoons extra-virgin olive oil

3 tablespoons balsamic vinegar

1 teaspoon sugar

1 teaspoon kosher salt

6 fresh bay leaves

10 fresh sage leaves

Maldon sea salt (or another flaky sea salt such as fleur de sel)

When I'm planning a dinner at my house in Panicale, the town in Italy where I have a home, I start by sitting down with a cup of coffee at the table outside my kitchen, looking out at the olive groves and my beautiful town behind them, to write my menu. Invariably, the first two things that I list are roasted tomatoes (see Slow-Roasted Roma Tomatoes with Garlic and Thyme, page 189) and these caramelized onions, which are glazed with balsamic vinegar and a tiny bit of sugar. It's a simple dish to make, and a total crowd-pleaser. Although you can use other types of onions, the dish is inspired by the Tropea, long, red torpedo onions from Calabria sold at every market and from trucks parked along the country roads throughout Umbria and Tuscany. When they're still fresh, the onion greens are braided together, so about a dozen onions hang off the braid like a giant strand of Christmas lights. I always buy a braid when I arrive; the onions look so pretty hanging on the wall in my kitchen until I get around to using them.

Agrodolce is the Italian concept of sweet and sour, in this case the sweetness of the onions and sugar comes together with the sourness of the vinegar. I nestle fresh bay and sage leaves between the onion wedges, which add a lovely aroma and look very pretty. In both Italy and Los Angeles, I go outside with a pair of scissors and pick fresh bay leaves from the bay laurel trees that grow in both yards. For me, this experience adds to the pleasure of making these onions, but those of you without a bay laurel tree can buy the leaves in the produce section; they're sold in little plastic clamshells with the other fresh herbs.

My preferred onions to use for this recipe are torpedo or spring onions, but any onions, including yellow Spanish onions or red onions, will do.

To make these onions, use a midlevel balsamic vinegar in the twenty-dollar range.

I like to serve these onions in the pan that I roast them in. If you want to serve them this way, reach for something you wouldn't mind putting on your buffet: I think they look pretty in a simple stainless steel sauté pan. Alternatively, transfer the finished onions to a platter to serve.

Adjust the oven racks so none are near the oven floor; you'll be putting a baking sheet directly on the oven floor. If you are using an electric oven or another oven where you can't put anything on the floor, adjust the oven racks so that one is closest to the floor and put a pizza stone on it, if you have one. Preheat the oven to 500°F.

Trim the root ends of the onions, trimming only the very bottom so the layers of the onions stay intact. Cut the onions into quarters or sixths (depending on size) through the root and stem ends. Cut off the greens, if you are using fresh onions with the greens attached, leaving a ½-inch "tail" on each onion.

Drizzle the olive oil and vinegar into a large ovenproof frying pan. Place the onions in the pan, sprinkle the onions with the sugar and kosher salt, and turn to coat the onion wedges on all sides with the seasonings. Arrange the onion wedges, cut side down, in a spiral, like a flower, with the stems pointed in the same direction. Nestle the bay leaves and sage leaves between the onion wedges. Cover the pan tightly with the lid or aluminum foil and put it on the oven floor or the lowest rack and roast the onions until they're tender, about 35 minutes.

To check for doneness, remove the pan from the oven and carefully lift up the lid or one segment of the foil. Use a small sharp knife to check to see if the onions are tender. If they're not done, replace the cover and return the onions to the oven until they're tender. Remove the onions from the oven and remove and discard the covering. Lift one of the onion halves to see if it is caramelized and glazed looking. If not, put the skillet on the stove top, uncovered, and cook over medium-high heat, until the liquid has cooked down to a molasses consistency and the sides of the onions touching the pan are caramelized.

To serve, use tongs to carefully turn the onions so the dark, caramelized sides are facing up in the same pan you cooked them in, or transfer the onions, dark sides up, to a medium round platter, arranging them in a spiral, flowerlike pattern on the platter, and scatter the bay and sage leaves over the onions. Sprinkle the onions with sea salt, and serve with a flat spatula or large spoon.

Marinated Lentils

1 pound Umbrian lentils
(or black or French lentils;
about 2¼ cups)

¼ pound prosciutto scraps
(or bacon or pancetta scraps)

1 tablespoon plus 1 teaspoon
kosher salt

2 fresh basil sprigs (each with
5 or 6 leaves)

1 medium fennel bulb

1 cup plus 2 to 4 tablespoons
finishing-quality extra-virgin
olive oil

Wedge of ricotta salata for shaving
(about 3 ounces; optional)

Before she opened multiple restaurants, including Lucques, Tavern and A.O.C., Suzanne Goin worked with me in the kitchen at Campanile, and she and I came up with this method of preparing black caviar lentils that involves gently boiling the lentils and then draining them and marinating them in extra-virgin olive oil. When they were done, they looked so pretty, like a bowl of shiny black caviar. Now that I've gone Italian, I more often stew lentils, but I still go back to this simple preparation from time to time. As a side dish, a bowl of these lentils is perfectly great on its own, although in Italy, I serve the lentils on a bed of shaved ricotta salata, salted aged ricotta. I made the cheese optional here so you can go either way. If you want to make it vegetarian, eliminate the prosciutto in the recipe.

This recipe calls for you to toss the finished lentils in high-quality olive oil; this may seem extravagant because it calls for so much oil, but the dish is so simple, it gets much of its flavor from the oil. I suggest you use Umbrian multicolored lentils, black lentils (also called caviar or beluga lentils), or French lentils. All of these are smaller and prettier than standard green lentils, and they hold their shape after they're cooked, where conventional green lentils get mushy. Having the tiny little "coins" or "caviar" is what makes a bowl of these special.

All beans harden slightly when they cool, but none more than lentils. The best way to know if lentils are properly cooked is to remove a spoonful from the pot, run them under cold water until they've cooled completely, and then bite the lentils for tenderness.

Put the lentils, prosciutto, and 1 tablespoon of the salt in a large saucepan. Add 3 cups water, or enough to cover the lentils by about ½ inch, and bring the water to a boil over high heat. Reduce the heat to low and simmer the lentils, uncovered, for about 1 hour, until they are tender but not falling apart, adding more water as necessary to keep the lentils covered by ¼ to ½ inch, and gently stirring occasionally to prevent the lentils from sticking to the pan.

While the lentils are cooking, put the basil sprigs in a large bowl or baking dish. Cut off the fronds from the fennel, if they are still attached, and discard or reserve them for another use. Remove any brown or unappealing outer layers and cut the fennel in half lengthwise. Trim the root end of the fennel and cut off ½ inch from the top to square it off. Discard all of the trimmed bits. Cut the fennel into ⅛-inch cubes and set aside.

When the lentils are done, strain them in a colander or fine-mesh strainer. Transfer the hot lentils to the bowl with the basil. Pour in 1 cup plus 2 tablespoons of the finishing-quality olive oil, and sprinkle the remaining 1 teaspoon salt over the lentils. Toss to coat the lentils with the olive oil and salt, and to distribute the basil leaves, adding the remaining 2 tablespoons olive oil if necessary to generously coat the lentils. Set the lentils aside to cool to room temperature. Add the fennel and toss to distribute it evenly. Remove and discard the prosciutto and basil.

To serve, if you are using the ricotta salata, shave it into paper-thin slices and arrange them on the bottom of a platter. Spoon the lentils on top of the cheese or directly onto the platter, and serve with a large spoon.

Chickpea Purée alla Massolino

**SERVES 8 OR MORE
MAKES ABOUT 4 CUPS**

1½ cups dried chickpeas, soaked overnight

½ cup extra-virgin olive oil

¼ cup kosher salt

1 small yellow Spanish onion, peeled and halved root to tip (root end intact)

1 carrot, cut into 2 or 3 segments

1 celery stalk, cut into 2 or 3 segments

1 garlic head, unpeeled, halved through the middle

5 fresh sage leaves

2 bay leaves (preferably fresh)

2 árbol chile pods

1 long fresh rosemary sprig, plus about 1 teaspoon finely chopped fresh rosemary needles for garnish

2 ounces cured pork scraps (such as prosciutto, pancetta, or salami; optional)

1 cup finishing-quality extra-virgin olive oil, plus more for serving

Garlic Crostini (page 275) or Fett'unta (page 274)

Chickpea purée is one of the traditional foods of the area around my little Italian town; you see chickpea crostini offered at every restaurant and bar in the area, and you see chickpeas themselves, harvested on the surrounding mountainsides, sold in stores throughout the region. Not a summer goes by that I don't cook a batch of chickpeas at my house in Italy. This purée, which I make both in Italy and at home, is based on one that I order every time I go to Ristorante Massolino, my favorite restaurant in Panicale. It's basically the Italian version of hummus, with the chickpeas cooked with rosemary and garlic and other aromatics, and puréed with olive oil instead of tahini. When the beans are done, I remove the carrot and celery from the cooking liquid, put them on a little plate, dress them with olive oil and sea salt, and offer them to my friends who come into the kitchen looking for a taste of what's cooking.

———

Drain the chickpeas and put them in a large Dutch oven or another large pot. Add enough water to cover the chickpeas by 1 to 1½ inches. Stir in the olive oil and salt. Add the onion, carrot, celery, garlic, sage leaves, bay leaves, chile pods, rosemary sprig, and pork.

Bring the water to a boil over high heat. Reduce the heat and simmer, skimming the foam off the top, and stirring occasionally until they are creamy and beginning to fall apart, about 2 hours, adding more water as necessary to keep the beans covered by 1 to 1½ inches. Turn off the heat and set aside to cool in the cooking liquid.

Remove the carrot, celery, and onion and discard (or season them with olive oil and sea salt and put them out for your friends to snack on as described above). Remove and discard the sage, bay leaves, chile pods, rosemary, and the pork, if you're using it. Remove the garlic halves, squeeze the garlic out of the skins onto a small plate, and discard the skins. Smash the garlic and return it to the pot with the remaining chickpeas. Use the chickpeas and garlic or refrigerate, submerged in the cooking liquid in a covered container, until you're ready to use them or for up to 4 days.

Strain the cooked chickpeas and garlic through a colander, reserving the cooking liquid.

Working in two batches, add half of the remaining chickpeas and garlic to the bowl of a food processor fitted with a metal blade. Turn on the machine and slowly drizzle in half of the finishing-quality olive oil and ½ cup of the reserved cooking liquid. Purée until smooth and velvety. Transfer the purée to a large fine-mesh strainer set in a bowl. Repeat, puréeing the remaining half of the chickpeas and garlic, the remaining olive oil, and another ½ cup cooking liquid in the same way, and add it to the strainer with the first batch. Pass the purée through the strainer into the bowl and stir together. Stir in more cooking liquid or olive oil (or both) as necessary to obtain a loose, spoonable but not thin consistency. You can make the purée to this point up to 3 days in advance. Put the purée and the leftover reserved cooking liquid in two separate covered containers and refrigerate until you're ready to serve the purée. Bring both to room temperature before serving. The purée may have solidified, so transfer it to a large mixing bowl and stir in enough cooking liquid to return the purée to a spoonable but not thin consistency.

To serve, spoon the purée into a medium deep serving bowl. Make a divot in the purée with the back of a large spoon and fill the divot with finishing-quality olive oil, letting some of the oil spill out around the divot. Sprinkle the chopped rosemary over the purée, and serve with crostini or fett'unta on the side and a spoon for guests to serve themselves.

Bean Salad with Celery Leaf Pesto

FOR THE PESTO

1 tablespoon pine nuts

1 medium or large garlic clove, peeled

¼ teaspoon kosher salt

¼ cup packed fresh Italian parsley leaves

1¾ cups packed fresh celery leaves (use as few of the darker leaves as possible)

1 cup extra-virgin olive oil, plus more as needed

¾ teaspoon fresh lemon juice

2 tablespoons finely grated Parmigiano-Reggiano

FOR THE SALAD

4 cups cooked white beans, borlotti beans, or chickpeas (see White Beans, page 36)

1 celery stalk, peeled and cut into ¼-inch dice

2 tablespoons white wine vinegar

1 teaspoon kosher salt

8 celery leaves (look for the lightest leaves you can find), stacked and thinly sliced

You can make this salad with chickpeas, white beans, or borlotti beans (also called cranberry beans), all of which are a big part of my cooking life in Panicale. Whichever variety of bean you use, cook them according to the recipe for White Beans (page 36). I love celery, and the leaves, combined with parsley leaves, make a refreshing alternative to the more common basil pesto.

You might not use all of the pesto for this salad. Serve leftover pesto with fresh burrata, or spoon it over grilled chicken or fish.

———

To make the pesto, adjust an oven rack to the middle position and preheat the oven to 325°F.

Spread the pine nuts on a baking sheet and toast them in the oven for 8 to 10 minutes, until they are fragrant and golden brown, shaking the baking sheet and rotating it from front to back halfway through the cooking time so the nuts brown evenly. Remove the pine nuts from the oven and set them aside to cool to room temperature.

To make the pesto using a large mortar and a pestle, transfer the pine nuts to the mortar. Using a fine Microplane, grate the garlic into the mortar and sprinkle with the salt. Using a pestle, grind the nuts and garlic to a paste. Finely chop the parsley and celery leaves by hand and add the chopped herbs to the mortar and pound with the pestle until the ingredients are mashed together and there are no visible chunks of any ingredients. Slowly stir in the olive oil, adding more if necessary to achieve a loose, spoonable pesto. Add the lemon juice and Parmigiano and stir to combine.

To make the pesto using a mini food processor or a blender, roughly chop the parsley and celery by hand. Transfer half of the chopped leaves to the bowl of a food processor fitted with a metal blade or to the jar of a blender. Add the pine nuts, salt, and ¼ cup of the olive oil. Using a fine Microplane, grate the garlic into the food processor or blender and pulse until the nuts and parsley are finely chopped but not puréed. Scrape down the sides of the food processor or blender and add the Parmigiano, lemon juice, and the remaining chopped leaves and pulse to combine. With the motor running, add the remaining ¾ cup olive oil. Purée (don't mix the pesto any longer than necessary as the blade heats up the garlic, turning it slightly bitter). Add more olive oil if necessary to achieve a loose, spoonable pesto. The pesto can made up to 1 day in advance. Refrigerate the pesto, covered, until you are ready to use it; bring it to room temperature and give it a stir to recombine the ingredients before using.

To make the salad, drain the beans of their cooking liquid and put them in a large bowl. Add the celery. Drizzle with the vinegar, sprinkle with the salt, and toss gently to combine the ingredients and to distribute the vinegar and salt. Add ¼ cup of the pesto to the bowl and toss gently to coat the beans without smashing them, adding more pesto until the beans are generously coated. Reserve the remaining pesto for another use.

To serve, transfer the beans to a deep bowl or bean pot, scatter the celery leaves over the top, and serve with a large spoon.

White Beans

2 cups dried white beans
(or borlotti beans, garbanzo
beans, or butter beans),
soaked overnight

1 cup extra-virgin olive oil

¼ cup kosher salt

1 small yellow Spanish onion,
peeled and halved root to tip
(root end intact)

1 garlic head, unpeeled, halved
through the middle

About 10 fresh thyme sprigs

1 large carrot, cut into
2 or 3 segments

1 celery stalk, cut into
2 or 3 segments

3 árbol chile pods

3 fresh sage sprigs

2 bay leaves (preferably fresh)

1 long fresh rosemary sprig

1½ ounces cured pork scraps
(such as prosciutto, pancetta,
or salami; optional)

I have a little plastic box in my refrigerator that, the day I arrive, I begin to stock with pretty wheels of cheese, big chunks of Parmigiano and pecorino, mortadella and local hand-sliced prosciutto that is sold at one of the two markets inside the town walls, and various *salumi* that I pick up on day trips in the region. I love to have a selection of these items to put out for guests coming for dinner or for a glass of wine, and of course for my family and houseguests to snack on. Each time I serve the cheese or *salumi,* I trim off the odd edges and make the pieces look appealing. But there's only so much trimming and reshaping that you can do, and as the summer evolves, I'm left with this box of odds and ends that nobody wants to eat. That's how the hunk of pork ended up in these beans. The beans gave me a way to use up what might otherwise have been thrown out, and in so doing, to add another layer of flavor to what I was cooking, which is the Italian way. But I certainly wouldn't suggest you go out and buy a chunk of pork just for this, and if you want to make this recipe without the pork to make it vegetarian, the beans will be equally delicious.

White beans are one of the handful of *contorni,* or side dishes, that you see in every restaurant in Italy, or at least in Umbria and Tuscany. I use these beans to make Stuffed Artichokes (page 113), and I also serve them as a side dish with beef, pork, chicken, or sausage.

When I'm in Italy, I just throw vegetables into the beans rather than tying them up in cheesecloth the way we do at the restaurant. When making these beans, I split a head of garlic and throw it, along with an onion, carrot, and celery stalk, into the pot. When the beans are done, I fish out the garlic, squeeze it out of its skin, smash the clove, and return it to the beans. When I serve these beans as a side dish (as opposed to as a component to another dish), I do as my friend the butcher Dario Cecchini does at his restaurants in Panzano, Italy: I put the whole pot of beans on the table with a bottle of good red wine vinegar, Dario's fragrant extra-virgin olive oil, and his Profumo del Chianti seasoned salt so each guest can put the finishing touches on his or her own serving.

This recipe calls for cannellini beans, but you could also use this recipe to cook borlotti beans (also called cranberry beans), garbanzo beans (chickpeas), or butter beans. If you like the flavor of pork with your beans, add some scraps to the pot.

Drain the beans and put them in a large Dutch oven or another large pot. Add enough water to cover the beans by 1 to 1½ inches. Stir in the olive oil and salt. Add the onion, garlic, thyme, carrot, celery, chile pods, sage, bay leaves, and rosemary. If you are using pork, add it to the pot. Bring the liquid to a boil over high heat, then reduce the heat so the liquid is gently simmering, skimming off and discarding the foam that will rise to the top. Simmer the beans for 2 hours, skimming as needed, stirring occasionally, and adding more water as needed to keep the beans covered by 1 inch, until they are tender and creamy but not mushy and falling apart, about 2 hours. (Take care when stirring the beans not to break or smash them, especially as they become more tender.) Turn off the heat and let the beans cool in the cooking liquid.

Remove and discard the pork if you used it. Remove the carrot, celery, and onion and discard (or season with olive oil and sea salt and put them out for your friends to snack on). Remove the garlic halves and squeeze the garlic out of the skins onto a small plate. Smash the garlic with a fork and return it to the pot with the beans; discard the skins. Use the beans or refrigerate, submerged in the cooking liquid in a covered container, until you're ready to use them, or for up to 4 days. If you are serving the beans as a side dish (rather than using them to make the stuffed artichokes) or using them in Bean Salad with Curly Leaf Pesto, warm the beans and cooking liquid over medium heat.

To serve the beans as a side dish, put the pot on the table with a ladle in it. Serve with a stack of bowls and a bottle of red wine vinegar, finishing-quality olive oil, and seasoned salt on the side for guests to personalize the dish for themselves.

FOR SERVING THE BEANS AS A SIDE DISH

Bottle of quality red wine vinegar

Bottle of finishing-quality extra-virgin olive oil

Antica Macelleria Cecchini Profumo del Chianti (available from online specialty food sources; or Maldon sea salt or another flaky sea salt such as fleur de sel)

Pan-Roasted Radicchio with Balsamic Vinaigrette

FOR THE VINAIGRETTE

Heaping ¼ cup minced shallot (from about 1 medium or large peeled shallot)

½ cup balsamic vinegar

1 teaspoon kosher salt

½ cup extra-virgin olive oil

FOR THE RADICCHIO

3 medium radicchio heads

¾ cup plus 2 tablespoons olive oil, or as needed

1 tablespoon plus 1 teaspoon kosher salt

3 long fresh rosemary sprigs

Finishing-quality extra-virgin olive oil

Maldon sea salt (or another flaky sea salt such as fleur de sel)

Radicchio is a grown-up vegetable; it's one of the more sophisticated flavors in the veggie world, and I would say definitely an acquired taste. It is also an example of a once-exotic vegetable that has worked its way into the mainstream. In this recipe, the radicchio, which you more often than not see raw, is pan-roasted. Roasting concentrates the flavor of any vegetable, so if you're not a radicchio fan, this concentrated version isn't for you. Even for someone like myself who likes radicchio, a little of this goes a long way, so while I could easily eat an entire plate of broccolini, I would be happy with just a wedge of roasted radicchio. I offer it as a little complementary dish, to add a touch of bitterness to balance the rich flavors on my tavola. I also like the deep purple color it brings to the table.

Use a midlevel balsamic vinegar in the $20 range for this recipe.

To make the vinaigrette, combine the shallot, vinegar, and salt in a small bowl. Add the olive oil in a slow, steady stream, whisking constantly to emulsify. Use the vinaigrette or refrigerate, covered, for up to 2 days. Bring the vinaigrette to room temperature and whisk to recombine the ingredients before using.

To prepare the radicchio, peel off and discard the outer leaves, and trim the stem ends of the radicchio heads, keeping enough of the cores intact that the leaves stay in place. Cut each radicchio head in half through the core and cut each half in half again, into 2 wedges. Put the radicchio wedges in a large bowl. Drizzle with ¼ cup of the olive oil, sprinkle with the kosher salt, and gently massage to coat the wedges evenly.

Heat 2 tablespoons of the remaining olive oil with the rosemary in a large heavy-bottomed sauté pan over high heat until the oil slides easily in the pan and the oil around the edges of the pan begins to smoke, 2 to 3 minutes. Put half of the radicchio wedges in the pan, cut side down, and sear them for about 3 minutes on each of the cut sides, until both cut sides are deep golden brown, turning them carefully with a metal spatula as they brown and adding as much as 3 tablespoons more oil to the pan, 1 tablespoon at a time, as the radicchio absorbs the oil and the pan becomes dry. Remove the radicchio wedges from the pan as they are done and put them on a small baking sheet, taking care to keep the wedges intact. Add 2 tablespoons of the remaining oil to the pan and heat it for about 1 minute, until the oil just begins to smoke around the edges of the pan. Add the remaining radicchio wedges and sear them in the same way you did the first batch, adding as much as 3 tablespoons more oil to the pan as needed. Remove the second batch of radicchio wedges from the pan and put them on the baking sheet with the first batch.

To serve, stack the wedges on a small or medium platter, with some of the wedges lying down and others propped up vertically against those. Drape the rosemary sprigs over the radicchio. Drizzle the radicchio with finishing-quality olive oil and sprinkle with sea salt. Whisk the vinaigrette to recombine and drizzle 1 tablespoon over the radicchio. Serve the radicchio with tongs and put the remaining vinaigrette in a small bowl. Serve with a small spoon for guests to drizzle on their servings.

Braised Garlic Cloves

SERVES 6 TO 8

2 large garlic heads, unpeeled, cloves separated and loose paper removed

1 tablespoon olive oil

¼ teaspoon kosher salt

1 cup Chicken Stock (page 59 or sodium-free store-bought stock), or as needed

8 fresh thyme sprigs

1 lemon, sliced into ¼-inch rounds, ends discarded

Finishing-quality extra-virgin olive oil

Maldon sea salt (or another flaky sea salt such as fleur de sel)

I'm a huge fan of whole cooked garlic cloves. Whether I'm roasting chicken, vegetables, or making Slow-Roasted Roma Tomatoes with Garlic and Thyme (page 189), I often scatter garlic cloves on the baking sheet and, after they're roasted, I pick them off the baking sheet and munch on them. In Italy, I cook garlic cloves on their own, both confit in olive oil or braised in stock as they are in this recipe, and serve them as a condiment. While Garlic Cloves Confit (page 42) are peeled, these are cooked and served in their skins. Maybe because I am such a garlic fanatic, for me, sucking the creamy garlic out of the skin just adds to the experience. I just pop a clove into my mouth, squeeze the garlic, and pull off the skin. The lemon and thyme that these are braised with impart a subtle flavor to the garlic, but just as important, they become part of the decoration when the garlic is served.

When shopping for garlic, look for plump, not shriveled heads, and certainly avoid bulbs that are sprouting. (The green sprouted centers are bitter.) In Italy, I could shop at the most unremarkable supermarket and the garlic would be fresh and delicious. Here, farmers' markets are your best guarantee of fresh garlic. I'm not a fan of elephant garlic; it doesn't have the same intense garlic flavor that smaller heads have. This recipe calls for sodium-free chicken stock. Use half of the salt in this recipe if you are using chicken stock that contains salt.

I like to serve braised garlic in a small pretty bowl. The important thing when choosing something to serve these in is that the serving vessel is small enough so the garlic cloves don't get lost in it, but instead look like little jewels nestled together.

Adjust an oven rack to the middle position and preheat the oven to 350°F.

Put the garlic cloves in a small sauté pan or baking dish. Drizzle with the olive oil, sprinkle with the kosher salt, and toss to coat the garlic. Pour the chicken stock around the garlic cloves until it comes halfway up the sides of the larger cloves. Lay the thyme sprigs and lemon slices over the garlic. Cover the pan tightly with the lid or aluminum foil and cook the garlic for 40 minutes. Remove the pan from the oven.

Increase the oven temperature to 450°F.

Remove the lid or foil, return the garlic to the oven, and cook, uncovered, for 25 to 30 minutes, until the cloves are a creamy, spreadable consistency, the texture of whipped butter. Remove the pan from the oven. You can cook the garlic cloves up to a few days in advance of serving them. Cool to room temperature, cover, and refrigerate. Bring the garlic to room temperature before serving it.

To serve, transfer the garlic cloves to a small deep serving bowl or dish, layering the lemon slices and thyme sprigs in with the cloves. Discard any liquid left in the pan. Drizzle finishing-quality olive oil over the garlic, sprinkle with sea salt, and serve with a small spoon.

Garlic Cloves Confit

MAKES ABOUT 1 CUP

1 cup extra-virgin olive oil

1 cup medium or large garlic cloves (about 40 cloves), peeled

2 árbol chile pods

2 bay leaves (preferably fresh)

1 (3-inch) fresh rosemary sprig

1 slice lemon zest (peeled with a vegetable peeler)

1 teaspoon kosher salt

In this recipe, whole peeled garlic cloves are cooked in olive oil very slowly, so the cloves cook evenly without browning, until they're creamy. The garlic, which becomes slightly sweet, is delicious spread on steak or toasted bread, or tossed in with grilled vegetables. We scatter them on pizza with leeks and goat cheese at the Pizzeria, and I use them in Egg Pie with Goat Cheese, Leeks, and Garlic Confit (page 134).

Heat the olive oil, garlic, chile pods, bay leaves, rosemary, lemon zest, and salt in a small saucepan over low heat until the oil begins to bubble around the edges. Reduce the heat to the lowest setting and cook the garlic in barely bubbling oil—only the edges should be bubbling; the oil shouldn't be simmering—for about 1 hour, until the garlic is soft and light golden. Turn off the heat and set the garlic aside to cool to room temperature in the oil. Serve the garlic, along with the chile pods, bay leaves, rosemary, and lemon zest, in a small deep bowl, with a generous amount of the oil drizzled around the cloves. Or remove and discard the chile pods, bay leaves, rosemary, and lemon zest and refrigerate the garlic cloves, submerged in the oil they were cooked in, covered, for up to 1 month.

Faith's Tomato Salad with Burrata and Torn Croutons

I learned to make this one summer when my friend Faith Willinger came to my house in Umbria for dinner. Faith, who is an authority on Italian cuisine, brought the tomatoes with her from Florence, where she lives, and proceeded to make a tomato salad in my kitchen unlike any I had ever seen. Instead of slicing the tomatoes as anyone else would have done, Faith passed the pulp through a strainer to catch the seeds and to juice the tomatoes. She roughly chopped the portion of tomato that was left after juicing them, and added the chopped tomatoes, olive oil, salt, and a few fresh basil leaves to the bowl with the juice. That was the salad. It was so unexpected, and a whole new approach to a tomato salad. The preparation couldn't be more direct. It also couldn't demand fewer skills; you don't even have to know how to hold a knife to make it.

Although Faith, being the traditionalist that she is, might not approve, after seeing all the delicious juice at the bottom of the bowl that the tomato salad was served in, I got the idea to present the tomatoes with gigantic croutons and fresh burrata or mozzarella on the side, turning the salad into a sort of build-your-own deconstructed panzanella.

As much as I like all the shapes, colors, and varieties of heirloom tomatoes found at farmers' markets, for this salad, because the tomatoes are juiced and then jumbled together, you want to stick to red tomatoes. However, feel free to use different varieties of red heirloom tomatoes. Look for tomatoes that are sweet, flavorful, and, most important, juicy. You don't want to use Early Girl tomatoes, for instance, which, although they are very sweet, are dry-farmed and contain virtually no juice at all. Ask for a sample of the tomatoes before you commit to a bagful. The world probably doesn't need another tomato recipe that starts with "Only make this when tomatoes are in season," but that's exactly what I'm telling you here. The salad is so simple that there is nothing to mask the flavor of inferior tomatoes.

Put a strainer inside a large serving bowl.

Cut out and discard the cores from the tomatoes. Cut the tomatoes in half through the stems. Pull the pulpy centers out of the tomato halves and drop the

SERVES 6 TO 8

3 pounds ripe red heirloom tomatoes or garden tomatoes

Modest handful small basil leaves; if you have access to only larger leaves, tear the leaves into small pieces

2 teaspoons kosher salt

½ teaspoon sugar, plus more to taste

½ cup finishing-quality extra-virgin olive oil

Torn Croutons (recipe follows)

12 to 18 ounces burrata (or mozzarella di bufala or mozzarella)

pulp into the strainer. Put the outsides of the tomatoes on a cutting board and set aside. When you've eviscerated the tomato halves, push the pulp through the strainer with your hand so the juice falls into the bowl and the seeds remain in the strainer. Discard the seeds. Roughly chop the tomatoes and put them in a separate large bowl. Add the basil.

Measure out ¼ cup of the strained tomato juice. (Discard or, better yet, drink the remaining juice; it's delicious.) Add the salt and sugar to the measured-out portion of juice and whisk to combine. Slowly add the olive oil in a thin stream, whisking constantly. Taste for seasoning and add more sugar if desired. Pour the seasoned juice over the tomatoes and basil and stir to combine.

To serve, transfer the tomato salad to a medium deep bowl and serve with a large spoon. Put the croutons in a bowl and the burrata on a small plate and serve them alongside the tomatoes for guests to build their own panzanella.

Torn Croutons

Makes about 3 cups

To make these croutons, I pull out the insides of a loaf of country bread, which is how I have been making croutons for years, maybe even decades. I've never understood why people cut bread into squares for croutons; it's like they go to all that effort to make croutons that look like they came from a box. By pulling the bread, you get irregularly shaped pieces with lots of nooks and crannies, which means more surface area, which means crispy, crunchy croutons after they're baked.

1 large loaf (1¾ to 2 pounds) of country bread	3 to 4 medium or large garlic cloves, peeled
¾ cup extra-virgin olive oil	1 teaspoon kosher salt

Adjust an oven rack to the middle position and preheat the oven to 350°F.

Cut the loaf of bread in half crossways to reveal the inside of the loaf. Pull the bread out in 1½- to 2-inch chunks and put the chunks in a large bowl. Reserve the crumbs and crusts for another use, such as to make bread crumbs.

Pour the olive oil into a large ovenproof sauté pan. Using a fine Microplane, grate the garlic into the pan and heat the oil and garlic over medium-high heat until the oil begins to bubble. Reduce the heat to medium and cook the garlic, stirring constantly so it doesn't brown, for about 3 minutes, until the garlic is fragrant. Add the bread chunks, season them with the salt, and toss to coat the bread. Increase the heat to medium-high and cook the croutons until they are light golden brown on the edges, turning them with tongs and tossing them in the pan so they brown evenly, about 3 minutes. Put the sauté pan in the oven and bake the croutons for 18 to 20 minutes, until they are golden brown and crispy, turning the pan a couple of times during the baking so the croutons brown evenly. Remove the sauté pan from the oven and set the croutons aside to cool to room temperature. You can make the croutons up to 1 day in advance of serving them. Store them, covered, at room temperature until you're ready to use them.

2

Sal's Roasted Pork Shoulder 48

Guacamole 50

Avocado Salsa 51

Charred Tomato Salsa 53

Tomatillo Salsa 55

Grilled or Roasted Spring Onions 56

Staff Meal Rice 58

Chicken Stock 59

Refried White Beans 60

Charred Italian or Mexican Peppers 62

Sal's Roasted Pork Shoulder

FOR THE RUB

3 tablespoons kosher salt

3 tablespoons freshly ground black pepper

3 tablespoons sweet smoked paprika

1 tablespoon cayenne pepper

FOR THE PORK

1 (12-pound) pork butt

3 tablespoons kosher salt

2 bunches radishes (preferably French breakfast radishes)

8 limes, quartered

Every year on November 13, the anniversary of the opening of Pizzeria Mozza in Los Angeles, we have a big celebration for the staff, our regular customers, and anyone else who happens to be dining at the Pizzeria at the end of the night, when the dining room turns into a party. Sal Jaramillo, the daytime sous-chef (aka "prep master") at the Osteria, along with some of the guys who work with him, started the tradition of making a roasted pork shoulder for the party. *Carnitas,* a Mexican dish of roasted pork shoulder, was Sal's inspiration. But rather than serving the meat in small chunks or shredded, as carnitas are, Sal presents the pork roast whole and lets guests tear off chunks as they serve themselves. The first time Sal served his pork shoulder, I knew it was the perfect thing for the occasion because it could be made in advance so the kitchen staff was able to enjoy the party. I also liked that it was Mexican, not Italian, because Italian is what we eat and work with at Mozza every day. The tradition of serving this pork shoulder at large staff parties continues to this day, not just for the Pizzeria anniversary, but anytime a beloved staff member leaves, or any other excuse we have to celebrate at the end of the night after we close our doors.

The pork roast is very simple to prepare, with only two "secrets." First, we cook a heritage-breed pig, which yields meat that is much more moist and flavorful than the meat of conventionally raised pigs. We also season the pork with a rub the night before we cook it. The rub really penetrates the fat layer of the roast. Then, as the pork cooks, the fat melts and the roast bastes itself in the spicy melted fat. The result is a pork roast that is as tender, juicy, and flavorful as one that is braised, but with much less effort.

The recipe for the rub may make more than what you will need, if you are using a smaller cut of meat. Use leftovers to season a whole chicken, chicken wings, pork chops, pork ribs, or even prawns. I call for a large pork butt, but roast whatever size pork butt you want. If you do cook a pork butt different in size from the one called for in this recipe, count on a ratio of ¾ teaspoon salt and 2 heaping teaspoons rub per pound of meat. The cooking time will also vary, so to ensure perfectly cooked pork butt, just be sure to cook it to an internal temperature of 195°F as stated in the recipe.

You will need a deep vessel, such as a stockpot or Dutch oven, to cook the pork in. Choose a vessel in which the pork fits snugly and no more than one-quarter of the roast peeks above the edges. The high sides are necessary to catch the enormous amount of fat rendered when the pork is cooked.

To make the rub, combine the salt, pepper, paprika, and cayenne in a large jar or another container with a cover and stir to thoroughly combine the ingredients. Close the jar and store at room temperature until you're ready to use it or for up to several months.

To prepare the pork roast, put it on a cutting board and sprinkle it all over with the salt and rub. Massage the seasonings into the meat with your hands. Wrap the pork in plastic wrap and refrigerate it overnight or for at least several hours.

Remove the pork from the refrigerator and remove and discard the plastic wrap. Put the pork roast in a deep vessel, such as a stockpot or Dutch oven, and set it aside for about 1 hour to come to room temperature.

Adjust an oven rack to the lowest position and remove any racks above it. Preheat the oven to 225°F.

Put the pork in the oven and forget about it for 4 hours. After 4 hours, check the temperature of the roast in several places. (There are pockets of fat in every roast; by checking the roast in several places, you ensure that you're not just checking the temperature of fat, which lags behind that of the meat.) Continue cooking the pork, checking the temperature every hour, until the internal temperature reaches 195°F, about 5 more hours, or 9 hours total, for a 12-pound roast. Remove the pork from the oven and let it rest in its own fat for at least 30 minutes.

Meanwhile, wash the radishes. Trim off all but the small pretty greens. Put the radishes in a small bowl.

To serve the pork in the pan you cooked it in, use a ladle to remove and discard most of the excess fat that will have rendered when the pork was cooked. (I like to leave a little in the pan to keep the pork moist.) Alternatively, use two metal spatulas to lift the pork roast and transfer it to a large serving platter or a cutting board with a moat for catching the juices. Using your hands, fold back a portion of the fat cap covering the roast to expose the meat beneath it. (The reason we don't peel it all back at once is that the fat cap acts as a heating blanket for the pork.) Serve the pork with the radish and lime quarters alongside in two separate bowls, and provide a pair of tongs or a serving fork for guests to rip off chunks of pork for themselves. Continue to fold back the fat cap as necessary to expose the pork roast.

Guacamole

½ cup roughly chopped fresh cilantro leaves (from about ½ bunch)

2 jalapeño peppers, halved (stems, seeds, and membranes removed and discarded) and roughly chopped

⅛ small yellow Spanish onion, peeled, root end trimmed and discarded, and roughly chopped

5 large ripe avocados, such as Hass, Pinkerton, or fuerte

1 tablespoon plus 1 teaspoon fresh lime juice

2 teaspoons fresh lemon juice

1½ teaspoons kosher salt

Guacamole is such a regular part of my outdoor entertaining spread that my assistant, Kate Green, says, "When Nancy puts guacamole on the table, you know it's a party." I have a lot of opinions about what makes great guacamole, starting with the fact that I don't like tomatoes in it. Chopped tomatoes make guacamole watery, and the texture I'm going for when I make guacamole is creamy. The additions I do like—including chiles, onion, and cilantro—I purée rather than chop. I got this idea from Carolynn, my coauthor, when she made guacamole for a local "Guac-Off" competition. Carolynn learned to make guacamole from a relative in Mexico City, who grinds the additions in a *molcajete*, a traditional Mexican mortar made of lava, into which the avocado is added. At Mozza, we adapted the recipe, using a blender to pulverize our additions, but the result is the same: the puréed onion, chile pepper, and cilantro are folded in with the avocados, seasoning them without interfering with their silky, buttery texture. We reached what I think is guacamole perfection—in the kitchen of an Italian restaurant, no less.

Put the cilantro, jalapeños, and onion in the bowl of a mini food processor fitted with a metal blade or in the jar of a blender and pulse until the ingredients are very finely chopped; you want them puréed almost to a paste but not so much that they become watery.

Cut the avocados in half lengthwise. Twist each half in opposite directions to separate them. Plunge the edge of a large sharp knife into the pit and twist the knife to release the pit from the avocado. Remove and discard the pits. Using a large spoon, scoop the flesh out of the avocados into a medium bowl. Add the lime juice, lemon juice, salt, and the contents of the food processor and mash everything together with a whisk or potato masher to combine the ingredients. Cover and keep the guacamole refrigerated until you are ready to serve it. (Chilling helps prevent avocados from turning brown.)

To serve, transfer the guacamole to one or several small pretty bowls. Serve alongside tortilla chips for dipping, or with a spoon for guests to use the guacamole as a condiment.

Avocado Salsa

A hybrid between tomatillo salsa and guacamole, this condiment is creamier than salsa and spicier, tangier, and a much looser consistency than guacamole. It's a nice choice if you love both tomatillo salsa and guacamole but feel like making only one of them. Serve it as a condiment for roasted pork or as a dip for chips.

This recipe calls for you to make the salsa in a food processor. If you have a Vitamix, that would also work, but if you have only a regular blender, you'll have to make the salsa in two batches and combine the batches in a large bowl before serving (a blender is too small to fit all of the ingredients at once).

———

Put the tomatillos, onion, jalapeños, garlic, and cilantro in the bowl of a food processor and pulse until the ingredients are just puréed but still have some texture, stopping a few times to scrape down the sides of the bowl.

Cut the avocados in half lengthwise. Twist each half in opposite directions to separate them. Plunge the edge of a large sharp knife into the pit and twist the knife to release the pit from the avocado. Remove and discard the pits. Using a large spoon, scoop the flesh out of the halves and discard the peels. Add half of the avocado halves and pulse to combine. Scrape down the sides of the bowl of the food processor, add the remaining avocado halves, and pulse until the salsa is puréed and creamy. Add the salt and lemon juice and pulse to combine. Serve or refrigerate the salsa, covered, for up to 3 hours. (Chilling helps prevent avocados from turning brown.)

To serve, transfer the salsa to one or several small pretty bowls. Serve the salsa with a spoon, if you are serving it as a condiment, such as alongside Sal's Roasted Pork Shoulder (page 48), or serve the bowl alongside a bowl of tortilla chips for dipping.

SERVES 12 OR MORE
MAKES ABOUT 4 CUPS

———

1 pound tomatillos, husks removed and discarded, rinsed

1 small yellow Spanish onion, peeled, root end trimmed and discarded, and roughly chopped

3 small jalapeño peppers, stems removed and discarded (for a less spicy salsa, cut the peppers in half and discard the membranes and seeds)

2 to 3 medium or large garlic cloves, peeled and roughly chopped

1½ cups roughly chopped fresh cilantro leaves and stems (from about 1½ bunches)

3 large ripe avocados, such as Hass, Pinkerton, or fuerte

1 tablespoon plus ½ teaspoon kosher salt

1 tablespoon fresh lemon juice

Charred Tomato Salsa

For this salsa, Sal blisters the tomatoes, jalapeño peppers, and onion, and then purées all of the ingredients together. It's far superior, in my opinion, to a chopped, pico de gallo style of salsa made with fresh tomatoes because it doesn't get watery over time the way pico de gallo does. The salsa is a staple at any feast featuring Sal's Roasted Pork Shoulder (page 48), Staff Meal Oven-Roasted Chicken Thighs (page 162), or anytime I am offering corn chips, guacamole, and salsa for guests to munch on before I put out dinner. Ideally, buy the tomatoes a few days before making the salsa and leave them out at room temperature to ripen and obtain their optimum red color. Salsa made with tomatoes straight from the refrigerator tends to have a dull brown color. This recipe makes a large batch; it can easily be halved if you want to make less. Better yet, make the entire batch and spoon it over roasted or grilled chicken or meat in the days to follow.

This recipe calls for you to make the salsa in a food processor. If you have a Vitamix blender, that would also work, but if you have only a regular blender, you'll have to make the salsa in two batches and combine the batches in a bowl to season them (a blender is too small to fit all of the ingredients at once).

———

Heat 1 tablespoon of the canola oil in a heavy-bottomed sauté pan over medium-high heat until it slides easily in the pan and the oil around the edges of the pan just begins to smoke, 2 to 3 minutes. Add the tomatoes and cook without touching them until they start to sizzle, brown, and blister, about 4 minutes. Begin turning the tomatoes as they are ready and cook for about 4 minutes, until they are brown and blistered all over. Remove the tomatoes from the pan as they are done and place them in a medium bowl or casserole dish. When you've removed all of the tomatoes, add the remaining 1 tablespoon oil to the pan and heat it for 1 minute. Add the jalapeños and onion and cook as you did the tomatoes, until they are brown and blistered all over, about 6 minutes total for the peppers, 12 minutes total for the onion. Remove the peppers and onion from the pan as they are done and add them to the bowl with the tomatoes. Set aside until the vegetables are cool enough to touch.

Roughly chop the jalapeños and onion and set aside.

Put the tomatoes, including any juices, in the bowl of a food processor and

SERVES 12 OR MORE
MAKES ABOUT 4 CUPS

———

2 tablespoons canola oil
(or another neutral-flavored oil)

6 medium red tomatoes, at room temperature

2 jalapeño peppers, stems removed and discarded (for a less spicy salsa, cut the peppers in half and discard the membranes and seeds)

½ red onion (halved root to tip), peeled, root end trimmed and discarded, and roughly chopped

5 to 6 medium or large garlic cloves, peeled and roughly chopped

½ cup roughly chopped fresh cilantro leaves and stems (from about ½ bunch), plus ½ cup finely chopped fresh cilantro leaves (from about ½ bunch)

1 tablespoon plus ½ teaspoon kosher salt

pulse a few times to break up the tomatoes. Add the jalapeños, onion, and garlic and blend until the ingredients are chunky. Add the roughly chopped cilantro and blend until the salsa is smooth and the cilantro appears like small flecks in the salsa. Transfer the salsa into a large bowl. Add the finely chopped cilantro leaves and salt and stir to combine. Use the salsa or refrigerate it, covered, for up to 2 days.

To serve, transfer the salsa to one or several small pretty bowls. Serve with a spoon, if you are serving it as a condiment, such as alongside Sal's Roasted Pork Shoulder (page 48), or serve with a bowl of tortilla chips for dipping.

Tomatillo Salsa

For this tomatillo salsa, Sal, our resident Mexican food guru, boils the tomatillos for just a short time, giving the salsa a pretty, light green color and a clean, bright flavor. Tomatillos have a citruslike flavor that cuts through the rich, fatty pork of Sal's Roasted Pork Shoulder (page 48) and other roasted or grilled meats.

This recipe calls for you to make the salsa in a food processor. If you have a Vitamix blender, that would also work, but if you have a regular blender, you'll have to make the salsa in two batches and combine the batches in a bowl to season them (a blender is too small to fit all of the ingredients at once).

———

Put the tomatillos in a large saucepan with 2 quarts water and 2 tablespoons of the salt. Bring the water to a boil over high heat. Add the jalapeños and boil the tomatillos and jalapeños until the tomatillos are tender and soft but still bright green and the skins have started to burst, but not so long that their skins peel off or they lose their bright color, 12 to 14 minutes. Drain the tomatillos and jalapeños in a colander, taking care not to let the tomatillos burst when you're draining them. Set aside to cool slightly.

Transfer the tomatillos and jalapeños to the bowl of a food processor fitted with a metal blade or to the jar of a blender. Add 2 teaspoons of the remaining salt and blend until smooth. Add the onion and garlic and blend until smooth. Add the cilantro and blend until the salsa is smooth and the cilantro appears like small flecks in the salsa. Transfer the salsa to a medium bowl. Add the sugar, the remaining 2 teaspoons salt, and the lime juice and stir to combine. Use the salsa or refrigerate, covered, for up to 2 days. Bring the salsa to room temperature before serving.

To serve, transfer the salsa to one or several small pretty bowls. Serve the salsa with a spoon, if you are serving it as a condiment, such as alongside Sal's Roasted Pork Shoulder (page 48), or serve with a bowl of tortilla chips for dipping.

SERVES 12 OR MORE
MAKES ABOUT 4 CUPS

2 pounds tomatillos
(about 12 large), husks removed
and discarded, rinsed

3 tablespoons plus 1 teaspoon
kosher salt

2 jalapeño peppers, stems removed
and discarded (cut the peppers in
half and remove and discard the
membranes and seeds for a less
spicy salsa)

¼ medium white onion (halved root
to tip), peeled, root end trimmed
and discarded, and roughly chopped

5 to 6 medium or large garlic
cloves, peeled and roughly chopped

2 cups roughly chopped fresh
cilantro leaves and stems
(from about 2 bunches)

½ teaspoon sugar

2 teaspoons fresh lime juice

Grilled or Roasted Spring Onions

SERVES 6

12 spring onions (or scallions)

½ cup packed fresh Italian parsley leaves

¼ cup extra-virgin olive oil

2 to 3 medium or large garlic cloves, peeled

½ teaspoon red chile flakes

2 teaspoons kosher salt

Finishing-quality extra-virgin olive oil

Maldon sea salt (or another flaky sea salt such as fleur de sel)

These onions are inspired by the charred green onions that you see being grilled along with thin sheets of *carne asada* at taco stands all over Southern California. When I can find them, I use spring onions, which are young onions; you eat both the bulb and the greens. I marinate the onions and then wrap them in aluminum foil before cooking, which allows the bulbs to get soft and sweet without the greens being charred to oblivion. I serve these on their own, taqueria style, alongside Sal's Roasted Pork Shoulder (page 48), and also use them as part of a more composed dish, Grilled or Roasted Spring Onions with Anchovies and Burrata (page 78).

Choose spring onions that are about the same size so they require the same cooking time. If you can't find spring onions, use the largest scallions you can find. When serving the onions on their own, count on two onions per person. You will need heavy-duty aluminum foil to make this.

To grill the onions, prepare a hot fire in a charcoal or gas grill. To prepare the onions in the oven, adjust the oven racks so none are near the oven floor; you'll be putting a baking sheet directly on the oven floor. If you are using an electric oven or another oven where you can't put anything on the floor, adjust the oven racks so that one is closest to the floor and put a pizza stone on it, if you have one. Preheat the oven to 500°F.

Trim and discard the hairy ends from the onions, trimming only as much as necessary so the onion bulbs stay intact, and trim off and discard the outer, slimy layer of the onions. Cut off the last inch or more of the green ends, including any yellowing or ugly parts; make sure the greens are the same length, and discard the trimmings. Put the onions in a bowl or shallow baking dish.

Combine the parsley, olive oil, garlic, and red chile flakes in the bowl of a mini food processor or in the jar of a blender fitted with a metal blade and blend until the ingredients are very finely chopped but not puréed. Drizzle the mixture over the onions, sprinkle with the kosher salt, and toss to coat. Set the onions aside to marinate for at least 30 minutes and up to overnight. (You won't notice much of a flavor difference in the longer marinating time, but you may find it convenient to do this in advance.)

Remove one onion from the marinade and use it to gauge the length of foil you will need. Cut a piece of aluminum foil that is the width of the roll and twice as long as the onions. Lay the foil on your work surface with the short end facing you. Remove the remaining onions from the marinade and lay them in a single layer with the bulbs lined up on the bottom edge of the foil. Fold the top edge to meet the bottom, creating a pocket for the onions, and fold only the sides closed.

If you are cooking the onions on a grill, put the foil pocket on the grill and cook until the onions are tender when pierced with a toothpick, 10 to 12 minutes for spring onions (about 8 minutes for scallions). Using tongs, slide the onions out of the foil so just the bulbs touch the grill grates and cook them until you see dark grill marks on the bulbs. Turn to color the bulbs on all sides, about 3 minutes. Remove the onions from the grill.

If you are cooking the onions in the oven, lay the foil pocket on a baking sheet and put the onions on the oven floor or the lowest rack to roast for 10 to 12 minutes for spring onions (about 8 minutes for scallions). Roast until the bulbs are blistered and tender when pierced with a toothpick, turning the onions halfway through the cooking time so they blister evenly. Remove the onions from the oven. Using tongs, slide the onions out of the foil so just the bulbs touch the baking sheet and cook them until you see dark marks on the bulbs. Turn to color the bulbs on all sides, about 5 to 7 minutes. Remove the onions from the oven.

To serve, carefully unwrap the foil to expose the onions. Transfer the onions with the bulbs facing one direction to a platter. Drizzle the onions with finishing-quality olive oil, sprinkle them with sea salt, and serve with tongs.

Staff Meal Rice

SERVES 8 TO 10
MAKES ABOUT 5 CUPS

2½ cups Chicken Stock
(recipe follows or sodium-free
store-bought stock)

2 tablespoons canola oil
(or another neutral-flavored oil)

2½ cups white basmati rice
(or another long-grain white rice)

½ small yellow Spanish onion,
peeled, root end trimmed and
discarded, and cut into ¼-inch dice
(about ½ cup)

1 celery stalk, cut into ¼-inch dice
(about ½ cup)

1 small carrot, cut into ¼-inch dice
(about ½ cup)

1 tablespoon kosher salt

In addition to a mainstay with his roasted pork feast, Sal serves this rice whenever he serves his Staff Meal Oven-Roasted Chicken Thighs (page 162). It's so flavorful that I was very surprised when I asked Sal for the recipe and learned that it didn't contain butter. Instead, the rice gets its delicious flavor from the homemade chicken stock it's cooked with. Sal also insists that the secret is in the rice he chooses; he uses basmati, which, because ours is an Italian, not an Indian, restaurant, we order strictly for staff meal. Make the rice as close to serving time as possible, because it is best warm, and you don't want to leave it covered to keep it warm; it will continue to cook and get mushy.

This recipe calls for sodium-free chicken stock. Use half of the salt in this recipe if you are using chicken stock that contains salt.

Heat the chicken stock with 1 quart water in a large saucepan over medium-high heat until it is hot but not boiling. Turn off the heat.

Put the canola oil in a large Dutch oven or another large pot over medium heat and add the rice while the oil is still cold. Cook the rice in the oil, stirring constantly, until the rice is lightly toasted, about 5 minutes. Reduce the heat to low, add the onion, and cook the rice and onion together, stirring constantly, until the onion is translucent, about 2 minutes. Add the warm liquid all at once. Add the celery, carrot, and salt and stir to combine. Increase the heat to medium and bring the liquid to a boil, scraping down the sides of the pot so all of the grains of rice are submerged. Reduce the heat to medium-low and simmer the rice, uncovered, for 5 minutes.

Reduce the heat to its lowest setting, put the lid on the pot (or cover the pot with aluminum foil), and cook the rice undisturbed for 10 minutes, or until there is no liquid at the bottom of the pot. (I suggest you use a timer for this as Sal does because, like Sal, you'll surely get busy doing something else, and you don't want to forget the rice.) To check for doneness, uncover the pot and, using a large spoon, dig down to see if there is any liquid at the bottom. If so, cover the pot and cook until the liquid is gone. Uncover the pot and use the spoon to fluff up the rice. Serve the rice in the pot you cooked it in or transfer it to a deep serving bowl and serve with a large spoon.

Chicken Stock

This is a basic, no-salt chicken stock and one of the backbones of the Mozza kitchens. We keep the flavor of the stock neutral because we use it in a variety of dishes, each of which will contain its own seasonings.

5 pounds chicken feet and chicken wings

1 large Spanish onion, peeled, root end trimmed and discarded, and quartered

1 large carrot, cut into large pieces

1 celery stalk, cut into large pieces

1 tablespoon black peppercorns

Put the chicken in a tall stockpot. Fill the pot with enough water to cover the chicken by several inches and bring the water to a boil over high heat. Boil the chicken, skimming off the gray foam that rises to the top, until very little foam rises from the stock, about 10 minutes. Add the onion, carrot, celery, and peppercorns. Reduce the heat to low and simmer the stock for about 2 hours, until the water has reduced by half and the stock is a light golden color.

Turn off the heat and let the stock cool slightly. Pour the stock through a fine-mesh strainer and discard the chicken and vegetables. Set the stock aside to cool to room temperature. Refrigerate the stock, covered, for up to several days, or freeze it for up to several months.

Refried White Beans

SERVES 8 TO 10
MAKES ABOUT 5 CUPS

2 cups dried white beans,
soaked overnight

¼ cup extra-virgin olive oil

¼ large yellow Spanish onion,
peeled, root end trimmed and
discarded, and roughly chopped

2½ ounces prosciutto,
finely chopped (about ½ cup)

5 árbol chile pods

1 tablespoon plus 1½ teaspoons
kosher salt

¼ cup canola oil
(or another neutral-flavored oil)

When Sal makes refried beans to go with his pork feast, because he is cooking from an Italian pantry, he uses white beans (cannellini) in place of traditional pinto beans, and prosciutto instead of lard. And let me tell you, he's on to something. His are the best refried beans I've ever had. What I like about them, besides the delicious flavor, is that they're soupy, not dry, like refried beans often are. Also, the creamy color of the white beans is really pretty prepared this way. I normally like to cook beans with just enough water to cover them, but we cook these beans as Sal does, with lots of water, and stir them often like risotto, which gives them a creamy quality as the beans begin break down. Until I saw Sal making them, I'd always thought that refried beans meant that the beans were cooked, then fried, and then fried again. But that's not the case. The beans are cooked and then fried only once, so to my mind they should be called *fried* beans, not *re*fried beans.

––––––––––

Drain the beans and put them in a large pot with 8 cups water. Add the olive oil, onion, prosciutto, 2 of the chile pods, and 1 tablespoon of the salt and bring the water to a boil over high heat. Reduce the heat to low and simmer the beans for 2 hours, stirring often. Add 2 cups water and continue cooking the beans, stirring often, until they are tender and creamy, not chalky or al dente, and the liquid is thick and cloudy, 30 minutes to 1 hour. (When you stir the beans, starch is released from them; the starch makes the finished beans creamier, which is a good thing with these beans.) To test the beans for doneness, press one bean between your fingers; if it is creamy and silky, it's done. If it seems dry or slightly chalky, keep cooking the beans until they're creamy. When the beans are done, reduce the heat to its lowest setting while you prepare the ingredients for frying them.

Heat the canola oil with the remaining 3 chile pods in a large Dutch oven or a large pot over low heat until the chiles are lightly fried (they will be a dark, reddish-brown color), 3 to 4 minutes, tilting the pan so the oil pools on one side and the chiles are submerged in the oil. Remove the chile pods from the oil and set them on a paper towel to drain. Increase the heat to medium-high and, using a slotted spoon or strainer, lift a big spoonful of beans out of the pot they were cooked in and transfer them to the pot with the oil, taking care because the oil will splatter when you add the beans. Use the back of a large spoon or a rubber spatula to smash the beans to a chunky consistency. Ladle 1 cup of the cooking liquid into the pot with the smashed beans and cook, stirring, until the liquid evaporates. Add another spoonful of beans, smash them, then add another cupful of liquid and cook until it evaporates. Continue adding the beans and liquid, smashing the beans before adding the next cupful of liquid, until you have added all of the beans to the pan. (You won't add all of the liquid; reserve it.)

Reduce the heat to low and simmer the beans until the liquid is thick and creamy but the beans are not dry looking, about 30 minutes. If you cook them too long and they do get dry looking, add more of the cooking liquid to loosen the beans to a creamy consistency. Finely chop the reserved chile pods and add one-fourth of the chopped chiles to the beans. Add the remaining 1½ teaspoons salt. Taste for seasoning and add more chopped chiles if desired.

The beans can be cooked up to 3 days in advance. Cool the beans and cooking liquid to room temperature, then refrigerate them in separate airtight containers. Warm the beans over medium-low heat, adding enough of the reserved liquid to loosen the beans to a creamy consistency.

Serve the beans in the Dutch oven in which you fried them, or transfer them to a bean pot or another deep serving bowl, and serve with a big long-handled spoon that won't fall into the pot.

Charred Italian or Mexican Peppers

SERVES 8 TO 12

1 pound sweet or mildly spicy peppers (such as Italian peppers, shishito, padrón, or other mild peppers) or spicy peppers (such as jalapeño, red jalapeño, Fresno, serrano, poblano, or Anaheim), stems left on

2 tablespoons olive oil

½ teaspoon kosher salt

Finishing-quality extra-virgin olive oil (for Italian peppers)

Maldon sea salt (or another flaky sea salt such as fleur de sel; for Italian peppers)

In Italy, charred peppers are served as a side dish, not as a condiment the way they are with Mexican food. I assume it's because Italian pepper varieties aren't spicy like Mexican pepper varieties are. The two types of peppers are cooked the same way, charred either in a sauté pan or on a grill. With Mexican peppers, I char them, steam them to soften them (a trick I learned from Sal), and serve the peppers without any further seasoning. Italian peppers I drizzle with olive oil and sprinkle with sea salt because it feels like the Italian thing to do.

When shopping for peppers, seek out a variety of shapes, sizes, and colors. Most important, commit to making either sweet Italian-style peppers or spicy Mexican peppers.

I suggest you use the grill if it's already fired up, otherwise, cook the peppers in a very hot grill pan or cast-iron skillet.

Put the peppers in a large bowl and drizzle them with 1 tablespoon of the olive oil, sprinkle with the kosher salt, and toss to coat the peppers.

Heat the remaining tablespoon olive oil in a large grill pan or cast-iron skillet over medium-high heat until it slides easily in the pan and the oil around the edges of the pan just begins to smoke, 2 to 3 minutes. Put the peppers in the pan and cook until they are browned all over and charred in places, about 5 minutes, turning the peppers so they color evenly. Remove the peppers from the pan.

If you are making Italian peppers, transfer them to a small serving dish, drizzle with finishing-quality olive oil, sprinkle with sea salt, and serve with small tongs or a fork.

For Mexican peppers, transfer the peppers to a plastic bag or to a bowl. Close the bag or cover the bowl with plastic wrap and set aside for the peppers to steam for 10 minutes. Pile the peppers in a small bowl or arrange them on a platter or cutting board and serve them with small tongs or a fork.

3

Niçoise Deconstructed: Olive Oil–Poached Albacore

I can't think of a salad that I like more or that is made of elements that taste better together than a Niçoise, a traditional French salad composed of tuna, anchovies, olives, green beans, potatoes, and eggs, and generally tossed together with mixed soft lettuces.

I was perfectly happy with the standard presentation of Niçoise until, at lunch at Bistro Jeanty in Yountville not long ago, I ordered a Niçoise that came to the table with all the elements of the salad presented in a single layer on a large flat platter. The server put the platter in the center of the table and my friends and I dug into it, family style, taking the elements we wanted and composing them on our individual plates. It was brilliant. That presentation inspired this meal, which consists of all the elements of a Niçoise salad, with each element in its own, stand-alone dish, and a simple bibb lettuce salad to pull all the elements together. It's basically a salad bar, but being the controlling person (when it comes to food) that I am, I'm not going to give anyone the option of creating a salad with combinations that would not appeal to me. No matter what you take off this table, what you're going to end up with is essentially a Niçoise, and as a hostess (and cookbook author), that's comforting to me.

As tempting as it is to buy poached tuna in a can or jar—and there are many good versions available for sale—I urge you to try making the tuna yourself using this recipe. It's really so simple to poach albacore, and once you do, you'll be astonished at how much more delicious it is than anything you can buy. The only thing that can go wrong in poaching tuna is that you overcook it, but if you follow this recipe, you will have perfectly poached albacore. It takes a lot of oil to make this; use the oil to poach up to two more batches of tuna, or to sauté fish, make mayonnaise for a tuna salad (see Garlic Mayonnaise, page 84), or in any other application where you wouldn't mind the mild flavor of tuna.

SERVES 6 TO 8

2 pounds (2-inch-thick) albacore tuna

1 tablespoon kosher salt

2 teaspoons fresh coarsely ground black pepper

2 lemons

3 cups olive oil

½ cup champagne vinegar (or white wine vinegar)

8 bay leaves (preferably fresh)

3 to 4 large garlic cloves, peeled and sliced ⅛ inch thick lengthwise

4 árbol chile pods

6 (2-inch-long) fresh rosemary sprigs

Maldon sea salt (or another flaky sea salt such as fleur de sel)

Adjust an oven rack to the middle position and preheat the oven to 350°F.

Cut the tuna into 3- to 4-inch chunks. Sprinkle with the kosher salt and pepper and set the tuna aside for 10 minutes to come to room temperature while you prepare the poaching ingredients.

Use a vegetable peeler to peel the outer skin of the lemons. Throw the peels into a large ovenproof saucepan. Slice the lemons into ¼-inch rounds, discarding the ends, and throw the rounds into the saucepan. Add the olive oil, remaining salt, pepper, vinegar, bay leaves, garlic, chile pods, and rosemary. Heat the oil over high heat until it begins to bubble around the edges. Turn the heat off and use a slotted spoon to carefully place the albacore chunks in the oil without the oil splattering. Put the lid on the pan, or cover tightly with aluminum foil, and put the pan in the oven for 10 minutes. Remove the pan from the oven, remove the lid or foil, and let the fish cool to room temperature in the oil.

Meanwhile, set a colander over a large bowl. Pour the contents of the pan into the colander. Reserve the oil for another use or to store leftover tuna, if you have any.

To serve, lay the tuna artfully on a medium rimmed platter, layering in the lemon, lemon peels, bay leaves, garlic, chiles, and rosemary sprigs in a way that looks pretty. Sprinkle the tuna with sea salt, and serve with tongs.

Bibb Salad with Soft Herbs

This light, herb-flecked salad is the base for the Niçoise salad. It's so simple and refreshing, you could serve it alongside almost any meal. Keep in mind that because bibb is a tender salad green, unlike in most of the salads in this book, you want to toss the salad as close to serving time as possible.

Chervil, also called French parsley, is a very delicate herb in the parsley family that, dried, is part of the spice blend fines herbes. If you can't find fresh chervil, substitute small fresh Italian parsley leaves and tarragon in equal parts for the chervil in this recipe.

―――――――

Remove and discard the outer unappealing leaves from the lettuce heads and remove and discard the cores. Put the lettuce leaves in a large bowl. Drizzle the lemon juice and sprinkle the salt over the lettuce and toss to coat the lettuce.

Drizzle one-third of the ½ cup vinaigrette over the lettuce. Reserve 4 or 5 chive batonettes. Sprinkle one-third of the remaining chives and one-third of the chopped chervil, dill, tarragon, and parsley over the salad and toss gently, massaging the vinaigrette into the leaves to distribute the herbs and coat the leaves with the vinaigrette. Continue adding the vinaigrette and herbs a third at a time, and tossing and massaging to distribute the herbs and coat the leaves with vinaigrette, until you have added all of the chopped herbs and ½ cup of the vinaigrette. Add the last 2 tablespoons vinaigrette only if needed to coat the greens.

To serve, transfer the salad to a large wide-mouthed bowl or a large platter. Sprinkle with the whole leaves of chervil, dill, tarragon, and parsley, and the reserved chives, and serve with tongs.

SERVES 6 TO 8

2 bibb lettuce heads

1 tablespoon fresh lemon juice

¾ teaspoon kosher salt

½ cup plus 2 tablespoons Lemon Vinaigrette (page 125)

25 (1-inch-long) fresh chive batonettes

2 tablespoons finely chopped fresh chervil leaves (from about ¼ cup packed whole leaves), plus several leaves for garnish

2 tablespoons finely chopped fresh dill leaves (from about ¼ cup packed whole leaves), plus several leaves for garnish

2 tablespoons finely chopped fresh tarragon leaves (from about ¼ cup packed whole leaves), plus several leaves for garnish

2 tablespoons finely chopped fresh Italian parsley leaves (from about ¼ cup packed whole leaves), plus several tiny leaves for garnish

Mixed Summer Beans with Chiles, Almonds, and Creamy Mustard Dressing

This is without a doubt a seasonal dish, consisting of tender, crunchy beans that are available only in the summer. The beans are coated in a mayonnaise-based dressing and tossed with thin slices of spicy fresh chiles and toasted almonds, which add elements of crunch and surprise. I call for a variety of beans in this recipe because the mix of shapes and colors makes the salad really pretty. Use one variety of beans if that's all you can find or want to cook. The recipe for the dressing makes half again as much as you will need. Save the leftover dressing for another salad, or make a bigger salad.

To make the dressing, combine the vinegar and lemon juice in a small bowl and whisk to combine. Combine the canola oil and olive oil in a measuring cup with a spout.

Put the egg yolk and mustard in the bowl of a mini food processor fitted with a metal blade. Using a fine Microplane, grate the garlic into the bowl with the egg, add the salt, and blend for about 30 seconds, until the yolk is pale yellow. Add a few drops of the combined oils and pulse to incorporate the oil into the egg mixture. With the machine running, begin adding the remaining oil a few drops at a time until the egg and oil are emulsified; you will have added 2 or 3 tablespoons of oil. Turn off the machine, take off the lid, scrape down the sides of the bowl with a rubber spatula, and add 2 teaspoons of the vinegar–lemon juice mixture. Return the lid and pulse to combine. Continue adding the oil a few drops at a time with the machine running constantly until you've added about half of the oil. Stop the machine again and add the remaining vinegar–lemon juice mixture and pulse to combine. Add the remaining oil in a slow, steady stream with the machine running constantly, stopping as soon as the dressing thickens. Use the dressing or refrigerate, covered, for up to 3 days.

To prepare the salad, adjust an oven rack to the middle position and preheat the oven to 325°F.

Spread the almonds on a baking sheet and toast them in the oven for 12 to 15 minutes, until they are fragrant and golden brown, shaking the baking sheet and rotating it from front to back halfway through the cooking time so the nuts brown evenly. Remove the almonds from the oven and set aside until they are

SERVES 6 TO 8

FOR THE DRESSING

2 teaspoons red wine vinegar

2 teaspoons fresh lemon juice

½ cup canola oil (or another neutral-flavored oil)

½ cup extra-virgin olive oil

1 extra-large egg yolk

3 tablespoons whole-grain mustard

2 to 3 large garlic cloves, peeled

½ teaspoon kosher salt

FOR THE SALAD

½ cup whole almonds, with skins

2 teaspoons extra-virgin olive oil

2½ teaspoons kosher salt, plus more for the blanching water

2 pounds mixed beans (any combination of string beans, haricots verts, yellow Romano beans, green Romano beans, Blue Lake beans, or yellow wax beans), stem ends trimmed and discarded, "tails" left intact

1 large shallot, peeled

(continued)

1 serrano chile, stem trimmed and discarded, sliced into paper-thin rounds

1 Fresno chile, stem trimmed and discarded, halved, seeds removed, and sliced very thin lengthwise

1 tablespoon fresh lemon juice

¼ cup packed small fresh Italian parsley leaves

cool enough to touch. Drizzle with the olive oil, sprinkle with 1 teaspoon of the salt, and toss to coat. Cut the almonds in half lengthwise and set them aside.

Meanwhile, fill a large saucepan with water, bring it to a boil over high heat, and salt the water to taste like the ocean, adding 1 tablespoon salt to each quart of water. Prepare an ice bath in a medium bowl and prepare a bed of paper towels.

If you are blanching only one type of bean, put the beans in the boiling water and blanch them. Times will vary depending on the type of beans you are cooking: green beans or Blue Lake beans will take about 1 minute; haricots verts will take about 45 seconds; yellow wax beans will take close to 2 minutes; and Romano beans will take 3 to 4 minutes. Your eyes are your best timer; no matter what kind of beans you're blanching, the moment the beans brighten in color, it's time to take them out and plunge them into the ice bath. Drain the beans in a colander and plunge them into the ice bath for 1 minute to cool them. Drain the beans in a colander, fish out and discard the ice cubes, and transfer the beans to the paper towels to dry.

If you are blanching more than one variety of bean, blanch each variety separately. One variety at a time, put the beans in a fine-mesh strainer and plunge the strainer with the beans directly into the boiling water using the times above as a guide. Plunge the strainer into the ice bath so you can use the same boiling water and ice bath for all of the beans. When all of the beans are blanched and dry, slice them into 2- to 3-inch segments on an extreme bias. If the haricots verts are small enough, leave them whole; otherwise, cut them in half on an extreme bias.

Cut the shallot in half root to tip and trim and discard the root end. Separate the layers of the shallot, stack 2 or 3 layers at a time on top of one another, and slice 1⁄16 inch thick lengthwise.

Put the beans, shallot slices, serrano chile, Fresno chile, and almonds in a large bowl. Drizzle with the lemon juice, sprinkle with the remaining 1½ teaspoons salt, and toss gently to combine the ingredients and coat them. Add 1 cup of the dressing, ¼ cup at a time, gently tossing the salad and massaging the dressing into the beans with your hands between additions. Add another ¼ cup if necessary for the beans to be evenly and generously coated. Add the parsley leaves and toss to distribute them.

To serve, using your hands, grab the beans from the mixing bowl and pile them into a wide-mouthed serving bowl or onto a large platter. Scatter the bits left in the bowl over the top of the salad and serve with tongs.

Marinated Pickled Italian Peppers with Anchovies and Olives

My recipe ideas never come from a dream; they're always inspired by an ingredient or by something I ate. This mélange of pickled peppers, anchovies, and olives is what came about after I was intrigued by an item I spotted on the menu at Frankies Spuntino in the West Village in New York City. It was a side dish of three-year-marinated peppers with anchovies, but the peppers specifically are what did it for me. I'm drawn to anchovies whenever I see them on a menu, but when I saw the aged peppers in this menu description, I had to order them—I'd never seen an age attached to marinated peppers. What came to the table were long, pale green peppers, each of which had been slashed and stuffed with a whole anchovy. I'm not even sure if my dinner companions got any because I remember devouring what seemed like the entire plate of them.

Because anchovies are the star, or rather the costar, of this dish, making it is a good excuse to seek out the super-special alici di Cetara (see A Note on Anchovies, page 9).

————

Remove the peppers from the oil, reserving the oil. Drape an anchovy fillet over each pepper and lay the peppers on a rectangular or round platter small enough that the peppers and anchovies won't get lost on it. When you've draped all of the peppers and put them on the platter, scatter the olives around them. Drizzle 2 teaspoons of the oil the peppers were marinated in over the peppers and anchovies, and serve with small tongs. Store leftover peppers in the oil. Use any remaining oil to make another batch of marinated pickled peppers or to make a spicy vinaigrette.

SERVES 6 TO 8

————

12 Marinated Pickled Italian Peppers (recipe follows)

12 Cetara anchovy fillets (or another quality anchovy)

½ cup (about 2 ounces) pitted black olives (such as Taggiasche, Niçoise, or Kalamata)

Marinated Pickled Italian Peppers

Makes 12 peppers

These peppers are my attempt at imitating three-year-marinated peppers that I tasted at Frankies Spuntino in New York City. Frankies doesn't normally sell the peppers—it's a restaurant, not a grocery store—but Frankies was kind enough to let me buy a jar. The peppers are produced on a very small scale in a little village in Italy, and every year, Frankies buys the entire production. Desperation breeds innovation, and when I found out I couldn't get them, I took my jar and set out to re-create the peppers in the Mozza kitchen.

We pickle the peppers for a week or more, and then pack them in olive oil and wait at least two weeks before serving them. The oil softens both the texture and flavor of the peppers, so they don't have the sharpness of pickled peppers, nor are they as crunchy. Yes, it takes some patience and planning ahead. At minimum it's a three-week pepper, but that's a lot better than a three-year pepper that you have no chance of buying.

Make the peppers not when you need them, but when you feel like taking on a pleasant, easy kitchen project. When you're planning a party or dinner, you can just reach for the jar and with very little effort, assemble an unusual and delicious appetizer. I make this composed appetizer using these peppers and also serve them as an accompaniment to sliced meats. It's such a nice dish to send to guests at my restaurants because the peppers are special, but they don't ruin anyone's appetite. A jar of these peppers, layered with anchovies and olives, would make a great gift for a foodie friend.

6 cups champagne vinegar
(or white wine vinegar)

2 tablespoons honey (preferably wildflower or another mild-flavored honey)

3 teaspoons black peppercorns

1½ teaspoons juniper berries

1½ teaspoons cloves

5 bay leaves (preferably fresh)

12 sweet (not spicy) Italian green peppers (long peppers, small green peperoncini, or yellow banana peppers)

2 cups extra-virgin olive oil, or as needed

Combine the vinegar, honey, peppercorns, juniper berries, cloves, bay leaves, and 2 cups water in a medium saucepan and bring the liquid to a boil over high heat. Reduce the heat to medium-low and simmer for 10 minutes to infuse the pickling liquid with the seasonings. Add the peppers, return the heat to high, and return the liquid to a boil. Reduce the heat to medium-low and simmer the peppers until they soften slightly, but not so long that they lose their shape, 4 to 6 minutes. Turn off the heat and set the peppers aside to cool in the pickling liquid.

Transfer the peppers to a 1-quart canning jar (or another container with a lid). Strain the pickling liquid into a large bowl. Add the pickling spices that are in the strainer to the jar with the peppers. Add enough of the pickling liquid to fill the jar, then discard the remaining liquid. Close the jar and refrigerate the peppers for 1 week.

Remove the peppers from the refrigerator and strain them, discarding the pickling liquid and spices. Return the peppers to the jar and add enough olive oil to cover them. Refrigerate the peppers for at least 1 day and up to several months. Bring the peppers to room temperature before serving.

Grilled or Roasted Spring Onions with Anchovies and Burrata

SERVES 6 TO 8

24 Grilled or Roasted Spring Onions
(page 54)

24 Cetara anchovy fillets
(or another quality anchovy)

Finishing-quality extra-virgin
olive oil

Maldon sea salt (or another flaky
sea salt such as fleur de sel)

Lemon for zesting

3 to 4 (2-ounce) balls burrata
(or mozzarella di bufala; optional),
or 1 (8-ounce) ball, cut into
3 or 4 segments

Anchovies and onions is a classic pairing, and for good reason: the sweet grassy taste of the onions and the salty fishy anchovies complement each other perfectly. This dish was inspired by one served at a luncheon that the chef Nancy Oakes served at her restaurant, Boulevard, in San Francisco. Ironically, it contained neither anchovies nor onions. Nancy's dish consisted of burrata garnished with fried butter beans, a combination of flavor and textures that went into the life-changing realm for me. I came back to Los Angeles determined to apply this idea at the Mozzarella Bar, and I created a composed plate with burrata in the middle, surrounded like a crown of thorns with marinated roasted spring onions, which were laced with long strands of anchovies; I scattered fried beans over the top and grated lemon zest over the entire dish. Even though the fried butter beans gave birth to this dish, at home I serve it without them, because they're too involved for home cooking. So Nancy Oakes's butter beans and burrata has evolved into an anchovy and onion dish, with even the burrata being optional.

Because anchovies are the star, or rather the costar, of this dish, making it is a good excuse to seek out the super-special Cetara (see A Note on Anchovies, page 9).

To serve this without burrata, cut grilled or roasted onions in half lengthwise on an extreme bias and lay them all facing one direction on a rectangular platter small enough so that the onions won't seem lost on it. Drape and tangle the anchovy fillets among the onions, drizzle with finishing-quality olive oil, and sprinkle with sea salt. Using a fine Microplane, grate a thin layer of lemon zest over the plate and serve with a small pair of tongs.

To serve this with burrata, line the burrata balls or segments down the center of a rectangular platter. Lay the onions around the burrata. Drape and tangle the anchovy fillets among the onions, drizzle with finishing-quality olive oil, and sprinkle with sea salt. Using a fine Microplane, grate a thin layer of lemon zest over the plate and serve with a large spoon.

Deviled Eggs with Pickled Mustard Seeds

Deviled eggs must be the most often brought-to-the-potluck appetizer in America, but I don't think I've ever heard of anyone making a batch for themselves. I love deviled eggs, but I have to say I, too, am guilty of making them only when I'm having company. I don't stray too far from the classic, but with these, I went wild and added pickled mustard seeds, which pop in your mouth like little eggs on a sushi roll. Carolynn made these to take to her family Thanksgiving dinner, and her sister called the mustard seeds a "game changer." That, to me, is the ultimate compliment.

I normally undercook hard-cooked eggs ever so slightly (see Perfect Hard-Cooked Eggs, page 82), but for deviled eggs, I cook the eggs all the way through so the yolks are dry enough to push through a strainer. To ensure that the yolky mixture is still creamy after I've added the wet mustard seeds, I call for an extra yolk, which means you have one pair of egg whites with no home. Find the two that didn't fare so well during the peeling process, sprinkle them with sea salt, and eat them. The eighth egg is a "tester egg" so you have one to break open and check for doneness.

**SERVES 6 OR MORE
MAKES 12 DEVILED EGGS**

1 tablespoon plus ¾ teaspoon kosher salt

8 extra-large eggs

⅓ cup Garlic Mayonnaise (page 84)

1 tablespoon Pickled Mustard Seeds (recipe follows), drained in a small strainer

2½ teaspoons Dijon mustard

1 teaspoon Tabasco sauce

Sweet smoked paprika or minced chives for garnish

Bring a large saucepan of water and 1 tablespoon of the salt to a boil over high heat. (The salt is added because it helps the whites to solidify quickly if there is a crack in an egg. The salt does not penetrate the egg shells and season the eggs.) Carefully add the eggs, lower the heat, and simmer for 7 minutes. Turn off the heat and let the eggs sit in the hot water for 5 to 6 minutes. To check for doneness, remove the tester egg after 5 minutes and crack it open to see if the white and the yolk are cooked through. The yolk should be bright yellow but not wet looking. If the yolk looks wet, leave the eggs in the hot water for another minute or two.

Meanwhile, create an ice bath in a medium bowl and create a bed of paper towels. Remove the remaining eggs from the hot water and transfer them to the ice water to cool completely. Remove the eggs from the ice bath, carefully peel them under running water, and put the peeled eggs on the paper towels to dry. Cut the eggs in half lengthwise, taking care to keep the whites intact because they are the vessel for the deviled eggs. Set the two most unattractive egg white halves aside and munch on them.

Put the remaining 12 egg white halves on a platter.

Press the egg yolks through a fine-mesh strainer into a medium bowl. Add the mayonnaise, mustard seeds, mustard, Tabasco, and the remaining ¾ teaspoon salt and mix with a rubber spatula until the ingredients are combined and the mixture is creamy. Using a small spoon, spoon the deviled egg yolks into the 12 egg whites.

Sprinkle each egg with a pinch of paprika or chives and serve, no utensil necessary.

Perfect Hard-Cooked Eggs

I am very specific about my hard-cooked eggs, but my demands when it comes to hard-cooked eggs are pretty simple: I don't like them overcooked. Most hard-cooked eggs are cooked to death, until the yolks are dry, chalky, and have a greenish-gray ring around them. I like the yolks to be cooked just enough that they are solid. Unless you are grating the eggs or making deviled eggs, the very center of the yolks should be the slightest bit undercooked and wet looking. I've worked out the timing for achieving perfect hard-cooked eggs. To make sure you get the eggs just right, I've called for you to put one extra egg in the pot. That's your "tester egg." After you've cracked it open to test its doneness, if it's cooked, sprinkle it with sea salt and eat it.

Bring a large saucepan of water to a boil over high heat. Add 1 tablespoon salt. (The salt is added because it helps the whites to solidify quickly if there is a crack in an egg. The salt does not penetrate the egg shells and season the eggs.) Carefully add the eggs, lower the heat, and simmer the eggs for 5 minutes. Turn off the heat and let the eggs sit in the hot water for 5 minutes. Remove one tester egg and crack it open. The yolk should be bright yellow and wet in the center. If the yolk is not yet set, leave the eggs in the hot water for another minute. While the eggs are cooling, create an ice bath in a medium bowl and create a bed of paper towels. Remove the remaining eggs from the hot water and transfer them to the ice water to cool completely. Remove the eggs from the ice bath, carefully peel them under running water, and place the peeled eggs on the paper towels to dry.

Pickled Mustard Seeds

Makes about 1¼ cups

Pickled mustard seeds are a relatively new discovery for me. They're so easy to make: just boil the pickling ingredients, pour them over the seeds, and a few hours later you have a game-changing condiment at your fingertips. I call for the pickled mustard seeds in Pickled Mustard Seed Mayonnaise (page 85) and in the deviled eggs. They also make a delicious condiment on their own, spooned onto a steak or burger or alongside cured meats.

½ cup mustard seeds

1 cup apple cider vinegar

1 tablespoon honey (preferably wildflower or another mild-flavored honey)

1 árbol chile pod

1½ teaspoons kosher salt

Put the mustard seeds in a 1-pint canning jar with a lid or in a heat-proof medium bowl.

Combine the vinegar, honey, chile pod, and salt in a small saucepan and bring the liquid to a boil over high heat. Turn off the heat and pour the boiling liquid over the mustard seeds and set aside for the liquid to cool to room temperature. Put the lid on the jar or cover the bowl tightly with plastic wrap and set the mustard seeds aside for 2 to 3 hours, until the pickling liquid has saturated the seeds (the finished condiment will look like a seedy syrup) and they pop like caviar in your mouth. Use the seeds or put the lid on the jar (or transfer to another covered container) and refrigerate for up to several months.

Garlic Mayonnaise

Makes about 1 cup

I use garlic mayonnaise (also called aioli) as a base for many salad dressings and dipping sauces at our restaurants and in this book. The trick to making mayonnaise successfully is to add the oils very slowly and to whisk vigorously the entire time you're adding them. Once you get a feel for that, which you will after making it two or three times, making mayonnaise is simple.

2 teaspoons champagne vinegar (or white wine vinegar)

2 teaspoons fresh lemon juice

¾ cup canola oil (or another neutral-flavored oil)

¼ cup extra-virgin olive oil

1 extra-large egg yolk

1 medium or large garlic clove, peeled

1 teaspoon kosher salt

Pour the vinegar and lemon juice in a small bowl and whisk to combine. Combine the canola oil and olive oil in a measuring cup with a spout.

Put the egg yolk in the bowl of a mini food processor fitted with a metal blade. Using a fine Microplane, grate the garlic into the bowl with the egg, add the salt, and blend for about 30 seconds, until the yolk is pale yellow. Add a few drops of the combined oil and pulse to incorporate the oil into the egg mixture. With the machine running, begin adding the remaining oil a few drops at a time until the egg and oil are emulsified; you will have added 2 or 3 tablespoons of oil. Turn off the machine, take off the lid, scrape down the sides of the bowl with a rubber spatula, and add a third tablespoon of the vinegar–lemon juice mixture. Return the lid and pulse to combine. Continue adding the oil a few drops at a time with the machine running constantly until you've added about half of the oil. Stop the machine again and add another third of the vinegar–lemon juice mixture in the same way that you did the first time. Add the remaining oil in a slow, steady stream with the machine running constantly, stopping when the mayonnaise thickens to add the remaining vinegar–lemon juice mixture and pulse to combine. Serve the mayonnaise or refrigerate, covered, for up to 3 days.

Mayonnaise Variations

For Pickled Mustard Seed Mayonnaise, increase the lemon juice to 1 tablespoon and stir 1 recipe Pickled Mustard Seeds (page 83) into the finished mayonnaise.

For Olive Anchovy Mayonnaise, double the amount of lemon juice and vinegar, decrease the salt to ¼ teaspoon, and stir ¼ cup pitted black olives (such as Taggiasche, Niçoise, or Kalamata), thinly sliced; 8 anchovy fillets (preferably salt-packed; rinsed, backbone removed if salt-packed), finely chopped and smashed to a paste with the side of a knife; and the finely grated zest of 1 lemon into the finished mayonnaise.

For Chipotle Mayonnaise, eliminate the lemon juice, double the amount of garlic, and stir the finely grated zest of 1 lime and 1 tablespoon plus 2 teaspoons chipotle purée (from 1 can of chipotle peppers in adobo sauce, puréed in a blender along with the canning liquid) into the finished mayonnaise.

For Dijonnaise, double the amount of garlic, eliminate the vinegar, and stir ¼ cup plus 1 tablespoon Dijon mustard into the finished mayonnaise.

For Sriracha Mayonnaise, double the garlic and stir 3 tablespoons plus 1 teaspoon Sriracha sauce into the finished mayonnaise.

For Old Bay Mayonnaise, substitute 1 teaspoon water for 1 teaspoon of the vinegar, add ¼ teaspoon finely grated garlic, and stir 1 tablespoon Old Bay Seasoning into the finished mayonnaise.

For Tabasco Mayonnaise, use 2 tablespoons Tabasco sauce and 1 teaspoon fresh lemon juice in place of the lemon juice and vinegar called for in the recipe, and double the amount of garlic.

For Dill Mayonnaise, double the amounts of fresh lemon juice, vinegar, and garlic, and stir ¾ cup finely chopped fresh dill into the finished mayonnaise.

Egg Salad with Bagna Cauda Toast

We use a lot of hard-cooked eggs at the Mozzarella Bar, and when we have a significant number left over, I turn them into egg salad for the staff and I serve it in a big bowl along with a platter of Fett'unta (page 274). The staff goes crazy for it. It's a very straightforward egg salad, made with eggs, salt, mayonnaise, and minced chives. What makes it special is just that every element of the salad is done correctly. The eggs are cooked so that the yolks are bright yellow and slightly moist in the center and the whites have a creamy texture. Then, instead of just mashing the yolks and whites together, I break the yolks in half and tear the whites into chunks, so the egg salad has texture. I bind the salad with homemade garlic mayonnaise instead of store-bought mayonnaise. And, probably the real secret to my egg salad: I add enough salt. When I serve egg salad to friends at home, I give it a more sophisticated presentation by serving it with crostini bathed in bagna cauda, warm anchovy and olive oil "bath." Egg salad is such a familiar comfort food: Who wouldn't want to come to a party and see a platter of toast with a big bowl of egg salad?

This egg salad is significantly better made with farmers' market fresh eggs.

———

To make the egg salad, break the eggs in half to separate the whites from the yolks. Break the yolks in half and drop them into a large bowl. Break the whites into small pieces (about 8 pieces per egg) and drop them into the bowl with the yolks. Sprinkle the eggs with the kosher salt. Add the mayonnaise, and aggressively stir the ingredients together using a rubber spatula until combined. (Stirring aggressively breaks down the egg yolks, which thickens the mayonnaise and ultimately makes for a creamier egg salad.) Serve the egg salad or cover and refrigerate until you're ready to serve it, or for up to 2 days.

To make the toast, adjust an oven rack to the middle position and preheat the oven to 350°F.

Lay the bread slices on a baking sheet, brush the tops with olive oil, and bake for 15 to 20 minutes, until the bread is golden brown and crispy. Remove the toast from the oven and rub the oiled side of each toast with the garlic clove.

To serve, transfer the egg salad to a medium deep serving bowl, piling it in a high mound. Sprinkle the egg salad generously with the chives and serve with a medium spoon. Give the bagna cauda a stir and spoon 1 tablespoon on each

SERVES 6 TO 8
MAKES ABOUT 4 CUPS

———

FOR THE EGG SALAD

13 extra-large eggs, hard-cooked (12 for the egg salad and 1 tester egg; see Perfect Hard-Cooked Eggs, page 82)

2 tablespoons kosher salt

½ cup Garlic Mayonnaise (page 84)

2 to 4 tablespoons minced fresh chives (depending on the dimensions of the platter or bowl in which you are serving the egg salad)

FOR THE TOAST

6 or 8 (½-inch-thick) slices from a loaf of country bread

Extra-virgin olive oil for brushing the bread

1 large garlic clove, peeled

Bagna Cauda (recipe follows)

Thinly sliced fresh Italian parsley leaves for garnish

Maldon sea salt (or another flaky sea salt such as fleur de sel)

piece of toast and put the remaining bagna cauda in a tiny saucepan or bowl with a small spoon. Sprinkle a pinch of parsley and a pinch of sea salt on each piece of toast, artfully stack the toast on a small platter or cutting board, and serve alongside the bowlful of the egg salad.

Bagna Cauda

Makes about 1 cup

Bagna cauda means "warm bath" in Italian, and is a classic condiment of warm olive oil, garlic, and anchovies. I love it. I serve it with Ella's Pinzimonio (page 20) and spoon it over toast for egg salad and over roasted and grilled vegetables, such as Pan-Roasted Cauliflower Wedges with Bagna Cauda (page 187).

8 tablespoons (1 stick) unsalted butter

½ cup extra-virgin olive oil

20 anchovy fillets, about 2 ounces (preferably salt-packed; rinsed, backbone removed if salt-packed),

finely chopped and smashed to a paste with the flat side of the knife

10 to 12 medium or large garlic cloves, peeled

Combine the butter, olive oil, and anchovies in a small saucepan. Using a fine Microplane, grate the garlic into the pan and cook over medium heat until the anchovies dissolve and the garlic is soft and fragrant, 5 to 6 minutes, stirring constantly so the garlic doesn't brown. Reduce the heat to low and cook the bagna cauda for another 2 to 3 minutes to meld the flavors. Turn off the heat and let the bagna cauda rest in the pan you cooked it in until you're ready to use it. Serve warm. Stir to recombine the ingredients before serving and from time to time when it's on the buffet or dinner table.

Black Olive Tapenade

I add orange and lemon zest to make this lively black olive tapenade, which, if I do say so myself, is the best I've ever tasted. If you choose to use olive purée to make the tapenade, avoid any labeled "olive tapenade," which generally has other ingredients in it, such as tomatoes, capers, or eggplant, and look for a product that contains only olives or olives and olive oil.

Put the olives in the bowl of a mini food processor fitted with a metal blade and finely chop. Turn them out into a medium bowl and add the sliced olives, anchovies, and capers. Using a fine Microplane, zest the orange and lemon directly into the bowl. Juice the lemon into the bowl, making sure not to let any seeds drop in, and stir to thoroughly combine the ingredients. Stir in the olive oil, adding more if necessary to obtain a loose, spreadable consistency. Use the tapenade or refrigerate, covered, for up to several weeks. Bring it to room temperature and stir in the parsley just before serving.

MAKES ABOUT 1 CUP

2 cups pitted black olives (such as Taggiasche, Niçoise, or Kalamata; or 1 cup store-bought black olive purée), plus ¼ cup olives, sliced

2 anchovy fillets (preferably salt-packed; rinsed, backbone removed if salt-packed), finely chopped and smashed to a paste with the side of a knife

1 tablespoon capers (preferably salt-packed; soaked for 15 minutes if salt-packed), rinsed, drained, and finely chopped

1 large orange

1 lemon

2 tablespoons extra-virgin olive oil, plus more as needed

¼ cup thinly sliced fresh Italian parsley leaves

4

Saturday Night Chicken Thighs with Italian Sausage and Spicy Pickled Peppers 92

Saturday Night Chicken Thighs with Italian Sausage and Spicy Pickled Peppers

SERVES 6 TO 8

8 bone-in, skin-on chicken thighs

1 tablespoon kosher salt

Freshly ground black pepper

3 tablespoons canola oil
(or another neutral-flavored oil)

1 pound sweet Italian sausage
(about 3 links)

10 to 12 medium or large garlic
cloves, peeled and grated on a
fine Microplane

12 Spicy Pickled Peppers
(recipe follows), stems trimmed,
seeds removed, and halved
lengthwise, plus 2 tablespoons
pickling juice

1 cup dry white wine

1 cup red wine vinegar

1½ cups Chicken Stock (page 59
or sodium-free store-bought stock),
or as needed

3 bunches broccolini
(or broccoli rabe or broccoli
di ciccio; about 1½ pounds)

Braised chicken with sausage is a traditional Italian preparation. We made the dish at the Pizzeria for the first time using a recipe of Lidia Bastianich's, an Italian cooking authority and mother of one of my partners, Joe Bastianich, for a party we hosted celebrating the publication of one of her cookbooks. After making and eating Lidia's dish, I decided to offer my own version of this classic as the Saturday night *piatto*, or entrée special, at the Pizzeria. We add pickled Fresno chiles to the braise for a touch of sweetness and acidity. Also, after the chicken comes out of the oven, we cook broccolini in the braising liquid so the vegetables take on all the delicious flavor of the liquid.

This recipe calls for sodium-free chicken stock. Use half of the salt in this recipe if you are using chicken stock that contains salt.

You will need a large cast-iron or another heavy-bottomed skillet to make this. This recipe calls for you to serve it in the pan it was cooked in, so reach for something you would feel good about putting on your table. You will also need a thin metal spatula, preferably a fish spatula, to turn the chicken without ripping the skin.

———

Adjust an oven rack to the middle position and preheat the oven to 350°F.

Lay the chicken thighs, skin side up, on a baking sheet. Season the skin sides with 1½ teaspoons of the salt and grind a light covering of pepper over the chicken. Turn the thighs and repeat, seasoning the flesh sides with 1½ teaspoons of the remaining salt and a light covering of pepper.

Pour the canola oil into a large cast-iron or another heavy-bottomed skillet and put the pan on the stove over low heat. Before the oil heats up, put the sausage links in the pan and cook them until they are deep brown all over and cooked through, 15 to 20 minutes. It's crucial that you cook them over low heat to prevent the casings from breaking. Remove the sausages to a plate.

Increase the heat to high and heat the fat in the pan for 1 minute, or until it begins to smoke around the edges of the pan. Put half of the chicken thighs, skin side down, in the pan and sear until the skins are golden brown, about 8 minutes, adding more thighs to the pan as those already in the pan shrink and make room for more. As the thighs are done, use a thin metal spatula to carefully remove them from the pan, taking care not to tear off the skin, and transfer the thighs, skin side up, to a plate.

Reduce the heat to low and drain and discard all but 1 tablespoon of fat from the pan. Tilt the pan so all of the fat is in one area. Add the garlic to the area of the pan with the fat, season with the remaining ½ teaspoon salt, and cook the garlic for 1 to 2 minutes, until golden and fragrant but not browned. Add the pickled peppers, and cook for 1 minute. Increase the heat to high, add the white wine, and use a spatula to scrape up the cooked bits on the bottom of the pan. Cook until the wine has completely evaporated, about 3 minutes. Add the vinegar and pickling juice and cook until the liquid is syrupy, about 3 minutes. Add 1 cup of the chicken stock and stir to combine the ingredients. Return the chicken thighs to the pan, skin side up, and add any juices that collected on the plate they were resting on. Nestle the sausages between the chicken thighs. Add enough stock as needed to come just to the top of the thighs without submerging the skin. Increase the heat to high and return the stock to a boil. Turn off the heat and put the lid on the pan or cover the pan tightly with aluminum foil. Put the pan in the oven for 1 hour. Remove the pan from the oven, uncover, and remove the sausages to a plate or cutting board to cool.

Increase the oven temperature to 450°F.

Return the chicken to the oven to cook, uncovered, until the skin is dark brown and crisp, 20 to 30 minutes. Remove the chicken from the oven and place the pan on the stove top.

While the chicken is cooking, trim and discard the dry stem ends of the broccolini; do this one at a time as each stalk of broccolini will need to be trimmed at a different place.

Using tongs, remove the chicken from the pan and put it, skin side up, on a plate. Add the broccolini to the pan you cooked the chicken in, completely submerging it in the liquid. Bring the liquid to a boil over high heat and cook the broccolini in the liquid until it is tender but still al dente and the liquid has reduced to a thick, saucy consistency. If the broccolini is done and the liquid needs to reduce further, remove the broccolini from the pan and continue to cook the liquid to the desired consistency. Turn off the heat. Return the broccolini to the pan.

Meanwhile, slice the sausages ½ inch thick on an extreme bias.

If you are serving the chicken in the pan you cooked it in, lay the chicken thighs, skin side up, in the pan on top of the broccolini, and nestle the sausage slices between the chicken thighs in a way that looks attractive. Alternatively, to serve the chicken thighs on a platter, using tongs, remove the broccolini from the pan to a large high-sided platter and pour the sauce over it. Lay the chicken on top of the broccolini and nestle the sausage slices around the chicken. Serve with a big spoon.

Spicy Pickled Peppers

Makes 2 cups

These chile peppers, which we use in a variety of dishes at both the Pizzeria and Osteria, are a key component to the Saturday Night Chicken Thighs. I also keep a container at home to put on sandwiches. The peppers are best if you let them rest for at least a few days before using them, and they will keep, refrigerated, for several months.

1 quart champagne vinegar (or white wine vinegar)

2 tablespoons honey (preferably wildflower or another mild-flavored honey)

2 teaspoons black peppercorns

1 teaspoon juniper berries

1 teaspoon cloves

4 bay leaves (preferably fresh)

¾ pound Fresno chiles, rinsed, stems left on

Combine the vinegar, honey, peppercorns, juniper berries, cloves, bay leaves, and 2 cups water in a medium saucepan and bring the liquid to a boil over high heat. Reduce the heat to medium-low and simmer for 10 minutes to infuse the liquid with the seasonings. Increase the heat to high, add the chile peppers, and return the liquid to a boil. Reduce the heat to medium-low and simmer the peppers for 4 to 6 minutes, until they soften slightly, but not so long that they lose their shape.

Turn off the heat and set the peppers aside for both the peppers and pickling liquid to cool to room temperature. Use the peppers, or transfer them to a 1-quart canning jar (or another covered container). Strain the pickling liquid into a large bowl. Add the pickling spices that are in the strainer to the jar with the peppers. Add enough of the pickling liquid to fill the jar and discard the remaining liquid. Close the jar and refrigerate the peppers for 1 to 2 days before using them, or for up to 6 months.

Marinated Olives and Fresh Pecorino

This dish of olives, marinated along with cubes of fresh pecorino cheese, allows you to add another element to your entertaining spread with minimal effort. I've had marinated olives many times, but the addition of cheese is a relatively new discovery. After seeing it for the first time in a Spanish restaurant, I knew I had to find a way to bring it into my repertoire. We serve this at Chi Spacca, the meat-centric restaurant in the Mozza group, to go with the cured meats.

I selected the olives that I suggest in this recipe for their variety of sizes, shapes, and colors, from tiny black Niçoise to big green Castelvetrano. Use whatever you want and whatever you can find. I'm all for driving around to three stores in three separate neighborhoods (or towns, if I'm in Italy) if that's what it takes to make a dish that I'm determined to make, but this is one that you should be able to knock out at one store. Fresh pecorino, also called cacio di Roma, is a young sheep's milk cheese from Rome. It's soft, like the texture of Jack cheese. It has a mild flavor, not to be confused with that of pecorino Romano, which is a very pungent, hard, grating cheese, and not what you want here. If you can't find fresh pecorino, use fresh provolone or quality Jack cheese.

You can serve these olives on a buffet table along with the main meal, or as a starter to almost any meal.

SERVES 10 OR MORE
MAKES ABOUT 1 QUART

1½ cups extra-virgin olive oil

¾ cup medium or large garlic cloves (about 30 cloves), peeled

4 cups mixed olives with pits (such as 1 cup each: Lucques, Castelvetrano, Niçoise, and Picholine), drained

4 fresh rosemary sprigs

3 árbol chile pods

4 bay leaves (preferably fresh)

½ teaspoon fresh coarsely ground black pepper

6½ ounces fresh pecorino (also called cacio di Roma; or another young mild white cheese, such as provolone), cut into ⅓- to ½-inch cubes (about 1 cup)

Fresh oregano leaves for garnish

Heat the olive oil in a medium sauté pan over medium-high heat until it slides easily in the pan and the oil around the edges of the pan begins to smoke, 2 to 3 minutes. Add the garlic cloves, reduce the heat to medium, and cook, stirring often, until the garlic cloves are deep golden brown and tender but not mushy when pierced with a small knife. Turn off the heat.

Combine the olives, rosemary, chile pods, bay leaves, and pepper in a large bowl and toss gently to combine. Add the garlic and its oil to the bowl with the olives and gently stir to coat the olives with the oil and combine the ingredients, being careful not to smash the garlic. You can make the olives to this point up to 2 weeks in advance. Refrigerate the olives in a covered container and bring them to room temperature before serving. Add the pecorino cubes and gently toss them into the mix just before serving. Transfer the olives to a small deep bowl and scatter the oregano leaves over the top. Serve the olives and cheese with a tiny fork for guests to grab the cheese cubes and a tiny bowl on the side for guests to put the pits in.

Mixed Chicories Salad with Mustard Vinaigrette

SERVES 6 TO 8

FOR THE VINAIGRETTE

1 large shallot, peeled

¼ cup plus 2 tablespoons apple cider vinegar

1 heaping tablespoon whole-grain mustard

1 heaping tablespoon Dijon mustard

1 teaspoon kosher salt

½ teaspoon freshly ground black pepper

¼ cup extra-virgin olive oil

FOR THE SALAD

3 large chicory heads (such as escarole, frisée, and radicchio)

A handful or two of arugula (preferably wild), optional

1 tablespoon fresh lemon juice

1½ teaspoons kosher salt

This winter salad made with chicories, a loose category of sturdy, slightly bitter lettuces that includes escarole, radicchio, endive, and frisée, is a refreshing accompaniment to a rich meal. It's a very simple salad consisting only of the chicories and the vinaigrette they're tossed with. It's one of the rare salads that I would put in the category of "overnight salads," meaning I still like it the day after it was tossed with vinaigrette. I wouldn't go so far as to say the salad *improves* overnight, but because the leaves are sturdy—chicories are prepared cooked as often as they are raw—the vinaigrette wilts them in a pleasant way. When you get up the morning after a dinner party, if you're anything like me, you undoubtedly forgot to eat and you'll say: "I'm starving. What is there to eat?" and if you're lucky, you'll find a container of this salad. You may not use all of the vinaigrette; use the rest within a few days of making it to dress a salad.

To make the vinaigrette, using a medium-holed Microplane, grate the shallot directly into a medium bowl. Add the vinegar, whole-grain mustard, Dijon mustard, salt, and pepper and stir to combine. Slowly add the olive oil, whisking constantly. Use the vinaigrette or refrigerate, covered, for up to 2 days. Bring the vinaigrette to room temperature and whisk to recombine the ingredients before using.

To prepare the salad, remove and discard the outer leaves from the heads of the escarole or frisée, using only the pale green leaves; discard the cores. Remove and discard the outer layers of the radicchio and discard the cores. Tear the leaves into 2- to 3-inch pieces and put them in a large bowl. Add the arugula if you are using it. Drizzle with the lemon juice, sprinkle with the salt, and toss to coat the chicories. Add ¼ cup of the vinaigrette and toss gently, massaging the dressing into the leaves. Add another ¼ cup vinaigrette, toss, and gently massage the vinaigrette into the leaves to coat them. Add another 2 tablespoons of the vinaigrette if necessary so the leaves are evenly coated and glistening but not overdressed or wilted. Transfer the salad to a large wide-mouthed serving bowl or pile it on a large platter and serve with tongs.

Twice-Roasted Smashed Potatoes with Rosemary and Sage

Smashed potatoes, with their craggy surface and crispy texture, is one of my favorite ways to enjoy potatoes, and one of the first *antipasti* I developed for the Pizzeria. We deep-fry them at the restaurant, but at home, I am able to achieve the same super-crunchy, deep golden exterior by roasting the potatoes on the oven floor. The nice thing about serving these at a dinner party is that unlike, say, French fries, the potatoes remain almost miraculously crisp even after they've cooled down. You will need a large (at least 13 x 9 inches) casserole dish to finish baking these in, preferably something that will look pretty on your table.

SERVES 6 TO 8

2 pounds baby Yukon gold or fingerling potatoes (choose potatoes that are roughly the same size as one another)

¼ cup plus 2 tablespoons olive oil

2 tablespoons plus 1 teaspoon kosher salt

6 (2- to 3-inch-long) fresh rosemary sprigs

6 fresh sage sprigs

8 tablespoons (1 stick) unsalted butter, cut into small cubes

Maldon sea salt (or another flaky sea salt such as fleur de sel)

Adjust the oven racks so none are near the oven floor; you'll be putting the casserole dish directly on the oven floor. If you are using an electric oven or another oven where you can't put anything on the floor, adjust the oven racks so that one is closest to the floor and put a pizza stone on it if you have one. Adjust another oven rack to the middle position and preheat the oven to 350°F.

Put the potatoes in a large bowl, drizzle with 2 tablespoons of the olive oil, sprinkle with 2 tablespoons of the kosher salt, and toss to coat the potatoes. Spread the potatoes out on a large baking sheet and put them on the middle rack to roast for 45 to 50 minutes, until they are very tender when pierced with a toothpick or fork. Remove the potatoes from the oven and set them aside until they are cool enough to touch.

Increase the oven temperature to 500°F.

One at a time, place the potatoes on a flat surface and use the heel of your hand to smash them to ¾ inch thick, pressing gently and evenly to prevent the potatoes from breaking apart. Slide (rather than lift) the smashed potatoes off the work surface and put them in a large bowl. Drizzle the potatoes with the remaining ¼ cup olive oil and the remaining 1 teaspoon kosher salt. Gently toss the potatoes to coat them, taking care not to break them up.

Lift the potatoes out of the bowl and transfer them to a table-worthy baking dish, layering in the rosemary and sage sprigs and the butter pieces so they are dispersed throughout. (The potatoes won't fit in a single layer; it's okay if they overlap.)

Return the potatoes to the middle rack of the oven and bake them for 20 minutes. Remove the baking dish from the oven, rotate it from front to back, and return it to the oven, this time placing it on the floor of the oven or the lowest rack. Roast the potatoes until they are golden brown and crispy, about 15 minutes, shaking the baking dish and rotating it from front to back halfway through the cooking time so the potatoes brown evenly. Remove the baking dish from the oven. Sprinkle the potatoes with sea salt, and serve them in the dish they were baked in.

Roasted Carrot and Wheat Berry Salad with Dill

I'm always looking for that one ingredient that will turn a familiar vegetable into something special and a little unexpected. In the case of this carrot and wheat berry dish, fresh dill turned out to be just the thing. Where parsley is often added for color, and rosemary or thyme add nice background flavor to braised meats, dill, like cilantro and tarragon, is a dish-changing herb. In this mix of carrots and wheat berries, the dill complements the other flavors and turns the overall dish into something memorable.

I call for wheat berries here, but you could use any chewy grain, such as farro, barley, rye berries, freekeh, or spelt. Use long, slender carrots, such as those you find at farmers' markets or those sold with the tops on at supermarkets. I spoon half of the grains onto the bottom of the platter and toss the other half with the carrots. It looks prettier this way, and I like the idea of people digging in for more.

Bring 1 quart water to a boil in a medium saucepan over high heat. Add 1 tablespoon of the kosher salt and the wheat berries and return the water to a boil. Reduce the heat to medium-low and simmer until the wheat berries are al dente, 30 to 50 minutes. (Cooking time varies greatly depending on the freshness of the grains.) Drain the wheat berries in a colander and transfer them to a small bowl. Drizzle with 2 teaspoons of the olive oil and toss gently to coat the grains. Set aside to cool to room temperature.

Adjust the oven racks so none is near the oven floor; you'll be putting the baking sheet directly on the oven floor. If you are using an electric oven or another oven where you can't put anything on the floor, adjust the oven racks so that one is closest to the floor and put a pizza stone on it, if you have one. Preheat the oven to 500°F.

Scrub the carrots and cut off the greens, leaving the last ¾ inch of the stems attached. Cut the carrots in half lengthwise (quarter them if you're using larger carrots) and put them in a large bowl. Drizzle the carrots with the remaining 3 tablespoons oil, sprinkle with the remaining 1 tablespoon kosher salt, and toss to coat them. Lay the carrots, cut side down, on a baking sheet. Toss the garlic and thyme in the bowl you tossed the carrots in and coat them with the oil left in the bowl. Scatter the garlic cloves and thyme sprigs around the carrots, taking

2 tablespoons kosher salt

½ cup wheat berries (or farro, barley, rye berries, freekeh, or spelt), soaked overnight and drained

3 tablespoons plus 2 teaspoons extra-virgin olive oil

3 pounds slender carrots (3 to 4 bunches; weighed with tops)

10 to 12 medium or large garlic cloves, peeled

10 fresh thyme sprigs

¼ cup fresh dill sprigs, chopped, plus a few sprigs for garnish

Finishing-quality extra-virgin olive oil

Maldon sea salt (or another flaky sea salt such as fleur de sel)

care that the garlic has as little contact with the tray as possible so it doesn't burn. Put the baking sheet on the floor of the oven or the lowest rack and roast the carrots and garlic until the carrots are fork-tender but not mushy, 10 to 15 minutes, shaking the baking sheet and rotating it front to back halfway through the cooking time so the carrots and garlic brown evenly. Remove the baking sheet from the oven and set it aside to cool to room temperature. (When cooking vegetables on the oven floor, a lot of steam is produced from the water released as a result of the vegetables cooking so quickly, so be careful of the steam that will arise when you open the oven door.)

Remove and discard the thyme sprigs and transfer the carrots and garlic to a large bowl. Add the chopped dill and toss gently to distribute it evenly. Add half of the wheat berries and toss again gently to distribute them.

To serve, spoon the remaining wheat berries onto the bottom of a large platter. Lift the carrots with the wheat berries out of the bowl and lay them on the platter on top of the bed of wheat berries. Scatter the dill sprigs on top of the salad, drizzle with finishing-quality olive oil, sprinkle with sea salt, and serve with a large serving spoon.

5

Grilled Lamb Shoulder Chops with Mint Yogurt Sauce

SERVES 8 TO 10

6 pounds lamb shoulder chops, cut ¾ inch thick

1 cup Tikka Marinade (recipe follows)

4 to 5 lemons

Olive oil for brushing the lemons

2 tablespoons kosher salt

Freshly ground black pepper

Finishing-quality extra-virgin olive oil

Maldon sea salt (or another flaky sea salt, such as fleur de sel)

Several long fresh cilantro sprigs

Mint Yogurt Sauce (recipe follows)

Today, there's a movement among restaurant chefs to try to utilize either the whole animal or at least some of the lesser-known and less-expensive cuts. At Chi Spacca, we serve lamb shoulder chops, marinated in an Indian-inspired yogurt-based marinade and quickly grilled or pan-seared, instead of the much more expensive and expected rib chops. The shoulder chops are the dish I'm most likely to order from that restaurant. I love to pick up the bone and gnaw on the meat closest to the bone, which is very flavorful. And I also really like the texture of the meat. Where lamb rib chops are tender, like beef tenderloin (not my favorite cut of meat), shoulder chops, cut as thin as they are and cooked correctly, are pleasantly chewy. Shoulder chops are widely available in butcher shops, of course, and also in supermarkets, where they are often sold simply as "lamb chops." You'll know them from lamb rib chops by their affordable price, and also they don't have the typical Fred Flintstone look of a rib chop. In this recipe, the chops are served with a simple yogurt sauce with mint. What could be simpler? Or easier?

These chops are best cooked over a very hot charcoal or wood fire. The point is to char the outsides very quickly before you cook the meat so long that it becomes tough. Most gas grills don't get hot enough, and in the length of time it takes to char the outsides, the meat will toughen up. If your gas grill does not get super hot, cook the chops instead in a searing-hot cast-iron skillet or grill pan, such as a 20-inch Lodge cast-iron grill/griddle. It fits over two burners and allows you to cook many chops at one time.

———

Put the chops in a large bowl and spoon the tikka marinade over them. Turn to coat the chops with the marinade and massage the marinade onto both sides of the chops with your hands. Cover the bowl and set it aside for the meat to marinate for 30 minutes; any longer and the marinade will cause the meat to break down and give it an unappealing, fuzzy texture.

While the meat is marinating, cut each lemon in half through the middle and trim and discard ½ inch from each end, so the lemon halves have two flat surfaces. Brush both cut ends of the lemon halves with the olive oil.

Prepare a hot fire in a charcoal grill. Alternatively, to cook the chops indoors, preheat a grill pan or cast-iron skillet over high heat. Cooking method and times will be the same as for grilling.

Remove the chops from the marinade and lay them in a single layer on a baking sheet. Season the chops with the kosher salt and a generous grinding of pepper on both sides.

Grill the chops until they are charred on both sides, about 3 minutes per side.

Place the lemon halves with the larger, middle side of the lemons facing down on the grill or in the grill pan with the chops for about 2 minutes, until golden brown. Turn and cook the smaller sides of the lemon halves for about 30 seconds just to warm them.

When all of the chops and lemons have been grilled, arrange the chops on a large rectangular platter. Nestle the lemon halves, middle side up, on the platter around the chops. Drizzle the chops with finishing-quality olive oil and sprinkle with sea salt. Scatter the cilantro sprigs over the chops and serve with the mint yogurt sauce in a bowl on the side for guests to serve themselves.

Tikka Marinade

Makes 1 cup

This Indian-inspired marinade is completely out of my usual flavor repertoire. Our former executive chef, Matt Molina, and I developed it when we were looking for a marinade for skinless chicken breasts that we were using to make Cobb salads and chicken sandwiches. It added great flavor to an otherwise not very flavorful cut of meat, and it also helped keep the meat moist, another challenge when it comes to skinless, boneless chicken breasts. Yogurt is a great tenderizer. I use this marinade for leg of lamb (see Lamb and Chicken Tikka Kebabs, page 270) and for Grilled Lamb Shoulder Chops. There is no salt in the marinade; salt causes the yogurt in the marinade to separate. For the same reason that yogurt tenderizes tough cuts of meat, you don't want to leave meat in this marinade for more than thirty minutes or the yogurt will turn the meat a mealy texture.

1 teaspoon fennel seeds

1 cup Straus Family Creamery Organic Greek Yogurt (or another whole-milk plain, not overly thick, Greek-style yogurt)

2 tablespoons finely chopped fresh mint leaves (from about ¼ cup packed whole leaves)

2 tablespoons finely chopped fresh cilantro leaves (from about ¼ cup packed whole leaves)

¾ teaspoon ground cardamom

¾ teaspoon sweet smoked paprika

½ teaspoon freshly ground black pepper

3 large garlic cloves

Toast the fennel seeds in a small sauté pan over medium heat for 1 to 2 minutes, until they are fragrant and golden brown, shaking the pan often so the seeds don't burn. Transfer the fennel seeds to a plate to cool to room temperature. Grind them in a spice grinder or use a mortar and a pestle.

Put the yogurt in a medium bowl and add the fennel, mint, cilantro, cardamom, paprika, and pepper. Using a fine Microplane, grate the garlic directly into the bowl and stir to thoroughly combine. The marinade can be made up to 2 days in advance. Refrigerate in a covered container until you're ready to use it.

Mint Yogurt Sauce

Makes about 1 cup

This refreshing condiment is easy to make and the perfect accompaniment to any lamb preparation.

1 cup Straus Family Creamery Organic Greek Yogurt (or another whole-milk plain, not overly thick, Greek-style yogurt)

2 tablespoons extra-virgin olive oil

1 tablespoon fresh lemon juice

½ teaspoon kosher salt

2 to 3 medium or large garlic cloves, peeled

¼ cup finely chopped fresh mint leaves (from about ½ cup packed whole leaves)

Combine the yogurt, olive oil, lemon juice, and salt in a small bowl. Using a fine Microplane, grate the garlic into the bowl and stir to combine. You can make the sauce to this point up to a day in advance. Refrigerate in a covered container. Stir in the mint just before serving. To serve, transfer the sauce to a small pretty bowl and serve with a small spoon.

Curry-Roasted Cauliflower

SERVES 6 TO 8

2 tablespoons coriander seeds

2 tablespoons caraway seeds

1 heaping teaspoon red chile flakes

1 cup apple cider vinegar

2 teaspoons curry powder

3 teaspoons kosher salt

2 large cauliflower heads
(about 2 pounds each),
cut into equal-size florets

½ cup plus 2 tablespoons olive oil

4 tablespoons (½ stick) unsalted
butter, cut into small cubes

½ cup packed fresh cilantro
leaves, picked from the stems with
about ½ inch of the stem still intact
(from less than ½ bunch)

15 to 20 large fresh mint leaves
(about ¼ cup packed), torn into
about ½-inch pieces

Recently a food writer asked me to name one of my favorite dishes served in a Los Angeles restaurant, and I named the Indian-spiced cauliflower at A.O.C. That dish, in which the cauliflower is broken up into florets and roasted with olive oil and Indian spices, is the inspiration for this recipe. Curry and cauliflower, a traditional Indian combination, work very well together: cauliflower's mild, lightly sweet flavor really picks up the flavor of the Indian spices. This cauliflower is delicious hot from the oven, at room temperature, and even cold. I love to snack on leftovers straight from the refrigerator. To make this a vegan dish, substitute olive oil for the butter called for in this recipe.

———

Adjust the oven racks so none are near the oven floor; you'll be putting the baking sheet directly on the oven floor. If you are using an electric oven or another oven where you can't put anything on the floor, adjust the racks so that one is closest to the floor and put a pizza stone on it if you have one. Adjust another oven rack to the middle position and preheat the oven to 500°F.

Toast the coriander seeds and caraway seeds in a small sauté pan over medium heat for 1 to 2 minutes, until they are fragrant and golden brown, shaking the pan often so they don't burn. Transfer the seeds to a plate to cool to room temperature. Grind the coriander seeds, caraway seeds, and red chile flakes in a spice grinder or use a mortar and a pestle and transfer to a medium bowl. Add the vinegar, curry powder, and 1½ teaspoons of the salt, and stir to thoroughly combine the ingredients.

Put the cauliflower florets in a large bowl. Drizzle with ½ cup of the olive oil, season with the remaining 1½ teaspoons salt, and toss well to coat all the florets.

Use your hands to lift the cauliflower florets out of the bowl and onto two large baking sheets, arranging the florets so the cut sides are facing down. Discard the cauliflower "crumbs" and liquid left in the bowl. Put one of the baking sheets on the oven floor or the lowest rack and roast for 10 to 15 minutes, until the florets start to brown. Remove the baking sheet from the oven. (When cooking vegetables on the oven floor, a lot of steam is produced from the water released as a result of the vegetables cooking so quickly, so be careful of the steam that will arise when you open the oven door.) Drizzle 1 tablespoon of the remaining olive oil over the cauliflower and dot with 2 tablespoons of the butter. Rotate the baking sheet from front to back and return to the oven, this time to the middle rack, and roast the cauliflower for 8 to 12 minutes, until the sides touching the baking sheet are deep brown and the cauliflower is tender but not mushy when pierced with a toothpick or fork. Remove the cauliflower from the oven and set it aside to cool for about 5 minutes.

Using a metal spatula, scrape the cauliflower off the baking sheet and into a large mixing bowl, making sure to get all the good bits stuck to the baking sheet. Repeat with the second batch of cauliflower florets. Remove from the oven and set the baking sheet aside to cool for about 5 minutes before scraping the florets off the baking sheet and into the bowl with the first batch of cauliflower. Add the cilantro and mint leaves and toss the cauliflower so the herbs are strewn throughout.

To serve, transfer the cauliflower to a large rimmed platter or wide-mouthed serving bowl, and serve with a large spoon.

Marinated Summer Squash Salad

SERVES 6 TO 8

1 pound baby or small summer squash (crookneck, yellow, green, or variegated zucchini, or pattypan squash)

1 tablespoon plus ¾ teaspoon kosher salt

½ cup champagne vinegar (or white wine vinegar)

1 tablespoon honey (preferably wildflower or another mild-flavored honey)

1 teaspoon coriander seeds

1 teaspoon mustard seeds

1 teaspoon fennel seeds

5 long fresh dill sprigs

½ teaspoon red chile flakes

½ cup finely chopped fresh Italian parsley leaves (from about 1 cup packed whole leaves)

5 to 6 medium or large garlic cloves, peeled and minced

1 cup finishing-quality extra-virgin olive oil

2 tablespoons fresh oregano leaves

I love taking a common vegetable and giving it an uncommon preparation, which is what I did with summer squash in this recipe. The squash is salted and set aside overnight to extract the excess water, concentrating the flavor and also softening the squash. The next day, the squash is tossed with an herb-infused marinade. The resulting vegetables seem as if they've been pickled, but they're much fresher than a pickle.

When shopping for squash, look for different varieties, shapes, and colors of baby summer squash. How you cut the squash will depend on their size and shape. Baby squash are ideal in that you will just cut them in half, preserving the unusual shapes of the squash and the pretty colors of their skins. This is a great side dish for a picnic, because the squash gets better as it sits in the marinade.

If you buy small rather than baby squash, a mandoline will make easy work of slicing the squash for this recipe.

———

If you are using baby squash, cut them in half or cut larger squash into 1½-inch segments and cut each segment into ½-inch-thick slices, ideally on a mandoline. Put the summer squash in a large bowl and sprinkle with 1 teaspoon of the salt. Toss to distribute the salt and set the squash aside for 1 hour. Put a cooling rack on a baking sheet, line the baking sheet with a thick layer of paper towels, and turn the squash out onto the towels. Put another baking sheet on top of the squash and put a large cast-iron skillet (or something equally flat and heavy) on top of the baking sheet. Put the whole package—baking sheets, skillet, and all—in the refrigerator for 12 to 24 hours to extract the water from the squash.

Combine the vinegar, honey, coriander seeds, mustard seeds, fennel seeds, dill sprigs, ¼ teaspoon of the red chile flakes, and 2 teaspoons of the remaining salt in a small saucepan over low heat and bring to a boil to melt the honey. Turn off the heat and set aside for 20 minutes to infuse the liquid with the seasonings. Pass the contents of the saucepan through a fine-mesh strainer into a large bowl and discard the solids. Set the liquid aside to cool to room temperature. Stir in the parsley, garlic, the remaining ¾ teaspoon salt, and the remaining ¼ teaspoon chile flakes. Add the olive oil in a slow, thin stream, whisking constantly.

Remove the squash from the refrigerator. Pat the squash dry with paper towels and add the squash to the bowl with the marinade. Toss to coat. Serve, or cover and refrigerate the squash until you're ready to serve it or for up to 1 day. Bring the squash to room temperature, add the oregano, and toss to distribute it just before serving.

To serve, transfer the squash and marinade to a medium deep serving bowl and serve with a large spoon.

Stuffed Artichokes

These globe artichokes are stuffed with a mixture including onion, toma-toes, and white beans, topped with crunchy panko bread crumbs, and baked. I serve them with grilled lamb, but they also make a lovely vegetarian main dish. Matt Molina, former executive chef at Osteria Mozza, made them for a special dinner we hosted at Pizzeria Mozza in Newport Beach, and it was love at first sight: as soon as I saw them lined up on a platter, I knew I wanted to serve them at home. Stuffed vegetables in general are just so appealing. Inside, there is always something sautéed and delicious, and, like these, they're pretty much always topped with crunchy bread crumbs and grated cheese. There is a substantial amount of effort that goes into making these, from prepping the artichokes to cooking the beans they're stuffed with. All that work pays off in that this is the rare artichoke dish that you can carve right through and eat with a knife and fork, because the choke has been removed. This is a luxury dish, no doubt, not in the price of the ingredients, but in the labor involved in making it.

You will need a 10 x 7-inch or an equivalent-size casserole dish or sauté pan to make these. (A standard 13 x 9-inch dish is too large and an 8 x 8-inch dish is too small.) Ideally, you'll serve the artichokes in the same pan you cook them in, so reach for something that you would feel good about putting on your table.

———

To prepare the artichokes, fill a large bowl with water. Cut the lemons in half, squeeze their juice into the water, and drop the lemon halves into the water. Working one at a time, trim and discard about ½ inch of the dry stem ends of the artichokes. Remove and discard the dark outer leaves from each artichoke until you see only bright greenish-yellow leaves. With a vegetable peeler shave each artichoke from halfway up the bulb, all the way down to the end of the stem so it's smooth and even and the entire artichoke is a pale yellowish-white color. Cut off and discard 1½ inches off the tip end of the artichoke to give it a flat top; you will be left with about 2 inches of artichoke from where the stem meets the body of the artichoke. Using a teaspoon, scrape the choke (the purple hairy fuzz in the center of the artichoke) out of each artichoke and discard it. Drop the prepped artichoke into the lemon water and prep the remaining artichokes in the same way.

FOR THE ARTICHOKES

2 lemons

8 globe artichokes

¼ cup chopped fresh mint leaves
(from about ½ cup whole leaves)

2 teaspoons kosher salt

1¼ cups extra-virgin olive oil,
or as needed

12 to 16 medium or large garlic
cloves, peeled

1 cup dry white wine

FOR THE STUFFING

1 small yellow Spanish onion,
peeled

3 tablespoons canola oil
(or another neutral-flavored oil)

1¼ teaspoons kosher salt

6 to 8 medium or large garlic
cloves, peeled

4 roasted tomatoes (see Slow-
Roasted Roma Tomatoes with
Garlic and Thyme, page 189)

1 cup cooked white beans
(see White Beans, page 36),
drained

1 tablespoon fresh oregano leaves,
chopped (about 1½ teaspoons)

(continued)

1 teaspoon fresh thyme leaves

⅛ teaspoon red chile flakes

FOR THE BREAD CRUMB TOPPING

½ cup panko bread crumbs

3 tablespoons extra-virgin olive oil

2 tablespoons thinly sliced fresh Italian parsley leaves (from about ½ cup packed whole leaves)

1 teaspoon kosher salt

When you have prepared all of the artichokes, remove them from the lemon water and pat them dry with paper towels. Put the mint, salt, and ¼ cup of the olive oil in a small bowl. Using a fine Microplane, grate the garlic directly into the bowl. Add the artichokes and toss gently to coat them with the seasonings.

Put the artichokes, flat sides down, in a large Dutch oven or another large pot (preferably one with a lid). Scrape the marinade out of the bowl and add it to the pan with the artichokes. Add the white wine and the remaining 1 cup olive oil, or enough so the artichokes are submerged, with only the stems sticking out of the liquid. Bring the liquid to a boil over medium heat. Reduce the heat to low so the liquid is barely simmering. Put a lid on the pot or cover it tightly with aluminum foil and cook the artichokes at a gentle simmer until they are tender when pierced at the widest part with a toothpick, about 40 minutes. Turn off the heat and let the artichokes cool, covered, to room temperature in the cooking liquid.

Remove the artichokes from the liquid and transfer them to a cutting board. Cut off the stems at the point where they meet the artichoke bottoms. Transfer the artichokes to a plate. Cut the stems into ¼-inch cubes and set them aside.

Pour the cooking liquid into a large measuring cup. Using a ladle, skim the oil off the top until the cup contains 1¼ cups of just the seasoned wine and vegetables and very little oil at the top. (If you don't have 1¼ cup liquid, add warm water to make up the difference.) Discard the skimmed oil.

Adjust an oven rack to the middle position and preheat the oven to 450°F.

To make the stuffing, trim and discard the root end of the onion and cut it in half root to tip. Cut each half in half again, root to tip, so the onion is quartered. Separate the layers of the onion, stack 2 or 3 layers at a time on top of one another, and slice ¼ inch thick lengthwise.

Heat the canola oil in a large sauté pan over medium heat. Add the onion and salt and cook, stirring frequently, until the onion is soft and tender but not browned at all, about 8 minutes, lowering the heat if the onion begins to brown. Using a medium-holed Microplane, grate the garlic into the pan and cook for 2 minutes, until the garlic is fragrant, stirring constantly so it doesn't brown. Add the tomatoes and ¼ cup water and cook the stuffing for about 5 minutes, stirring and breaking up the tomatoes with a wooden spoon, until the liquid has reduced to a thick, saucy consistency. Add the beans, cubed artichoke stems, oregano, thyme, red chile flakes, and ¾ cup of the reserved cooking liquid and stir to combine. Cook the stuffing, stirring frequently, until the liquid has reduced to a thick, saucy consistency, 5 to 6 minutes.

To make the bread crumb topping, combine the bread crumbs, olive oil, parsley, and salt in a small bowl and stir to thoroughly combine the ingredients.

To assemble the artichokes, spread 1 cup of the stuffing to cover the bottom of a 10 x 7-inch (or equivalent-size) casserole dish. Stir the remaining cooking liquid and spoon 1 tablespoon of the liquid, including the onion and other seasonings, over each artichoke; discard the remaining liquid. Working one at a time, fill each artichoke with 3 tablespoons of the stuffing and place it, filled side up, in the dish, gently nestling it into the stuffing on the bottom of the dish. Fill the remaining artichokes in the same way. When you've filled all of the artichokes, top each with a light sprinkling of the bread crumbs, about 2 tablespoons on each.

Bake the artichokes for 10 to 15 minutes, rotating the baking dish from front to back halfway through the cooking time, until the bread crumbs are golden brown and crunchy. Remove the artichokes from the oven.

Serve the artichokes in the dish you cooked them in, or transfer them to a large round platter, arranging them in a flowerlike pattern on the platter. Serve with a flat spatula or large spoon.

Farro Salad with Fresh Herbs and Feta

SERVES 6 TO 8

FOR THE FARRO

1 cup farro

2 tablespoons extra-virgin olive oil

1 tablespoon kosher salt

FOR THE VINAIGRETTE

¼ cup plus 1 tablespoon red wine vinegar

1 tablespoon fresh lemon juice

2 tablespoons dried oregano

½ teaspoon kosher salt

¼ teaspoon freshly ground black pepper

2 to 3 medium or large garlic cloves, peeled

½ cup extra-virgin olive oil

FOR THE SALAD

½ medium red onion (halved root to tip), peeled

¾ pound Persian or Japanese cucumbers, halved lengthwise and thinly sliced on an extreme bias (about 2 cups)

1 cup small sweet tomatoes (such as Sun Golds, Sweet 100s, or grape tomatoes), halved through the stems

This salad has all the components of a Greek salad—tomatoes, cucumbers, red onion, and feta—with the addition of farro, an ancient Tuscan grain similar to barley, which makes the salad more substantial. I love the nutty flavor and toothsome texture of farro. I serve this salad with lamb because when I think Greek, I think lamb, but it would be equally delicious alongside any grilled meat or fish. It's the perfect salad to put on a buffet or bring to a picnic because it gets even better with time, as the farro absorbs the tangy oregano vinaigrette. The vinaigrette recipe makes more vinaigrette than you may need for this; use any left over within the next few days to dress another salad.

If you have parchment paper, use it to line the baking sheet to toast the farro; it makes it so easy to get the grains off the baking sheet without spilling any. Just pull the entire sheet of parchment off the baking sheet and fold it up to create a sort of funnel to pour the farro into the pot once it's toasted.

To cook the farro, adjust an oven rack to the middle position and preheat the oven to 350°F. Line a baking sheet with parchment paper, if you are using it.

Put the farro on the baking sheet, drizzle with 1 tablespoon of the olive oil, and toss to coat the grains. Spread the farro out on the baking sheet and toast in the oven until it's golden brown and slightly fragrant, 8 to 10 minutes, shaking the baking sheet and rotating it from front to back halfway through the cooking time so the farro browns evenly. Remove from the oven.

Meanwhile, bring 2 quarts water to a boil in a medium saucepan over high heat. Add the salt and farro and return the water to a boil. Reduce the heat to medium-low and simmer the farro until it is al dente, 18 to 22 minutes. Drain the farro in a colander and transfer to a large bowl. Drizzle the farro with the remaining 1 tablespoon olive oil and toss to coat the grains. Set aside to cool to room temperature.

To make the vinaigrette, combine the vinegar, lemon juice, oregano, salt, and pepper in a medium bowl. Using a fine Microplane, grate the garlic directly into the bowl and whisk to combine the ingredients. Add the olive oil in a slow, thin, stream, whisking constantly to emulsify. Use the vinaigrette or refrigerate, covered, for up to 3 days. Bring the vinaigrette to room temperature and whisk to recombine the ingredients before using.

To prepare the salad, trim and discard the root end of the onion and cut the onion half in half root to tip so it is quartered. Separate the layers of the onion, stack 2 or 3 layers at a time on top of one another, and slice 1/16 inch thick lengthwise. Place the onion slices in a small bowl of ice water and set them aside for 5 to 10 minutes; this draws out some of the bitterness. Before using them, drain them on and pat them dry with paper towels.

To assemble the salad, add the cucumbers, tomatoes, parsley, basil, and onion slices to the bowl with the farro. Holding the radishes by the stems, thinly slice on a mandoline or with a sharp knife and discard the stems. Add the radish slices to the bowl with the other salad ingredients.

Drizzle the lemon juice and sprinkle the salt over the salad and toss gently to coat the grains and vegetables. Drizzle all but 2 tablespoons of the vinaigrette over the salad. Toss gently to combine the ingredients and coat the salad with the vinaigrette; add the remaining vinaigrette if needed to coat the grains and vegetables and toss again gently. Add the feta and toss gently to distribute the cheese, taking care not to mash it.

To serve, transfer the salad to a large platter or wide-mouthed serving bowl and scatter the petite basil leaves over the top, if you are using them. Serve with a big spoon.

½ cup thinly sliced fresh Italian parsley leaves (from about 1 cup tightly packed whole leaves)

12 fresh basil leaves, stacked and thinly sliced lengthwise, plus several leaves of petite basil, or the smallest leaves from the bunch, for garnish (optional)

10 to 12 radishes (preferably French breakfast radishes)

2 tablespoons fresh lemon juice

1 teaspoon kosher salt

¾ cup crumbled feta cheese (about 4 ounces)

Roasted Asparagus with Herb Vinaigrette

SERVES 6 TO 8

2 pounds medium asparagus, stems snapped off at their natural breaking point and discarded

2 tablespoons olive oil

2 teaspoons kosher salt

10 fresh thyme sprigs

Herb Vinaigrette (recipe follows)

Maldon sea salt (or another flaky sea salt such as fleur de sel)

I love roasted vegetables seasoned with just good olive oil and sea salt, but I also get excited when I find a condiment that transforms roasted veggies into a more finished dish.

When shopping for asparagus, look for spears that would fall in the middle, standard-size range, neither pencil asparagus nor jumbo asparagus. To trim, just snap the end of each spear at its natural breaking point. The asparagus tells you where it wants to be broken. If you have a grill fired up, cook these on a grill instead; cooking times will be the same.

———

Adjust the oven racks so none is near the oven floor; you'll be putting the baking sheet directly on the oven floor. If you are using an electric oven or another oven where you can't put anything on the floor, adjust the oven racks so that one is closest to the floor and put a pizza stone on it, if you have one. Preheat the oven to 500°F.

Put the asparagus on a large baking sheet. Drizzle with the olive oil, sprinkle with the kosher salt, and toss to coat the spears. Scatter the thyme over the asparagus. Put the baking sheet on the oven floor or the lowest rack and roast the asparagus until it is tender (the best test for doneness is to bite into one spear) and the part touching the baking sheet is brown, 8 to 10 minutes, shaking the baking sheet and rotating it from front to back halfway through the cooking time so the asparagus browns evenly. Remove the asparagus from the oven and set it aside to cool to room temperature. (When cooking vegetables on the oven floor, a lot of steam is produced from the water released as a result of the vegetables cooking so quickly, so be careful of the steam that will arise when you open the oven door.)

To serve, lay the asparagus with the spears facing one direction on a long rectangular platter. Use the back of a spoon to paint the asparagus spears with a light coating of herb vinaigrette, sprinkle with sea salt, and serve the rest of the vinaigrette on the side with a small spoon for people to serve themselves.

Herb Vinaigrette

Makes about 2 cups

I developed this herb vinaigrette when I was looking for something to dress up asparagus. Made with equal parts champagne vinegar and prosecco, loads of herbs (including basil, chervil, tarragon, and chives), and a little bit of sugar, it perfectly complements the grassy flavor of asparagus. One day, looking for other uses for the vinaigrette, I saw some roasted eggplant in the kitchen and a light went off in my mind—I just knew that the vinaigrette would be equally delicious on the eggplant. I tried it, and my hunch was right.

If you can't find fresh chervil, substitute fresh Italian parsley and tarragon in equal parts for the chervil in this recipe.

½ cup packed fresh basil leaves

½ cup packed fresh chervil leaves

½ cup packed fresh tarragon leaves

½ cup packed fresh chives

¾ cup extra-virgin olive oil

1 tablespoon plus 1 teaspoon kosher salt

¼ cup minced shallot (from about 1 medium peeled shallot)

1 tablespoon sugar

¼ cup plus 2 tablespoons champagne vinegar (or white wine vinegar)

¼ cup plus 2 tablespoons prosecco or sparkling white wine

2 tablespoons grated lemon zest (from 3 lemons), plus 2 tablespoons fresh lemon juice

Put the basil, chervil, tarragon, and chives on a cutting board and very roughly chop them. Transfer the herbs to the bowl of a mini food processor fitted with a metal blade. Add ½ cup of the olive oil and 1 tablespoon of the salt and pulse until the herbs are chopped to tiny flecks but not to a paste or purée.

Transfer the contents of the food processor to a medium bowl. Add the shallot, sugar, and the remaining 1 teaspoon salt and stir to combine. Add the vinegar, prosecco, lemon zest, and lemon juice and stir to combine. Add the remaining ¼ cup oil in a slow, thin stream, whisking constantly to emulsify. Serve or refrigerate the vinaigrette, covered, for up to 1 day; any longer and the herbs will brown. Bring the vinaigrette to room temperature before serving.

Roasted Eggplant with Herb Vinaigrette

I give you two separate recipes here, one for roasting baby eggplants and another for roasting giant eggplants. Which you choose is entirely a matter of personal taste. The small eggplants are halved, roasted, and drizzled with herb vinaigrette, so each guest takes an entire half. The large eggplants are halved, roasted, and served cut side up, family style, so guests spoon out the creamy insides and drizzle their portion with the vinaigrette, like an eggplant version of mashed potatoes and gravy. Do you want your guests to grab a piece and go: a nice, compact, and clean experience? Or to dig into something for a more communal and dramatic presentation. I guess you have to figure out what personality type you are before you go any further with this recipe.

If you are using baby eggplants, cut each eggplant in half lengthwise. Score the cut sides of the eggplants ⅛ inch deep in a diagonal crosshatch pattern. Lay the eggplant halves, cut sides up, on a baking sheet. Drizzle 2 teaspoons of the olive oil and 2 teaspoons of the kosher salt on the cut sides and massage the oil and salt into the eggplant flesh.

Heat 2 tablespoons of the olive oil in a large heavy-bottomed sauté pan over medium-high heat until it slides easily in the pan and the oil around the edges of the pan just begins to smoke, 2 to 3 minutes. Lay half of the eggplant halves, cut sides down, in the pan and cook without moving them, until they are deep brown, about 2 minutes. Add 2 to 3 more tablespoons of the oil to the pan, 1 tablespoon at a time, as the pan becomes dry. Turn the eggplant halves with a spatula or tongs. Sprinkle 1 teaspoon of the remaining kosher salt over the eggplants and sear the skin sides for about 1 minute, until the skin is deep brown but not charred. Remove the eggplants from the pan and transfer them, cut sides up, to a baking sheet. Add 2 tablespoons of the olive oil to the pan you cooked the first batch of eggplants in and let the oil heat up for about 1 minute until it's smoking hot. Lay the remaining eggplant halves, cut sides down, in the pan and cook and season them with salt the same way you did the first batch, adding more to the pan as needed. Transfer the second batch of eggplants to the baking sheet with the first batch.

To serve, lay the eggplant halves, cut sides up, in a single layer on a large round or rectangular platter. Use the back of a spoon to paint a light coat of herb vin-

FOR BABY EGGPLANTS

4 baby or Japanese eggplants

2 teaspoons olive oil, plus more for cooking the eggplant

1 tablespoon plus 1 teaspoon kosher salt

Herb Vinaigrette (page 119)

Maldon sea salt (or another flaky sea salt such as fleur de sel)

(continued)

**2 large eggplants
(1 to 1½ pounds each)**

1 tablespoon plus 1 teaspoon olive oil, plus more for cooking the eggplant

1 tablespoon plus 1 teaspoon kosher salt

Maldon sea salt (or another flaky sea salt such as fleur de sel)

Herb Vinaigrette (page 119)

aigrette on each eggplant half, sprinkle with sea salt, and serve the rest of the vinaigrette on the side with a small spoon for guests to serve themselves.

———————

If you are using large eggplants, adjust an oven rack to the middle position and preheat the oven to 350°F.

Cut the eggplants in half lengthwise. Score the cut sides of the eggplants ⅛ inch deep in a diagonal crosshatch pattern. Lay the eggplant halves, cut sides up, on a baking sheet. Drizzle with the 1 tablespoon plus 1 teaspoon of the olive oil, sprinkle 1 teaspoon of the kosher salt, and massage the oil and salt into the eggplant flesh with your hands.

Heat 2 tablespoons of the olive oil in a large heavy-bottomed sauté pan over medium-high heat until it slides easily in the pan and the oil around the edges of the pan begins to smoke, 2 to 3 minutes. Lay 2 of the eggplant halves, cut sides down, in the pan and cook over medium-low heat until the cut sides of the eggplant are golden brown, about 5 minutes. Add 2 to 3 more tablespoons of oil to the pan, 1 tablespoon at a time, as the eggplants absorb the oil and the pan becomes dry. After cooking only one side, remove the eggplant halves from the pan and place them, cut sides up, on a baking sheet. Add 2 tablespoons of the olive oil to the pan and heat it over high heat for about 1 minute until it's smoking hot. Turn off the heat and lay the remaining 2 eggplant halves, cut sides down, in the pan. Cook the eggplants in the same way you cooked the first 2, adding as much as 3 tablespoons more oil to the pan as necessary. Remove the eggplant halves from the pan and transfer them, cut sides up, to the baking sheet with the other halves.

Put the baking sheet in the oven and roast the eggplant halves for 12 to 15 minutes, until they collapse slightly and the skin is very thin and papery to the touch. Remove the eggplants from the oven.

To serve, nestle the eggplant halves, cut sides up, in a large shallow bowl or on a rimmed platter. Drizzle the eggplant halves with herb vinaigrette and sprinkle them with sea salt. Serve with a spoon for guests to scoop out the creamy insides of the eggplants and a bowl of the remaining herb vinaigrette for guests to serve themselves.

Spring Gem Salad with Soft Herbs and Labneh Toasts

I started adding herb leaves to salads in the eighties, when I made a butter lettuce salad with fresh herbs and a simple lemon vinaigrette. I used that salad as an inspiration for this, but added spring vegetables, including raw asparagus, sugar snap peas, and English peas, to make it more substantial than a side salad. It's the first tell on the Osteria menu that spring has sprung in Los Angeles. I welcome any excuse to eat with my hands, especially when I'm eating salad—and this one, made with sturdy leaves of Little Gem lettuce, which is similar to romaine, invites that. The shape of the leaves catches the herbs and other vegetables like little lettuce tacos, and I serve the salad with toast slathered in Labneh (page 126), so I can hold the toast in one hand and the lettuce in the other. The only thing that might improve the situation would be a third hand for a glass of wine.

If you can't find fresh chervil, substitute additional tarragon.

———————

To make the toasts, adjust an oven rack to the middle position and preheat the oven to 350°F.

Place the bread slices on a baking sheet, brush the tops with olive oil, and bake for 15 to 20 minutes, until the toasts are golden brown and crispy, rotating the baking sheet from front to back halfway through the cooking time so the toasts brown evenly. Remove the toasts from the oven and set aside to come to room temperature while you make the salad.

To make the salad, fill a large saucepan with water, bring the water to a boil over high heat, and salt it to taste like the ocean, adding 1 tablespoon salt to each quart of water. Prepare an ice bath in a medium bowl and prepare a bed of paper towels.

Put the peas in a fine-mesh strainer and plunge them into the boiling water to blanch for 2 minutes, until tender but not mushy. Lift the strainer out of the water and immediately plunge the strainer into the ice bath for about 1 minute to cool the peas. Remove the strainer from the water and turn the peas out onto the paper towels to drain.

Starting at the tip and keeping the entire tip intact, slice the entire stalk of

SERVES 6 TO 8

———————

FOR THE TOASTS

6 to 8 (½-inch-thick) slices from a *bâtard* or fat baguette (or 4 slices from a loaf of country bread, halved or quartered depending on size)

Extra-virgin olive oil for brushing the bread

FOR THE SALAD

¾ teaspoon kosher salt, plus more for the blanching water

⅔ cup shelled English peas (from about ½ pound in the pods)

3 ounces medium asparagus, stems snapped off at their natural breaking point and discarded

3 ounces sugar snap peas

6 radishes (preferably French breakfast radishes)

1 recipe Lemon Vinaigrette (recipe follows)

3 Little Gem lettuce heads (or hearts of romaine)

1 tablespoon fresh lemon juice

(continued)

2 tablespoons finely chopped fresh chervil leaves (from about ¼ cup packed whole leaves), plus several leaves for garnish

2 tablespoons finely chopped fresh dill leaves (from about ¼ cup packed whole leaves), plus several leaves for garnish

2 tablespoons finely chopped fresh tarragon leaves (from about ¼ cup packed whole leaves), plus several leaves for garnish

2 tablespoons finely chopped fresh Italian parsley leaves (from about ¼ cup packed whole leaves)

15 to 20 (1-inch-long) fresh chive batonettes

FOR FINISHING THE TOASTS

Heaping ½ to ¾ cup chilled Labneh (page 126, or store-bought)

Finishing-quality extra-virgin olive oil for drizzling

Sweet smoked paprika for garnish

Chervil leaves or other microgreens for garnish (optional)

asparagus on an extreme bias ⅛ inch thick. Put the sliced asparagus and the tips in a medium bowl.

Remove and discard the strings from the sugar snap peas and slice ⅛ inch thick on an extreme bias. Put the sugar snap peas in the bowl with the asparagus. Holding the radishes by the stems, thinly slice on a mandoline or with a very sharp knife and discard the stems. Add the radish slices to the bowl with the other vegetables. Drizzle the vegetables with 3 tablespoons of the lemon vinaigrette, toss gently, and set aside to marinate the vegetables while you prepare the rest of the salad.

Remove and discard the outer, limp, dark green leaves from the lettuce. Pull the remaining leaves from the cores; discard the cores and put the leaves in a large bowl.

Sprinkle the lettuce leaves with the lemon juice and salt, and toss to coat the lettuce. Drizzle all but 2 tablespoons of the remaining vinaigrette over the salad. Add the chopped chervil, dill, tarragon, parsley, and chives and gently massage the vinaigrette and herbs into the lettuce leaves with your hands. Add the remaining vinaigrette if necessary to coat the leaves.

To finish the toasts, slather a heaping tablespoon of labneh on each toast, leaving the edges of the toast visible. (This is purely for aesthetic reasons, but for me, that's as good a reason as any.) Drizzle the labneh with finishing-quality olive oil, sprinkle each toast with a pinch of paprika, and top with a few leaves of chervil, if you are using it.

To serve, lift the largest lettuce leaves and herbs out of the bowl they were tossed in and put them on a large platter, laying them so they're like tacos with the "bowls" facing upright and the leaves slightly overlapping one another. Scatter one-third of the marinated vegetables over the lettuce. Continue building the salad, using the medium leaves next, topping with a third of the marinated vegetables, and the smallest leaves last. Scatter the remaining marinated vegetables into each lettuce cup and sprinkle the whole herb leaves over the top. Serve with tongs and the labneh toasts on a separate platter.

Lemon Vinaigrette

Makes 1 cup

We use this simple vinaigrette to dress many salads at Mozza, and also as a base for other vinaigrettes.

¼ cup minced shallot (from about 1 medium peeled shallot)

¼ cup fresh lemon juice

1 tablespoon champagne vinegar (or white wine vinegar)

1 teaspoon kosher salt

½ teaspoon freshly ground black pepper

½ cup extra-virgin olive oil

Combine the shallot, lemon juice, vinegar, and salt in a small bowl. Add the olive oil in a slow, steady stream, whisking constantly to emulsify. Use the vinaigrette or refrigerate, covered, for up to 2 days. Bring the vinaigrette to room temperature and whisk to recombine the ingredients before using.

Labneh

SERVES 8 TO 10 AS A SIDE DISH
MAKES ABOUT 3 CUPS

1 quart Straus Family Creamery
Organic Greek Yogurt (or another
whole-milk plain, not overly thick,
Greek-style yogurt)

1 tablespoon finely grated lemon
zest (about 1 medium lemon,
grated on a Microplane),
plus 3 tablespoons fresh
lemon juice

¾ teaspoon kosher salt

Labneh is a fresh cheese traditional to Middle Eastern cuisine. It's made by straining whole-milk plain yogurt through cheesecloth to drain out the whey, which completely changes the product; nobody who didn't know would ever guess that when you serve them labneh, what they are eating is essentially yogurt.

Because it's made almost entirely of yogurt (there is a bit of lemon juice and salt added), the better the yogurt, the better the labneh. If you have access to a place that sells homemade yogurt, use that. Otherwise, our preferred yogurt is Straus Family Creamery Organic Greek Yogurt, which is available at specialty food stores. Unlike most Greek-style yogurts, the one made by Straus is not super thick. If you can't get Straus, use another whole-milk plain yogurt, but not a thick Greek yogurt. This recipe calls for a quart of yogurt because you need the weight of the yogurt for it to drain, so it's impossible to make a smaller quantity. I use labneh as a condiment with lamb and chicken; I spread it on toast to serve alongside the refreshing Spring Gem Salad with Soft Herbs and Labneh Toasts (page 123); and I shape it into cheese balls, which are rolled in walnuts and included in a salad with marinated radicchio and beets.

You will need kitchen twine, a long-handled wooden spoon, and a tall container, such as a stockpot, to make this.

Combine the yogurt, lemon zest, lemon juice, and salt in a medium bowl and stir with a rubber spatula.

Line a second bowl with a double layer of cheesecloth with enough cheesecloth left over to flop over the top of the bowl. Pour the yogurt mixture over the cheesecloth and gather the edges of the cheesecloth at the middle to form a loose bundle. You don't want the bundle so tight that the yogurt squishes out of the cheesecloth. Tie the bundle closed at the top with kitchen twine. Stick the handle of a long wooden spoon or a skewer through the cheesecloth, piercing the cloth just under the knot so the handle goes all the way through and the bundle hangs from it. Drop the pouch down into a tall container, such as a stockpot, so the spoon handle rests across the top of the container and the pouch hangs down into the container with at least 2 inches of clearance at the bottom to allow the whey to drain out of the yogurt. You don't want the yogurt pouch to touch the bottom of the container; if it does, you need to use a taller container.

Put the container with the yogurt in the refrigerator and let it sit for 3 days to drain the whey out of the yogurt.

Remove the yogurt from the refrigerator. Untie and unwrap the cheesecloth; remove the labneh from the cheesecloth and discard the cheesecloth. Use the labneh or refrigerate, covered, for up to 1 week.

6

Eggs for Anytime

When I first came back to the States after studying at Le Cordon Bleu in London, a couple who were friends of my parents asked me to cater a few lunches for them, applying the ideas and techniques I'd learned in school. Maybe my parents put them up to it to see if their investment had paid off. However it came about, I was really intimidated by the prospect. I felt like they were saying, "Show us the money." For the first lunch, I wanted to strike a balance between playing it safe and doing something slightly fancy or impressive. And this being 1977, I landed on quiche. Quiche Lorraine was just starting to hit some of the trendiest fern bars in Los Angeles. For me, quiche just felt like a safer bet than making, say, a lamb crown roast, which would cost a lot more money and where a lot more could go wrong. I made the quiches in a very low, fluted tart mold, and I'm pleased to report that they turned out beautifully. The recipes here are basically quiches. At the Pizzeria, where we serve them on weekends, we call them torta rustica, or, rustic tarts, because the name "quiche" just didn't seem to fit in an Italian restaurant. In these recipes I call them egg pies because that seems to be the clearest description of what they are.

The great thing about an egg pie (or a torta rustica or a quiche) is that it's equally delicious hours after its been cooked as it is still warm from the oven. You could serve these for brunch, lunch, dinner, or take them to a picnic. The sides I serve them with make the pies feel more like lunch or brunch items. The meal in its entirety would make a lovely spread for Easter brunch. To stick with the 1970s California theme, I serve them with Spiced Carrot Cake with Molasses Cream Cheese Frosting (page 348). An egg pie with a Bibb Salad with Soft Herbs (page 71) is my dream idea of a weeknight dinner.

Egg Pie with Bacon, Potato, and Caramelized Onion

The caramelized onions for this take a long time to make. I suggest you double the amount of onions and use the extra to make another egg pie within a few days, or throw them into scrambled eggs or on burgers. The pie can be made up to several hours in advance of serving it.

SERVES 6 TO 8

Trim and discard the root end of the onion and cut the onion in half root to tip. Cut each half in half again root to tip so the onion is quartered. Separate the layers of the onion, stack 2 or 3 layers at a time on top of one another, and slice ¼ inch thick lengthwise.

Warm the canola oil in a large sauté pan over medium heat for 1 minute just to warm it slightly. Add the onion slices and sprinkle them with 1 teaspoon of the salt. Reduce the heat to low and cook the onion slices, stirring often, for 45 minutes to 1 hour, until they are dark brown and soft. Turn off the heat.

Adjust an oven rack to the middle position and preheat the oven to 350°F.

Prepare a bed of paper towels. Lay the bacon on a baking sheet and bake until the bacon is cooked all the way through but not crisp, 15 to 17 minutes, rotating the baking sheet from front to back halfway through the cooking time so the bacon cooks evenly. Remove the bacon from the oven and transfer it to the paper towels to drain and to cool to room temperature. Tear the bacon into 1-inch pieces.

Whisk the whole eggs and egg yolks in a medium bowl to break up the yolks. Add the cream, milk, crème fraîche, cayenne, and the remaining 1 teaspoon salt and whisk to combine the ingredients.

Steam the potatoes until they are tender when pierced with a small sharp knife, about 20 minutes. Transfer the potatoes to a plate until they are cool enough to touch. Use the back of a small knife to remove the peel from the potatoes and discard the peels.

Put the par-baked pie shell on a baking sheet. Reserve a small handful of the Gruyère and sprinkle the rest over the bottom of the pie shell. Scatter the bacon pieces over the cheese. Break the potatoes into rough ¾-inch pieces directly over the pie, scattering the potato pieces evenly over the surface of the pie. Spread the caramelized onion slices over the potatoes. Starting in the middle and going around the sides, slowly pour or ladle the custard into the shell; if you dump the

1 large yellow Spanish onion, peeled

1½ tablespoons canola oil (or another neutral-flavored oil)

2 teaspoons kosher salt

3 thick-cut applewood-smoked bacon slices (about 2½ ounces)

3 extra-large eggs plus 2 extra-large egg yolks

1 cup heavy cream

½ cup whole milk

3 tablespoons crème fraîche (or sour cream)

¼ teaspoon cayenne pepper

¼ pound small fingerling potatoes

1 All-Butter Par-Baked Pie Shell (recipe follows)

4 ounces Gruyère, shredded (about 1 cup)

1 tablespoon fresh thyme leaves (from 10 to 12 sprigs)

custard into the shell all at once, the toppings will scatter randomly instead of being evenly dispersed throughout. Sprinkle the reserved cheese on top of the pie and sprinkle the thyme leaves over the cheese.

Bake the pie for 50 to 55 minutes, until the top is golden brown and the custard is set (it will jiggle like firm Jell-O but won't be liquidy when you gently shake the baking sheet), turning the pie halfway through the baking time so it browns evenly. Remove the baking sheet from the oven and set aside to cool for at least 45 minutes before slicing the pie; any sooner and the filling will all spill out.

To serve, put the pie on a buffet or dining table with a long knife and pie server for guests to cut the size pieces they want. Serve slightly warm or at room temperature.

All-Butter Par-Baked Pie Shell

You will need a deep 9½-inch pie dish, parchment paper or large paper coffee filters, and pie weights or rice (to use as pie weights) to make this.

2 cups pastry flour (or unbleached all-purpose flour), plus more for dusting

2 teaspoons kosher salt

8 ounces (2 sticks) cold unsalted butter, cut into small cubes

2 tablespoons heavy cream

3 tablespoons ice-cold water, or as needed

Combine the flour and salt in the bowl of a standing mixer fitted with the paddle attachment and mix on low speed for a few seconds to distribute the salt. Add the butter and cream and mix on low speed until the mixture resembles the consistency of coarse cornmeal with small chunks of butter visible, about 2 minutes. Add the ice water and mix on medium speed until the dough is smooth, 2 to 3 minutes, being careful not to work the dough any more than necessary. Turn off the machine.

Dust a flat work surface with flour and turn the dough out onto the dusted surface. Knead the dough gently, just enough to bring it together into a ball. Pat the dough into a disk, wrap it in plastic wrap, and refrigerate it for at least 2 hours and up to 3 days; or freeze the dough for up to 2 months and defrost it overnight in the refrigerator.

Take the dough out of the refrigerator and cut it into a few chunks. Dust a flat work surface with flour and knead the chunks on the floured surface to soften the dough until it is the texture of Play-Doh. Bring the chunks together into one ball. Dust a rolling pin with flour, dust the work surface again, and roll the dough out to a 15-inch circle. Fold the dough circle in half and lift it into a 9½-inch pie dish. Unfold it to line the pie dish. Using scissors, trim the dough, leaving 2 inches of dough hanging over the edge of the pie dish. Working your way around the pie, fold the dough edge under itself so that 1 inch of the dough is doubled, creating a thick border of dough and making the crust 1 inch taller than the pie dish. Pinch the border of dough together between your thumb and index finger into a sturdy wall around the pie. Refrigerate the pie shell for at least 30 minutes and up to overnight.

Adjust an oven rack to the middle position and preheat the oven to 425°F.

Remove the pie shell from the refrigerator. Line the shell with parchment paper or coffee filters and weigh it down with pie weights or rice. Put the shell in the oven to bake until the edges of the crust are brown and the bottom is light golden brown, 15 to 20 minutes, turning the shell from front to back halfway through the baking time so it browns evenly. Remove the pie shell from the oven and carefully remove and discard the parchment paper; reserve pie weights or rice to use (as pie weights only) another time. Return the pie shell to the oven and bake until golden brown, 8 to 10 minutes. Remove the pie shell from the oven and set aside to cool to room temperature.

Egg Pie with Goat Cheese, Leeks, and Garlic Confit

This egg pie contains four members of the *allium* (or, onion) family: scallions, leeks, garlic, and chives. It can be made up to several hours in advance of serving.

SERVES 6 TO 8

¾ pound leeks (about 2 medium)

4 tablespoons (½ stick) unsalted butter, cut into chunks

2 teaspoons kosher salt

3 extra-large eggs plus 2 extra-large egg yolks

1 cup heavy cream

¾ cup finely grated Parmigiano-Reggiano (about 3 ounces)

½ cup whole milk

3 tablespoons crème fraîche (or sour cream)

¼ teaspoon cayenne pepper

2 bunches scallions

1 All-Butter Par-Baked Pie Shell (page 132)

¼ cup Garlic Cloves Confit (page 42; about 12 large cloves)

3 ounces crumbled fresh goat cheese (about ⅓ cup lightly packed)

30 (2-inch-long) fresh chive batonettes

Adjust an oven rack to the middle position and preheat the oven to 350°F.

Trim and discard the hairy ends and the tough dark green outer layers of the leeks. Cut the leeks in half lengthwise. Lay one half flat and, starting at the light end, slice the leeks ½ inch thick on an extreme bias, stopping when the leeks become dark green. Discard the dark green ends and slice the rest of the leeks in the same way. Wash and dry the leek slices and separate the layers.

Put the leeks, butter, and 1 teaspoon of the salt in a large sauté pan and cook the leeks over medium heat for 20 to 30 minutes, until they are soft and melted, stirring often so they don't brown. Turn off the heat and set the leeks aside to cool to room temperature.

Whisk the whole eggs and egg yolks in a medium bowl to break up the yolks. Add the cream, Parmigiano, milk, crème fraîche, cayenne, and 1 teaspoon of the remaining salt and whisk to combine the ingredients.

Trim and discard the root ends and any wilted greens from the scallions. Slice the white parts of the scallions 1/16 inch thick on an extreme bias and discard the remaining dark greens.

Put the par-baked pie shell on a baking sheet. Spread the leeks over the bottom of the pie shell. Sprinkle the scallions over the leeks. Scatter the garlic and goat cheese in clumps over the scallions. Starting in the middle and going around the sides, slowly pour or ladle the custard into the shell; if you dump the custard into the shell all at once, the toppings will scatter randomly instead of being evenly dispersed throughout. Scatter the chives over the pie like pickup sticks.

Bake the pie for 50 to 55 minutes, until the top is golden brown and the custard is set (it will jiggle like firm Jell-O but won't be liquidy when you gently shake the baking sheet), turning the pie halfway through the baking time so it browns evenly. Remove the baking sheet from the oven and set aside to cool for at least 45 minutes before slicing the pie; any sooner and the filling will all spill out.

To serve, put the pie on the buffet or dining table with a long knife and pie spatula for guests to cut the size pieces they want. Serve slightly warm or at room temperature.

Egg Pie with Braised Swiss Chard and Ham

This is my take on a classic French combination of ham, Gruyère, and spinach. I use braised Swiss chard in place of the spinach because I like its robust flavor, and also the different textures that you get from the leaves and stems of chard. I smear a layer of whole-grain mustard over the bottom of the pie shell before adding the filling, which gives the pie a kick, and what I think is a decidedly French flavor. The pie can be made up to several hours in advance of serving it. You won't use all of the chard for the pie, but I like to cook the entire bunch. The leftovers are great on their own, or topped with a fried egg.

———

Pull the chard leaves from the ribs. Trim and discard the ends of the ribs and slice the ribs 2 inches wide on an extreme bias. Tear the chard leaves into 2-inch pieces.

Trim and discard the root end of the onion half and cut the half in half again root to tip so it is quartered. Separate the layers of the onion, stack 2 or 3 layers at a time on top of one another, and slice ¼ inch thick lengthwise.

Heat the olive oil in a large sauté pan over medium-high heat until it slides easily in the pan and the oil around the edges of the pan begins to smoke, 2 to 3 minutes. Add the chard ribs, onion, garlic, and chile pods. Season with ½ teaspoon of the salt and cook until the vegetables are tender and translucent, about 15 minutes, stirring often so the vegetables don't brown. Add the chard leaves, season with 1 teaspoon of the remaining salt, and cook, folding the chard leaves in with the cooked vegetables, until they wilt enough so that they fit in the pot, 5 to 8 minutes. Reduce the heat to low, cover the pot, and cook for an additional 20 minutes, or until the chard stems and onion are soft and melted.

Place a colander in the sink and drain the chard in the colander. Leave the chard in the colander to cool to room temperature and drain. Remove and discard the chile pods. Measure out 1 cup of the chard and reserve the rest for another use. The chard can be made up to 3 days in advance. Refrigerate, covered, until you are ready to use it.

Meanwhile, adjust an oven rack to the middle position and preheat the oven to 350°F.

Whisk the whole eggs and egg yolks in a medium bowl to break up the yolks. Add the cream, Parmigiano, milk, crème fraîche, cayenne, and the remaining 1 teaspoon salt and whisk to combine the ingredients.

SERVES 6 TO 8

1 pound Swiss chard
(about 1 bunch)

½ large yellow Spanish onion
(halved root to tip), peeled

¼ cup olive oil

10 to 12 large garlic cloves, peeled
and sliced ⅛ inch thick lengthwise

2 árbol chile pods

2½ teaspoons kosher salt

3 extra-large eggs plus 2 extra-large egg yolks

1 cup heavy cream

¾ cup finely grated Parmigiano-Reggiano (about 3 ounces)

½ cup whole milk

3 tablespoons crème fraîche
(or sour cream)

¼ teaspoon cayenne pepper

1 All-Butter Par-Baked Pie Shell
(page 132)

¼ cup plus 2 tablespoons
whole-grain mustard

4 ounces Gruyère, shredded
(about 1 cup)

½ pound thinly sliced prosciutto
cotto (Italian cooked ham or
another quality cooked ham)

Put the par-baked pie shell on a baking sheet. Spread the mustard over the bottom of the pie shell and scatter the Gruyère over the mustard. Reserve 7 or 8 of the cooked chard leaves and lay the remaining chard mixture over the cheese. Scatter the prosciutto over the chard. Starting in the middle and going around the sides, slowly pour or ladle the custard into the shell; if you dump the custard into the shell all at once, the toppings will scatter randomly instead of being evenly dispersed throughout. Drape the reserved chard leaves on top of the custard.

Bake the pie for 50 minutes to 1 hour, until the top is golden brown and the custard is set (it will jiggle like firm Jell-O but won't be liquidy when you gently shake the baking sheet), turning the pie halfway through the baking time so it browns evenly. Remove the baking sheet from the oven and set aside to cool for at least 45 minutes before slicing it; any sooner and the filling will all spill out.

To serve, put the pie on the buffet or dining table with a long knife and pie server for guests to cut the size pieces they want. Serve slightly warm or at room temperature.

Croissant Bread Pudding with Creamed Spinach and Ham

SERVES 10 TO 12

¾ pound leeks (about 2 medium)

3 tablespoons unsalted butter

1 tablespoon plus 1 teaspoon kosher salt

6 cups lightly packed spinach (about 6 ounces), rinsed and dried thoroughly

8 extra-large eggs

5 cups whole milk

2 tablespoons fresh thyme leaves

6 medium plain butter croissants (about 12 ounces), halved horizontally like hamburger buns

6 ounces Comté (or fontina) cheese, shredded (about 1½ cups)

3 ounces thinly sliced prosciutto cotto (or another quality cooked ham), torn into long, thin strips

½ cup finely grated Parmigiano-Reggiano (about 2 ounces)

4 tablespoons (½ stick) unsalted butter, cut into small cubes

If someone asked me to bring something to a brunch, I wouldn't have to think twice about it: this croissant bread pudding, made with ham, cheese, and creamed spinach and leeks, is what I would bring. It can be served for breakfast or brunch or as an easy, eggs-for-dinner option. When I was perfecting this pudding, I made two versions—one with half again as much spinach and ham in it as the other—and tasted them side by side. Much to my surprise, I liked the one with less filling best, because it made room for these nice pockets of custard throughout. Plus, it felt more French, since the French clearly value subtlety over abundance, at least when it comes to food and portion sizes.

The nice thing about using croissants to make bread pudding is that the most difficult task—making the croissants—has already been done by the baker. And croissants, being buttery and soft as they are, make for a bread pudding that is pretty much guaranteed to be tender and delicious. You don't need to use award-winning croissants for this, but you do need to use croissants made with all butter.

You will need a 13 x 9-inch or equivalent-size casserole dish to make this. You will be serving it in the dish in which it was baked, so look for a dish you would feel comfortable presenting on your table.

Trim and discard the hairy ends and the tough dark green outer layers of the leeks. Cut the leeks in half lengthwise. Lay one half flat and, starting at the light end, slice the leeks ½ inch thick on an extreme bias, stopping when the leeks become dark green. Discard the dark green ends and repeat, slicing the rest of the leeks in the same way. Wash and dry the leek slices thoroughly and separate the layers.

Heat the butter in a large sauté pan over medium heat until it just melts. Add the leeks, season with ½ teaspoon of the salt, and sauté the leeks for about 5 minutes, until they're soft and translucent, stirring often so they don't brown. (Lower the heat if the leeks begin to brown before they are soft.) Add the spinach, season it with ½ teaspoon of the remaining salt, and gently fold the spinach in with the leeks so it wilts and fits in the pan. Continue to cook the spinach, stirring often, until all the water released from the spinach during cooking has evaporated, about 5 minutes. Transfer the vegetables to a plate and set aside to cool to room temperature.

Adjust an oven rack to the middle position and preheat the oven to 300°F.

Whisk the eggs in a medium bowl to break up the yolks. Add the milk, 1 tablespoon of the thyme leaves, and the remaining tablespoon salt and whisk to combine the ingredients.

Lay the croissant bottoms, cut side up, in the bottom of a 9 x 13-inch casserole dish, trimming them as necessary to make them fit in a single layer like pieces of a puzzle. Pour 2 cups of the custard over the surface of the croissants, pouring it over the entire surface, not dumping it in one place, and press gently on the croissants with your fingers to help them absorb the liquid. Sprinkle two-thirds (4 ounces) of the Comté over the croissants and pour 2 cups of the remaining custard over the cheese, pouring it over the entire surface. Lay the ham strips in an even layer and scatter the spinach and leeks over the ham, spreading them in an even layer (the best way to do this is with your hands). Lay the croissant tops, cut sides down, on top of the filling, again cutting them as needed so they fit in the dish. Pour the remaining custard over the entire surface of the croissants.

Combine the remaining 2 ounces Comté and the Parmigiano in a small bowl and sprinkle it over the top of the croissants. Press down on the croissants to nestle them tightly in the dish and to push out any air bubbles. Scatter the butter pieces and sprinkle the remaining thyme leaves over the top of the bread pudding.

Put the bread pudding on a baking sheet and bake for 1 hour 10 minutes to 1 hour 20 minutes, until the top is golden brown and an instant-read thermometer inserted into the center registers 165°F, rotating the baking sheet from front to back halfway through the cooking time so the bread pudding browns evenly. Remove the bread pudding from the oven and set it aside to rest for 45 minutes to 1 hour before serving.

To serve, put the baking dish on the buffet or dining table with a long knife and pie server or a large flat spoon for guests to cut the size pieces they want. Serve slightly warm or at room temperature.

Avocado Toasts with Garlic Mayonnaise and Toasted Coriander

Even though I grew up in Southern California, where avocados are in abundance, I didn't start eating avocados on a regular basis until the 1970s, when I went away to college at Sonoma State. Back then, smearing avocados on whole-grain bread was just something that we did; we didn't call it avocado toast, as people do now. When I make avocado toast, rather than spreading mashed avocado on bread, I put half of a ripe avocado that has been scored with a knife on the toast and then smash it with a fork. (If your avocados aren't soft enough, smash the avocados on a plate with a fork and then transfer them to the toast so you don't smash the toast in an effort to smash the avocado.) I sprinkle my avocado toast with a bit of toasted coriander seeds; the little bits of toasted spice take the flavor of avocado toast to the next level. When shopping for avocados, note that one of the keys to the success of these toasts is that you use avocados that are ripe but not mushy or watery. If you live in or near an avocado-growing region, such as Southern California or Florida, this is the perfect reason to go to a farmers' market and find flavorful, seasonal, and less common varieties, such as fuerte or Pinkerton, in addition to the very common and very flavorful Hass.

Toast the coriander seeds in a small sauté pan over medium heat for 1 to 2 minutes, shaking the pan often, until the seeds are fragrant and golden brown. Transfer the seeds to a cutting board to cool to room temperature. Use the underside of a heavy skillet to crack the seeds, or grind them in a spice grinder or use a mortar and a pestle, to about one-quarter of their original size.

Preheat a grill pan or cast-iron skillet over high heat until it's smoking hot or adjust the oven racks to the middle position and preheat the oven to 350°F.

If you are toasting the bread on a grill or grill pan, brush the bread slices liberally on both sides with olive oil. Lay the bread in the grill pan and toast it for about 2 minutes per side, until it's crispy and golden brown, almost black in places. If you are making the toast in the oven, put the slices (without the oil) on a baking sheet and cook for 30 minutes, turning the bread after 15 minutes so that it is golden brown and crispy on both sides. Rub the garlic clove on one side

SERVES 6

1 tablespoon coriander seeds

6 (½-inch-thick) slices from a large loaf of whole-grain or country bread

Extra-virgin olive oil for brushing the bread

1 large garlic clove, peeled

¼ cup plus 2 tablespoons Garlic Mayonnaise (page 84)

3 large ripe avocados

1 lime or ½ lemon

Finishing-quality extra-virgin olive oil

Maldon sea salt (or another flaky sea salt such as fleur de sel)

of the toast and lay the toast with the garlic-rubbed side facing up on a flat work surface. Set the toast aside for about 1 minute to cool slightly.

Spoon 1 tablespoon garlic mayonnaise on each piece of toast and use the back of the spoon to spread the mayonnaise over the toast, leaving the edges of the toast visible.

Cut the avocados in half lengthwise. Twist each half in opposite directions to separate them. Plunge the edge of a large sharp knife into the pit and twist the knife to release the pit from the avocado. Remove and discard the pits. With the avocado halves still in the skin, score the avocados crosshatch style, making the cuts ½ inch apart and not all the way through to the avocado skins. Working one at a time, use a large spoon (not a measuring spoon) to scoop the avocado flesh out of the skin and put it domed side up on a piece of toast. Use the back side of a fork to smash the avocado on the toast, leaving a small border of the mayonnaise visible around the edges of avocado, and taking care to maintain some height to the avocado. Repeat, smashing the remaining avocado halves on the remaining toasts in the same way. Squeeze a few drops of lime juice over the avocado on each piece of toast and drizzle the avocado lightly with finishing-quality olive oil. Sprinkle a pinch of sea salt and a pinch of coriander over the avocado on each toast.

To serve, arrange the avocado toasts nicely on a small pretty cutting board or platter—no serving utensil necessary.

Fava, Pea, and Mint Salad with Fresh Pecorino

Fava beans and fresh pecorino is a classic combination in Italian cooking. The cheese comes to ripeness in the springtime, the same time of year that fava beans come into season. Because I'm never in Italy in the spring, I re-create the combination in Los Angeles. I add peas and mint to the traditional combo and, where most often the pecorino is sliced for the salad, I cut it into cubes to mirror the size of the peas. I don't have to tell you to make this salad only in the springtime because I doubt you'd find fresh favas when they aren't in season. This is dressed with nothing but olive oil, so it's a call to break out the best stuff you have, or to buy that bottle you've always wanted.

When most people hear "pecorino," they automatically think "pecorino Romano," which is a hard, dry grating cheese, similar in texture to Parmigiano. But *pecorino*, which comes from *pecora*, meaning "sheep," can refer to any sheep's milk cheese. For this, you want to use fresh pecorino, also called cacia di Roma, which you'll find at a well-stocked cheese counter, or substitute fresh provolone.

SERVES 6 TO 8

1 teaspoon kosher salt, plus more for the blanching water

2 cups shelled English peas (from about 1½ pounds in the pods)

1½ cups shelled fava beans (from about 1½ pounds in the pods)

7 ounces fresh pecorino (also called cacio di Roma; or another young mild white cheese, such as provolone), cut into ⅓-inch cubes (about 1¼ cups)

1 cup fresh mint leaves, stacked 4 or 5 at a time, rolled, and thinly sliced

¼ cup finishing-quality extra-virgin olive oil

Fill a large saucepan with water, bring the water to a boil over high heat, and salt it to taste like the ocean, adding 1 tablespoon salt to each quart of water. Prepare an ice bath in a medium bowl and prepare two beds of paper towels.

Put the peas in a fine-mesh strainer and plunge them into the boiling water to blanch for 2 minutes. Lift the strainer out of the water and plunge the strainer into the ice bath to cool the peas. Remove the strainer from the ice bath and turn the peas out onto the paper towels to drain.

Put the fava beans in the strainer and plunge them into the boiling water to blanch for 3 to 6 minutes, depending on their size, until they are tender and bright green. Lift the strainer out of the water and plunge it into the ice water to cool the fava beans. Remove the strainer from the ice water and turn the fava beans out onto a separate bed of paper towels to drain. Peel and discard the outer skins from the fava beans and put the shelled beans in a large bowl.

Add the peas, pecorino, and mint to the bowl with the fava beans. Sprinkle with the salt, drizzle with the olive oil, and toss to combine the ingredients and to coat the vegetables and cheese.

To serve, transfer to a small deep serving bowl and serve with a big spoon.

7

The Ultimate Hamburger

SERVES 6

3 pounds coarsely ground beef
(see headnote)

2 tablespoons kosher salt

2 teaspoons fresh coarsely ground
black pepper

¼ cup Dijon mustard (for animal-
style burgers cooked in a cast-iron
skillet)

12 thick-cut applewood-smoked
bacon slices (about 10 ounces)

6 soft hamburger buns
(preferably sesame seed buns)

4 tablespoons (½ stick) unsalted
butter

2 tablespoons canola oil
(or another neutral-flavored oil)

6 slices Gruyère
(or another cheese; optional)

Ultimate Hamburger Onions
(page 149)

Seasoned Avocado Halves
(page 321)

Liz's Secret Sauce (page 152)

Garlic Mayonnaise (page 84)

Pickled Mustard Seed Mayonnaise
(page 85)

When I first started entertaining a lot in my home in Los Angeles, unless told otherwise, guests could pretty much count on being served hamburgers. I make the burger spread special by serving it with a selection of condiments, including a variety of flavored mayonnaises, a few special mustards, "secret sauce," bacon, caramelized onions, and avocados. I offer all of the options here; pick as many as you like.

In the past, I've always grilled my burger patties in my outdoor fireplace, but recently, I discovered the appeal of cooking burgers "animal style." Angelenos are obsessed with the burger chain In-N-Out, and you often hear the term *animal style*, a phrase coined by that chain, in reference to burgers. I always thought that the term referred to a burger served with lettuce in place of a bun, but, in fact, it's a mustard-crusted burger patty. To get the mustard to form a crust, the patty has to be cooked on a solid surface, such as a cast-iron skillet or griddle, where the meat has direct, even contact with the heat. (If you want to cook the burgers outside, put the skillet or griddle on the grates of your grill, fire up the grill, and then cook the burgers on the cast-iron surface.) The first time I tried an animal-style burger, I thought, "I love that flavor, but . . . what *is* it?" Although I couldn't place it, the charred mustard brought the flavor of the burger to another level. Also, when seared, the mustard gives the burger an additional crustiness, which is ideal for me, because I eat my burgers so rare that it's hard to get the outside as crusty as I like it without overcooking the meat. This method does the trick.

Naturally, the real foundation of a great burger is great burger meat. My burger blend, which is sold at my local butcher shop, Huntington Meats, and called Nancy Silverton's Backyard Burger Blend, consists of chuck ground with 10 percent extra fat. The butcher Pat LaFrieda, who is famous on the East Coast for his burger blend, uses equal parts short rib, chuck, and brisket. Whatever blend you use, aim for a 75–25 meat-to-fat ratio. In addition to the condiments listed here, set jars of Dijon and whole-grain mustards on the table for guests to use to dress their burgers.

To make the burgers, form the meat into six 8-ounce patties. If you want perfect-looking burgers, put them into a 4-inch round pastry mold and press down gently on the meat to form solid patties. If you are free-forming the patties, pat them just enough so the patties won't break apart when you flip them.

Lay the patties on a baking sheet. Season each patty on the side facing up with ½ teaspoon of the salt. Sprinkle 1 teaspoon of the pepper over the 6 patties, dividing it evenly. For animal-style burgers, spoon 1 teaspoon of the Dijon mustard on each patty and use the back of the spoon to spread the mustard over the surface of the patty. Turn the burgers and season them the same way on the second side: ½ teaspoon salt on each patty, 1 teaspoon pepper divided among the 6 patties, and, for animal-style burgers, smear 1 teaspoon mustard on the second side of each patty.

Meanwhile, adjust an oven rack to the middle position and preheat the oven to 350°F.

Prepare a bed of paper towels. Lay the bacon on a baking sheet and bake until it is cooked all the way through but not crisp, 15 to 17 minutes, rotating the baking sheet from front to back halfway through the cooking time so the bacon cooks evenly. Remove the bacon from the oven and transfer it to the paper towels to drain and cool to room temperature. Set aside to serve on your burger spread.

For animal-style burgers, melt one-third of the butter in a large sauté pan over medium heat. Add 2 buns to the sauté pan, cut side down, and cook until they are lightly toasted, about 2 minutes. Remove the buns from the pan. Add another third of the butter, let it melt in the pan, and toast 2 more buns. Melt the remaining butter in the pan and toast the last 2 buns.

Pour enough canola oil into a large cast-iron skillet or griddle to barely cover the bottom and heat it over high heat until it's almost smoking, about 2 minutes. Lay 3 or 4 of the hamburger patties in the pan—make sure not to overcrowd the pan—and cook them until a crust forms on the bottom side, about 3 minutes for medium-rare burgers. Using a spatula, gently flip the burgers. Reduce the heat to medium and lay the cheese on the burgers, if you are using it. Put the lid on the pan to melt the cheese and cook the burgers for 3 to 4 minutes for medium-rare. (For a more well-done burger, cook it for 1 to 2 more minutes on each side; cook it for 2 minutes on the second side before adding the cheese.) Remove the patties from the pan and cook the remaining patties in the same way, adding more oil to the pan if it is dry and letting it heat up before adding the meat to the pan.

If you are grilling your burgers, prepare a hot fire in a charcoal grill.

Put the burgers on the grill and sear until they can be turned without sticking

Dijonnaise (page 85)

Olive Anchovy Mayonnaise (page 85)

Chipotle Mayonnaise (page 85)

Spicy Tarragon Mustard (page 154)

6 large leaves iceberg lettuce

to the grill. Turn the patties and cook for 4 minutes for rare burgers (5 minutes for medium-rare, 6 minutes for medium). Remove them from the grill.

Melt the butter in a small saucepan over medium heat. Brush the burger buns with the melted butter and put them on the grill, cut side down, until the cut sides are lightly toasted. Remove them from the grill.

To assemble the burgers, put a burger patty, cheese side up, on each toasted bun. Rest the top bun on the burger but off to the side a bit, inviting guests to dress up their burgers the way they like them. Serve the bacon, caramelized onions, avocado halves, secret sauce, iceberg lettuce, and whatever mayos and mustards you've chosen to make, as well as the jarred Dijon and whole-grain mustards, on the side for people to dress their burgers the way they want them.

Ultimate Hamburger Onions

These onions are cooked low and slow, until they're meltingly tender and sweet. It may seem like too many onions to fit in your pan, but the onions will break down and shrink in volume as they cook, and after about 10 minutes of cooking, there will be plenty of room.

2 yellow Spanish onions, peeled

2 tablespoons unsalted butter

6 long fresh thyme sprigs

½ teaspoon kosher salt

Slice the onions into ¾-inch-thick rounds, keeping the rings intact, and discard the ends.

Warm the butter with the thyme sprigs in a large sauté pan over medium heat for about 1 minute, until the butter begins to bubble. Add the onion slices and season with the salt. Increase the heat to medium-high and cook until the butter begins to brown. Add 2 tablespoons water, cover the pot, and cook without turning the onions for 10 to 15 minutes, adding more water in 2-tablespoon increments, until the onions are light golden and soft. Remove them from the pan as they are done. (You will be checking the onions to see if the pan needs more water and checking for doneness every few minutes; tilt the pan as the onions cook so they don't stick to the bottom of the pan and so they color evenly.) Carefully transfer the onions to a small platter or bowl, keeping them intact, and put the thyme sprigs on top for garnish. Serve with small tongs or a fork.

Liz's Secret Sauce

Makes about 1½ cups

Liz worked hard on this secret sauce with the single goal of imitating the secret sauce served at In-N-Out.

1 extra-large egg yolk

2 tablespoons Heinz Tomato Ketchup

¾ teaspoon kosher salt

2 to 3 medium or large garlic cloves, peeled

1 cup plus 3 tablespoons canola oil (or another neutral-flavored oil)

2 tablespoons plus 1 teaspoon pickle juice (from the cornichons below)

1 medium shallot, peeled

12 cornichons (also called baby gherkins), minced (about ¾ cup)

1 tablespoon capers (preferably salt-packed; soaked for 15 minutes if salt-packed), rinsed, drained, and finely chopped

Put the egg yolk in the bowl of a mini food processor fitted with a metal blade and pulse for about 30 seconds, until the yolk is pale yellow. Add the ketchup and salt. Using a fine Microplane, grate the garlic cloves directly into the bowl and pulse to combine. Add a few drops of the canola oil and pulse to incorporate the oil into the egg. Begin adding the remaining oil, a drop at a time, running the machine constantly, until the oil and egg are emulsified; you will have added 2 or 3 tablespoons of oil. Turn off the machine, take off the lid, scrape down the sides of the bowl with a rubber spatula, and add 1 tablespoon of the pickle juice. Return the lid and pulse to combine. Continue adding the oil a few drops at a time with the machine running constantly until you've added about half of the oil and the sauce is very thick. Stop the machine again, take off the lid, scrape down the sides of the bowl, and add the remaining 1 tablespoon plus 1 teaspoon pickle juice. Drizzle the remaining oil in a slow, steady stream until all the oil has been added. Using a fine Microplane, grate the shallot into the sauce and pulse to incorporate. Spoon the sauce into a small bowl and stir in the cornichons and capers. Serve the secret sauce in the bowl with a small spoon, or refrigerate, covered, for up to 1 day.

Spicy Tarragon Mustard

Makes about 1½ cups

Tarragon and mustard is one of those perfect combinations. I always have a bottle of tarragon mustard in my refrigerators in both Los Angeles and Italy for sandwiches and burgers. It wasn't until I started eating and serving tarragon mustard with Staff Meal Oven-Roasted Chicken Thighs (page 162) that I decided to try to make my own.

1 cup Dijon mustard

1 cup lightly packed tarragon leaves, very roughly chopped

3 tablespoons fresh lemon juice

3 tablespoons apple cider vinegar

1 teaspoon sugar

½ teaspoon kosher salt

Put the mustard, tarragon, lemon juice, vinegar, sugar, and salt in the jar of a blender and purée until the tarragon is finely chopped and the mustard is green from the tarragon. Serve the mustard or refrigerate, covered (I like to put it in a canning or recycled mustard or jam jar), until you're ready to serve it or for up to 3 weeks.

Serve the mustard straight from the jar, if you used one, or transfer it to a very small pretty bowl and serve with a tiny spoon, preferably a wooden spoon.

Potato Chips with Atomic Horseradish Cream

Over the years as a chef, I've fixated on various ingredients. But I'd never given horseradish a second thought until fairly recently, when I became obsessed with the horseradish cream that my friend the chef Suzanne Tracht serves at her restaurant, Jar. I dine there often, and every time I tasted that sauce, which she serves with her famous pot roast and as a dip for the potato chips she offers at the bar, I was blown away by how strong the burn was from the horseradish. I loved it.

Because Suzanne and I use the same produce purveyor, Mohammed, the next time I saw Mohammed, I asked what kind of horseradish Suzanne used. I expected him to hand me some knobby root of an extra-special variety of horseradish that alone would offer me the pungent, up-the-nose quality that made Suzanne's horseradish cream so special. "Atomic," he said casually, as if I'd know what he was talking about. "What variety is *that*?" I asked. And Mohammed walked outside to his truck and came back holding a giant jar.

Before I go on record saying that my favorite horseradish comes from a jar, I feel like I can at least partially redeem myself by saying that it's not just *any* jar, but the Atomic itself. Where most prepared horseradish brands contain just horseradish and vinegar, Atomic also contains grated parsnips, which give the condiment a slightly sweet flavor, and—the ingredient responsible for that eye-watering heat that makes this brand inimitable—mustard oil. Atomic is so much better than any other prepared horseradish, it's the only one I will ever use again. It is available at many conventional supermarkets, specialty food stores, and butcher shops, and from mail-order sources. There is no substitute.

I serve this sauce as a condiment with meats and with potato chips for dipping. My favorite supermarket chips, in this order, are: Kettle Sea Salt & Vinegar; Kettle Krinkle Cut Sea Salt & Freshly Ground Pepper; Lay's Classic; and Ruffles.

MAKES ABOUT 2½ CUPS

2 cups crème fraîche (or sour cream), plus more as needed

¼ cup plus 1 tablespoon drained and packed Atomic Extra Hot Horseradish Sauce

2 tablespoons fresh grated horseradish (from a 2- to 2½-inch piece, peeled and grated on a medium-holed Microplane)

2 teaspoons kosher salt

1 teaspoon fresh coarsely ground black pepper

1 teaspoon fresh lemon juice

1 teaspoon Tabasco sauce

1 teaspoon Worcestershire sauce

Potato chips (see headnote)

Mix the crème fraîche, horseradish sauce, horseradish, salt, pepper, lemon juice, Tabasco, and Worcestershire sauce in a bowl, stirring to thoroughly combine. Serve or refrigerate, covered, for up to 2 days. The sauce will thicken when refrigerated. Thin with crème fraîche to loosen. Transfer to a small bowl and serve along with your favorite potato chips.

Iceberg Wedge Salad with Gorgonzola Dressing

SERVES 6

FOR THE DRESSING

5 ounces Gorgonzola dolce

1 tablespoon plus 1 teaspoon
Spanish sherry vinegar

1 cup Straus Family Creamery
Organic Greek Yogurt (or another
whole-milk plain, not overly thick,
Greek-style yogurt)

2 tablespoons well-shaken
buttermilk, plus more as needed

1 teaspoon fresh lemon juice

1 teaspoon fresh thyme leaves,
finely chopped

1½ teaspoons kosher salt

¼ teaspoon freshly ground black
pepper

3 to 4 medium or large garlic
cloves, peeled

This wedge salad is present at many of my Los Angeles parties, especially those where I cook outdoors, but it is a requisite on my burger spread, where it serves two purposes. Guests who want lettuce on their burger can just borrow a leaf from their wedge salad. And those who don't put lettuce on their burger have a delicious, crunchy, flavorful salad to put on their plate.

Iceberg was vilified for a long time, but there's a lot to love about it. It's crunchy. It's sturdy enough to hold its own against any dressing, no matter how thick. It has a mild, slightly sweet, grassy flavor that is a great vehicle for pungent dressings, such as the classic blue cheese or, in this case, Gorgonzola. It's also easy to find and inexpensive. As you can see, I'm a fan.

This salad would be equally good made with Little Gem, romaine hearts, or standard iceberg wedges, but my all-time favorite is baby iceberg. You'll most likely find baby heads of iceberg, which are about the size of a softball, at farmers' markets. Rather than cutting one head into six wedges, you cut the baby heads in half. Inside, the leaves of baby iceberg are more loosely packed than larger heads, so the dressing gets down into the crevices, which means more dressing on your salad, and more dressing on an iceberg salad is a good thing.

The way the halves or wedges are garnished in this recipe, each is a perfect, composed salad itself, so your guests are guaranteed to get all the components with each serving.

To make the dressing, combine half of the Gorgonzola and the vinegar in a medium bowl and mash them together with a fork until the cheese is smooth. Add the yogurt and buttermilk and use a whisk to stir the ingredients together. Add the lemon juice, thyme, salt, and pepper. Using a fine Microplane, grate the garlic directly into the bowl and stir to combine. Break the remaining Gorgonzola into small pieces into the bowl and stir gently with a rubber spatula to incorporate the chunks of cheese into the dressing but not so much that they disintegrate into it. Refrigerate the dressing, covered, until you're ready to use it, or for up to 1 week. Stir the dressing to recombine the ingredients and add more buttermilk if necessary to thin out before using it.

To prepare the salad, adjust the oven rack to the middle position and preheat the oven to 350°F.

Prepare a bed of paper towels. Lay the bacon on a baking sheet and bake until it is cooked all the way through but not crisp, 15 to 17 minutes, rotating the baking sheet from front to back halfway through the cooking time so the bacon cooks evenly. Remove the bacon from the oven and transfer it to the paper towels to drain and cool to room temperature. Slice the bacon into ¼-inch-wide threads on an extreme bias and set aside.

Trim and discard the root end of the onion. Separate the layers of the onion, stack 2 or 3 layers at a time on top of one another, and slice ¹⁄₁₆ inch thick lengthwise. Place the onion slices in a small bowl of ice water and set them aside while you prepare the rest of the ingredients. Drain the onion slices and pat them dry with paper towels before adding them to the salad.

If you are using a large head of iceberg, remove and discard the outer leaves. Cut each head of baby iceberg or Little Gem lettuce in half through the core; if you are using a large head of iceberg, cut it in half through the core and cut each half into thirds.

To serve, spoon 2 tablespoons of the dressing onto each half or wedge of iceberg or Little Gem and gently massage the dressing with your hands so it coats the lettuce thoroughly. Smear 1 tablespoon of the dressing on a long rectangular or large round flat platter or cutting board, preferably something dark colored to accentuate the light color of the lettuce and dressing. Rest the lettuce, cut side up, on the dressing, nestling it into the dressing to help it stay in place. Repeat, dressing the remaining lettuce, smearing a tablespoon at a time of the dressing on the platter, and nestling one lettuce half or wedge on each smear of dressing in the same way you did the first. When you have dressed all the lettuce halves or wedges and they are all on the platter, scatter the onion slices and tomatoes over the lettuce, dividing them evenly. Scatter the bacon over the lettuce, then the thyme, being sure to get an equal amount of all the components on each wedge. Coarsely grind a few turns of pepper over each half or wedge and serve the salad with tongs.

FOR THE SALAD

4 thick-cut applewood-smoked bacon slices (about 3 ounces)

¼ medium red onion (quartered root to tip), peeled

3 baby iceberg lettuce heads (or 3 Little Gem lettuce heads or 1 big iceberg head)

24 small sweet tomatoes (such as Sun Golds, Sweet 100s, or grape tomatoes), halved through the stem ends

1 tablespoon fresh thyme leaves

Fresh coarsely ground black pepper

Sliced Heirloom Tomatoes with Sweet Onion Dressing

This salad is both an heirloom tomato salad and a novel presentation of a burger condiment. Dressing the tomatoes as they are in this recipe makes it so that those who don't want tomatoes on their burgers, or those who aren't eating burgers at all, can still enjoy the tomatoes. The flat presentation was inspired by a photograph I saw on the cover of *Bon Appétit* magazine, where a variety of heirloom tomatoes was beautifully arranged to create a sort of sliced tomato rainbow. In deciding how to dress this salad, I searched through my mental recipe index as far back as I could for an acidic, emulsified, but not creamy dressing. I stopped when I got to the 1970s and remembered a tart poppy seed dressing that I used to enjoy at a restaurant called Poppy's in Westwood Village. That's where I would go to see first-run movies—movies always started out in Westwood in those days—and I would always stop at Poppy's for a salad. I leave out the poppy seeds in this version, but otherwise, this dressing is unchanged. I spoon the dressing on the platter, so it's underneath the tomato slices, not on them, which helps to prevent the tomatoes from getting watery after sitting out for a while on the buffet.

To make the dressing, combine the vinegar, grated onion, lemon juice, and kosher salt in a medium bowl and set aside for 5 to 10 minutes to marinate the onion. Stir in the mayonnaise, sugar, and mustard. Add the canola oil in a thin, steady stream, whisking constantly to emulsify. Use the dressing or refrigerate, covered, for up to 3 days. Bring the dressing to room temperature and stir in the minced onion just before using.

To prepare the salad, slice the large tomatoes ¼ inch thick. (Reserve the top and bottom slices to snack on, drizzled with olive oil and sprinkled with sea salt.) Cut the small tomatoes in half through the stem ends, drizzle with the olive oil, sprinkle with the kosher salt, and toss gently to coat the tomatoes.

Stir the dressing to recombine the ingredients and spoon 2 to 3 tablespoons of the dressing on a medium oval platter, or enough to generously cover the surface of the platter. Lay the sliced tomatoes on top of the dressing, arranging them nicely with the various colors, shapes, and sizes distributed in a pretty way. Distribute the small tomatoes in clusters over the sliced tomatoes. Sprinkle the tomatoes with sea salt and serve with a flat spoon and the remaining dressing in a small bowl on the side with a small spoon for guests to serve themselves.

SERVES 6 TO 8

FOR THE DRESSING

½ cup plus 2 tablespoons champagne vinegar (or white wine vinegar)

½ cup grated yellow Spanish onion (grated on a medium-holed Microplane), plus ½ cup minced yellow Spanish onion

3 tablespoons fresh lemon juice

2 teaspoons kosher salt

2 tablespoons Garlic Mayonnaise (page 84 or store-bought mayonnaise)

2 tablespoons sugar

2 teaspoons Dijon mustard

¼ cup canola oil (or another neutral-flavored oil)

FOR THE SALAD

3 large heirloom tomatoes (preferably different colors)

1 cup small heirloom tomatoes (preferably different colors or another sweet tomato such as Sun Golds)

1 tablespoon extra-virgin olive oil

¼ teaspoon kosher salt

Maldon sea salt (or another flaky sea salt such as fleur de sel)

Spicy Cucumber Pickles

I recently made sliced pickles to go with an autostrada sandwich (my name for a pressed sandwich made with sliced meats and provolone) that I served at a sandwich demonstration at a food festival in South Carolina. Bringing pickles to the South felt a bit like bringing coals to Newcastle, so I was pleasantly surprised that the southerners at the festival loved them. And I was reminded once again that there is just nothing like homemade pickles. There are a lot of great pickles for sale out there, and believe me, when I have a big crowd of people coming, I feel perfectly fine going to Huntington Meats in Los Angeles to pick up Guss' pickles, from New York City, along with my burger blend. But it's fun to look at a sandwich or a spread of food and be able to say, "I made every single thing myself."

You will need parchment paper or large paper coffee filters for this recipe. If you have a mandoline, use it to make easy work of slicing the garlic.

Combine the vinegar, sugar, salt, and garlic in a medium saucepan. Add 2 cups water and bring the liquid to a boil over high heat. Reduce the heat to low and simmer for 10 minutes to infuse the liquid with the seasonings. Add the red chile flakes and simmer for another minute. Turn off the heat.

Put the ice in a large high-sided vessel, such as a stockpot, Dutch oven, or roasting pan. Add the pickling liquid to the vessel with the ice, then add the cucumbers. Lay a sheet of parchment paper or coffee filters on top of the cucumbers and put a plate on top of that to keep the pickles submerged while they cool. Transfer the pickles, stacked vertically, to a 1-quart canning jar (or another container with a lid). Strain the pickling liquid into a large bowl. Add the pickling spices in the strainer to the jar with the cucumbers. Add enough of the pickling liquid to fill the jar and discard the remaining liquid. Close the jar and refrigerate the pickles for 1 to 2 days before serving them or for up to 6 months.

MAKES 1 QUART

1 quart champagne vinegar (or white wine vinegar)

1 cup sugar

¼ cup kosher salt

½ cup large garlic cloves (about 20 cloves), peeled and sliced ¹⁄₁₆ inch thick lengthwise, preferably on a mandoline

1 tablespoon red chile flakes

2½ cups ice cubes

5 pounds Persian or Japanese cucumbers

8

Staff Meal Oven-Roasted Chicken Thighs

SERVES 6 TO 8

12 bone-in, skin-on chicken thighs

1 medium yellow Spanish onion, peeled

1 cup medium or large garlic cloves (about 40 cloves), peeled

1 large lemon, sliced into ¼-inch rounds

15 fresh thyme sprigs

4 (3-inch long) fresh rosemary sprigs

2 tablespoons kosher salt

2 teaspoons freshly ground black pepper

Every morning when I walk into the restaurant, when I see Sal, our daytime chef at the Osteria, the first thing I do is ask, "Sal, what's for lunch?" If Sal says chicken, he means these oven-roasted chicken thighs. It's not a fancy preparation, but if you're in the mood for a super-moist, very flavorful, comforting chicken dish, it doesn't get any better. My friend and Mozza's (unofficial) chief security officer, Michael Krikorian, plans his day around what time Sal's chicken is going to come out of the oven so he can stop by the restaurant for lunch. These chicken thighs couldn't be easier to make—just season them, throw them into the oven, and they cook while you put the rest of the meal together. The only catch is that you have to plan ahead. Sal's trick for achieving a crispy skin is to dry the skin out first, which he does by leaving the chicken in the refrigerator overnight, uncovered.

I serve the chicken with the side dishes that I brought to Thanksgiving dinner at my sister's house one year, as well as Tomatillo Salsa (page 55), whose citrusy flavor is the perfect complement to the chicken. It's such a simple, home-style preparation that, depending on the season and what you like, you could serve this with any vegetables or salads in this book. The serving size of this recipe depends entirely on how much each guest eats, but don't worry, it's an easy recipe to expand for a larger number of guests.

Pat the chicken thighs dry with paper towels and lay them, skin side up, in a single layer on a baking sheet. Put the baking sheet in the refrigerator, uncovered, and refrigerate the chicken overnight or for at least 8 hours. Take the chicken thighs out of the refrigerator 45 minutes before you're ready to cook them, to bring them to room temperature.

Adjust an oven rack to the middle position and preheat the oven to 500°F.

Trim and discard the root end of the onion and cut the onion in half root to tip. Cut each half in half again root to tip so the onion is quartered. Separate the layers of the onion, stack 2 or 3 layers at a time on top of one another, and slice ¼ inch thick lengthwise.

Spread the onion slices and garlic cloves in a single layer in the center of a large baking sheet to create a bed large enough to nestle the chicken thighs in a single layer. Lay the lemon slices on top of the onion and garlic and scatter the thyme sprigs and rosemary sprigs on top of the lemon.

Prepare a double bed of paper towels on a flat work surface to put the chicken on. Remove the chicken thighs from their baking sheet and put them, skin side down, on the paper towels. Sprinkle 1 tablespoon of the salt and 1 teaspoon of the pepper over the bone side of the chicken thighs. Turn the chicken thighs and sprinkle 1 tablespoon of the salt and 1 teaspoon of the pepper on the skin side of the chicken. Transfer the chicken thighs from the paper towels to the baking sheet, nestling them, skin side up, snugly next to one another on the bed of onions and seasonings. Once you've laid down all the chicken thighs, push the onions inward with your hands so they are not spread out wider than the thighs. If the chicken skins appear wet, pat the thighs dry with paper towels and season them again.

Roast the chicken for 40 to 50 minutes, until the juices run clear when the chicken is pierced with a small knife. Turn the oven to the broiler setting and move the chicken so it is closest to the broiler. Broil the chicken for about 5 minutes, until the skin is deep golden and crispy.

To serve, move the chicken thighs off the bed of seasonings and fish out and discard the lemon slices. Spoon the thyme, rosemary, onions, and garlic onto a large round or rectangular serving platter. Using tongs, lift the chicken thighs off the baking sheet and lay them on the bed of onions and garlic. Serve with tongs.

Balsamic-Glazed Mushrooms

SERVES 6 TO 8

1 cup balsamic vinegar, plus
2 tablespoons if needed

1 large shallot, peeled

½ cup olive oil, or as needed

2 pounds cremini mushrooms
(also called baby portobello;
or white button mushrooms),
caps wiped clean with damp paper
towels and stems trimmed at the
base and discarded

1½ teaspoons kosher salt

¼ cup fresh tarragon leaves,
half of the leaves finely chopped,
half left whole

Balsamic vinegar was one of my dad's very favorite foods, so when I brought these balsamic-glazed mushrooms to Thanksgiving dinner at my sister's house one year, I knew they would have at least one fan. If I were leafing through a book and saw this recipe, I might be turned off, thinking that a mushroom drenched in vinegar would be overly sweet, and an unappealing black color. And although they wouldn't win any beauty contests, these mushrooms are neither drenched nor overly sweet. They do indeed turn out black—not the most appetizing color in a vegetable, I admit—because the mushrooms are cooked whole, the little black globes are pretty in their own way. Both their look and flavor are brightened up with fresh tarragon leaves that are tossed with the mushrooms after they're cooked.

When shopping for the mushrooms for this dish, choose those that are firm, with unopened caps (you don't see gills under the caps). When choosing white button mushrooms, pick those on the larger end of the spectrum.

Divide the balsamic vinegar in half so you have two ½-cup containers. Have the vinegar handy.

Cut the shallot in half root to tip; trim and discard the root end. Separate the layers of the shallot, stack 2 or 3 layers at a time on top of one another, and slice 1⁄16 inch thick lengthwise.

Heat 2 tablespoons of the olive oil in a large sauté pan over medium-high heat until it slides easily in the pan and the oil around the edges of the pan begins to smoke, 2 to 3 minutes. Add half of the mushrooms, caps down, to the pan. Season with ¾ teaspoon of the salt and cook the mushrooms for about 10 minutes, until they are golden brown, turning them as they brown and adding 2 tablespoons of the remaining oil, 1 tablespoon at a time, as the pan becomes dry. Pour one-third of one portion of the balsamic vinegar into the pan and cook the mushrooms for 3 to 4 minutes, shaking the pan and turning the mushrooms to coat them evenly with the vinegar, until the mushrooms have absorbed the vinegar. Add half of the remaining vinegar from the same portion you're working from and cook the mushrooms in the same way, shaking the pan and turning the mushrooms to coat them evenly until the newly added vinegar has been absorbed, 3 to 4 minutes. Add the remaining vinegar from the portion you're working from and cook until the vinegar left in the pan is syrupy and caramel-like, but not overly thick and sticky, 2 to 3 minutes. (Lift the pan off the heat so the bubbles subside and you are better able to see the consistency of the vinegar.) If the vinegar is over-reduced to a sticky mess, add another tablespoon of vinegar and cook it for about 1 minute, or just long enough to integrate it with the balsamic in the pan.

Turn off the heat and add half of the shallot slices to the pan. Gently stir to combine the shallot slices with the mushrooms and to coat the shallot with the balsamic glaze. Transfer the mushrooms and shallot slices to a large bowl. Cook the remaining mushrooms in the same way, using the remaining ¼ cup oil, ¾ tea-spoon salt, and the second portion of the vinegar, and adding the remaining shallot slices at the end as you did when cooking the first batch of mushrooms. When the second batch is done, add it to the bowl with the first batch. Sprinkle the chopped tarragon over the mushrooms and shallot slices and toss gently to combine.

To serve, pile the mushrooms and shallot slices, making sure the mushrooms are cap side up, 2 to 3 high, in a large shallow bowl or a rimmed platter. Scatter the whole tarragon leaves over the top and serve with a large spoon.

Roasted Vegetable Medley with Yogurt Dressing

I developed this recipe for Thanksgiving when I wanted to serve roasted vegetables to my family and friends, but to present them in a way that felt worthy of a special occasion. Roasting, which brings out the natural sweetness in vegetables, is hands down my favorite vegetable preparation. For this dish, I roast four different batches of vegetables: mushrooms, root vegetables, winter squash, and Brussels sprouts leaves, which I layer with a farro and flaxseed mélange and, finally, drizzle with a tangy yogurt dressing. The result is a beautiful mix of colors, sizes, and shapes. This recipe might seem a bit involved, and for everyday it is, but think of it as inspiration. You could roast only the mushrooms, root vegetables, or squash, or eliminate the farro mélange altogether, and the dish would still be beautiful and taste great. Or substitute vegetables that you have on hand or that you see in the market, such as carrots, cauliflower, or turnips, for the vegetables I call for in the recipe. The roasted Brussels sprouts leaves add a lovely textural component and also add to the autumnal feel of the dish, looking as they do like fallen leaves.

I call for you to toss the vegetables with seasonings in a bowl and then to transfer them to a baking sheet, but if you have enough baking sheets, you can toss them directly onto the baking sheets and save yourself the trouble of washing the bowl. If you have parchment paper, use it to line the baking sheet to toast the farro; it makes it so easy to get the grains off the baking sheet without spilling any. Just pull the entire sheet of parchment off the baking sheet and fold it up to create a sort of funnel to pour the farro into the pot once it's toasted.

———

To cook the farro, adjust an oven rack to the middle position and preheat the oven to 350°F. Line a baking sheet with parchment paper, if you are using it.

Put the farro on the baking sheet, drizzle with 2 teaspoons of the olive oil, and toss to coat the grains. Spread the farro out on the baking sheet and toast in the oven until it's golden brown and slightly fragrant, 8 to 10 minutes, shaking the baking sheet and rotating it from front to back halfway through the cooking time so the farro browns evenly. Remove from the oven.

Meanwhile, bring 1 quart water to a boil in a medium saucepan over high heat. Add 1½ teaspoons of the salt and the farro and return the water to a boil. Reduce the heat to medium-low and simmer until the farro is al dente, 18 to 22 minutes.

SERVES 6 TO 8

———

FOR THE FARRO

½ cup farro, soaked overnight and drained

1 tablespoon plus 1 teaspoon extra-virgin olive oil

2 teaspoons kosher salt

½ cup brown flaxseeds

1 teaspoon fresh lemon juice

FOR THE MUSHROOMS

¾ pound mixed mushrooms (such as chanterelles, hen of the woods, or beech), caps wiped clean with damp paper towels and tough stems trimmed and discarded; if you are using beech mushrooms, keep the stems bundled

10 fresh thyme sprigs

¼ cup olive oil

1 teaspoon kosher salt

FOR THE ROOT VEGETABLES

2 parsnips (about 1 pound), trimmed and peeled

2 small celery roots (about 1 pound), trimmed and peeled

10 to 12 medium or large garlic cloves, peeled

(continued)

10 fresh thyme sprigs

¼ cup olive oil

1 teaspoon kosher salt

1 tablespoon unsalted butter,
cut into small cubes

FOR THE WINTER SQUASH

2 pounds butternut squash
(or another winter squash such
as kabocha or acorn)

10 to 12 medium or large garlic
cloves, peeled

12 fresh sage leaves

10 fresh thyme sprigs

¼ cup plus 2 tablespoons olive oil

1 teaspoon kosher salt

2 tablespoons unsalted butter,
cut into small cubes

FOR THE BRUSSELS SPROUTS

1¼ pounds Brussels sprouts

¼ cup plus 2 tablespoons olive oil

1 teaspoon kosher salt

1 recipe Yogurt Dressing
(recipe follows)

Drain the farro in a colander and transfer it to a small bowl. Drizzle the farro with the remaining 2 teaspoons olive oil and toss to coat the grains. Set aside to cool to room temperature.

Toast the flaxseeds in a small sauté pan over medium heat without moving them for 1 to 2 minutes, until they start to pop in the pan. Shake the pan so the seeds don't burn and continue to toast the seeds for 2 to 3 minutes, shaking the pan often, until they darken in color and start to release a nutty aroma. Transfer the seeds to a plate to cool to room temperature. Add the flaxseeds to the baking sheet with the farro and set aside.

Drizzle with the lemon juice and the remaining ½ teaspoon salt, and toss to combine the ingredients and to distribute the salt.

To prepare the mushrooms, adjust the oven racks so none are near the oven floor; you'll be putting a baking sheet directly on the oven floor. If you are using an electric oven or another oven where you can't put anything on the floor, adjust the oven racks so that one is closest to the floor and put a pizza stone on it, if you have one. Preheat the oven to 500°F.

Put the mushrooms and thyme sprigs in a medium bowl. Drizzle with the olive oil, sprinkle with the salt, and toss to coat the vegetables. Spread the mushrooms in a single layer on a large baking sheet and put the baking sheet on the floor of the oven or the lowest rack and roast the mushrooms until they are golden brown all over, 8 to 12 minutes, shaking the baking sheet and rotating it from front to back halfway through the cooking time so the mushrooms brown evenly. Remove the baking sheet from the oven and set aside. (When cooking vegetables on the oven floor, a lot of steam is produced from the water released as a result of the vegetables cooking so quickly, so just be careful of the steam that will arise when you open the oven door.) If you need the baking sheet to roast the other vegetables, transfer the vegetables to a large bowl or a baking dish to cool.

To prepare the root vegetables, starting at the thin root end of the parsnips, cut 2 or 3 (depending on how thin the root tip is) ½-inch-thick slices on an extreme bias. Cut the fatter remainder of the parsnip in half lengthwise and slice both halves into ½-inch-thick half-moons on an extreme bias. (Cutting the parsnips this way ensures the slices are roughly the same size and therefore require the same cooking time.) Repeat with the second parsnip. Put the parsnips in the bowl you tossed the mushrooms in.

Cut the celery roots in half down the middle. Lay one half of the celery root flat and cut ¼-inch-thick slices across it. Repeat with the remaining halves. Lay the slices down, stacking 2 or 3 at a time, and cut them in half down the middle.

Cut the halves into 1½-inch-wide slices. Add the celery roots to the bowl with the parsnips. Add the garlic cloves and thyme sprigs. Drizzle the vegetables with the olive oil, sprinkle with the salt, and toss to coat the vegetables evenly.

Spread the vegetables in a single layer on a large baking sheet. Put the baking sheet on the floor of the oven or the lowest rack and roast until the vegetables are tender when pierced with a toothpick and the sides touching the pan are caramelized, about 30 minutes, shaking the baking sheet and rotating it from front to back halfway through the cooking time so the vegetables brown evenly. Remove the baking sheet from the oven, scatter the butter pieces over the vegetables, and return the baking sheet to the oven for 5 minutes to melt the butter. Remove the baking sheet from the oven, toss to coat the vegetables with the melted butter, and set aside. If you need to use the baking sheet again, transfer the vegetables to another large mixing bowl or baking dish to cool.

To prepare the squash, peel it with a vegetable peeler, or cut off the peel with a knife. Cut it in half and scoop out and discard the seeds. With the flat sides of the squash facing down, cut it into 1½-inch cubes. Put the squash cubes in the bowl you tossed the other vegetables in. Add the garlic cloves, sage leaves, and thyme sprigs. Drizzle the vegetables with the olive oil, sprinkle with the salt, and toss to coat the vegetables.

Spread the vegetables in a single layer on a large baking sheet. Put the baking sheet on the floor of the oven or the lowest rack and roast the squash until it is tender when pierced with a toothpick and the sides touching the pan are caramelized, about 30 minutes, and shake the baking sheet. Rotate it from front to back halfway through the cooking time so the squash browns evenly; make sure not to cook it so much that it is mushy. Remove the baking sheet from the oven, scatter the butter pieces over the squash, and return the baking sheet to the oven for 5 minutes to melt the butter. Remove the baking sheet from the oven and toss to coat the vegetables with the melted butter. If you need to use the baking sheet again, transfer the vegetables to another large mixing bowl or baking dish to cool.

To prepare the Brussels sprouts, using a paring knife, cut off the stems from each sprout. Cut each sprout in half through the core, and cut out and discard the cores from the sprouts. Separate the Brussels sprouts leaves and drop them into the bowl you tossed the other veggies in. Drizzle with the olive oil, sprinkle with the salt, and toss to coat the leaves.

Spread the leaves in a single layer on a large baking sheet, nestling them close to one another to prevent them from burning. Put the baking sheet on the floor of the oven or the lowest rack and roast the leaves until they are browned around the edges but still mostly green, 8 to 10 minutes. Shake the baking sheet and rotate it from front to back halfway through the cooking time so the leaves brown evenly. Remove the baking sheet from the oven and set aside.

Pick out and discard the thyme stems. Place all the vegetables except the Brussels sprouts leaves in a large bowl and toss gently.

To serve, scatter one-third of the Brussels sprouts leaves over the surface of a large rimmed platter or wide-mouthed bowl. Spoon one-third of the farro mixture over the Brussels sprouts, leaving ½ inch of the leaves exposed around the edges. Spoon one-third of the roasted vegetables out of the bowl and pile them in an even layer on top of the farro, leaving ½ inch of the farro exposed around the rim. Drizzle with 3 tablespoons of the dressing. Build a second layer identical to the first: a layer of Brussels sprouts leaves, then a layer of farro, and then a layer of roasted vegetables, always leaving a little bit of the previous layer visible when you add the next layer. Drizzle with 3 tablespoons of the dressing. Build a third layer using the remaining Brussels sprouts leaves, farro, and roasted vegetables. Drizzle 2 tablespoons of the dressing over the salad and pour the rest into a small pretty bowl. Serve the salad with a big spoon and the dressing with a small spoon for guests to serve themselves.

Yogurt Dressing

Makes 1¼ cups

This tangy, lemony, yogurt dressing is delicious drizzled on any roasted vegetable.

2 tablespoons minced shallot
(from about 1 small peeled shallot)

2 tablespoons fresh lemon juice

2 teaspoons champagne vinegar
(or white wine vinegar)

1 teaspoon kosher salt

¼ teaspoon freshly ground black pepper

¼ cup extra-virgin olive oil

½ cup Straus Family Creamery Organic Greek Yogurt (or another whole-milk plain, not overly thick, Greek-style yogurt)

Combine the shallot, lemon juice, vinegar, salt, and pepper in a small bowl. Add the olive oil in a slow, steady stream, whisking constantly to emulsify. Put the yogurt in a medium bowl and gradually add the contents of the first bowl, whisking constantly to emulsify. Use or refrigerate the dressing, covered, for up to 2 days.

Baked Japanese Sweet Potatoes with Fried Sage Leaves and Bacon

In my opinion, there is no better side dish than a baked potato with all the usual trimmings. That said, I don't serve baked potatoes when I entertain because they're truly magnificent only straight from the oven. Enter the sweet potato, specifically, the yellow-fleshed sweet potatoes and purple-fleshed yams that you find at farmers' markets and specialty food stores. These sweet potatoes are much creamier than regular potatoes, and the texture isn't compromised when they cool in the way it is with, say, russet potatoes. In this recipe, the potatoes are topped with butter, thin threads of cooked bacon, fried sage leaves, and a light dusting of Parmigiano. They make a great side dish to bring to Thanksgiving dinner in lieu of their cloying, marshmallow-topped cousins.

I cook the potatoes on mounds of kosher salt, which serves two purposes: it helps to conduct the heat and it keeps the potatoes from flattening, which causes the juices to run out of them, as they bake. Yellow-fleshed sweet potatoes and purple yams are much easier to find than they were even a few years ago. If you can't find them, use small garnet yams instead.

———

Adjust an oven rack to the middle position and preheat the oven to 350°F.

Prepare a bed of paper towels. Lay the bacon on a baking sheet and bake until it is cooked all the way through but not crisp, 15 to 17 minutes, rotating the baking sheet from front to back halfway through the cooking time so the bacon cooks evenly. Remove the bacon from the oven and transfer it to the paper towels to drain and cool to room temperature. Slice the bacon into ¼-inch-wide threads on an extreme bias and set aside.

Put the sweet potatoes or yams in a large bowl, drizzle them with the olive oil, and rub the oil to coat the potatoes or yams. Pour six ¼-cup mounds of the salt on a baking sheet, leaving at least 6 inches between each, and nestle one sweet potato or yam on each mound. Sprinkle ½ teaspoon of the remaining salt over each of the potatoes or yams.

Bake the sweet potatoes or yams for 1 hour to 1 hour 15 minutes, until they're tender when pierced with a toothpick. Depending on their size and shape, some of the sweet potatoes or yams may be done sooner than others; remove each one from the oven as it's done. Set the potatoes or yams aside until they're cool

SERVES 6

4 thick-cut applewood-smoked bacon slices (about 3 ounces)

6 medium yellow-fleshed sweet potatoes or purple yams

1 tablespoon plus 1 teaspoon olive oil, plus more for frying the sage leaves

1½ cups plus 1 tablespoon plus 2½ teaspoons kosher salt

½ cup fresh sage leaves

6 tablespoons (¾ stick) unsalted butter

Wedge of Parmigiano-Reggiano for grating

enough to touch. You can bake the sweet potatoes or yams up to several hours in advance. Store them, uncovered, at room temperature. Before serving, warm them in a 350°F oven enough so that butter melts on them.

Meanwhile, if you have one, fasten a deep-fry thermometer onto a small deep pot. Fill the pot 3 to 4 inches deep with olive oil. Heat the oil over medium-high heat until the thermometer registers 350°F, or until a sage leaf sizzles immediately when dropped into the pot. While the oil is heating, line a plate with paper towels.

Add half of the sage leaves to the pot. Fry the sage for about 30 seconds, until it is crispy but not brown. Lift the sage leaves out of the oil with a slotted spoon or spider, transfer to the paper towels to drain, and sprinkle with ½ teaspoon of the remaining salt. Repeat with the remaining sage leaves. Turn off the heat and let the oil cool. Transfer the oil to a covered container and reserve to cook with.

Remove the sweet potatoes or yams from the baking sheet, tap and wipe them to remove the salt, and put them on a cutting board. Cut a 1-inch-deep slit lengthwise into each potato or yam. Squeeze the edges of the potatoes or yams toward each other to push the insides up out of the skins. Sprinkle ¼ teaspoon of the remaining salt on each sweet potato or yam. Put 1 tablespoon of the butter on each potato or yam. Using a fine Microplane, grate a generous layer of Parmigiano over each potato. Sprinkle the bacon slices and scatter the fried sage leaves over the potatoes, dividing both evenly.

To serve, transfer the sweet potatoes to a medium round or rectangular platter. Serve with tongs only if you think your guests would mind grabbing a potato with their hands.

Endive Salad with Date Anchovy Dressing

SERVES 6 TO 8

FOR THE DRESSING

10 Medjool dates, pitted and roughly chopped (about 1 cup)

10 anchovy fillets, about 1 ounce (preferably salt-packed; rinsed, backbone removed if salt-packed), roughly chopped and smashed to a paste with the flat side of a knife

3 tablespoons red wine vinegar

1 small orange for zesting, plus 3 tablespoons fresh orange juice

1 lemon for zesting, plus 1½ tablespoons fresh lemon juice

3 to 4 medium or large garlic cloves, peeled

1 teaspoon kosher salt

1 cup extra-virgin olive oil

FOR THE SALAD

2 large fennel bulbs

2 tablespoons fresh lemon juice

1 teaspoon kosher salt

5 Belgian endive heads (preferably red)

Wedge of Parmigiano-Reggiano for grating

For those who like sweet and savory flavors together, this is your salad. It's composed of sliced fennel and crisp, sturdy endive leaves, coated in a thick dressing made of puréed dates and anchovies. The recipe for the dressing makes more than you will need to dress this salad. Use it to make another, smaller salad later in the week, or as a dip for raw vegetables. Although I included a version of this dressing in my book *Twist of the Wrist*, this dressing is so delicious and unusual, I thought it worth repeating here.

You will need a mandoline to slice the fennel for this recipe.

———

To make the dressing, put the dates, anchovies, and 1 tablespoon of the vinegar in the bowl of a mini food processor fitted with a metal blade or in the jar of a blender and purée to a chunky paste. Using a fine Microplane, zest the orange and lemon directly into the bowl. Use the Microplane to grate the garlic directly into the food processor and purée to a smooth paste. Add the orange juice, lemon juice, salt, and the remaining 2 tablespoons vinegar and pulse to combine. Transfer the contents of the food processor to a medium bowl. Add the olive oil and stir to combine. (The dressing may separate and look a bit pasty, but don't worry, that's just the nature of it.) Use the dressing or refrigerate, covered, for up to 3 days. Bring the dressing to room temperature before serving.

To prepare the salad, cut off the fronds from the fennel bulbs, if they are still attached, and discard them or reserve for another use. Trim ¼ inch of the cut (root) end of the fennel, making sure not to trim too much; you want the layers of the fennel to remain intact. Remove any outer layers that are brown and unappealing. Using a mandoline, slice the fennel slightly less than ¼ inch thick vertically; the shape of the fennel will stay intact. Transfer the fennel slices to a medium bowl, drizzle with 1 tablespoon of the lemon juice, sprinkle with ½ teaspoon of the salt, and toss to coat. (The lemon juice prevents the fennel from browning after it's been sliced.)

Trim the stem ends from the endive and tear the leaves from the cores. Cut the larger leaves crosswise into 3 segments and the smaller leaves into 2 segments. Put the endive in a separate bowl. Drizzle the remaining 1 tablespoon lemon juice and sprinkle the remaining ½ teaspoon salt over the endive. Toss gently to coat the leaves.

Pour ⅓ cup of the dressing over the fennel and pour ½ cup of the dressing over the endive. Gently toss each vegetable, massaging the dressing onto each fennel slice and endive leaf.

To build the salad, scatter one-third of the endive leaves over the bottom of a large flat platter. Lay one-third of the fennel slices over the endive and grate a generous layer of Parmigiano over the fennel. Repeat, building two more layers with the remaining endive and fennel and ending with a generous dusting of Parmigiano. Serve with tongs and place the wedge of Parmigiano and the Microplane on a plate next to the salad for guests to grate more cheese on their portions.

Carrot and Rice Salad with Ginger Sumac Dressing

SERVES 8 TO 12
MAKES ABOUT 10 CUPS

FOR THE DRESSING

½ cup fresh lime juice,
plus 2 tablespoons grated lime zest
(from about 2 limes, grated on a
fine Microplane)

½ cup sumac

¼ cup plus 2 tablespoons
champagne vinegar
(or white wine vinegar)

2 ounces fresh ginger
(one 3- to 4-inch piece), peeled
and grated on a medium-holed
Microplane (about 2 tablespoons)

2 teaspoons kosher salt

1 teaspoon red chile flakes,
ground in a spice grinder
or use a mortar and a pestle

FOR THE RICE

1½ teaspoons kosher salt

½ cup Forbidden (Thai black) rice

1 tablespoon extra-virgin olive oil

½ cup Thai red rice

½ cup brown jasmine or brown
basmati rice

At one time in the culinary history of this country, if I'd said to a friend, "I'll bring a carrot salad," my friend would have imagined me carrying a bowlful of shredded carrots tossed with black raisins and bound with a sweet mayonnaise-based dressing. This is my twenty-first-century version of a carrot salad, made with matchsticks of carrots tossed with rice and a tangy lime dressing seasoned with fresh ginger and sumac. I brought the salad to Thanksgiving one year, along with four other side dishes and salads, and this stood out as the crowd favorite because the flavor and the entire concept of the dish were so unexpected.

This recipe calls for three types of rice—red, black, and brown. Each needs to be cooked separately, because they cook for different lengths of time. If you wanted to simplify the story, use two types of rice, or even one. Just make sure you cook the total amount of rice called for. Sumac, a red berry ground into a spice, is widely used in Middle Eastern cooking. It has become somewhat trendy in recent years and today is widely available. Try to buy yours at a specialty spice store, where the freshness of the spice results in noticeably more intense flavor.

You will need a mandoline to slice the carrots for this salad.

To make the dressing, combine the lime juice, lime zest, sumac, vinegar, ginger, salt, and ground chile flakes in a medium bowl and whisk to combine.

To cook the rice, bring 1 cup water to a boil in a small saucepan over high heat. Add ½ teaspoon of the salt and the black rice and return the water to a boil. Reduce the heat to low, cover the pan, and simmer the rice, using the cooking time indicated on the package as a guide, until all the liquid is absorbed. Turn off the heat and let the rice rest for 10 minutes. Drizzle with 1 teaspoon of the olive oil and use a fork to fluff up the rice and distribute the oil. Dump the rice onto a baking sheet, spread the rice out into a thin layer, and set aside to cool.

Cook the red rice in the same way: bring 1 cup water to a boil, season with ½ teaspoon of the remaining salt, and cook until the water is absorbed, using the cooking time indicated on the package as a guide. Drizzle the red rice with 1 teaspoon of the remaining oil and fluff it with a fork. Push the black rice to the side of the baking sheet and transfer the red rice to the baking sheet alongside the black rice. Spread the red rice out on the baking sheet and set aside to cool.

Repeat, cooking the brown rice in the same way you cooked the black and red rice, seasoning the water with the remaining ½ teaspoon salt and tossing the cooked rice with the remaining 1 teaspoon olive oil. Push the red rice aside with the black rice and spread the brown rice on the baking sheet. Put the baking sheet in the refrigerator until all the rice is chilled. Use the rice or refrigerate, covered, for up to 2 days.

To prepare the salad, toast the flaxseeds in a small sauté pan over medium heat without moving them for 1 to 2 minutes, until they start to pop in the pan. Shake the pan so the seeds don't burn and continue to toast the seeds for 2 to 3 minutes, shaking the pan often, until they darken in color and start to release a nutty aroma. Transfer the seeds to a plate to cool to room temperature.

Cut the carrots into 3- to 4-inch-long segments. Using a mandoline, slice the segments ¹⁄₁₆ inch thick lengthwise. Stack the slices and slice with a large knife into ¹⁄₁₆-inch batons.

Remove the rice from the refrigerator and transfer it to a large bowl. Add the flaxseeds and carrots. Drizzle with the finishing-quality olive oil, season with the salt, and toss to coat the rice and carrots. Give the dressing a quick whisk to distribute the ginger and sumac and pour the dressing over the salad. Toss the salad gently to coat the ingredients with the dressing. Pile the salad in a tall mound in a large shallow serving bowl or on a large rimmed platter and serve with a large serving spoon.

FOR THE SALAD

1 cup brown flaxseeds

1½ pounds carrots (about 4 medium), trimmed and peeled

¼ cup finishing-quality extra-virgin olive oil

1½ teaspoons kosher salt

9

Sicilian Swordfish Spiedini 181

Sicilian Swordfish Spiedini

Spiedini means "skewers" in Italian. The first place in Italy that I saw spiedini was Sicily, where you see assembled spiedini of meat and fish varieties for people to buy to cook at home. This recipe is based on those we serve at Chi Spacca, but we use amberjack, a steaklike fish similar to swordfish. Because amberjack can prove elusive to the home cook, we adapted this recipe to work with swordfish or ahi tuna. These skewers would be delicious with any of the Italian-leaning vegetables in this book.

If you are not cooking these on an outdoor grill, you will need a square or rectangular grill pan, such as a 20-inch Lodge reversible grill/griddle, to cook on because you can fit only one skewer in a round grill pan. You will also need 8 to 10 long (at least 10 inches) skewers, preferably metal (if you're using wooden skewers, soak them in water for at least 1 hour before assembling the spiedini), and a mandoline to slice the zucchini as thinly as it needs to be sliced. You can find fresh bay leaves sold in small plastic containers along with other fresh herbs in most supermarkets.

———

To make the marinade, combine the parsley, olive oil, garlic, and red chile flakes in the bowl of a mini food processor fitted with a metal blade or in the jar of a blender and purée. Set aside.

To prepare the spiedini, cut the stems and tips off each zucchini and slice ⅛ inch thick lengthwise on a mandoline.

Organize the zucchini slices, bay leaves, fish cubes, and skewers (see headnote) on a flat work surface to create an assembly line. Building one skewer at a time, put a bay leaf on a skewer, pushing the leaf toward the bottom of the skewer. Stack two zucchini slices, roll them like a fruit roll-up, and spear them on the skewer, pushing the rolled zucchini slices to meet the bay leaf. Add another bay leaf, then a cube of fish. Build two more layers, adding another bay leaf, doubled zucchini-slice roll, bay leaf, a second cube of fish, bay leaf, zucchini roll, bay leaf, third cube of fish, bay leaf, zucchini roll, and finishing with a bay leaf. Assemble all of the skewers in the same way.

Divide the spiedini between two large sealable plastic bags, taking care not to puncture the bags with the skewers, or put them in a large nonreactive baking dish. Pour the marinade into the bags, dividing it evenly, or over the skewers

SERVES 6 TO 8

FOR THE MARINADE

2 cups packed fresh Italian parsley leaves

1 cup extra-virgin olive oil

10 large garlic cloves, peeled

½ teaspoon red chile flakes

FOR THE SPIEDINI

1½ pounds zucchini

48 to 60 fresh bay leaves

3½ pounds (1½-inch-thick) skinless swordfish or ahi tuna steaks (or amberjack), cut into 1½- to 2-inch cubes

4 lemons

Oil for brushing the lemons

2 teaspoons kosher salt

Freshly ground black pepper

Finishing-quality extra-virgin olive oil

Maldon sea salt (or another flaky sea salt such as fleur de sel)

1 tablespoon finely chopped fresh Italian parsley leaves (from about 2 tablespoons packed whole leaves)

in the dish. Turn the spiedini to coat the fish on all sides and gently massage the marinade into the fish with your hands. If you are marinating the fish in bags, put the bags in a baking dish to catch any marinade that might leak out of them. Set the fish aside to marinate at room temperature for 30 minutes, or in the refrigerator for up to 2 hours. Bring the spiedini to room temperature before grilling.

Prepare a hot fire in a charcoal or gas grill. Alternatively, preheat a square or rectangular grill pan over high heat. Cooking method and times will be the same as for grilling.

Cut the lemons in half through the middle and cut ½ inch off the pointed ends so each lemon half has two flat surfaces. Brush both cut ends of the lemon halves with the olive oil.

Remove the spiedini from the marinade. Sprinkle with the kosher salt and a light coat of pepper; discard the marinade. Put the spiedini on the grill or in the grill pan and cook for 14 to 16 minutes for swordfish, about 12 minutes for tuna, turning the skewers halfway through the cooking time to cook both sides evenly, until the fish is cooked through. It will be firm to the touch and no longer stick to the grill. (The most surefire way to test for doneness is to remove one cube of fish from a skewer and tear it open; it's done when it is opaque throughout.) Remove the skewers from the grill as the fish is done.

While the spiedini are grilling, place the lemon halves on the grill or in the grill pan with the fish with the larger, middle side of the lemons facing down, for about 2 minutes, until the lemons are golden brown. Turn the lemon halves and cook the smaller sides for about 30 seconds just to warm them through.

To serve, lay the spiedini facing in one direction on a large rectangular or square cutting board or platter. Drizzle the spiedini with finishing-quality olive oil and sprinkle them with sea salt and the parsley. Nestle the lemon halves, middle cut sides up, around the spiedini on the platter and serve—no serving utensil necessary.

Couscous Salad with Root Vegetables and Ricotta Salata

This salad dates back to early La Brea Bakery days when, for a few years, we had a small deli in the store where each day we offered a selection of four or five salads for customers to buy and take home. The couscous salad was one of the most popular, and my personal favorite. What I like about it is that the vegetables are cut up small, to mirror the size of the couscous. If they were any larger, instead of the vegetables integrating with the grains of couscous, the couscous would coat the veggies, which I wouldn't like. The finished salad could seem a bit sparse, but it's very flavorful and elegant in its minimalism. Because it was originally sold from a deli case, the salad had to hold up over time, which means it also works on a buffet table. I serve it with Sicilian Swordfish Spiedini (page 181) because the North African influence of the couscous complements the Sicilian-inspired skewers. Though I don't have as much control over how my guests serve themselves as I might like, the idea is that they'll lay the skewer on a bed of the couscous as you'd traditionally see skewers on a bed of rice.

A lot of people think that couscous is a grain, but it's actually a very small semolina pasta. When we serve couscous at Chi Spacca, we make the pasta by hand, but when I make couscous at home, I go to the other extreme and use instant. Couscous is the rare ingredient that, unlike, say, oatmeal or polenta, doesn't suffer from being instant. It's so easy to make and is perfectly cooked every time.

Ricotta salata is an Italian cheese made from the whey left over from making whole sheep's milk cheeses. It is salted, pressed, and aged for at least ninety days. It is not as pungent nor as hard as Parmigiano, but like Parmigiano, ricotta salata is usually sliced, shaved, and grated and used in salads and pasta dishes.

You will need a mandoline to slice the carrots and parsnips for this salad.

SERVES 6 TO 8

2 tablespoons extra-virgin olive oil

3 tablespoons kosher salt

2 cups instant couscous (such as Casbah Organic Whole Wheat CousCous)

1 large carrot, trimmed and peeled

1 large parsnip, trimmed and peeled

10 scallions

2 tablespoons canola oil (or another neutral-flavored oil)

7 ounces ricotta salata, cut into ⅛-inch cubes (about 1½ cups)

5 large radicchio leaves (about ½ medium head), stacked and thinly sliced (about 1 cup)

1 cup packed fresh Italian parsley leaves

2 tablespoons fresh lemon juice

1 recipe Lemon Vinaigrette (page 125)

Put 3 cups water in a medium saucepan. Add the olive oil and 2 tablespoons of the salt and bring the water to a boil over high heat. Add the couscous and cover the pan. Turn off the heat and let the couscous sit, covered, for 5 minutes. Uncover the pan, transfer the couscous to a large bowl, and fluff up the couscous with a fork.

Cut the carrots into 3- to 4-inch-long segments. Using a mandoline, slice the segments ⅛ inch thick lengthwise. Stack the slices and slice with a large knife into ⅛-inch-thick batons, and then across the batons into ⅛-inch cubes. Set aside. Cut the parsnips in the same way. Keep the carrots and parsnips separate.

Trim and discard the root ends from the scallions and remove any wilted greens. Starting at the green ends and moving toward the white ends, slice the scallions ⅛ inch thick on an extreme bias. Set the scallions aside.

Line a plate with paper towels. Heat 1 tablespoon of the canola oil in a large sauté pan over high heat until the oil slides easily in the pan and the oil around the edges of the pan begins to smoke, 2 to 3 minutes. Add the carrot cubes, sprinkle with ½ teaspoon of the remaining salt, and cook for about 3 minutes, until the carrots have softened slightly but are still al dente and the edges are starting to brown, tossing the pan or stirring with a rubber spatula so the carrot cubes cook evenly. Transfer the carrot cubes to the paper towel–lined plate. Add the remaining 1 tablespoon canola oil and heat it as you did for the carrots. Add the parsnip, sprinkle with ½ teaspoon of the remaining salt, and cook as you did the carrot cubes, until the edges are starting to brown and the parsnip cubes have softened slightly but are still al dente, about 3 minutes. Add the parsnip cubes to the plate with the carrot cubes. Allow to cool.

Add the scallions, ricotta salata, radicchio, parsley, carrot cubes, and parsnip cubes to the bowl with the couscous. Drizzle the lemon juice and sprinkle the remaining 2 teaspoons salt over the salad and toss gently to combine the ingredients and coat the couscous and vegetables. Drizzle the lemon vinaigrette over the salad using only enough as necessary and toss gently to coat the couscous and vegetables.

To serve, transfer the couscous salad to a wide serving bowl and serve with a large spoon.

Pan-Roasted Cauliflower Wedges with Bagna Cauda

I've always been a fan of cauliflower, and it makes me very happy to see that its popularity is on the rise. For so long, cauliflower was a forgotten vegetable: pale, boiled, covered with melted cheese, and pretty forgettable. These days, cauliflower is being treated by chefs in all sorts of creative ways, from how it's cut to the manner in which it's seasoned and cooked. In this preparation, which we offer at Chi Spacca, the head of cauliflower is cut into large wedges to mirror the dramatic meat presentations served at that restaurant. The wedges are blanched and then seared, bringing out the natural sweetness of the cauliflower, and finally drizzled with bagna cauda, a warm anchovy and olive oil "bath."

Even though technically cauliflower does have a season—late fall—you can find it year-round in supermarkets, and it's one of the rare vegetables where the supermarket version tastes just as good as carefully sourced cauliflower. Whether you're running a restaurant or hosting a dinner party in your home, you need those easy-to-get, inexpensive vegetables whose quality and flavor you can count on.

SERVES 6

2 teaspoons kosher salt, plus more for the boiling water

1 large cauliflower head (about 2 pounds)

¾ cup olive oil, or as needed

Bagna Cauda (page 88)

1 tablespoon finely chopped fresh Italian parsley leaves (from about 2 tablespoons packed whole leaves)

1 lemon

Fill a large pot with water, bring the water to a boil over high heat, and salt it to taste like the ocean, adding 1 tablespoon salt to each quart of water. Prepare an ice bath in a large bowl and line a plate or baking sheet with paper towels.

Trim about 1 inch from the stem of the cauliflower, trimming as little of the core as possible so the cauliflower stays intact when cut into wedges. Only remove and discard the large leaves from the cauliflower if necessary, leaving as much green as possible. Cut the cauliflower in half through the core and cut each half through the core into 3 wedges.

Plunge the cauliflower wedges into the boiling water and cook until they are tender when pierced with a toothpick or fork, 2 to 3 minutes. Drain the cauliflower wedges in a colander and transfer them to the ice bath to cool. Drain the cauliflower wedges and transfer them to the paper towels to dry.

Put the cauliflower wedges in a large bowl, drizzle with 2 tablespoons of the olive oil, and sprinkle with the salt. Gently massage the cauliflower wedges to coat the them evenly.

Heat 2 tablespoons of the remaining oil in a large heavy-bottomed sauté pan over medium-high heat until it slides easily in the pan and the oil around the edges of the pan just begins to smoke, 2 to 3 minutes. Add half of the cauliflower wedges, cut sides down, and sear them for 3 to 5 minutes on each of the cut sides, until both cut sides are deep golden brown, adding as much as 3 tablespoons more oil to the pan, 1 tablespoon at a time, as the cauliflower absorbs the oil and the pan becomes dry. Remove the cauliflower wedges from the pan and put them on a small baking sheet as they are done. Add 2 tablespoons of the remaining oil to the pan and heat it for about 1 minute, until the oil just begins to smoke around the edges. Add the remaining cauliflower wedges and sear them in the same way you did the first batch, adding as much as 3 tablespoons oil as needed. Remove the second batch of cauliflower wedges from the pan and put them on the baking sheet with the first batch.

To serve, line up the cauliflower wedges in a single layer on a long rectangular serving platter. Spoon 2 tablespoons of the bagna cauda on each wedge of cauliflower and sprinkle the chopped parsley over the tops. Using a citrus zester, zest long thin strands of lemon over the cauliflower, and serve with the remaining bagna cauda in a small bowl with a spoon for guests to help themselves.

Slow-Roasted Roma Tomatoes with Garlic and Thyme

I don't think I ever serve an Italian meal at home without serving some kind of roasted tomatoes. I roast small tomatoes on the vine when I can find them, but Roma tomatoes, halved, dressed with herbs from my garden and roasted until they're collapsed and sweet are the staple, because they're available year-round at every kind of supermarket both in Italy and here. This recipe makes a large quantity—sixteen tomato halves. I like to have some around to eat with the leftovers I'm bound to have after any feast or to put on sandwiches. Store leftover tomatoes one tomato deep on a plate or in a casserole dish so they maintain their shape. Cover with plastic wrap and refrigerate the tomatoes for up to several days. Bring them to room temperature before serving them.

I like to serve these tomatoes in the pan in which they are roasted. If you want to serve them this way, reach for something you wouldn't mind putting out on your buffet.

———

Adjust an oven rack to the middle position and preheat the oven to 250°F.

Put the tomatoes and garlic in a large table-worthy baking dish or on a baking sheet. Drizzle with the olive oil, sprinkle with the kosher salt, and toss to coat the tomatoes. Transfer the garlic to a small bowl and set aside. Arrange the tomatoes, cut side down, and scatter the thyme sprigs over and around them.

Roast the tomatoes for 40 minutes. Remove the baking dish from the oven and scatter the garlic cloves around the tomatoes, making sure the cloves are touching the pan, not lying on top of the tomatoes. Return the baking dish to the oven, rotating it from front to back. Roast the tomatoes and garlic for 50 minutes to 1 hour, until the tomatoes are shriveled and golden brown around the edges and the garlic is golden brown, rotating the baking dish once halfway through the cooking time so that they brown evenly. Remove the dish from the oven and set the tomatoes aside to cool slightly.

Serve the tomatoes in the dish you cooked them in or transfer the tomatoes to a medium rimmed serving dish, either way turning them so they're cut side up. Scatter the garlic cloves around the tomatoes and the thyme sprigs over them. Drizzle the tomatoes with finishing-quality olive oil, sprinkle with sea salt, and serve with a big spoon.

SERVES 12 OR MORE

———

8 fresh Roma tomatoes, halved through the cores, stems removed and discarded

10 to 12 medium or large garlic cloves, peeled and smashed with the flat side of a knife

½ cup extra-virgin olive oil

1 tablespoon kosher salt

20 to 25 fresh thyme sprigs

Finishing-quality extra-virgin olive oil

Maldon sea salt (or another flaky sea salt such as fleur de sel)

Gino Angelini's Braised Artichokes

SERVES 8 OR MORE
MAKES 20 ARTICHOKES

2 lemons

20 small or Italian artichokes

1 large yellow Spanish onion, peeled
and finely chopped

2 to 3 medium or large garlic
cloves, peeled and minced

½ cup finely chopped fresh Italian
parsley leaves (from about 1 cup
packed whole leaves)

2½ cups extra-virgin olive oil,
or as needed

2¾ teaspoons kosher salt

Maldon sea salt (or another flaky
sea salt such as fleur de sel)

The braised artichokes that Gino Angelini serves at Angelini Osteria are legendary in Los Angeles. I don't think I could go to Angelini without ordering them, so I was very pleased when I asked Gino if he would share his recipe, and he invited me to come into his kitchen to make the artichokes with him. Unlike marinated artichokes, which taste mostly of the marinade, these have an intense, unadulterated artichoke flavor. The dull, grayish green that would be unappealing in another vegetable is totally appetizing in these artichokes. After you've eaten them once, to look at them or even to think about them will be to taste them. The artichokes are cooked submerged in olive oil, so it takes a lot of oil to make them. After making the artichokes, use the oil to sauté anything in which you don't mind a little artichoke flavor: fish, chicken, or vegetables; to make another batch of these artichokes within the week; or to make an artichoke-infused mayonnaise (see Garlic Mayonnaise, page 84).

Use small or Italian artichokes for this recipe, not baby artichokes and not the common globe artichokes.

———

To prepare the artichokes, fill a large bowl with water. Cut the lemons in half, squeeze their juice into the water, and drop the lemon halves into the water. Working one at a time, trim and discard about ½ inch of the dry stem ends of each artichoke. Remove and discard the dark outer leaves from the artichokes until you see only bright greenish-yellow leaves. With a paring knife, shave the artichoke from halfway up the bulb all the way down to the end of the stem so it's smooth and even and the entire artichoke is a pale yellowish-white color. Cut off and discard 1½ inches from the tip end of the artichoke to give it a flat top; you will be left with about 1½ inches of artichoke from where the stem meets the body of the artichoke. Drop the prepped artichoke into the lemon water and prep the remaining artichokes in the same way.

Combine the onion, garlic, and parsley in a medium bowl. Add ¼ cup of the olive oil and ¾ teaspoon of the kosher salt and stir to combine the ingredients. Transfer the contents of the bowl to a medium Dutch oven or another large high-sided (at least 4 inches deep), heavy-bottomed pot and spread the aromatic vegetables out to create a level bed. Drain the artichokes and put them into the bowl in which you tossed the aromatic vegetables. Drizzle the artichokes with

¼ cup of the remaining olive oil and sprinkle with the remaining 2 teaspoons kosher salt. Toss to coat the artichokes. Transfer the artichokes to the pot with the aromatic vegetable mixture, laying them on their sides in an even layer on top of the aromatic vegetables. Add the remaining 2 cups olive oil, or enough to just cover the artichokes.

Bring the oil to a boil over medium-low heat. (It's important to bring the oil to a boil slowly so you don't inadvertently fry the artichokes.) Reduce the heat to its lowest setting so that the oil barely bubbles, and only around the edges. Cover the pot and cook the artichokes for 25 minutes, or until thoroughly cooked but not mushy, swirling the pot two or three times during the cooking time so the artichokes cook evenly and to prevent the aromatic vegetables from sticking to the bottom of the pot. Turn off the heat. Remove the lid and set the artichokes aside to cool to room temperature in the oil.

The artichokes can be made up to several days in advance. Refrigerate them, submerged in the oil they were cooked in and covered, until you are ready to serve them. Bring the artichokes and the oil to room temperature before serving.

To serve, use a small spoon to lift the artichokes out of the oil, taking care to keep them intact, and transfer them to a small serving dish (preferably oval) with a 1-inch lip. Pour the cooking oil through a fine-mesh strainer and reserve the oil to store any artichokes you will have leftover or for another use. Spoon the onion-parsley mixture in the strainer over the artichokes, sprinkle with sea salt, and serve with a small spoon.

10

Garlic-Rubbed Skirt Steak with Scallion Vinaigrette

SERVES 8 TO 12

6 medium or large garlic cloves, peeled

¼ cup kosher salt

1 tablespoon freshly ground black pepper

4 pounds skirt steak

¼ cup olive oil, plus more for drizzling and as needed

Finishing-quality extra-virgin olive oil

Maldon sea salt (or another flaky sea salt such as fleur de sel)

This steak, rubbed in garlic and seared in a hot pan, is the centerpiece of a feast inspired by Santa Maria barbecue. Santa Maria is a city north of Santa Barbara, and the surrounding area is known for a regionally specific type of barbecue that includes a grilled tri-tip steak, green salad, grilled bread, and stewed beans. Tri-tip is an inexpensive triangular-shaped cut, but I decided to go with skirt steak instead. Skirt steak is without a doubt one of my favorite cuts of beef, second only to a rib steak, which is about twice the price. A lot of people confuse flank steak with skirt, but they're two completely different cuts; flank steak is chewy, not particularly flavorful, and definitely *not* a favorite. Skirt steak is juicy and flavorful, and you don't need to be an expert to cook it correctly: sear it on both sides over high heat and you're pretty much guaranteed to end up with a perfectly cooked medium-rare steak. Even if skirt steak is slightly overcooked, it's still juicy, where an overcooked rib steak, or tri-tip for that matter, would be dry and unappealing. Because skirt steak is so thin, it takes quickly to a marinade or rub.

In keeping with the Santa Maria theme, I serve this steak with friend and former Mozza sous-chef Chris Feldmeier's Santa Maria–Style Beans (page 200) and other side dishes that seem like something I would find on the central California ranch.

This recipe yields a lot of meat, but it's an easy recipe to cut in half if you want to make less. I love having leftover steak in the refrigerator to snack on or for making sandwiches.

You will need a large grill pan or a cast-iron skillet to cook the steaks. If you have a square or rectangular grill pan, even better, as you will be able to fit more steaks in the pan at one time. A Lodge cast-iron reversible grill/griddle is my favorite surface to cook skirt steak on, placed either over two hot burners or on a wood or gas grill. It's 20 inches long so I can cook the steaks in one piece rather than having to cut them into segments.

Put the garlic in the bowl of a mini food processor fitted with a metal blade and pulse to mince it. Add the kosher salt and pulse again just to combine. Alternatively, put the garlic in a small mortar. Sprinkle with the kosher salt and pound to break up the garlic. Or mince it very fine by hand, adding the kosher salt midway through mincing to help the garlic break down. Stir in the pepper.

Lay the skirt steaks on a flat work surface. Spoon the garlic rub onto the steaks, using about 1 tablespoon of rub per pound of meat, and rub it all over with your hands, putting more rub on the thickest parts of the steak. Turn the steaks to coat the other sides with the rub. Set the steaks aside for at least 30 minutes to marinate, or cover and refrigerate them as long as overnight. Bring the steaks to room temperature before cooking them.

If necessary, cut the skirt steaks into segments that will fit in the pan you're cooking them in.

Heat 2 tablespoons of the olive oil in a large grill pan or cast-iron skillet over high heat until it slides easily in the pan and the oil around the edges of the pan just begins to smoke, 2 to 3 minutes. Drizzle a thin layer of the olive oil on both sides of the steak. Working in batches, lay the skirt steak in the pan in a single layer and sear each side until it is deep brown and caramelized, 3 to 4 minutes per side for medium-rare. Remove the steaks from the pan and put them on a baking sheet or plate to rest while you sear the remaining steaks. Add 2 more tablespoons of the remaining oil to the pan and heat the oil for about 1 minute, until it starts to smoke around the edges of the pan, before adding the remaining steaks and searing them in the same way.

To serve, transfer the steaks to a cutting board with a moat to catch the juices. Slice the steaks against the grain ½ inch thick on the bias. Drizzle the meat with finishing-quality olive oil, sprinkle with sea salt, and serve on the cutting board, with a carving or serving fork.

Scallion Vinaigrette

Makes about 2 cups

I use this vinaigrette to dress the Charred Broccolini with Salami and Burrata (page 203) and as a condiment to spoon over the garlic-rubbed skirt steak, two dishes that conveniently (but not coincidentally) I serve together at the same meal. I like the grassy flavor that the scallions impart to both dishes.

½ pound scallions (about 3 bunches)

½ cup plus 2 tablespoons champagne vinegar (or white wine vinegar)

2 teaspoons kosher salt

1 teaspoon red chile flakes, ground in a spice grinder or use a mortar and a pestle

1 cup extra-virgin olive oil

Trim and discard the root ends and any wilted greens from the scallions. Finely chop the scallions and put them in a bowl. Add the vinegar, salt, and ground red chile flakes. Add the oil in a slow, steady stream, whisking constantly. Serve or refrigerate the vinaigrette, covered, for up to 1 day; any longer and the color of the scallions will fade. Bring the vinaigrette to room temperature before serving.

Skillet Corn Bread with Honey Butter and Scallion Butter

I've been making different versions of corn bread for as long as I've been baking. Corn bread wasn't a part of my family table; my only association with it was the corn bread that made a weekly appearance at the summer camp I attended for five years with my friend Margy Rochlin. Years ago, when I decided to add corn bread to the repertoire at La Brea Bakery, I didn't have much to go on, but I was determined to turn this simple quick bread into something more sophisticated and delicious than any I'd ever eaten. I browned the butter. I made creamed corn and stirred that into the batter. I added fresh sage leaves. But the one thing I'd neglected to experiment with or to upgrade, which decades later I would realize was *the* secret to a great corn bread, was the cornmeal itself.

I figured this out after tasting the corn bread made by Sean Brock, the chef/owner of Husk Restaurants in Charleston, South Carolina, and Nashville, Tennessee. Sean is a very talented young chef who specializes in upgrading iconic southern dishes with better ingredients. Tasting his corn bread was an "Aha!" moment for me. Suddenly I realized that it wasn't corn that was supposed to give corn bread its intense corn flavor—much less sage or brown butter. It was corn*meal*. It seems so obvious now.

After tasting Sean's corn bread, with the help and patience of one of my pastry cooks, Carrie Whealy, I went back to the corn bread drawing board. We started with my original recipe, threw out the fancy 1980s additions, and flipped the ratio of cornmeal to flour so there was more cornmeal than flour. We also stole from Sean the idea of inverting the corn bread, so the top, originally the bottom, is beautifully brown and crispy, which we achieved by preheating the skillet and cooking the bread for part of the time on the oven floor. I serve the corn bread with two compound butters: sweet honey butter and a savory scallion butter.

I like to use freshly milled cornmeal, specifically "artisan handmade fine yellow polenta" (*polenta* is just Italian for "cornmeal") from Anson Mills. Even though it's called "fine," because it's stone ground, this cornmeal still has quite a bit of texture.

You will need a 10-inch cast-iron skillet to make this. Because of the number of chiles you will be slicing for this recipe, it's important that you wear thin rubber gloves.

SERVES 8 TO 10

¾ cup plus 2 tablespoons medium-ground cornmeal or polenta

½ cup plus 2 tablespoons unbleached all-purpose flour

3 tablespoons sugar

1½ teaspoons kosher salt

½ teaspoon baking soda

1½ teaspoons baking powder

1½ cups well-shaken buttermilk

2 extra-large eggs

4 tablespoons (½ stick) unsalted butter, melted and cooled to room temperature

¼ pound Fresno chiles, halved (stems, seeds, and membranes removed and discarded) and julienned lengthwise

3 tablespoons vegetable oil

Honey Butter (recipe follows)

Scallion Butter (recipe follows)

Adjust the oven racks so one is in the uppermost position. Make sure there is no oven rack near the oven floor; you'll be baking the corn bread on the oven floor. If you are using an electric oven or another oven where you can't put anything on the floor, adjust one rack so that it is closest to the floor and put a pizza stone on it, if you have one. Put the skillet in the oven and preheat the oven and skillet to 375°F. Set up a cooling rack.

Combine the cornmeal, flour, sugar, salt, baking soda, and baking powder in a large bowl and stir to distribute the ingredients.

Whisk the buttermilk and eggs together in a small bowl.

Make a well in the dry ingredients and pour the buttermilk and eggs into the well, whisking, working from the center outward, until no flour is visible. Add the melted butter and whisk to incorporate it into the batter. Add the chiles and stir with the whisk to incorporate them into the batter.

Remove the skillet from the oven and use a wad of paper towels or a pastry brush to grease the inside with vegetable oil, being careful of the hot skillet. Pour the batter into the skillet and place it on the floor of the oven or the lowest rack. Bake the corn bread for 30 minutes, rotating it halfway through the baking time so it browns evenly. Check the corn bread after 20 or 25 minutes. If you notice it is browning around the edges, proceed to the next step.

Increase the oven temperature to 425°F.

Transfer the corn bread to the rack in the upper part of the oven and bake it for 10 to 15 minutes, until it's golden brown and a toothpick inserted into the center comes out clean, rotating the corn bread halfway through that time so it bakes evenly.

Remove the corn bread from the oven and immediately invert it onto the cooling rack. (It's important to take the corn bread out of the skillet right away; otherwise the crust will soften.)

To serve, put the corn bread on a rustic cutting board with a knife for guests to slice the size piece they want, and bowls of honey butter and scallion butter on the board alongside the corn bread.

Honey Butter

I use wildflower honey to make this; use whatever variety of honey you like or that is available where you live. I stir the honey into the softened butter by hand, because I don't like the airiness of whipped butter.

8 tablespoons (1 stick) unsalted butter, softened at room temperature

2 tablespoons honey (preferably wildflower or another mild-flavored honey), or more to taste

¼ teaspoon kosher salt

Place the butter, honey, and salt in a small bowl and stir to combine the ingredients. Add more honey to taste. Transfer the honey butter to a pretty vessel just large enough to hold it, so it looks abundant. Cover and refrigerate the butter until you're ready to serve it, or for up to several weeks. Soften it slightly at room temperature before serving. Serve with a small butter or cheese knife.

Scallion Butter

Makes about ½ cup

2 scallions

¼ teaspoon kosher salt

8 tablespoons (1 stick) unsalted butter, softened at room temperature

Trim and discard the root ends and any wilted outer greens from the scallions. Mince the white and light green parts of the scallions and discard the remaining dark ends. Combine the scallions, butter, and salt in a small bowl and stir to incorporate the scallions and salt into the butter. Transfer the scallion butter to a pretty vessel just large enough to hold it, so it looks abundant. Cover and refrigerate the butter until you're ready to serve it, or for up to several weeks. Soften it slightly at room temperature before serving. Serve with a small butter or cheese knife.

Chris Feldmeier's Santa Maria–Style Beans

SERVES 10 TO 12
MAKES ABOUT 10 CUPS

¼ cup olive oil

2 large yellow Spanish onions, peeled and halved root to tip (root ends intact)

1 to 2 jalapeño peppers (depending on your taste), stem ends cut off (to expose the seeds inside) and discarded

1 pound bacon scraps, cut into 2-inch chunks

2 tablespoons plus 2 teaspoons kosher salt

20 fresh thyme sprigs, tied in a bundle with kitchen twine

½ cup medium or large garlic cloves (about 20 cloves), peeled

¼ cup tomato paste (one 2-ounce can)

1½ pounds dried pinto beans, soaked overnight

4 quarts Chicken Stock (page 59 or sodium-free store-bought stock), or as needed

Our former sous-chef Chris Feldmeier made these beans for a one-night Santa Maria barbecue-themed dinner we hosted in the space that is now Chi Spacca. The beans traditionally served at a Santa Maria barbecue are a tiny variety, about half the size but similar in color, shape, and flavor to pinto beans, but Chris makes these with the easier-to-find pintos. Unlike most beans that accompany barbecue, they are not sweet and molasses-y, which is one of the reasons I like them.

I serve these beans in the Dutch oven they're cooked in. When I serve these or any other beans, I put the pot near my outdoor fireplace or on a cool part of the grill to keep them warm throughout the meal. Chris cooks the beans the day before he serves them. He warms them with chicken stock and stirs in a bit of salt just before serving. I think anytime you can get an entire dish out of the way, it's a good thing, and slow-cooked foods such as beans always taste better a day or two after they're made.

This recipe calls for sodium-free chicken stock. Use half of the salt in this recipe if you are using chicken stock that contains salt.

Heat the olive oil in a large Dutch oven or another large heavy-bottomed pot over medium-high heat until it slides easily and the oil around the edges of the pan just begins to smoke, 2 to 3 minutes. Put the onions, cut side down, in the pan. Add the jalapeños and bacon and sprinkle the onions and jalapeños with 2 teaspoons of the salt. (The pan will be crowded at first, but as the bacon starts to render, it will shrink, creating more surface area in the pan.) Cook the onions, jalapeños, and bacon over medium-high heat for 12 to 15 minutes, turning the ingredients with tongs, until all of the ingredients are browned on both sides. Add the thyme, make room for the garlic in the bottom of the pan, and add the garlic to the space you created in the pan. Cook for about 4 minutes, until the garlic is golden brown, stirring and turning the garlic to brown all sides. Create a space in the pan as you did for the garlic and add the tomato paste to the space created in the pan. Cook the tomato paste, stirring with a rubber spatula, for about 1 minute, to concentrate the flavor and caramelize it slightly, but be careful not to burn it.

Add the beans and enough chicken stock to just cover them. Stir in the remaining 2 tablespoons salt. Increase the heat to high and bring the stock to a boil. Reduce the heat to low and simmer the beans until they are tender and creamy, not chalky or al dente, stirring often and adding more stock to the pan as needed to keep the beans covered at all times, about 3 hours. (When you stir the beans, starch is released from them; the starch makes the finished beans creamier, which is a good thing with these beans.) To test beans for doneness, press one bean between your fingers; if it is creamy and silky, it's done. If it seems dry or slightly chunky, keep cooking the beans until they're creamy.

Remove and discard the onions, jalapeños, and thyme bundle. Fish out the bacon pieces and set them aside until they're cool enough to touch. Shred the bacon, discarding any sinew or fat chunks. Return the shredded bacon to the pot with the beans.

You can cook these beans up to 3 days in advance. Cool the beans to room temperature, cover, and refrigerate them in the pot you cooked them in. When you're ready to serve them, warm the beans over medium-low heat, adding chicken stock to loosen the beans and stirring often, until they are warmed through.

Serve the beans in the pot you cooked them in, close to a fire if possible, with a long-handled ladle for serving.

Charred Broccolini with Salami and Burrata

Broccolini, a hybrid of broccoli and *kai-lan* (Chinese broccoli) is one of my favorite vegetables—it's flavorful and perfectly crunchy when cooked properly. I eat broccolini almost every night for dinner at the Osteria. It's hard to believe that fifteen years ago, it was just beginning to find its way onto supermarket shelves. As much as I like and eat broccolini, and even though I work creating dishes utilizing burrata all night long, five nights a week, I never would have thought of putting broccolini, salami, and burrata together until I saw the combination at the Los Angeles restaurant The Pikey, on the Sunset Strip, where I was having lunch. They served only the florets of flowering broccoli and laid them out in a composed style with slices of soppressata, dollops of burrata, and a sprinkling of red chile flakes—none of the ingredients touching one another. The flavors were so unexpected and so satisfying, and the combination so unique, I used that austerely presented appetizer as an inspiration for this much more rustic side dish.

I use only four ounces of burrata when I make this, but when my daughter, Vanessa, made it using this recipe, she informed me that because burrata is sold in eight-ounce portions, it made more sense to add all of the burrata rather than have four ounces left over. If you want to go wild with the burrata like Vanessa suggests, be my guest.

———

Adjust the oven racks so none are near the oven floor; you'll be putting the baking sheet directly on the oven floor. If you are using an electric oven or another oven where you can't put anything on the floor, adjust the oven racks so that one is closest to the floor and put a pizza stone on it, if you have one. Preheat the oven to 500°F.

Trim and discard the dry stem ends of the broccolini; do this one at a time as each stalk will need to be trimmed at a different place. Put the broccolini on a large baking sheet, drizzle with the canola oil, sprinkle with 1½ teaspoons of the salt, and toss to coat the broccolini. Spread the broccolini out onto a baking sheet, put the baking sheet on the floor of the oven or the lowest rack, and roast until the broccolini is slightly charred and the stems are tender (the best test of broccolini for doneness is to bite into one), 10 to 12 minutes, shaking the baking sheet and rotating it from front to back halfway through the cooking time so the

SERVES 6 TO 8

2 bunches broccolini
(or broccoli rabe or broccoli
di ciccio; about 1 pound)

2 tablespoons canola oil
(or another neutral-flavored oil)

2 teaspoons kosher salt

4 ounces hard salami
(such as Fra' Mani Toscana salami),
sliced ¹⁄₁₆ inch thick (15 to 18 slices)

¾ cup plus 1 tablespoon Scallion
Vinaigrette (page 196)

4 ounces burrata (see headnote)

broccolini browns evenly. When cooking vegetables on the oven floor, a lot of steam is produced from the water released as a result of the vegetables cooking so quickly, so just be careful of the steam that will arise when you open the oven door. Remove the baking sheet from the oven and set it aside for the broccolini to cool to room temperature.

If you are using salami 1¼ inches or less in diameter, cut the slices in half to form half-moons. If you are using a larger salami, cut the rounds into quarters.

Put the salami in a large bowl. Add the broccolini and toss so the two are tangled together. Whisk the vinaigrette to recombine the ingredients and drizzle ¾ cup of the scallion vinaigrette over the broccolini and salami. Sprinkle with the remaining ½ teaspoon salt. Toss gently and massage the vinaigrette into the broccolini to make sure all the florets are coated.

To serve, scatter one-third of the broccolini and salami in a medium round bowl. Using a spoon to break it apart, spoon the burrata in random bite-size clumps over the broccolini. Scatter more broccolini and salami onto the platter, making sure the first layer of burrata is still visible, and continue layering the broccolini-salami and the burrata clumps until you've used all of both. Use a spoon to drizzle the remaining 1 tablespoon vinaigrette over the burrata clumps and serve with tongs.

Corn and Fava Bean Succotash Salad

Succotash is a mix of vegetables that traditionally includes corn and lima beans. I use fava beans in place of limas for this recipe, but lima beans will also work. The other big difference between this and traditional succotash is that where most succotash is served warm, this is more of a salad, tossed with an herb and garlic–infused mayonnaise. This succotash is most definitely something that you can make only in the summer, when corn, green beans, and fava beans are in season.

My preferred way of making the dressing is to pound the herbs in a mortar, then make the dressing in a blender and combine the herbs and dressing at the end. Pounded in a mortar, the herbs release liquid, which stains the mayonnaise rather than the mayonnaise just being dotted with the color of the herbs. If you don't mind the fifteen minutes or more of elbow grease required to pound the herbs, you'll be rewarded with a dressing vibrant in both color and flavor. You may not need all of the dressing for the salad; use the rest to dress another salad, or as an herb mayonnaise, within the next two days. If you can't find fresh chervil, substitute fresh Italian parsley and tarragon in equal parts for both the dressing and the salad portions of this recipe.

––––––––––

To make the dressing, combine the vinegar and lemon juice in a small bowl. Combine the olive oil and canola oil in a measuring cup with a spout.

Put the egg yolk and salt in the bowl of a mini food processor fitted with a metal blade. Using a fine Microplane, grate the garlic into the bowl with the egg and salt, and blend for about 30 seconds, until the yolk is pale yellow. Add a few drops of the combined oil and the anchovy and pulse to incorporate the oil and anchovy into the egg.

Begin adding the remaining oil, a drop at a time, running the machine constantly, until the oil and egg are emulsified; you will have added 2 or 3 tablespoons. Turn off the machine, take off the lid, scrape down the sides of the bowl with a rubber spatula, and add 1 tablespoon of the vinegar–lemon juice mixture. Return the lid and pulse to combine. Continue adding the oil a few drops at a time with the machine running constantly until you've added about half of the oil and the dressing is very thick. Stop the machine again, take off the lid, scrape down the sides of the bowl, and add 1 tablespoon water. Return the lid and pulse

SERVES 8 TO 10

FOR THE DRESSING

1½ teaspoons champagne vinegar (or white wine vinegar)

1½ teaspoons fresh lemon juice

½ cup extra-virgin olive oil

½ cup canola oil (or another neutral-flavored oil)

1 extra-large egg yolk

½ teaspoon kosher salt

2 to 3 medium or large garlic cloves, peeled

1 anchovy fillet (preferably salt-packed; rinsed, backbone removed if salt-packed), finely chopped and smashed to a paste with the flat side of a knife

1 tablespoon finely chopped fresh chervil leaves

1 tablespoon finely chopped fresh tarragon leaves

1 tablespoon minced fresh chives

1 tablespoon finely chopped fresh Italian parsley leaves

FOR THE SUCCOTASH

1 tablespoon plus 2 teaspoons kosher salt, plus more for the blanching water and to taste

(continued)

9 ounces green beans
(preferably haricots verts
or another tender green bean),
stem ends trimmed and discarded,
tails left intact

2 cups shelled small fava beans
(or lima beans; from about 2 pounds
in the pods)

½ cup canola oil
(or another neutral-flavored oil)

8 cups fresh-cut corn kernels
(from about 8 ears of corn)

2 cups ¼-inch diced red onions
(from about 1 large peeled onion)

2 cups ¼-inch diced red bell pepper
(from about 1 large bell pepper,
cored and seeded)

¼ cup finely minced fresh chervil
leaves (from about ½ cup packed
whole leaves)

¼ cup finely minced fresh tarragon
leaves (from about ⅔ cup packed
whole leaves)

¼ cup finely minced fresh basil
leaves (from about ½ cup packed
whole leaves)

¼ cup finely minced fresh chives
(from about 20 whole chives)

¼ cup finely chopped fresh Italian
parsley leaves (from about ½ cup
packed whole leaves)

2 tablespoons fresh lemon juice

to incorporate the water. Drizzle the remaining oil in a slow, steady stream until all the oil has been added.

Spoon half of the dressing from the food processor into a medium bowl. Add the chervil, tarragon, chives, and parsley to the food processor with the remaining dressing and pulse to incorporate the herbs. Turn the herb-flecked dressing out of the food processor into the bowl with the plain dressing and stir to combine. Cover and refrigerate the dressing for up to 2 days.

To make the succotash, fill a large saucepan with water, bring the water to a boil over high heat, and salt it to taste like the ocean, adding 1 tablespoon salt to each quart of water. Prepare an ice bath in a medium bowl and prepare a bed of paper towels.

Put the green beans in a fine-mesh strainer and plunge them into the boiling water to blanch for about 1 minute, until they turn bright green but are still crunchy. Lift the strainer out of the water and plunge the strainer into the ice water for about 1 minute, until the beans have cooled completely. Remove the strainer from the ice water and turn the beans out onto the paper towels to dry completely. Slice the green beans ¼ to ½ inch long on an extreme bias and put them in a large bowl.

Put the fava beans in the strainer and plunge them into the boiling water to blanch for 3 to 5 minutes, until they are tender and bright green. Lift the strainer out of the water and plunge the strainer into the ice water to cool the beans. Remove the strainer from the ice water and turn the beans out onto a separate bed of paper towels to drain. Peel and discard the outer skins from the fava beans and add the shelled beans to the bowl with the green beans.

Line a large plate or baking sheet with paper towels.

Put 2 tablespoons of the canola oil and half of the corn in a large sauté pan. Sprinkle with 1 teaspoon of the salt and cook the corn over medium-low heat, stirring constantly to avoid browning the corn, for 3 to 5 minutes, just to take off the raw edge. Transfer the corn to the paper towels. Repeat, adding another 2 tablespoons of the remaining oil and the remaining corn, seasoning it with 1 teaspoon of the remaining salt, and cooling it in the same way.

Line two small plates with paper towels. Pour 2 tablespoons of the remaining oil into the pan you cooked the corn in. Add the onion, sprinkle with ½ teaspoon of the remaining salt, and cook over medium-low heat for about 5 minutes, stirring constantly, until the onions are barely translucent but still crunchy. Transfer the onions to one of the paper towel–lined plates to cool to room temperature. Add the remaining 2 tablespoons oil to the pan, add the bell peppers, sprinkle with ¼ teaspoon of the remaining salt, and cook and cool them the same way you did the corn and onions.

Add the corn, onions, bell peppers, chervil, tarragon, basil, chives, and parsley to the bowl with the green beans and fava beans. Drizzle the lemon juice and sprinkle the remaining 2¼ teaspoons salt over the vegetables. Toss gently to combine the ingredients and coat the vegetables. Spoon the dressing over the vegetables and toss to coat the vegetables.

To serve, transfer the succotash to a medium bowl and serve with a big spoon.

11

Dean Fearing's Frito Pie

Whole Leaf Caesar Salad with Fried Parsley Leaves and Anchovy Croutons

Other Menu Options

Dean Fearing's Frito Pie

SERVES 12 OR MORE
MAKES ABOUT 4 QUARTS

FOR THE CHILI PASTE

¼ cup unsalted skinless peanuts

10 ancho chiles, stems and seeds removed and discarded

2 pasilla chiles, stems and seeds removed and discarded

2 tablespoons cumin seeds

2 tablespoons coriander seeds

1 tablespoon canola oil (or another neutral-flavored oil), plus more for frying

3 corn tortillas, cut into ½-inch-wide strips

½ large yellow Spanish onion, peeled, root end trimmed and discarded, and cut into ¼-inch dice

1 large carrot, cut into ¼-inch dice

1 celery stalk, cut into ¼-inch dice (about ¾ cup)

1 medium shallot, peeled and cut into ¼-inch dice (about ½ cup)

3 medium or large garlic cloves, peeled and smashed with the flat side of a knife

2 teaspoons kosher salt

1 (12-ounce) bottle dark ale (or another dark beer)

1 cup fresh orange juice

One of the things I love most about participating in food events, which I do often, is walking around and seeing and tasting what other chefs are serving. It was at one of these festivals that I had the life-altering experience that is Dean Fearing's Frito pie. If I'd seen a description for Frito pie in a magazine—beef chili ladled over Fritos and topped with the usual chili fixings—I definitely would have flipped the page, thinking it would be similar to those layered dips you might be served at a Super Bowl party. But I've known Dean Fearing, for decades considered to be one of the pioneers of southwestern cuisine, since our paths crossed at an event during my early days at Spago. I know him as an excellent chef with the highest standards, so I knew that whatever he was serving, it had to be special. Dean was serving his chili directly in the Fritos bag, which I had never seen before, and I thought it was just such an adorable presentation. To seal the deal, if you ask me what my guilty pleasure is in the snack department, it is definitely Fritos. I took a bag of Dean's Frito pie, dug my spoon down into it so I penetrated all the layers, and took a bite. I just loved it—the hot chili with the cold sour cream and crunchy Fritos. At first bite, I knew that I would have to make and serve Frito pies one day in my own backyard.

Luckily, Dean gave me his chili recipe and this is it, pretty much exactly as he offered it. It is authentic Texas-style chili, which means it starts with cubed sirloin, not ground beef, and it doesn't contain beans. For the seasonings, Dean starts with dried chiles, which are toasted, rehydrated, and puréed into a paste along with fried tortillas and peanuts, among other ingredients. In a million years I wouldn't have thought to put fried tortillas and peanuts in my chili, but they give the chili a rich, complex flavor. This is why I always try to stay curious about and open to what other chefs are doing: there is always something to discover and learn. Dean uses sirloin to make the chili, which isn't a great cut of meat, but it works perfectly in this recipe. After being cooked for more than an hour in the chili "gravy," the meat becomes tender, but the cubes aren't mushy and they don't fall apart like more tender cuts of meat might. You still need teeth to eat it.

To serve the chili, it's important that you use the smallest bags of Fritos. I call it the five-cent size but I don't think anything is five cents anymore. You can buy them as part of a variety pack at supermarkets or order just the

Fritos from online sources. Obviously, you could also serve the chili in a bowl, though it means more to wash up, and it's not nearly as charming a presentation.

I serve the chili with a big Caesar salad. Just those two items, with Mexican Wedding Cookies (page 362) for dessert, make for a perfect casual party. If you really wanted to go wild, you could also offer tortilla chips with Guacamole (page 50) and any of the salsas in this book.

This recipe calls for sodium-free chicken stock. Use half of the salt in the chili portion of this recipe if you are using chicken stock that contains salt.

———

To make the chili paste, adjust an oven rack to the middle position and preheat the oven to 325°F.

Spread the peanuts on a baking sheet and toast them in the oven for 8 to 10 minutes, until they are fragrant and golden brown, shaking the baking sheet and rotating it from front to back halfway through the cooking time so the nuts brown evenly. Remove the peanuts from the oven and set them aside to cool to room temperature.

Put the ancho and pasilla chiles in a single layer on a baking sheet and toast them in the oven for about 3 minutes, until the chiles are warm and fragrant. Remove the baking sheet from the oven and set it aside until the chiles are cool enough to touch. Roughly chop the chiles.

Toast the cumin seeds and coriander seeds in a small sauté pan over medium heat for 1 to 2 minutes, until the seeds are fragrant and golden brown, shaking the pan often so they don't burn. Transfer the seeds to a plate to cool to room temperature. Grind the seeds in a spice grinder or use a mortar and a pestle.

Fasten a deep-fry thermometer onto a medium saucepan and fill the saucepan 3 to 4 inches deep with the canola oil. Heat the oil over medium-high heat until the thermometer registers 350°F. While the oil is heating, line a baking sheet with paper towels.

Carefully drop half of the tortilla strips into the oil and fry until they are golden brown and curl slightly, 3 to 4 minutes, turning them to brown evenly. Use a slotted spoon to remove the strips from the oil and transfer them to the prepared baking sheet to drain. Repeat, frying the remaining tortilla strips in the same way.

Heat the 1 tablespoon canola oil in a large sauté pan over medium-high heat until it slides easily in the pan and the oil around the edges of the pan begins to smoke, 2 to 3 minutes. Add the onion, carrot, celery, shallot, and garlic. Sprinkle

FOR THE CHILI

½ cup plus 2 tablespoons canola oil (or another neutral-flavored oil)

4 pounds beef sirloin, cut into ½-inch cubes

6 teaspoons kosher salt

3 large yellow Spanish onions, peeled, root ends trimmed and discarded, and cut into ½-inch dice

3 cups Chicken Stock (page 59 or sodium-free store-bought stock), or as needed

1 can chipotle peppers in adobo sauce

1 heaping tablespoon Aleppo pepper (or ancho chili powder)

2 tablespoons fresh lime juice

FOR THE FRITO PIES

2 cups crumbled queso fresco (fresh Mexican cheese, about 10 ounces)

2 cups shredded yellow Cheddar cheese (about 8 ounces)

1 medium white onion, peeled, root end trimmed and discarded, and finely chopped

1 cup crema (Mexican sour cream; or crème fraîche or sour cream)

Picked leaves from 2 bunches fresh cilantro

12 or more (1-ounce) bags of Fritos

with 1 teaspoon of the salt and cook the vegetables for about 5 minutes, stirring occasionally, until the onion is translucent and the vegetables are tender. Add the ground cumin, ground coriander, chopped ancho chiles, and chopped pasilla chiles and stir to combine. Add the beer and orange juice and bring the liquid to a boil, scraping up any brown bits from the bottom of the pan. Reduce the heat to medium and cook for about 5 minutes, until the liquid has reduced by half. Stir in the remaining 1 teaspoon salt, reduce the heat to low, and cook for 5 minutes. Stir in the peanuts and tortilla strips and cook for 2 to 3 minutes, stirring occasionally, until the liquid has evaporated and the tortilla strips are soggy. Turn off the heat and set aside to cool slightly.

Transfer the contents of the sauté pan to the bowl of a food processor fitted with a metal blade or to the jar of a blender and purée until you have a smooth paste. (If you put the ingredients in the food processor or blender while they're still piping hot, the heat will cause them to explode in the machine.) You can make the chili paste up to 4 days in advance; cool the paste to room temperature, then transfer it to a container and refrigerate until you're ready to use it.

To make the chili, heat 2 tablespoons of the canola oil in a large Dutch oven or another high-sided, heavy-bottomed pan over medium-high heat until it slides easily in the pan and the oil around the edges of the pan just begins to smoke, 2 to 3 minutes. Working in batches, add 1 pound (one-quarter) of the beef, season with 1 teaspoon of the salt, and cook until the meat is seared all over, 8 to 10 minutes, stirring or turning the meat pieces to brown all sides. Remove the meat from the pan and transfer it to a baking sheet. Repeat three more times, cooking the remaining meat 1 pound at a time, for each batch adding 2 tablespoons of the oil to the pan, heating the oil until it smokes around the edges of the pan before adding the meat, and seasoning each pound of meat with 1 teaspoon of the salt.

When you have cooked all of the meat, reduce the heat to medium-low, add the remaining 2 tablespoons oil, and heat it until it begins to smoke around the edges of the pan. Add the onions, season them with 1 teaspoon salt, and cook them for about 10 minutes, until they're tender and translucent, stirring often so they don't brown. Reduce the heat to medium-low. Return the meat to the pot with the onions. Stir in 3 cups of the chili paste and 1 cup of the chicken stock, or enough so the meat doesn't look dry. (Use the remaining chili paste to make a quick, small batch of chili or stew, or use it to marinate chicken or beef.) Increase the heat to medium-high and bring the liquid to a simmer. Reduce the heat to low and simmer the meat in the liquid for about 1 hour 30 minutes, stirring occasionally, scraping the bottom of the pan so the chili doesn't burn and adding more stock as necessary when the chili looks dry (you will add about

3 cups total), until the meat is tender and there is just enough liquid to form a thick sauce binding the meat.

While the meat is cooking, dump the can of chipotle peppers, including the liquid the peppers are packed in, into the jar of a blender or the bowl of a mini food processor fitted with a metal blade and purée. Add 2 tablespoons of the chipotle purée, the Aleppo pepper, lime juice, and the remaining 1 teaspoon salt to the chili and stir to combine. Taste for seasoning and add more chili paste if needed. Transfer the remaining chipotle purée to a covered container. Drizzle enough olive oil to cover the surface, cover the container, and refrigerate until you are ready to use it, or for up to several months. My favorite way to use leftover chipotle purée is to make Chipotle Mayonnaise (page 85).

To serve, put each of the toppings, including the queso fresco, Cheddar cheese, white onion, crema, and cilantro leaves, in its own bowl with a spoon in it. Put the chili on a buffet table or on the stove over low heat with a ladle in it for guests to serve themselves. Line up the toppings next to the chili. Put the bags of Fritos in a basket and let your guests assemble their own.

Whole Leaf Caesar Salad with Fried Parsley Leaves and Anchovy Croutons

Carolynn, my coauthor, has for years bragged to me that she makes the best Caesar salad in the land. Carolynn is from Tijuana and her father owned a restaurant there, across the street from the Caesar Hotel, where the salad was purportedly invented. Hers was not only the most delicious, she told me, but also the classic. Because Carolynn had the credentials, I asked her to share her recipe with me, and when she did, I was delighted to learn that I had been making mine Carolynn's way all along. We both start with whole romaine lettuce leaves, and only the innermost, sturdy parts of the romaine. (If I've said it once, I'll say it again: my favorite way to eat a salad is with my fingers, and the long sturdy hearts of romaine leaves invite you to pick them up.) We both use a very thick, mayonnaiselike dressing that really coats the leaves, and lots of black pepper. We both use lime juice, where it's more common to see Caesar salad made with lemon juice, and we both add anchovy to the croutons, which Carolynn insists is the way it was originally done.

Because I love nothing more than tinkering with a dish to see if I can make the great greater, I have recently made two non-Carolynn-sanctioned additions to my otherwise pretty classic Caesar. The first idea I got from April Bloomfield, who serves a Caesar salad at The Breslin in New York laced with fried parsley leaves. The parsley doesn't give you a powerful flavor punch, but the contrast between the firm, pale green hearts of romaine leaves and the delicate, dark green fried parsley leaves really adds to the visual appeal of the salad. I made the parsley optional in this recipe. Second, from an idea I got from a Caesar salad I was served at another restaurant, I grate orange zest over the finished salad.

To make the croutons, adjust an oven rack to the middle position and preheat the oven to 350°F.

Cut the loaf of bread in half crossways to reveal the inside of the bread. Pull the bread out in 1- to 1½-inch chunks and put the chunks in a large bowl. Reserve the crumbs and crusts for another use, such as to make bread crumbs.

Combine the olive oil and anchovies in a large ovenproof sauté pan. Using a fine Microplane, grate the garlic directly into the pan and heat the oil over high

SERVES 8 TO 10

FOR THE ANCHOVY CROUTONS

1 small (about 9 ounces) loaf of country bread

½ cup extra-virgin olive oil

10 anchovy fillets, about 1 ounce (preferably salt-packed; rinsed and backbones removed if salt-packed), finely chopped and smashed to a paste with the side of a knife

6 medium or large garlic cloves, peeled

½ teaspoon kosher salt

FOR THE DRESSING

2 tablespoons red wine vinegar

2 tablespoons fresh lime juice (preferably from Mexican or key limes)

30 drops (10 or 15 shakes) Tabasco sauce

¼ teaspoon Worcestershire sauce

¾ cup canola oil (or another neutral-flavored oil)

¼ cup extra-virgin olive oil

1 extra-large egg yolk

2 teaspoons kosher salt

(continued)

3 large garlic cloves, peeled

10 anchovy fillets, about 1 ounce (preferably salt-packed; rinsed, backbones removed if salt-packed), finely chopped and smashed to a paste with the flat side of a knife

½ teaspoon fresh coarsely ground black pepper

6 ounces (about 1½ cups) Parmigiano-Reggiano, grated using a fine Microplane

FOR THE FRIED PARSLEY (OPTIONAL)

Canola oil (or another neutral-flavored oil) for frying

Leaves and small stems from 1 bunch fresh Italian parsley (about 2 cups), dried thoroughly

½ teaspoon kosher salt

FOR THE SALAD

3 hearts of romaine heads (about 2 pounds)

3 tablespoons fresh lime juice

1 teaspoon kosher salt

Wedge of Parmigiano-Reggiano for grating

Fresh coarsely ground black pepper

1 orange for grating

heat until it begins to bubble. Reduce the heat to medium and cook the anchovies and garlic, stirring constantly so the garlic doesn't brown, for about 3 minutes, until the anchovies have completely melted into the oil and the garlic is fragrant. Add the bread chunks, season them with the salt, and toss to coat the bread with the seasoned oil. Increase the heat to medium-high and cook the croutons until they are light golden brown on the edges, about 3 minutes, turning them with tongs and tossing them in the pan so they brown evenly. Put the sauté pan in the oven and bake the croutons for 18 to 20 minutes, until they are golden brown and crispy, turning the pan and shaking the croutons twice during the time so the croutons brown evenly. Remove the sauté pan from the oven and set the croutons aside to cool to room temperature. You can make the croutons up to 1 day in advance of serving them. Store, covered, at room temperature until you're ready to use them.

To make the dressing, place the vinegar, lime juice, Tabasco, and Worcestershire sauce in a small bowl and whisk to combine. Combine the canola oil and olive oil in a measuring cup with a spout.

Put the egg yolk and salt in the bowl of a mini food processor fitted with a metal blade. Using a fine Microplane, grate the garlic into the bowl with the egg and salt, and blend for about 30 seconds, until the yolk is pale yellow. Add a few drops of the combined oil and the anchovies and pulse to incorporate the oil and anchovies into the egg.

Begin adding the remaining oil, a drop at a time, running the machine constantly, until the oil and egg are emulsified; you will have added 2 or 3 tablespoons. Turn off the machine, take off the lid, scrape down the sides of the bowl with a rubber spatula, and add 1 tablespoon of the vinegar–lime juice mixture. Return the lid and pulse to combine. Continue adding the oil a few drops at a time with the machine running constantly until you've added about half of the oil and the dressing is very thick. Stop the machine again and add another tablespoon of the vinegar–lime juice mixture in the same way you did the first time. Return the lid to the machine and add the remaining oil in a slow, steady stream with the machine running constantly, stopping when the dressing thickens again to add the remaining vinegar–lime juice mixture, and pulse to combine. Transfer the dressing to a medium bowl and stir in the pepper and Parmigiano. Use the dressing or refrigerate, covered, for up to 3 days.

To fry the parsley, if you are making it, fill a small deep saucepan 3 to 4 inches deep with canola oil. Fasten a deep-fry thermometer, if you have one, to the side of the pan. Heat the oil over medium-high heat until the thermometer registers

350°F, or a parsley leaf sizzles immediately when dropped into the oil. Line a plate with paper towels and place a colander or strainer over a small heat-proof bowl.

Turn off the heat and carefully add half of the parsley leaves to the pot, stepping back as you add them because the natural moisture in the parsley will cause the oil to splatter. Count to four, then use a slotted spoon or spider to lift the parsley leaves out of the oil and transfer the leaves to the paper towels, spreading them out evenly, to drain. Season with ¼ teaspoon of the salt. Repeat, frying, draining, and salting the remaining parsley leaves in the same way. Turn off the heat and let the oil cool. Strain the oil, allow it to cool, and transfer to a covered container, and reserve to cook with.

To prepare the salad, remove and discard the outer limp leaves from the hearts of romaine. Trim and discard the limp dark green tips, 2 to 3 inches from the top, so that only the sturdy, light green hearts remain. Pull the remaining leaves from the cores.

Put the romaine leaves in a giant mixing bowl. Sprinkle the leaves with the lime juice and salt and toss to coat the lettuce. Drizzle the dressing over the leaves, toss gently, and massage the dressing into the leaves with your hands to coat the leaves thoroughly. Add the croutons and gently toss the salad again to distribute them.

To serve, heap one-third of the dressed lettuce leaves and croutons into a large wide-mouthed serving bowl, distributing the croutons evenly. Using a medium-holed Microplane, grate a light dusting of Parmigiano, grind a generous amount of pepper, and scatter a third of the parsley leaves, if you are using them, over the salad. Build another layer, adding another third of the lettuce leaves and croutons to the serving bowl. Grate a light dusting of Parmigiano, grind a generous amount of pepper, and scatter a third of the remaining parsley leaves, if you are using them, over the second layer. Build a third layer just like the first two, using the remaining lettuce leaves, croutons, and fried parsley. Grate a generous blanket of Parmigiano, grind a generous amount of pepper, and using a fine Microplane, grate the zest of the orange (colored part only) over the finished salad. Serve with tongs and place the wedge of Parmigiano and the Microplane on a plate next to the salad for guests to grate more cheese onto their portions.

12

Braised Oxtails

SERVES 6 TO 8

8 pieces round-cut oxtails
(about 4 pounds)

1 tablespoon plus 2 teaspoons
kosher salt

1 teaspoon freshly ground black
pepper

½ pound medium cipollini onions

1 medium yellow Spanish onion,
peeled

¼ cup plus 2 tablespoons olive oil

1 large carrot, halved lengthwise
and sliced ½ inch thick on an
extreme bias

5 to 6 large garlic cloves, peeled
and sliced ¹⁄₁₆ inch thick lengthwise,
preferably on a mandoline

2 árbol chile pods

1 tablespoon tomato paste
(preferably double concentrated)

1 cup dry red wine

16 ounces (2 cups) peeled
tomatoes (preferably San Marzano),
including juice

2 cups Chicken Stock (page 59
or sodium-free store-bought stock),
or as needed

10 fresh thyme sprigs

Finishing-quality extra-virgin
olive oil

Oxtail is a culinary term that refers to the tail of cattle. Traditionally, the cattle used for cooking were castrated and called oxen, which is how the cut got its name. Oxtails must have the least amount of meat on them of any bone you'll ever cook, but the meat is so delicious and tender when braised that oxtails are without a doubt worth the effort it takes to both make them and eat them. In this recipe, the oxtails are presented in the same dish they're braised in. Put the dish in the center of the table and guests can pick up a bone and pick the meat off it.

Oxtails are definitely not something you'd want to serve your boss, or your soon-to-be in-laws the first time you have them over. But it is the perfect thing for an intimate Sunday supper with close friends and family—served and eaten with lots of napkins.

When asking your butcher for oxtails, request the fattest ones available. Count on each person eating one oxtail, but some hungry carnivores may have the patience to eat two. This recipe calls for sodium-free chicken stock. Use half of the salt in this recipe if you are using chicken stock that contains salt. Cipollini are small, flat Italian onions. If you can't find them, use pearl onions instead.

You need a large Dutch oven or a deep straight-sided sauté pan (preferably one with a lid) to make this. If you don't have one, use another large heavy-bottomed pot and heavy-duty aluminum foil to cover it. If you are going to serve the oxtails, as well as the celery, in the same pan you braised them in, use one that you would feel good about putting on your table. If you have a mandoline, use it to make easy work of slicing the garlic for this recipe.

———

Put the oxtails in a single layer in a nonreactive baking dish and season them all over with the 1 tablespoon plus 1 teaspoon of the salt and the pepper. Set aside to come to room temperature or cover the dish with plastic wrap and refrigerate the oxtails overnight. Bring the meat to room temperature before cooking it.

Adjust an oven rack to the lower third of the oven and preheat the oven to 350°F.

Remove the papery skins from the cipollini. Trim and discard the dry root ends, leaving the roots so the onions stay intact. Cut each cipollini into quarters.

Trim and discard the root end of the Spanish onion and cut the onion in half root to tip. Cut each half in half again root to tip so the onion is quartered. Separate the layers of the onion, stack 2 or 3 layers at a time on top of one another, and slice ¼ inch thick lengthwise.

Heat 2 tablespoons of the olive oil in a large Dutch oven or another large heavy-bottomed pan over medium-high heat until it slides easily in the pan and the oil around the edges of the pan begins to smoke. Put half of the oxtails, flat side down, in the pan to sear for 10 to 15 minutes, until they are seared on all sides (round and flat), turning them with tongs as they brown. Remove the oxtails to a baking sheet. Add 2 tablespoons of the remaining oil to the pan and heat the oil for about 1 minute, until it smokes around the edges of the pan, before adding the remaining oxtails. Cook the remaining oxtails in the same way and remove them to the baking sheet with the first batch.

Drain the oil from the pan. Wipe out the pan only if the bits on the bottom are burned. Add the remaining 2 tablespoons oil and heat it over medium-high heat until the oil around the edges of the pan is almost smoking. Add the cipollini onions, sliced Spanish onion, carrot, garlic, and chile pods, and season with ½ teaspoon salt. Cook for about 5 minutes, stirring often to prevent the vegetables from browning, until the onions are tender and translucent but not mushy. Move the vegetables to create a bare spot in the pan and add the tomato paste to the space you created in the pan. Cook the tomato paste, stirring with a rubber spatula, for about 1 minute, to concentrate the flavor and caramelize it slightly, but be careful not to burn it. Add the red wine and increase the heat to high. Bring the wine to a boil and boil it until it reduces by half, about 5 minutes. Add the tomatoes and their juices and use a wooden spoon to crush the tomatoes slightly. Cook until the tomatoes come to a simmer. Stir in the remaining ½ teaspoon salt.

Return the oxtails to the pot. Add enough chicken stock to come just to the top of the oxtails, pouring it around, not over, the oxtails. Bring the chicken stock to a simmer over high heat. Turn off the heat and scatter the thyme sprigs over the oxtails. Put the lid on the pot or cover the pot tightly with aluminum foil.

Put the oxtails in the oven to braise for 2 hours. Halfway through the cooking time, remove the oxtails from the oven and remove the lid or foil. Use tongs to turn each oxtail. Return the lid or foil to the pot and return the pot to the oven for 1 to 2 more hours, until fork-tender. Remove the pot from the oven and uncover. Let the oxtails rest for at least 20 minutes, uncovered, before serving.

To serve, spoon some of the veggies and sauce from around the oxtails over them, and drizzle with the finishing-quality olive oil. Serve the oxtails in the pot you cooked them in with a large spoon.

Braised Celery

SERVES 6

3 celery heads

¼ cup olive oil

½ teaspoon kosher salt

1½ cups Chicken Stock
(page 59 or sodium-free
store-bought stock), or as needed

1 lemon, sliced into ¼-inch rounds,
ends discarded

10 fresh thyme sprigs

Finishing-quality extra-virgin
olive oil

Maldon sea salt (or another flaky
sea salt such as fleur de sel)

Celery is one of the most undercelebrated vegetables I can think of. People throw it into mirepoix or *soffritto* (the French and Italian versions, respectively, of a combination of onion, carrot, and celery that is a foundation for many soups and sauces), and it gets used raw in tuna salad and smeared with peanut butter to make a crunchy snack. But celery is rarely given the respect that other vegetables are, cooked and admired on its own. I am one of celery's biggest champions (see Bean Salad with Celery Leaf Pesto, page 34), and I especially like its mineral quality in contrast to beef. In this recipe, hearts of celery are used in place of leeks in what would otherwise be a classic braised leek preparation, and served along with Braised Oxtails (page 220). I dare you to try it. You'll never look at celery the same way again.

This recipe calls for sodium-free chicken stock. Use half of the salt in this recipe if you are using chicken stock that contains salt.

You will need a 13 x 9-inch baking dish or a similar-size baking dish as well as heavy-duty aluminum foil to make this.

Adjust an oven rack to the middle position and preheat the oven to 300°F.

Remove the outer stalks from the celery heads so that only the very lightest green, almost white core remains and reserve the removed stalks for another use. Trim the root ends of the celery, leaving enough of it to hold the heads intact. Peel the outer, exposed stalks with a vegetable peeler and cut each head in half lengthwise.

Put the celery in a shallow baking dish just large enough to hold them in a single layer, such as a 13 x 9-inch baking dish. Drizzle the celery with the olive oil and massage the oil into the celery with your hands to coat the stalks all over. Sprinkle the celery with the salt and toss gently to distribute the salt. Arrange the celery, cut side up, in a single layer in the baking dish. Add enough chicken stock to come three-fourths of the way up the sides of the celery, pouring it around, not over, the celery. Lay the lemon slices over the celery and scatter the thyme sprigs on top. Cover the dish tightly with heavy-duty aluminum foil.

Cook the celery for 1½ hours. Remove the baking dish from the oven.

Increase the oven temperature to 500°F.

Remove and discard the foil. Remove and discard the thyme sprigs and the lemon slices. Return the celery to the oven, uncovered, for 40 minutes, or until the top of the celery is golden brown and glazed looking and the liquid in the pan has evaporated. Remove the celery from the oven.

To serve, transfer the celery to a medium rectangular platter or serve it in the dish you cooked it in. Drizzle the celery with finishing-quality olive oil, sprinkle with sea salt, and serve with tongs.

Braised Cabbage Wedges with Bacon

SERVES 6 TO 12
MAKES 12 HALVES

6 baby or 2 large savoy cabbage heads

¾ cup plus 1 tablespoon olive oil, plus more as needed

2 teaspoons kosher salt

6 ounces slab bacon, fat trimmed and discarded, or thick-cut applewood-smoked bacon, cut into ¼-inch dice

2 medium carrots, cut into ¼-inch dice

3 celery stalks, cut into ¼-inch dice

1½ cups Chicken Stock (page 59 or sodium-free store-bought stock), or as needed

Finishing-quality extra-virgin olive oil

Maldon sea salt (or another flaky sea salt such as fleur de sel)

Monday is an exciting day at Mozza because Monday is when Dragan comes. Dragan is a produce purveyor whose job it is to drive up and down California and its surrounding states, visiting small family farms and farmers' markets and picking up the most beautiful, unusual, and flavorful vegetables he can find. Like a door-to-door salesperson, Dragan drives into big cities to the back doors of some of the finer restaurants in the state, and we're fortunate enough to be one of those restaurants. When he pulls up at Mozza and opens the doors of his truck, the chefs and cooks from all three restaurants as well as the pastry kitchen hop on board to see what Dragan has brought with him. It's like the best farmers' market in the entire world, brought straight to our kitchens. One week, Dragan had some beautiful baby savoy cabbages, about the size of a doll's head. Our former chef Matt bought a case, and he invented this braised cabbage dish as a way to use them. This is what it means to be inspired by ingredients.

This recipe calls for sodium-free chicken stock. Use half of the salt in this recipe if you are using chicken stock that contains salt.

It's nice to make this in a pan you can also serve it in. Liz Hong takes the dish from start to finish in a five-quart Le Creuset braiser. If you use a pan without a lid, use heavy-duty aluminum foil to cover the pan.

————————

Adjust an oven rack to the middle position and preheat the oven to 350°F.

Remove and discard any unappealing outer leaves from the cabbages. Trim the dry ends of the cabbage stems, leaving as much of the cores intact as possible so the wedges stay intact. If you are using baby heads, cut each head in half through the core. If you are using large heads, cut each head in half through the core and cut each half into 3 wedges. Put the cabbage halves or wedges in a large bowl. Drizzle with 3 tablespoons of the olive oil, sprinkle with the kosher salt, and gently massage the cabbages to coat them evenly.

Prepare a bed of paper towels. Put 1 tablespoon of the remaining oil and the bacon in a large heavy-bottomed sauté pan and cook the bacon over medium heat for 3 to 5 minutes, until the fat is rendered and the bacon is crisp, stirring often to cook the bacon on all sides and prevent it from burning. Fish out the bacon with a slotted spoon and put it on the paper towels to drain.

Increase the heat to medium-high and put half of the cabbage wedges in the pan, cut side down. Sear the cabbage for about 3 minutes on each of the cut sides, or until both cut sides are deep golden brown, turning them carefully with a metal spatula as they brown and adding as much as 3 tablespoons more oil to the pan, 1 tablespoon at a time, as the cabbage absorbs the oil and the pan becomes dry. Remove the cabbage wedges from the pan and put them on a baking sheet, taking care to keep the wedges intact. Add 2 tablespoons of the remaining oil to the pan and heat it for about 1 minute, until the oil just begins to smoke around the edges. Add the remaining cabbage wedges and sear them in the same way you did the first batch, adding as much as 3 tablespoons more oil to the pan as needed. Remove the second batch of cabbage wedges from the pan and put them on the baking sheet with the first batch.

Add the remaining 1 tablespoon oil to the pan and heat it for about 1 minute over medium-high heat until it just begins to smoke around the edges of the pan. Add the carrots and celery and cook for about 1 minute, stirring constantly, just to coat them with the oil and soften them very slightly. Return the cabbage wedges to the pan, curved side down, arranging them attractively in a single layer. Add enough chicken stock to come one-third of the way up the sides of the cabbage wedges, pouring it around, not over, the cabbage wedges. Bring the liquid to a boil over high heat. Put the lid on the pot or cover it tightly with heavy-duty aluminum foil.

Put the cabbages in the oven to cook for 25 minutes. Remove the pot from the oven.

Increase the oven temperature to 500°F.

Remove the lid or foil. Scatter the bacon pieces around the cabbage wedges. Return the pot to the oven, uncovered, and cook until the cabbage wedges are browned and blistered in places, about 10 minutes. Remove the cabbages from the oven.

To serve, using tongs, remove the cabbage halves or wedges to a rimmed round or rectangular platter with the cut sides facing up. Spoon the sauce and other goodies from the bottom of the pan over the cabbage. Drizzle the cabbage with finishing-quality olive oil, sprinkle with sea salt, and serve with a large spoon.

Pan Cotto

SERVES 6 TO 8

1 pound broccolini (or broccoli rabe or broccoli di ciccio; about 2 bunches)

Small loaf of stale country bread (about 6 ounces; crusts cut off and weighed without the crust), cut into ¼-inch cubes

½ cup plus 1 tablespoon extra-virgin olive oil

10 to 12 large garlic cloves, peeled and sliced ¹⁄₁₆ inch thick lengthwise, preferably on a mandoline

1½ tablespoons plus ½ teaspoon kosher salt

4 árbol chile pods

½ to 1 teaspoon red chile flakes (depending on how spicy you like your food)

Finishing-quality extra-virgin olive oil

I don't know if this sounds snobby to say, or if it just makes me sound old, but I've been around, and I've eaten so many things at so many restaurants that very seldom do I eat something that really amazes me. On the rare occasion that I do fall absolutely in love with a dish, without fail, it's something simple, comforting, and accessible, never something that has been overmanipulated. This pan cotto is the perfect example. *Pan cotto*, which means "cooked bread," is an Italian *contorno*, or, side dish, made of fried bread, broth, and vegetables. I had never seen or heard of it until it was one of myriad dishes served for lunch at an *agriturismo* in Tuscany that Faith Willinger, a friend and an authority on Italian cuisine, suggested I visit. What came to the table was a sort of crunchy, earthy, vegetable-laced pancake—just the sort of humble dish I get excited about. And as high as my expectations were, the pan cotto tasted even better than it looked.

I was having lunch with my friends Caryl Lee and Margy Rochlin, and my daughter, Vanessa. We were all talking and eating, and at some point we each found ourselves saying, "Did you taste the broccoli?" "Pass the broccoli." "What's up with that broccoli?" I knew from taste and sight what I was eating was made from some variety of broccoli, bread, and red chile flakes, but beyond that, I was mystified. It wasn't cooked vegetables with bread crumbs mixed in, and it wasn't *ribollita*—minestrone soup thickened with bread—but it was something indescribably unique and delicious.

I knew that something had been done in the cooking process to get these three ingredients to taste as exceptional as they did, but I didn't know what. Determined to learn how to make this dish, I told Faith about my experience. Faith explained that what I had eaten was a classic Tuscan use for stale bread and that she makes it every few days because it's a favorite of her husband, Massimo. Faith invited me to her house and spent an entire afternoon teaching me how she makes pan cotto. When I got back to Los Angeles, I took what I'd learned from Faith and played with the cooking process until, after about a dozen attempts, I finally got a pan cotto that had the combination of a crunchy bread exterior and comforting, soft pieces of bread strewn throughout that had so captivated me at the *agriturismo* in Tuscany. The instructions look involved, but the pan cotto is not remotely difficult to make. It's just one of those God-is-in-the-details cooking techniques, the kind of detail that normally a grandmother would tell you by standing next to you while she taught you how to make something. Just as Faith acted as my "Italian grandmother," I'll have to stand in for yours for now. If your pan cotto doesn't come out as perfectly uniform as I describe, no worries; the combination of flavors is utterly delicious and will make up for its lack of aesthetic appeal. It's equally delicious warm or at room temperature.

If your bread is not stale, leave the cubes, uncovered, at room temperature overnight to stale.

You will need a 9-inch nonstick sauté pan, as well as a slightly smaller pot or pan that fits inside it, to make this. If you don't have a pot or pan that will fit inside the larger one, use a heat-resistant plate and weigh it down with cans or whatever you like. If you have a mandoline, use it to make easy work of slicing the garlic for this recipe.

———————

Trim and discard the dry stem ends of the broccolini; do this one at a time as each stalk will need to be trimmed at a different place. Cut the broccolini in half, separating the florets and the stems. Cut the stems in half lengthwise and cut them into 2-inch-long segments. Put the bread cubes in a medium bowl. Add ½ cup of the olive oil, the garlic, and ½ teaspoon of the salt and toss to coat the bread with the oil and to distribute the garlic and salt.

Combine 2 quarts water in a medium saucepan; if you have a pot whose bottom is slighly smaller than the sauté pan you will be using in the next step, clean the bottom and use that. Add the remaining 1½ tablespoons salt and the árbol chile pods and bring the water to a boil over high heat. Add the broccolini, return the water to a boil, and cook the broccolini until the stems are soft but not mushy, about 3 minutes. (Broccoli rabe and broccoli di ciccio will take about 1 minute longer to cook.) Turn off the heat. Using a strainer, fish the broccolini out of the water and transfer it to a large bowl, reserving the cooking water in the pot. (You will use the pot of water to weigh down the pan cotto.) Remove and discard the árbol chile pods. Sprinkle the broccolini with the red chile flakes and toss to distribute the chile.

Pour the remaining 1 tablespoon of olive oil into a 9-inch nonstick sauté pan. Add the bread to the sauté pan, scraping all of the garlic and oil into the pan. Spread the bread so it is in an even layer in the pan. Put the pan over high heat and leave it untouched until you hear the oil begin to sizzle, 3 to 4 minutes. Continue to cook the bread over high heat, swirling the pan often and gently stirring the bread once or twice so the bread doesn't stick to the pan and it cooks evenly, until the edges of the bread are golden brown, 3 to 4 minutes. Add the broccolini and reduce the heat to medium. Using tongs, gently spread the broccolini, mixing it in with the bread so that they are evenly dispersed in the pan with as much bread as possible touching the surface of the pan. Add ¾ cup of the reserved broccolini cooking water to the pan and swirl the pan to prevent the bread from sticking to the surface.

Put the pot with the cooking water or whatever you are using as a weight (see headnote) in it directly on top of the broccolini and bread to weigh it down and force it to bind together. Cook the bread and broccolini with the pot weighing it down for 3 to 4 minutes, until the bread has come together into the shape of a pancake and the broccolini is melded into the bread. Remove the pot used to weigh down the ingredients. Reduce the heat to medium-low and cook the pancake for about 20 minutes, swirling the pan every few minutes to prevent the bread from sticking and pressing on the pancake with a metal spatula, working from the center out (the edges will become higher than the center; if the edges are higher than the edge of the pan, gently pat them down to the level of the pan), until you begin to hear the oil in the pan sizzle. (By pressing on the pancake, you will be pressing the water out from the bread and vegetables, so it can cook off. Once all the water has cooked off, you will begin to hear the oil sizzle in the pan.) After the oil begins to sizzle, increase the heat to medium and cook the pancake, swirling the pan and pressing on the pancake, until the pancake is deep golden brown and crispy and smells like toasted (but not burned) bread, about 5 minutes.

To serve, turn off the heat and slide the pan cotto out of the pan onto a round dinner plate in one swift motion. Put a second dinner plate over the first and flip the plates to invert the pancake so the crispy bottom side is facing up. (If, when you invert the pancake, you find that the top is not brown and crispy, return it with the original side on the surface of the pan and cook it over medium-low heat for a few more minutes, until it is brown and crispy.) Serve the pan cotto with a large spoon for guests to spoon out the size portion they want, or cut it like a pie into 6 or 8 wedges and serve with a cake spatula. Place a bottle of finishing-quality olive oil alongside for guests to drizzle on for themselves.

Shaved Brussels Sprouts Salad with Pecorino and Toasted Almonds

Shaved Brussels sprouts are very trendy right now, but I believe that my friend the great chef Jonathan Waxman put them on the map. Jonathan always has a shaved raw vegetable salad on the menu at his restaurant Barbuto, in the West Village in New York: shaved cauliflower, long ribbons of asparagus or summer squash, or, yes, shaved Brussels sprouts, depending on the season. I channeled my inner Jonathan to create this salad, which we offer at the Osteria. It's definitely a crowd-pleaser.

You will need a mandoline to shave the Brussels sprouts for this salad.

———

Adjust an oven rack to the middle position and preheat the oven to 325°F.

Spread the almonds on a baking sheet and toast them in the oven for 12 to 15 minutes, until they are fragrant and golden brown, shaking the baking sheet and rotating it from front to back halfway through the cooking time so the nuts brown evenly. Remove the almonds from the oven and set aside until they are cool enough to touch. Drizzle with the olive oil, sprinkle with 2 teaspoons of the salt, and toss to coat. Coarsely chop the almonds and set them aside.

Remove and discard the unappealing outer leaves from the Brussels sprouts. Holding a Brussels sprout by the root end with the rounded head facing the mandoline blade, shave the sprout as thinly as possible until you reach the part that you're holding; discard. Repeat with the remaining Brussels sprouts.

Put the shaved Brussels sprouts and mint in a large bowl. Drizzle with the lemon juice, sprinkle with the remaining 2 teaspoons salt, and toss to coat the leaves. Drizzle the finishing-quality olive oil over the salad, toss, and gently massage the oil to coat the leaves. Check for seasoning, adding more salt and oil to taste.

To serve, using a Microplane (preferably a ribbon Microplane), grate a thin layer of pecorino to cover the surface of a large rimmed platter or large shallow serving dish. Mound the salad on top of the cheese and gently flatten the mound to make an even circle. Grate a thin layer of the cheese over the salad and scatter the chopped almonds over the cheese. Drizzle a few drops of lemon juice and grind several turns of pepper over the salad. Serve with a big spoon and the cheese and grater on the side for guests to grate more cheese over their own servings.

SERVES 6 TO 8

———

1 cup whole almonds with skins

1 tablespoon extra-virgin olive oil, plus more to taste

1 tablespoon plus 1 teaspoon kosher salt, plus more to taste

4 pounds Brussels sprouts

1 cup thinly sliced fresh mint leaves

2 tablespoons fresh lemon juice, plus more for squeezing on the finished salad

¼ cup plus 2 tablespoons finishing-quality extra-virgin olive oil

Wedge of pecorino Romano for grating

Freshly ground black pepper

13

**Dave's Oven-Roasted Grouper
with Spicy Tomato Marmalade and Tahini**

Dave's Oven-Roasted Grouper with Spicy Tomato Marmalade and Tahini

SERVES 10

FOR THE TAHINI SAUCE

1 cup cooked chickpeas
(see White Beans, page 36,
or from a can), drained

1 cup tahini (preferably made with
whole unhulled seeds stirred or
shaken so the oil is integrated)

6 tablespoons fresh lemon juice

3 teaspoons kosher salt

1½ cups ice-cold water

FOR THE FISH

1 medium yellow Spanish onion,
peeled

½ cup olive oil

5 to 6 large garlic cloves, peeled
and sliced ⅟₁₆ inch thick lengthwise,
preferably on a mandoline

1 tablespoon plus 2¼ teaspoons
kosher salt

Big pinch of saffron threads
(about ¼ teaspoon)

1 pint small red cherry or grape
tomatoes, halved through the stems

1 to 2 jalapeño peppers
(depending on taste; stems,
seeds, and membranes removed
and discarded), cut into quarters
lengthwise, and seeds and ribs
removed and discarded

On my annual trip to Singapore to visit my restaurants there last fall, Dave Almany, our former chef in Singapore, made a fish dish for me based on one he'd had on a recent trip to Tel Aviv. Israeli food is definitely on the rise; there are more than a handful of Israeli chefs and restaurants being talked about, and Dave had the opportunity to eat at many of those restaurants. At The Salon, Dave had a version of this fish dish, and the chef, Eyal Shani, was nice enough to talk Dave through the process of making it. When Dave returned home to Singapore, he made the dish for me, asking if I would approve of his putting it on the menu. The fish is oven roasted with onions, jalapeño peppers, saffron, and tomatoes that are cooked down until they're sweet and jammy, and then it is drizzled with tahini sauce. I told Dave that the only way he could put the fish dish on his menu at the Osteria was if he also agreed to teach me how to make it, so I could serve it at home and include it in this book. We had a deal.

I'm usually a stickler for cooking dried beans rather than using canned, but in this recipe, where the chickpeas (my addition) play such a minor role, I will turn a blind eye if you want to use canned.

This dish is served in the pan in which it is cooked. So choose a pan that will look pretty on your dining or buffet table. If you have a mandoline, use it to make easy work of slicing the garlic for this recipe. Ask your fishmonger to scale and portion your fillets.

———

To make the tahini sauce, combine the chickpeas, tahini, lemon juice, salt, and 1 cup of the ice water in the jar of a blender and purée, adding more water as needed, until creamy, but not runny, and lighter in color. Serve at room temperature.

To prepare the fish, trim and discard the root end of the onion and cut the onion in half root to tip. Cut each half in half again root to tip so the onion is quartered. Separate the layers of the onion, stack 2 or 3 layers at a time on top of one another, and slice ¼ inch thick lengthwise.

Pour 2 tablespoons of the olive oil into a large heavy sauté pan (not non-stick). Add the onion and garlic, season with 1 teaspoon of the salt, and cook over medium-low heat, stirring often, until the onion and garlic are very soft but not brown, about 15 minutes, lowering the heat if the onion and garlic begin to brown. Stir in the saffron and cook for about 5 minutes, until the threads have dissolved and the onion is stained with the saffron. Turn off the heat. Remove the onion and garlic from the pan, put them on a plate, and set aside.

Add 2 tablespoons of the remaining oil to the pan you cooked the onion and garlic in. Heat the oil over medium-high heat until it slides easily in the pan and the oil at the edges of the pan just begins to smoke, 2 to 3 minutes. Add the halved cherry tomatoes and the jalapeños, sprinkle with ½ teaspoon of the remaining salt, and cook without stirring until the tomatoes begin to caramelize on the surface of the pan, about 3 minutes. Stir and scrape up any brown bits stuck to the bottom of the pan and continue to cook the tomatoes and jalapeños, stirring occasionally, for 10 to 12 minutes, until the tomatoes are shapeless. Add the white wine and cook until the pan is almost dry, 5 to 8 minutes. Add the chickpeas, return the onion and garlic to the pan, and stir to combine the ingredients. Add the crushed tomatoes and season with the sugar, ½ teaspoon of the pepper, and ¾ teaspoon of the remaining salt. Bring the liquid to a boil, reduce the heat to low, and simmer the sauce, stirring often, for 15 to 20 minutes, until it is the thickness of porridge. Turn off the heat.

While the sauce is cooking, adjust an oven rack to the middle position and preheat the oven to 450°F.

Cut the fish in half either lengthwise or crosswise, depending on what seems more natural given the shapes of the fillets. Set the fish aside while you make a rub.

Put the fennel pollen, dried oregano, the remaining 1 teaspoon pepper, and 1½ teaspoons of the remaining salt in a small bowl and stir to combine the ingredients.

Lay the fish, skin side down, on a flat work surface. Sprinkle the flesh side with the rub and pat gently so the rub adheres. Turn the fish skin side up and sprinkle the skin with the remaining 1½ teaspoons salt. Nestle the fish, skin side up, in a single layer in the pan with the tomato sauce and drizzle with the remaining ¼ cup olive oil.

Bake the fish for 15 minutes. Turn the pan from front to back, increase the heat to 500°F, and bake until the fish skin is golden brown and crisp and the sauce is jammy, about 5 minutes. Remove the fish from the oven.

With the fish still in the pan, drizzle the finishing-quality olive oil over and around the fish and spoon 1 tablespoon of the tahini sauce over each fillet. Using scissors, snip a few fresh oregano leaves over each fish fillet.

Serve the fish in the pan you baked it in with a big spoon for guests to dish out a portion of the fish and serve the remaining tahini sauce in a small bowl with a spoon for guests to drizzle over their fish.

½ cup dry white wine

1 cup cooked chickpeas (see White Beans, page 36, or from a can), drained

1½ cups canned crushed tomatoes (preferably San Marzano)

Big pinch of sugar

1½ teaspoons freshly ground black pepper

5 (8-ounce) grouper fillets (or bass, cod, or another firm white fish), scales removed

1 tablespoon fennel pollen (or ground fennel seeds)

1 tablespoon dried oregano

Finishing-quality extra-virgin olive oil

Fresh oregano leaves for garnish

Roasted Radishes and Turnips with Radish Sprouts and Dill

SERVES 6

1½ pounds radishes
(preferably French breakfast
radishes) and turnips
(about 1 bunch each), greens
attached

¼ cup olive oil

1 teaspoon kosher salt

1 cup radish sprouts (about 1 ounce)

16 fresh dill sprigs

1 teaspoon finishing-quality extra-
virgin olive oil, plus more
for drizzling

1 lemon for grating, plus
½ teaspoon fresh lemon juice

Maldon sea salt (or another flaky
sea salt such as fleur de sel), plus
more for sprinkling

One of the creative advantages to having three restaurants side by side is that I'm constantly walking back and forth through the kitchens, and as I do so, I'm doing mental research. Out of the corner of one eye I might see a cook performing a task I think he or she could do better; out of the corner of the other I may see an ingredient that inspires me in that moment. One day, thinking about ways to brighten this wintery dish of roasted turnips and radishes, I saw some radish sprouts in one of the kitchens. I picked up a handful, then grabbed a few dill sprigs from the walk-in refrigerator, and tossed them together into a delicate little salad condiment that turned out to be just the thing to liven up the dish in terms of flavor and visually as well.

It's very trendy to talk about nose-to-tail cooking, but being more of a vegetable person myself, I'm equally obsessed with root-to-leaf cooking, or using all parts of the vegetable, as I do with this dish, where the radishes and turnips are roasted with their leaves still attached. You rarely see radishes served any way but raw. Where raw radishes are crunchy and watery, when roasted they become creamy and sweet and seem almost like a starchy vegetable. Because you'll be utilizing the entire vegetable, including the greens, I think you'll have the best luck if you shop for the radishes and turnips at farmers' markets, where the greens attached to the vegetables will be more appealing.

Adjust the oven racks so none are near the oven floor; you'll be putting the baking sheet directly on the oven floor. If you are using an electric oven or another oven where you can't put anything on the floor, adjust the oven racks so that one is closest to the floor and put a pizza stone on it, if you have one. Preheat the oven to 500°F.

Wash the radishes and turnips thoroughly, making sure to get all the dirt off the leaves. (The best way to do this is to soak them in a sink or bowlful of water and let the dirt fall to the bottom. Drain and repeat until you no longer see sand on the bottom of the sink.) Put the turnips and radishes on a bed of paper towels to dry and pat the leaves with paper towels to dry them completely.

Trim and discard any yellow or wilted leaves from the radishes and turnips. Cut each vegetable in half through the middle, keeping the leaves intact as much as possible, and save any leaves that fall off. Put the radishes, turnips, and stray leaves on a large baking sheet. Drizzle with 3 tablespoons of the olive oil, sprinkle with the kosher salt, and gently massage the bulbs and leaves to coat them. Arrange the bulbs, cut side down, on a baking sheet and drizzle the remaining 1 tablespoon oil over just the bulbs. Put the baking sheet on the oven floor or the lowest rack and roast the vegetables for 12 to 16 minutes, until the bottoms of the bulbs are deep brown, shaking the baking sheet and rotating it from front to back halfway through the cooking time so the vegetables brown evenly. (When cooking vegetables on the oven floor, a lot of steam is produced from the water released as a result of the vegetables cooking so quickly, so just be careful of the steam that will arise when you open the oven door.) Remove the vegetables from the oven and set them aside to cool to room temperature.

Put the radish sprouts and dill sprigs in a small bowl, drizzle with the finishing-quality olive oil and lemon juice, sprinkle with the sea salt, and toss to coat and combine the ingredients.

To serve, lay one-third of the radishes and turnips on a medium rectangular platter with the caramelized sides facing up. Tangle a small handful of the sprouts and dill garnish in between the leaves of the radishes and turnips. Continue adding more radishes and turnips, layering in the sprouts and dill garnish, until you've put all the radishes and turnips on the platter, reserving a small amount of the garnish for the top. Drizzle the vegetables with finishing-quality olive oil and sprinkle with sea salt. Use a fine Microplane to grate a thin layer of lemon zest over the vegetables. Scatter the reserved sprouts and dill over the top and serve with tongs.

Grilled Escarole with Salsa Rustica

SERVES 6 TO 8

3 pounds escarole
(or romaine lettuce)

1½ cups olive oil

12 to 14 medium or large garlic cloves, peeled and roughly chopped

2 large shallots, peeled and roughly chopped

¼ cup plus 2 tablespoons kosher salt

Finishing-quality extra-virgin olive oil

Maldon sea salt (or another flaky sea salt such as fleur de sel)

Salsa Rustica (recipe follows)

This dish, a cousin to the grilled romaine Caesar that has become popular in recent years, is a cross between a salad and a cooked vegetable side dish. You don't see grilled escarole nearly as often as you see grilled romaine, which is a shame, as escarole has a lot more character both in flavor and texture than romaine. In this recipe, after being grilled, the escarole is dressed with salsa rustica, which is salsa verde with chopped hard-cooked eggs and almonds stirred in. I think of this as a side dish. Once you grill a vegetable, it's not a salad.

If you can't find escarole, substitute romaine lettuce heads (not hearts of romaine). I call for you to cook this on the stove top for convenience, but you can also cook the escarole on an outdoor grill.

———

Cut the heads of escarole in half through the middle at the base and then pull both halves like a wishbone to split each head in half. Put the escarole in a large bowl or casserole dish.

Combine the olive oil, garlic, and shallots in the jar of a blender and purée until the garlic and shallots are very finely chopped. Pour the marinade over the escarole and sprinkle with the kosher salt. Toss to coat the escarole using your hands to massage the marinade so it coats the leaves and between the layers. You can prepare the escarole to this point up to several hours in advance. Cover and refrigerate until you're ready to grill it.

Preheat a grill pan or cast-iron skillet over high heat.

Working in batches, lay the escarole halves in a single layer in the grill pan and cook until the halves are charred in places and cooked through but still al dente (to test, break off a leaf and bite into the thickest portion), 8 to 10 minutes, turning the escarole several times during the cooking time so it cooks evenly and doesn't burn to a crisp. Remove the escarole from the grill pan and cook the remaining halves in the same way.

To serve, tear the escarole halves into manageable pieces, tearing each half into 4 sections (if you're cooking romaine, you will tear each half into thirds), leaving the leaves attached to the root. As you tear the escarole, lay the sections, all facing the same direction, on a large rectangular platter. Drizzle with finishing-quality olive oil and sprinkle with sea salt. Smear a spoonful of the salsa rustica on each section of escarole, using the back of a spoon to paint the salsa onto the escarole so that you can see small chunks of salsa peeking out from between the leaves, but not so much that the salsa hides the escarole or falls off onto the platter. Transfer the remaining salsa to a small pretty bowl. Serve the escarole with tongs and the remaining salsa on the side with a spoon for guests to serve themselves.

Salsa Rustica

Makes about 1½ cups

Salsa rustica—salsa verde with almonds and hard-cooked egg stirred in—is something I was introduced to what seems like a hundred years ago at the legendary Zuni Cafe in San Francisco. I liked the name as much as I liked the sauce, and I immediately brought it into my repertoire. It was only recently that I realized that in all these years, I'd yet to see salsa rustica in Italy or at another Italian restaurant. From the name, I'd always assumed it was a classic sauce, but as it turns out, Judy Rodgers, the late chef and owner of Zuni, invented it and just gave it that classic-sounding name.

¼ cup whole almonds, with skins

2 hard-cooked extra-large eggs (see Perfect Hard-Cooked Eggs, page 82)

1 cup packed fresh oregano leaves

1 cup packed fresh mint leaves

3 medium or large garlic cloves

2 teaspoons kosher salt

2 anchovy fillets (preferably salt-packed; rinsed, backbones removed if salt-packed), finely chopped and smashed with the flat side of a knife

1 cup plus 1 tablespoon extra-virgin olive oil, plus more as needed

1 teaspoon capers (preferably salt-packed; soaked for 15 minutes if salt-packed), rinsed, drained, and finely chopped

Adjust an oven rack to the middle position and preheat the oven to 325°F.

Spread the almonds on a baking sheet and toast them in the oven for 12 to 15 minutes, until they are fragrant and golden brown, shaking the baking sheet and rotating it from front to back halfway through the cooking time so the nuts brown evenly. Remove the almonds from the oven and set them aside to cool to room temperature. Roughly chop the almonds and set aside.

Peel the eggs and separate the whites and yolks. Roughly chop the egg whites and put them in a small bowl. Roughly chop the egg yolks and add them to the bowl with the whites; set the eggs aside.

To make the salsa using a large mortar and a pestle, finely chop the oregano and mint by hand. Transfer the chopped herbs to the mortar. Using a fine Microplane, grate the garlic directly into the mortar. Add the salt and anchovies and pound with the pestle until the ingredients are mashed together and there are no visible chunks of any ingredients. Slowly stir in the olive oil, adding more oil if necessary to achieve a loose, spoonable salsa.

To make the salsa using a mini food processor or blender, very roughly chop the oregano and mint leaves by hand. Transfer the herbs to the bowl of a food processor fitted with a metal blade or to the jar of a blender. Using a fine Microplane, grate the garlic directly into the bowl. Add the salt and anchovies and pulse to roughly chop the ingredients. Scrape down the sides of the bowl. With the motor running, gradually add the olive oil through the feed tube, stopping after you've added half of the oil to scrape down the bowl of the food processor again, then adding the rest of the oil. Transfer the salsa to a medium bowl. Stir in more oil if necessary to achieve a loose, spoonable salsa.

The salsa can be made to this point up to 1 day in advance. Refrigerate the salsa in a covered container until you're ready to use it. Bring it to room temperature before using. Gently stir in the almonds, capers, egg yolks, and egg whites just before serving.

Mixed Grain and Seed Salad

One of the early dishes at Campanile was a grilled quail entrée served with a grain salad. At that time I had seen quail paired with wild rice on menus and in cookbooks so often that to go one step further and pair quail with a mixed grain salad that included wild rice just didn't seem like a huge leap. The dish had its fans, myself among them, but it was never as popular as I would have liked. The salad would fit right into today's grain-obsessed world, where the more unusual the grain, the more sought after it is, which is why I decided to resurrect it and serve it as a side dish at home.

This salad calls for three different grains—quinoa, farro, and wild rice—in addition to fregola sarda, which is a small round pasta shape from Sardinia. Use whatever combination of grains you like, including wheat berries, freekeh, amaranth, brown rice, orzo, or millet, in addition to those I call for here. Make sure to keep the amount of total uncooked grains/fregola the same as it is in the recipe. Each type of grain, rice, or pasta cooks for a different length of time, so each must be cooked separately. You can cook them one at a time or have them all going on your stove top, depending on how many saucepans you have. This recipe has bacon in it, but I hereby grant you permission to leave it out and turn this into a vegan side dish.

If you have parchment paper, use it to line the baking sheet to toast the farro; it makes it so easy to get the grains off the baking sheet without spilling any. Just pull the entire sheet of parchment off the baking sheet and fold it up to create a sort of funnel to pour the farro into the pot once it's toasted.

To prepare the salad, adjust an oven rack to the middle position and preheat the oven to 350°F. Line a baking sheet with parchment paper, if you are using it.

Put the farro on the baking sheet, drizzle with 1½ teaspoons of the olive oil, and toss to coat the grains. Spread the farro on the baking sheet and toast it in the oven until it's golden brown and slightly fragrant, 8 to 10 minutes, shaking the baking sheet and rotating it from front to back halfway through the cooking time so the farro browns evenly. Remove from the oven.

Meanwhile, bring 2 cups water to a boil in a medium saucepan over high heat. Add 1 teaspoon of the salt and the farro and return the water to a boil. Reduce the heat to medium-low and simmer until the farro is al dente, 18 to 22 minutes.

SERVES 6 TO 8

¼ cup farro

1 tablespoon extra-virgin olive oil

2 tablespoons plus 2½ teaspoons kosher salt

6 thick-cut applewood-smoked bacon slices (about 5 ounces)

¼ cup quinoa (tricolored if you can find it), rinsed thoroughly

¼ cup wild rice, rinsed thoroughly

¼ cup fregola sarda

¼ cup natural, unhulled sesame seeds

¼ cup golden flaxseeds

½ large radicchio head (halved through the core)

2 bunches scallions

2 tablespoons fresh lemon juice

½ cup Lemon Vinaigrette (page 125)

Drain the farro in a colander and transfer it to a baking sheet. Drizzle the farro with the remaining 1½ teaspoons olive oil and toss to coat the grains.

Prepare a bed of paper towels. Lay the bacon on a baking sheet and bake until it is cooked all the way through but not crisp, 15 to 17 minutes, rotating the baking sheet from front to back halfway through the cooking time so the bacon cooks evenly. Remove the bacon from the oven and transfer it to the paper towels to drain and to cool to room temperature. Slice the bacon into ⅛-inch-wide threads on an extreme bias and set aside.

Combine the quinoa with 1 cup water and 1 teaspoon of the remaining salt in a medium saucepan and bring the water to a boil over high heat. Reduce the heat to low and simmer the quinoa until it is tender and fluffy and all the water is cooked off, 15 to 18 minutes. Turn off the heat and let the quinoa rest in the pot for 5 minutes, then transfer it to the baking sheet with the farro to cool.

Combine 1 quart water and 1 tablespoon of the remaining salt in a medium saucepan and bring the water to a boil over high heat. Add the wild rice and let the water come back to a boil. Reduce the heat to low and simmer, uncovered, until tender, about 25 minutes. Drain the wild rice and transfer it to the baking sheet with the farro and quinoa to cool.

Combine 1 quart water with 1 tablespoon of the remaining salt in a medium saucepan and bring the water to a boil over high heat.

Drop the fregola into the boiling water and stir to prevent it from sticking together. Boil the fregola, using the time indicated on the package instructions as a guide, until it's al dente. (Fregola tends to harden as it cools, so to test for doneness, put a couple of fregola in the ice water to cool completely, then taste it for doneness.) Drain the pasta and transfer it to the baking sheet with the grains.

Toast the sesame seeds in a small sauté pan over medium heat for 1 to 2 minutes, until they are fragrant and golden brown, shaking the pan often so they don't burn. Transfer the seeds to a plate to cool to room temperature.

Toast the flaxseeds in a small sauté pan over medium heat without moving them for 1 to 2 minutes, until they start to pop in the pan. Shake the pan so the seeds don't burn and continue to cook the seeds for 2 to 3 minutes, shaking the pan often, until they darken in color and start to release a nutty aroma. Transfer the seeds to a plate to cool to room temperature.

Remove and discard the outer leaves from the radicchio and cut out and discard the core. Separate the leaves, stack 2 or 3 leaves at a time on top of one another, and slice ¼ inch thick lengthwise.

Trim and discard the root ends and any wilted greens from the scallions. Slice the white parts of the scallions 1/16 inch thick on an extreme bias and discard the remaining greens.

Put the farro, quinoa, wild rice, fregola, sesame seeds, flaxseeds, radicchio, bacon, and scallions in a large bowl. Drizzle the lemon juice and sprinkle the remaining 1/2 teaspoon salt over the salad. Toss gently to combine the salad ingredients and to coat them with the lemon and salt. Drizzle 1/2 cup of the lemon vinaigrette over the salad and toss gently to combine the ingredients and coat them with the vinaigrette. Transfer the salad to a large wide-mouthed serving bowl or rimmed platter and serve with a large spoon.

Roasted Carrots and Chickpeas with Cumin Vinaigrette

FOR THE VINAIGRETTE

¼ cup cumin seeds

¼ cup red wine vinegar

1 tablespoon fresh lemon juice

2 teaspoons kosher salt

7 to 9 medium or large garlic cloves, peeled

¾ cup extra-virgin olive oil

FOR THE CARROTS

2 pounds slender carrots (about 3 bunches)

3 tablespoons olive oil

3 teaspoons kosher salt

1 teaspoon fresh coarsely ground black pepper

10 fresh thyme sprigs

The first restaurant job I had was as a server at a small café in Sonoma County, where I went to college, called A Chez Nous, run by an Algerian family: the mom, dad, and son, Hubert. The only dish I remember from that restaurant experience was the freebie that we served to every table, which was a small plate of shredded carrots tossed with a lot of olive oil, lemon juice, and cumin. At the time, it must have been the most exotic flavor combination I'd ever had, and I loved it. It has remained ingrained in me, and since then, every time I think about what I want to do with carrots, the first thing that comes to mind is cumin. I try other things, but the cumin always wins out.

The carrots I use to make this are slender carrots, which are sold with the tops on at farmers' markets. If you can't make a trip to the farmers' market, buy the slenderest carrots you can find from the supermarket. If you find bunches of rainbow carrots, note that each color requires a different cooking time. Bunch rainbow carrots together by color on the baking sheet and pull each color off the sheet as it is done; dark red carrots usually take the longest.

To make the vinaigrette, toast the cumin seeds in a small sauté pan over medium heat for 1 to 2 minutes, until the seeds are fragrant and golden brown, shaking the pan often so they don't burn. Transfer the seeds to a plate to cool to room temperature. Grind the cumin seeds in a spice grinder or use a mortar and a pestle.

Combine the vinegar, lemon juice, salt, and 1 tablespoon plus 1 teaspoon of the ground cumin in a medium bowl. (Reserve the remaining ground cumin for seasoning the carrots.) Using a fine Microplane, grate the garlic directly into the bowl and whisk to thoroughly combine the ingredients. Add the olive oil in a slow, steady stream, whisking constantly to emulsify.

To prepare the carrots, adjust the oven racks so none are near the oven floor; you'll be putting a baking sheet directly on the oven floor. If you are using an electric oven or another oven where you can't put anything on the floor, adjust the oven racks so that one is closest to the floor and put a pizza stone on it, if you have one. Preheat the oven to 500°F.

Scrub the carrots and cut off the greens, leaving the last ¾-inch of the stems attached. Cut the carrots in half lengthwise (or quarter them if you're using larger carrots) and put them on a large baking sheet. Drizzle the carrots with the olive oil, sprinkle with the salt, pepper, and the remaining ground cumin (about 2 tablespoons plus 2 teaspoons) and toss to coat. Add the thyme sprigs and toss again to distribute. Arrange the carrots and thyme so the carrots are cut side down in a single layer with the thyme sprigs scattered over them. Put the baking sheet on the floor of the oven or the lowest rack and roast the carrots until they are fork-tender but not mushy, 10 to 15 minutes, shaking the baking sheet and rotating it front to back halfway through the cooking time so the carrots brown evenly. (When cooking vegetables on the oven floor, a lot of steam is produced from the water released as a result of the vegetables cooking so quickly, so be careful of the steam that will arise when you open the oven door.) Remove the carrots from the oven and set them aside to cool to room temperature. Remove and discard the thyme sprigs and transfer the carrots to a large bowl.

Meanwhile, to prepare the salad, cut the onion half in half root to tip so it is quartered. Separate the layers of the onion, stack 2 or 3 layers at a time on top of one another, and slice ¹⁄₁₆ inch thick lengthwise. Place the onion slices in a small bowl of ice water and set them aside while you prepare the rest of the ingredients for the salad or for at least 10 minutes.

Add the chickpeas and parsley to the bowl with the carrots. Drain the onion slices, pat them dry with paper towels, and add them to the bowl with the carrots and chickpeas. Drizzle the lemon juice and vinaigrette into the bowl with the carrots and chickpeas and toss gently to coat the carrots and chickpeas. Set aside for 15 minutes to marinate.

Five to 10 minutes before serving, using your hands or a slotted spoon, lift the salad out of the bowl and put it on a plate. Leave the excess vinaigrette in the bowl and reserve it for another use. Let the salad sit on the plate for 5 minutes to let the excess vinaigrette drain out.

To serve, using your hands, lift the carrots and chickpeas off the plate on which they were draining and pile them attractively on a large rimmed platter. Serve with a big spoon.

FOR THE SALAD

½ small red onion (halved root to tip), peeled and root end trimmed and discarded

1 cup cooked chickpeas (see White Beans, page 36, or from a can), drained

Heaping ¼ cup thinly sliced fresh Italian parsley leaves (from 1 heaping cup packed whole leaves)

1 tablespoon fresh lemon juice

Blistered Green Beans with Yogurt Dressing

SERVES 6 TO 8

6 large shallots (about 12 ounces), peeled

1½ pounds haricots verts (or another tender, tiny green or yellow wax bean)

¼ cup plus 2 tablespoons olive oil

2½ teaspoons kosher salt

1 recipe Yogurt Dressing (page 170)

1 lemon

At one time in the culinary history of the green bean, blistering them as I do here would have been considered an unconventional preparation. Green beans were usually blanched, which maintains and even brightens their color, whereas in this preparation, the beans are charred until they have a black tinge and are starting to shrivel. It must be the perfect nightmare to a classically trained chef. I appreciate both schools, but charring the beans is definitely more my style. First, it's a lot simpler: toss them in oil, throw them on a baking sheet, and put them in the oven. Blanching takes a bit more time and a lot more attention. Blistering them doesn't change the flavor drastically the way it does with some vegetables, such as cauliflower and winter squash, but I really like the rustic look of the charred beans. Where blanching them feels more French, charring them feels more like what an Italian would do, and we all know that I'm a wanna-be Italian. The shallots that are tossed with the beans make a pretty and flavorful addition; they're cut so the layers stay together and, when tossed with the beans, fan out among them. The beans are drizzled with a lemony yogurt dressing, with additional dressing served on the side. The entire presentation is just very refreshing and definitely a crowd-pleaser. The dressing makes enough for twice as many vegetables as this recipe calls for. If you're a vegetable lover as I am, double the shallot and green bean portions of this recipe and enjoy the leftovers.

Adjust the oven racks so none are near the oven floor; you'll be putting the baking sheet directly on the oven floor. If you are using an electric oven or another oven where you can't put anything on the floor, adjust the oven racks so that one is closest to the floor and put a pizza stone on it, if you have one. Preheat the oven to 500°F.

Trim the very ends of the roots of the shallots, leaving as much as possible so the layers of the shallots stay intact. Cut the shallots in half root to tip. Lay each half cut side down and cut each half into thirds root to tip. Trim and discard the stem end of the beans, leaving the "tail" end attached.

Put the shallots and green beans on a large baking sheet, drizzle with the olive oil, sprinkle with 2 teaspoons of the salt, and toss to coat the vegetables. Spread the shallots and beans in a single layer with the flat sides of the shallots facing down. Put the baking sheet on the floor of the oven or the lowest rack and roast until the beans are tender and blistered in places but not soggy, 10 to 12 minutes, shaking the baking sheet and rotating it from front to back halfway through the cooking time so the vegetables cook evenly. (When cooking vegetables on the oven floor, a lot of steam is produced from the water released as a result of the vegetables cooking so quickly, so be careful of the steam that will arise when you open the oven door.) Remove the baking sheet from the oven and set it aside for the vegetables to cool to room temperature.

Transfer the green beans and shallots to a large mixing bowl, sprinkle with the remaining ½ teaspoon salt, and toss gently, taking care not to break up the shallots. Drizzle ¼ cup of the yogurt dressing, like abstract art, over the vegetables and toss just a couple of times to distribute the vinaigrette but not so much that the vegetables are evenly coated; you want to see the color of the beans peeking through.

To serve, using your hands, lift one-third of the vegetables out of the bowl and pile them onto a medium serving platter or in a medium wide bowl. Drizzle 2 tablespoons of the remaining dressing over the vegetables, then pile another one-third of the vegetables onto the platter. Drizzle another 2 tablespoons of the remaining dressing on the salad, then pile the remaining vegetables on the platter. Drizzle 1 tablespoon of the remaining dressing over the top of the salad and transfer the remaining dressing to a small pretty bowl. Using a fine Microplane, grate a thin layer of lemon zest over the salad, and serve with tongs and the remaining dressing on the side with a spoon for guests to drizzle more on if they wish.

14

Eggplant Lasagne

Lasagne is a perfect party dish because it can be prepared in advance and heated up when guests arrive. Plus, who doesn't like lasagne? As much as I love a well-prepared, traditional lasagne Bolognese, if I'm going to serve it at home, I want it to be vegetarian, should the rare vegetarian friend happen to arrive. This eggplant lasagne is not the typical vegetarian version with a mishmash of vegetables, but a hybrid of eggplant Parmesan and classic lasagne. Because eggplant has a satisfying, meaty quality to it that broccoli and zucchini do not possess, even a meat lover such as myself doesn't miss the meat. This takes some time and effort to make, but it has a good payoff. When you serve this rich dish, you don't have to serve a lot of other items. For a casual Sunday dinner with friends, all you need is a salad.

The eggplant is seasoned with za'atar, a Middle Eastern spice blend made of dried herbs, sumac, and sesame seeds. Za'atar is not something I normally use, but it turns out to be the perfect complement to both the eggplant and the tomato sauce in this recipe. Look for za'atar that doesn't contain salt; if the za'atar you use does contain salt, hold back slightly on the salt called for in this recipe and add more to taste. And if you can't find za'atar, substitute dried oregano.

We cut the lasagne before it goes into the oven, a trick we learned from the great Italian chef Gino Angelini, who is famous in Los Angeles for his lasagne Bolognese. Gino taught us that cutting the lasagne before it goes into the oven ensures clean, even portions; it also prevents the entire top layer of cheese from sliding off with the first piece served.

You will need a 13 x 9-inch or other similarly sized baking dish to make this—ideally, something pretty enough so that you feel comfortable taking it to the table. If you have a mandoline, use it to make easy work of slicing the garlic for this recipe.

––––––––––

To prepare the eggplants, adjust the oven racks so none are near the oven floor; you'll be putting the baking sheet directly on the oven floor. If you are using an electric oven or another oven where you can't put anything on the floor, adjust the oven racks so that one is closest to the floor and put a pizza stone on it, if you have one. Preheat the oven to 500°F.

SERVES 9 TO 12

FOR THE EGGPLANTS

2 large eggplants (2 to 2½ pounds)

1 cup extra-virgin olive oil

3½ teaspoons kosher salt

½ cup large garlic cloves (about 20 cloves), peeled and sliced ¹⁄₁₆ inch thick lengthwise, preferably on a mandoline

1 (28-ounce) can crushed tomatoes (preferably San Marzano)

1½ teaspoons sugar

½ cup pitted small black olives (such as Taggiasche, Niçoise, or Kalamata; about 3 ounces)

3 tablespoons za'atar (or dried oregano)

½ teaspoon freshly ground black pepper

¼ teaspoon red chile flakes

FOR THE CHEESE SAUCE

½ large yellow Spanish onion (halved root to tip), peeled

4 tablespoons (½ stick) unsalted butter

1 árbol chile pod

2 bay leaves (preferably fresh)

¼ cup unbleached all-purpose flour

(continued)

1 quart whole milk

2 teaspoons kosher salt

12 ounces shredded low-moisture mozzarella (about 3 cups)

8 ounces fresh ricotta (about 1 cup)

½ cup finely grated Parmigiano-Reggiano (about 2 ounces)

2 extra-large eggs, lightly beaten

FOR THE PASTA AND ASSEMBLING THE LASAGNE

6 tablespoons kosher salt

1 (16-ounce) package dried lasagna noodles

Olive oil, if needed

1 cup finely grated Parmigiano-Reggiano (about 4 ounces)

Trim and discard the tip and stem ends of the eggplants and cut the eggplants into 1-inch cubes. Divide the eggplants between two large baking sheets. Drizzle each portion with ¼ cup plus 2 tablespoons of the olive oil. Toss and gently massage the cubes to coat the eggplants. Spread the eggplant cubes out in a single layer on the baking sheets. Cooking one batch at a time, put one baking sheet on the oven floor or the lowest rack and cook for 15 to 20 minutes, until the cubes are dark brown all over and beginning to lose their shape, rotating the baking sheet from front to back and moving the cubes with a metal spatula halfway through the cooking time so they don't stick to the baking sheet. (When cooking vegetables on the oven floor as you do in this recipe, a lot of steam is produced from the water released as a result of the vegetables cooking so quickly, so just be careful of the steam that will arise when you open the oven door.) Remove the baking sheet from the oven, season with 1 teaspoon of the salt, and set aside. Cook the second batch of eggplant in the same way. Remove the baking sheet from the oven, season the cubes with 1 teaspoon of the salt, and set aside.

Combine the garlic and the remaining ¼ cup oil in a large Dutch oven or another large high-sided pot over medium heat. Cook until the garlic is soft and very light golden brown, stirring constantly so it doesn't burn, about 5 minutes. Add the tomatoes, sugar, and the remaining 1½ teaspoons salt, stir to combine, and cook the tomatoes for 5 to 6 minutes, until they thicken slightly. Spoon out and reserve ½ cup of the tomato sauce. Add the roasted eggplants, olives, za'atar, pepper, and red chile flakes. Stir to combine and cook until the eggplants have taken on the color of the sauce, about 5 minutes, adding ½ cup to ¾ cup water if the sauce is dry and sticky. Turn off the heat and set aside while you make the cheese sauce.

To make the cheese sauce, trim and discard the root end of the onion half. Cut the onion half in half again root to tip so the onion is quartered. Separate the layers of the onion, stack 2 or 3 layers at a time on top of one another, and slice ¼ inch thick lengthwise.

Combine the butter, onion, chile pod, and bay leaves in a medium heavy-bottomed saucepan over medium-low heat. Cook, stirring often, until the butter is melted and the onion is soft but not brown, about 10 minutes, stirring often to prevent the onion from browning. Add the flour, whisking constantly to remove any lumps, and cook for 2 minutes to cook off the flour flavor. Gradually add 1 cup of the milk, whisking constantly to prevent lumps. Increase the heat to high and cook the sauce, whisking constantly, until it begins to thicken, about 1 minute. Add another cup of the remaining milk, whisking constantly. Return the sauce to a boil and add the remaining 2 cups milk, whisking constantly. Return the sauce to a boil, reduce the heat to low, and simmer, whisking or stirring constantly, until the sauce is thick enough to coat the back of a spoon, 3 to 4 minutes.

Turn off the heat and stir in the salt. Pour the sauce through a fine-mesh strainer into a medium bowl and discard the contents of the strainer. Ladle out 1 cup of the white sauce (this is a béchamel) and set it aside. Add the mozzarella, ricotta, Parmigiano, and eggs to the bowl with the remaining béchamel and gently whisk to integrate the additions into the sauce.

Meanwhile, to cook the pasta and assemble the lasagne, adjust the oven racks so one is in the middle position. Unless the broiler is in a different section of the oven, put another rack closest to the broiler. Preheat the oven to 350°F.

Combine 6 quarts water and 6 tablespoons salt in a a large soup or pasta pot and bring to a boil over high heat. If you are not using a pasta pot, place a colander in the sink. Prepare an ice bath in a large bowl and create a large bed with paper towels or clean dish towels to lay the pasta on after it's cooked.

Drop the lasagna into the boiling water and stir to prevent the sheets of pasta from sticking together. Boil the pasta using the time indicated on the package instructions as a guide, until it's al dente. Quickly drain the pasta in the colander or lift out the pasta pot insert. Immediately transfer the pasta to the ice water to cool completely; this is especially important when making baked pasta such as this because the pasta will cook more when you bake the lasagne. Lift the noodles out of the ice bath with your hands and lay the sheets of pasta in a single layer on the towels to dry. Lightly oil the noodles before placing a second layer on top if you need to stack them. Pat the top sides dry with paper towels.

Spread the ½ cup reserved tomato sauce over the bottom of a 13 x 9-inch baking dish. Lay 3 sheets of lasagna on the bottom of the pan to cover it. Add half of the tomato and eggplant sauce (about 2½ cups) and use a wooden spoon or rubber spatula to spread it evenly over the pasta. Spoon half of the cheese sauce over the sauce and use another clean spoon or spatula to spread it in an even layer to the edges and into the corners of the pan. Lay 3 sheets of lasagna on top of the cheese sauce. Press gently down on the pasta sheets with the palms of your hands to ensure that the layers are flat and even, and that there aren't any air bubbles in the lasagna. Spoon the remaining tomato and eggplant sauce on top of the pasta and spread it out as you did the first layer. Spoon the remaining cheese sauce over the tomato and eggplant sauce and spread it out to cover as you did the first layer. Lay a final layer of pasta on top of the cheese sauce. You can make the lasagne to this point up to 1 day in advance. Cover the pan and refrigerate the lasagne until you're ready to bake it, but note that it will take a bit longer to cook.

Using a rubber spatula, gently spread the reserved béchamel evenly over the top of the lasagne and sprinkle the Parmigiano over the béchamel. Using a long sharp knife, cut the lasagne into 9 or 12 equal-size servings.

Put the lasagne on a baking sheet and put it in the oven to bake for 35 to 45 minutes, until the edges are golden brown and puffed up a bit, rotating the pan from front to back halfway through the baking time so the lasagne browns evenly.

Turn the oven to the broiler setting.

Remove the lasagne from the oven and set it aside for 5 to 10 minutes to pre-heat the broiler.

Put the lasagne on the rack closest to the broiler or to the broiler section of the oven and cook until the top is golden brown around the edges, 5 to 10 minutes; check the lasagne often while it is under the broiler because broilers vary greatly and the lasagne could quickly go from brown to burned. Remove the lasagne from the oven and let it cool for at least 1 hour before serving.

Serve the lasagne in the dish it was cooked in, with a spatula for guests to dig out a portion for themselves.

Prosciutto Mozzarella Parcels

Prosciutto and fresh mozzarella are nothing new together, but with the prosciutto slices wrapped around the cheese into neat little packages as they are here, the common pairing is transformed into a special, two-bite treat. The first time I made these, I found myself suddenly enthusiastic about a combination I'd eaten a million times before. The parcels are a nice way to serve mozzarella as a party appetizer because guests can easily grab one and pop it into their mouths—no fork, knife, or plate necessary. I drizzle the platter that the parcels are served on with olive oil and a few drops of balsamico, which is just enough to make the flavors come alive.

When shopping for this recipe, buy prosciutto that is sliced paper thin to order rather than presliced, packaged prosciutto. You don't want the slices so thin that they tear into shreds when you lift them off the paper they're wrapped in, but you want them thin enough that they roll easily and are easy to eat. Having the person behind the deli counter hand you a slice of prosciutto to inspect (and eat!) is one of the great perks of shopping for prosciutto. Use a midlevel balsamic for this; not a super-expensive *condimento*-level balsamic, but one that is thick and viscous, not watery.

**SERVES UP TO 16
MAKES 16 PARCELS**

8 thin prosciutto slices
(about ¼ pound)

1 pound fresh mozzarella
(cow's milk mozzarella, burrata,
or mozzarella di bufala), cut into
16 (1-ounce) pieces

1 pound wild arugula
(or baby arugula)

3 lemons

1 tablespoon finishing-quality
extra-virgin olive oil, or as needed,
plus the bottle of oil to serve on
the side

2 teaspoons balsamic vinegar,
plus the bottle of vinegar to serve
on the side

Maldon sea salt (or another flaky
sea salt such as fleur de sel)

Choose a platter on which the parcels will fit snugly in a single layer.

Tear a slice of prosciutto in half lengthwise and wrap it around a piece of cheese. Put the cheese parcel, seam side down, on a cutting board or countertop, which will help to keep the parcel together. Continue wrapping the remaining cheese with the remaining prosciutto slices in the same way.

Put the arugula in a large wooden bowl. Cut the lemons in half through the stems and cut each half lengthwise into 3 wedges. Put the lemons in a small pretty bowl.

To serve, drizzle the olive oil and balsamic vinegar on the platter, using more of each for a larger platter. Transfer the cheese parcels, seam side down, to the platter, nestling them closely together. Scatter a handful of arugula over the parcels. Serve the platter of cheese parcels with the bowls of arugula, lemon wedges, the bottles of olive oil and balsamic vinegar, and a little bowl or box of sea salt on the side for guests to make their own salads to go with the cheese parcels.

Radicchio Salad with Bacon and Egg

SERVES 6 TO 8

1 pound slab bacon, cut into 1-inch-wide, 1½-inch-long, ¼-inch-thick pieces (or ½ pound thick-sliced bacon, slices left whole)

1 pound radicchio (about 2 large heads)

2 tablespoons fresh lemon juice

2 teaspoons kosher salt

¾ cup Lemon Vinaigrette (page 125)

5 large hard-cooked eggs (4 for the salad plus 1 tester egg; see Perfect Hard-Cooked Eggs, page 82)

Wedge of pecorino Romano for grating

Freshly ground black pepper

2 tablespoons minced fresh chives (from about 10 whole chives; optional)

As a chef and restaurateur, I often get my inspiration from eating in restaurants, but it's rare that I try something that I want to copy exactly. I usually see an idea that I like but I want to add or take out an ingredient, or to alter the way it's presented. That was not the case with this salad. I ordered it at a restaurant in Portland, Oregon, Tasty n Alder, where I was having lunch with my friend Margy Rochlin when we were visiting my son, Oliver, who attends Reed College there. The salad was served in a big glass bowl, so you could see the pretty, contrasting colors of radicchio, hard-cooked eggs, and bacon all layered in the bowl. I loved the way it looked, and after I took the first bite, I knew it was a winner. I snapped a picture and said to Margy, "I'm putting that salad on the Pizzeria menu." It's like an Italian cousin to the frisée salad with lardons and poached egg served at every French bistro on the planet, but because radicchio is Italian, I felt justified in offering this salad at a pizzeria.

If I were having a meal of just a salad (which I often do), I would choose this salad. The bacon and egg make it feel substantial, and the flavor combination is so satisfying that I wouldn't wish I had something else to eat. With a slice of Fett'unta (page 274) and a glass of red wine, it would be a perfect meal. If you served it with Avocado Toasts (page 141) in place of fett'unta, you'd have something like a deconstructed Cobb salad.

Ideally, you'll be able to track down slab bacon from a butcher or another specialty source, but if not, thick-cut bacon will have to do. In either case, you want to cook the bacon so that it's meaty and chewy—not leathery or crispy. (Thinner slices of bacon won't give you the meatiness of slab bacon, no matter how perfectly you cook it.) Also, don't worry if there's a pool of dressing at the bottom of the bowl after you toss the salad; this is a salad that needs to be overdressed. The radicchio needs the salt and other flavors in the dressing to counter its bitterness, and the pecorino soaks up a lot of the dressing, so if there isn't enough, the salad will be dry. At the Pizzeria, we top the salad with minced chives, but I made them optional here. If you have them, great—they add a nice splash of color—but if you don't, no need to run out and buy them just for this.

Adjust an oven rack to the middle position and preheat the oven to 350°F.

Prepare a bed of paper towels. If you are using slab bacon, lay the bacon pieces in a single layer on a baking sheet and put the bacon in the oven to cook for 30 to 35 minutes, until it is cooked through, chewy, and golden in places but not crispy, turning each piece of bacon with tongs and rotating the baking sheet from front to back halfway through the cooking time so the bacon cooks evenly. Remove the bacon from the oven and set it aside to cool to room temperature. If you are using thick-cut bacon, lay the bacon on a baking sheet and bake until it is cooked all the way through but not crisp, 15 to 17 minutes, rotating the baking sheet from front to back halfway through the cooking time so the bacon cooks evenly. Remove the bacon from the oven and transfer it to the paper towels to drain and cool to room temperature. Cut the bacon slices into 2-inch lengths and set aside.

Remove and discard the outer limp leaves from the radicchio. Cut each head in half and cut out and discard the cores. Cut each half in half again to create 4 wedges from each head, and cut each wedge in half crosswise to create roughly 2-inch squares. Put the radicchio in a large bowl. Drizzle the lemon juice and sprinkle the salt over the radicchio and toss to coat the leaves. Add ½ cup of the lemon vinaigrette and toss to coat, massaging the vinaigrette into the leaves with your hands and adding another ¼ cup vinaigrette halfway through tossing.

To serve, scatter one-third of the radicchio onto the bottom of a large shallow bowl or platter. Break 2 of the eggs into thirds (first break them in half, then break the larger half in half to create 3 pieces), and nestle the 6 pieces over the first layer of radicchio, trying to keep the yolks and whites together as much as possible. Nestle a third of the bacon around the eggs. Using a fine Microplane, grate a healthy layer of pecorino over the salad. Repeat, building two more layers of radicchio, egg, and bacon. Finish the salad with a thin grating of the cheese so it looks like a blanket of snow light enough that you can still see everything the "snow" is covering through it. Grind a generous amount of pepper over the salad. If you are using chives, snip them into 2-inch pieces directly over the top. Serve with tongs and place the wedge of pecorino and the Microplane on a plate next to the salad for guests to grate more cheese on their portions.

15

Backyard Peel 'n' Eat Shrimp Boil 258

Celery Root Remoulade with Fresh Horseradish and Toasted Almonds 260

Remoulade 262

Green Potato Leek Salad with Scallion Vinaigrette 263

Corn on the Cob with Chile Butter 266

Other Menu Options

Pimento Cheese with Celery Sticks 328

Husk-Style Pickled Green Beans 332

Pickled Carrots 333

Pickled Shallots 334

Tabasco Mayonnaise, Sriracha Mayonnaise, Old Bay Mayonnaise 85

Potato Chips with Atomic Horseradish Cream 155

Twice-Roasted Smashed Potatoes with Rosemary and Sage 97

Corn and Fava Bean Succotash Salad 205

Coleslaw with Green Goddess Dressing 338

Backyard Peel 'n' Eat Shrimp Boil

SERVES 8 TO 10

3 to 6 pounds fresh large shrimp in the shells (preferably 16/20 per pound)

3 limes

1 cup champagne vinegar (or white wine vinegar)

1 large yellow Spanish onion, peeled and quartered root to tip (root end intact)

1 carrot, cut in half

1 celery stalk, cut in half

10 to 12 medium or large garlic cloves, peeled

2 tablespoons plus 1 teaspoon kosher salt

2 tablespoons celery seeds

2 tablespoons fennel seeds

2 tablespoons black peppercorns

12 fresh thyme sprigs

2 árbol chile pods

15 dried bay leaves

OPTIONAL DIPPING SAUCES

Old Bay Mayonnaise (page 85)

Dill Mayonnaise (page 85)

Remoulade (page 262)

Sriracha Mayonnaise (page 85)

Tabasco Mayonnaise (page 85)

I like to work for my food, whether it's shelling peanuts over an *aperitivo* at Bar Gallo in the piazza in Panicale, or digging into a platter of peel 'n' eat shrimp like these. I also like the warm, casual atmosphere that comes with serving foods that guests have to eat with their hands. When everyone is up to their elbows in shrimp shells, there's really no putting on airs. For these shrimp, Liz and I created a flavorful poaching liquid using the ingredients that we read from the back of the can of Old Bay, the classic crab boil spice blend, and applied it to shrimp, which are both easier to cook and to eat than crab. This is one of the few meals in this book that I don't serve buffet style. Instead, I plop it down in the center of my long patio table and let my friends sit around peeling and dipping away. I use my favorite outdoor metal plates because they seem to fit the vibe, but you could mimic the classic shrimp boil: cover the table with newspaper, dump the shrimp out onto it, and serve the meal without any plates or bowls for shells. When you're done, just wrap up the newspaper with all the remnants of the feast and throw it away.

You can cook three to six pounds of shrimp using this recipe, without changing the seasonings. Count on a half pound per person.

Using a small knife, make a slit through the shell down the back of each shrimp and pull out and discard the veins.

Put 5 cups water in a large soup pot or stockpot. Using a fine Microplane, grate the zest from the limes into the pot. Cut the limes in half, squeeze the juice into the pot, and drop the juiced lime halves into the pot. Add the vinegar, onion, carrot, celery, garlic, salt, celery seeds, fennel seeds, peppercorns, thyme sprigs, and chile pods to the pot. Using your hands, crush the bay leaves over the pot so they crumble into the pot. Bring the liquid to a boil over high heat, reduce the heat to low, and simmer for 30 to 40 minutes to steep the liquid with the seasonings. Increase the heat to high and return the liquid to a boil. Add the shrimp and cook them for 3 minutes. Drain the shrimp in a colander. Pick the shrimp out of the colander, transfer them to a bowl, and discard the contents of the colander. Put the shrimp in the refrigerator to cool completely. (This method of chilling the shrimp prevents them from overcooking without washing away the seasonings as it would if you were to plunge the shrimp into an ice bath or run them under cold water.)

To serve, line your patio or picnic table with newspapers and dump the shrimp in a large pile on the papers, or transfer the shrimp to a large platter and put the platter in the middle of your dining table. Set bowls with your choices of dipping sauces around the shrimp and serve with small bowls for people to put discarded shells in, and lots of napkins for guests to wipe their hands with.

Celery Root Remoulade with Fresh Horseradish and Toasted Almonds

SERVES 6 TO 8

¾ cup whole almonds with skins

1 tablespoon extra-virgin olive oil

2¼ teaspoons kosher salt

1½ pounds celery root

2 tablespoons fresh lemon juice

Remoulade (recipe follows)

1 (3- to 4-inch) piece fresh horseradish (about 2 ounces)

Classic celery root remoulade is a traditional French bistro dish of julienned celery root tossed in Dijonnaise. These days, you most often see celery root remoulade served as a condiment alongside crab cakes or something else that begs for mayonnaise. But I hadn't had this dish for ages until fairly recently, when I walked across the street from Mozza to the twenty-seat bistro Petit Trois. I'd ordered an omelet for lunch, and the chef, Ludovic Lefebvre, sent me a plate of celery root remoulade to enjoy with it. Until that plate arrived, I'd completely forgotten that traditionally celery root remoulade was served on its own, as an appetizer, and, in fact, I may have forgotten about celery root remoulade altogether. At Petit Trois, they added toasted almonds and topped the celery root with a blanket of grated fresh horseradish. I was completely taken with the thought of these two knobby roots sitting side by side in the kitchen in order to make the dish, and the two also tasted delicious together. After lunch, I marched right back across the street, determined to make my own version of this classic, borrowing Ludo's ideas for both the almonds and the horseradish. I added pickle, onion, capers, and fresh herbs to the mayonnaise both for the added flavors and so that I could say that I didn't copy Ludo's dish exactly. Nevertheless, *merci*, Ludo!

The recipe for the remoulade, or, dressing, makes almost double what you will need for the salad. Better to have some left than not to have enough. Use the leftover dressing to make a similar salad or on a sandwich in place of mayonnaise within two days. I serve this salad in a wide-mouthed bowl or on the biggest platter I can get my hands on. The wider the bowl or larger the platter, the larger the surface area onto which to grate a larger blanket of horseradish.

You will need a mandoline to slice the celery root for this recipe.

Adjust an oven rack to the middle position and preheat the oven to 325°F.

Spread the almonds on a baking sheet and toast them in the oven for 12 to 15 minutes, until they are fragrant and golden brown, shaking the baking sheet and rotating it from front to back halfway through the cooking time so the nuts brown evenly. Remove the almonds from the oven and set aside until they are

cool enough to touch. Drizzle with the olive oil, sprinkle with ¼ teaspoon of the salt, and toss to coat. Finely chop the almonds and set aside.

Peel the celery root with a vegetable peeler. Using a mandoline, slice the celery root ¼ inch thick. Stack a few slices at a time and cut the slices into ¼-inch-wide matchsticks with a knife. Repeat with the remaining slices of celery root.

Combine the celery root and almonds in a large bowl. Drizzle with the lemon juice, sprinkle with the remaining 2 teaspoons salt, and toss gently to combine the ingredients and coat the celery root and nuts. Add 1½ cups of the remoulade and toss to coat, adding the remaining dressing if necessary to coat the celery root.

To serve, pile the celery root remoulade in a wide-mouthed bowl or on a large rimmed platter. Using a Microplane, grate a thick layer of horseradish over the top and serve with tongs.

Remoulade

Makes about 1½ cups

We use this as a dressing for Celery Root Remoulade, and it also makes a terrific dipping sauce for Backyard Peel 'n' Eat Shrimp Boil (page 258).

1 recipe Garlic Mayonnaise (page 84)

1 tablespoon finely chopped fresh Italian parsley leaves (from about 2 tablespoons packed whole leaves)

1 tablespoon finely chopped fresh tarragon leaves (from about 2 tablespoons packed whole leaves)

⅛ cup minced red onion

⅛ cup minced cornichon (also called baby gherkin; or another sour pickle; about 1 cornichon)

1½ teaspoons minced fresh chives (from 2 to 3 whole chives)

1 tablespoon capers (preferably salt-packed; soaked for 15 minutes if salt-packed), rinsed, drained, and finely chopped

¾ teaspoon Dijon mustard

Combine the mayonnaise, parsley, tarragon, onion, cornichon, chives, capers, and mustard in a medium bowl and stir with a whisk to thoroughly combine the ingredients. You can make the remoulade up to 2 days in advance. Refrigerate, covered, until you're ready to use it.

Green Potato Leek Salad with Scallion Vinaigrette

Potatoes and leeks form a perfect marriage in the classic vichyssoise, or, potato leek soup, and likewise, they meld together beautifully in this salad. I call it green potato salad because the scallion vinaigrette turns the potatoes a very appealing, bright shade of green. This potato salad is lighter compared with more traditional, mayonnaise-based potato salad such as Erik Black's Potato Salad (page 340). It makes great picnic food, because it can be left at room temperature longer than a mayonnaise-based potato salad.

———

To make the vinaigrette, trim and discard the root ends and any wilted greens from the scallions. Roughly chop the scallions and put them in a food processor fitted with a metal blade or in a blender. Add the vinegar and pulse until the scallions are muddled, like mint in a glass for a cocktail, but not puréed. Transfer the scallion-vinegar mixture to a medium bowl and stir in the salt. Add the olive oil in a slow, steady stream, whisking constantly.

To make the salad, trim and discard the hairy ends and the tough, dark green outer layers of the leeks. Cut the leeks in half lengthwise. Cut each halved leek crosswise into 3-inch segments. Flatten each segment and cut each segment lengthwise into ½-inch-wide strips. Wash the leeks thoroughly.

Fill a medium saucepan with water, bring the water to a boil over high heat, and salt it to taste like the ocean, adding 1 tablespoon salt to each quart of water. Prepare an ice bath in a medium bowl and prepare a bed of paper towels.

Put the leeks in the boiling water and blanch for 1 minute. Drain the leeks and plunge them into the ice bath for about 1 minute to cool. Drain the leeks from the ice bath, pick out the ice, and squeeze the leeks in your fists to release the excess water. Transfer the leeks to the paper towels and set aside for at least 5 minutes to drain completely.

Put the leeks in a small bowl, sprinkle with 1½ teaspoons of the salt, and drizzle with ½ cup of the vinaigrette. Massage the salt and vinaigrette into the leeks with your fingers and run your fingers through the leeks to separate them as you would to untangle your hair.

Steam the potatoes until they are tender when pierced with a small knife,

SERVES 8 TO 10

FOR THE VINAIGRETTE

½ pound scallions
(about 3 bunches)

½ cup plus 2 tablespoons
champagne vinegar
(or white wine vinegar)

2 teaspoons kosher salt

1 cup extra-virgin olive oil

FOR THE SALAD

½ pound leeks

2 tablespoons kosher salt,
plus more for the blanching water

3 pounds small, thin-skinned,
waxy potatoes (such as small red
rose, fingerlings, or Yukon gold),
not peeled

1 cup minced fresh chives
(from one ¾-ounce clamshell)

1 packed cup fresh Italian parsley
leaves, roughly chopped

about 20 minutes. Remove the potatoes to a plate until they are cool enough to touch. Use a small knife to remove and discard the peel from the potatoes.

Break the potatoes with your hands into 1-inch pieces and let them drop into a medium bowl. Add the chives, parsley, and leeks, including any marinade left in the bowl the leeks were marinated in. Add the remaining 1½ tablespoons salt and ¾ cup of the remaining vinaigrette. Toss gently to coat the vegetables and to distribute the salt, being gentle with the potatoes to prevent them from breaking up too much and adding another ¼ cup or more vinaigrette as you toss the salad if the potatoes look dry.

To serve, transfer the potato salad to a large platter or serving bowl and serve with a large spoon.

Corn on the Cob with Chile Butter

SERVES 8

8 ounces (2 sticks) unsalted butter, softened at room temperature

1 teaspoon kosher salt

2 ounces Fresno chiles (about 3 chiles), halved (stems, seeds, and membranes removed and discarded)

1 medium or large garlic clove, peeled

8 ears corn on the cob

Maldon sea salt (or another flaky sea salt such as fleur de sel)

Nothing says "summer" to me more than grilled corn on the cob. In this recipe, the corn is dressed with a compound butter made with Fresno chiles, garlic, and salt. Make this only with delicious, farm-fresh corn when it's in season.

To turn this into Mexican-style corn on the cob, which I do when serving it with Sal's Roasted Pork Shoulder (page 48) or Garlic-Rubbed Skirt Steak with Scallion Vinaigrette (page 194), squeeze lime juice over the corn after it's cooked, roll it in finely grated Parmigiano or queso cotija, and top the corn with a dollop of crema (Mexican sour cream) or crème fraîche.

If you are not cooking these on an outdoor grill, you will need a square or rectangular grill pan such as a 20-inch Lodge reversible grill/griddle.

Put the butter and kosher salt in a medium bowl. Finely chop the chiles until they are almost pulverized. Scrape the chiles off the cutting board using the side of a knife to get even the smallest bits and add the chiles to the bowl with the butter. Using a fine Microplane, grate the garlic directly into the bowl and stir with a rubber spatula or wooden spoon until the additions are thoroughly incorporated. Set the butter aside if you are using it right away, or cover and refrigerate for up to 3 days. Soften it at room temperature before using it.

Pull back the husks from the corn and remove and discard the silks, leaving the husks attached. Slather the corn with chile butter, wrap the husks around the corn, leaving 1 inch of the corn kernels exposed, and tie the husks at the top with twine.

Prepare a hot fire in a charcoal or gas grill to high heat. Alternatively, preheat a cast-iron skillet or grill pan over high heat until it is smoking hot.

Put the corn on the grill or in the skillet and cook for 5 to 7 minutes, until the corn is cooked through, turning the corn to cook it evenly on all sides.

Remove the corn from the grill or skillet and put it on a large baking sheet. Peel the husks back to expose the kernels and leave the husks attached to use as a handle. Slather 1 tablespoon of the butter on each ear of corn and sprinkle generously with sea salt.

To serve, transfer the corn cobs to a long serving platter, no serving utensil necessary.

16

Lamb and Chicken Tikka Kebabs

SERVES 8

1½ pounds leg of lamb, trimmed of excess fat and sinew and cut into 2-inch cubes

½ recipe Tikka Marinade (page 106)

1½ pounds boneless, skinless chicken thighs, trimmed of excess fat and cut into 2-inch cubes

2 lemons

Olive oil for brushing the lemons

2 tablespoons plus 1 teaspoon kosher salt

Freshly ground black pepper

Finishing-quality extra-virgin olive oil

Maldon sea salt (or another flaky sea salt such as fleur de sel)

Anyone who knows me well knows that my secret last-minute dinner party "recipe" is takeout. But not just any takeout. When I want to have friends over and have absolutely no time to cook, I put together a spread curated from some favorite spots in Los Angeles, including wood-fired whole chickens, cut up, that I buy from a stand called Pollo alla Brasa, and a selection of side dishes from my favorite Middle Eastern restaurant, Carousel, in Hollywood. These skewers were inspired by those they serve at Carousel. Likewise, the Carousel sides were the inspiration for the side dishes that I serve with these kebabs.

Kebabs in general make great party food, because the meat is already portioned out and guests just grab one and move along. Kebabs also look nice on a platter, and the presentation stays neat and clean even as the number of kebabs diminishes. Because the meat is cut into small pieces, giving it more surface area, the tikka marinade used on these kebabs penetrates the pieces entirely, so the flavor isn't only on the surface of the meat. In this recipe, I call for half lamb and half chicken, but you can grill twice as much of just one type of meat if you wish. Or you can double the recipe easily; the recipe for the marinade makes enough to marinate twice the amount of meat called for in this recipe.

If you are not cooking these on an outdoor grill, you will need a square or rectangular grill pan such as a 20-inch Lodge reversible grill/griddle because you can fit only one skewer in a round grill pan. You will need 8 long (at least 10 inches) skewers, preferably metal, to make these. If you're using wooden skewers, soak them in water for at least 1 hour before assembling the kebabs.

Put the cubed lamb in a large bowl and spoon ¼ cup of the tikka marinade over it. Toss the lamb to coat the meat and gently massage the marinade into the meat with your hands. Put the cubed chicken in another bowl and spoon the remaining ¼ cup marinade over it. Toss to coat the chicken and massage the marinade into the chicken with your hands. Cover the bowls and set them aside for the meats to marinate for 30 minutes; any longer and the marinade will cause the meat to break down and give it an unappealing, fuzzy texture.

While the meat is marinating, cut the lemons in half through the middles and cut ½ inch off the pointed ends so each lemon half has two flat surfaces. Brush both cut ends of the lemon halves with olive oil.

Prepare a hot fire in a charcoal or gas grill. Alternatively, preheat a square or rectangular grill pan over high heat. Cooking method and times will be the same as for grilling.

Starting with the lamb, remove the meat from the bowl and put 5 cubes of meat (about 6 ounces) on each skewer, dividing the meat evenly among the skewers and putting similar-size pieces on the same skewer so they cook evenly. Put the skewers on a baking sheet as you finish them. When you've laced all the meat onto skewers, season the side facing up with 2 teaspoons of the kosher salt and grind a generous amount of pepper on them. Turn the skewers and season the other side with 2 teaspoons of the kosher salt and a generous grinding of pepper.

Repeat, lacing the chicken onto the remaining skewers in the same way. Season them with 1 teaspoon of the remaining kosher salt and a generous grinding of pepper on each side. (If you are cooking 3 pounds of only one type of meat, use all 4 teaspoons of salt on the one type of meat.)

Grill the lamb kebabs for 7 to 10 minutes for medium-rare, turning the kebabs with a metal spatula to brown all sides. The best way to test for doneness is to sacrifice a cube of lamb and cut into it. Remove the lamb kebabs from the grill and put them on a baking sheet.

Grill the chicken kebabs for 12 to 15 minutes, turning the kebabs with a metal spatula to brown all sides, until the juices run clear when the chicken is pierced with a small knife. The best way to test for doneness is to sacrifice a cube of chicken and cut into it. Remove the chicken kebabs from the grill or grill pan and put them on a baking sheet.

Meanwhile, place the lemon halves, with the larger, middle sides of the lemons facing down, on the grill or in the grill pan for about 2 minutes, until golden brown. Turn and cook the smaller sides of the lemon halves for about 30 seconds just to warm them.

To serve, lay the kebabs, separating the chicken from the lamb, on one or two large platters and nestle the lemon halves, middle cut sides up, around the kebabs. Drizzle the meat with finishing-quality olive oil, sprinkle with sea salt, and serve—no serving utensils necessary.

Fire-Roasted Eggplant Caviar

SERVES 8 OR MORE
MAKES ABOUT 1 QUART

3 pounds eggplants
(about 3 medium or 2 large
eggplants)

½ cup sherry vinegar

¼ cup minced shallot
(from about 1 medium peeled
shallot)

3 tablespoons fresh lemon juice

2 teaspoons sugar

2 tablespoons plus ¾ teaspoon
kosher salt

5 to 7 medium or large garlic
cloves, peeled

½ cup extra-virgin olive oil

12 to 15 fresh mint leaves

Garlic Crostini (page 275), Fett'unta
(page 274), or toasted pita bread

Eggplant caviar was something my mother served in the 1950s, the era of rumaki and Chinese chicken salad. It was a time in which there were far fewer cookbooks, fewer food magazines, no Internet, obviously, and in general, far fewer recipes and ideas to choose from. You can just imagine women such as my mother planning their cocktail party menus and running across something called eggplant caviar. How sophisticated and exotic that must have seemed! Since those days, I always knew that eggplant caviar referred to a purée of roasted eggplant, but it wasn't until last year, when I picked up Yotam Ottolenghi's book *Jerusalem*, that I learned that eggplant caviar got its name because the eggplant seeds resemble caviar, however vaguely.

The focal point of Ottolenghi's recipe for eggplant caviar was to very carefully scoop out the seeds, which are contained almost as if in their own "sac," after the eggplant is cooked. Ottolenghi puts the sac of seeds in a bowl and adds the other ingredients, so the seeds really are the star of the dish. If I hadn't read that recipe, I would have scooped out the seeds and tossed them out the same way I do with tomatoes, cucumbers, and peppers, whose seeds tend to be bitter; I also would have thought I didn't want the texture of the seeds to interfere with the smooth purée. But, in fact, the seeds add an appealing flavor and texture to eggplant purée.

In this recipe, I borrow Ottolenghi's method of incorporating the seeds into the purée, and also the idea of roasting eggplant directly over an open flame. I've charred red peppers this way my entire cooking life, but it had never occurred to me to cook eggplant that way, again, until I saw it in *Jerusalem*. I knew it was a brilliant idea the moment I read it, and when I tried it and tasted the resulting eggplant, which takes on a smoky flavor from the fire, I knew that Ottolenghi had changed my eggplant world forever.

This recipe calls for you to char the eggplant directly on the burners of a gas stove, but you can also char them on an outdoor grill or in a preheated grill pan or cast-iron skillet. If you have an electric stove, choose one of the alternatives. (You can always roast them in the oven, but you won't achieve the smoky flavor.)

Preheat the oven to 500°F.

Turn as many burners of a gas stove to high heat as you have eggplants. Put one eggplant directly on each of the burners and cook, turning the eggplants as they char, until the skins are charred on all sides, about 10 minutes. Put the charred eggplant on a baking sheet and put them in the oven to bake until they are mushy, about 15 minutes, turning them and rotating the baking sheet from front to back halfway through the cooking time. Remove the baking sheet from the oven and transfer the eggplants to a large bowl or plastic bag. Cover the bowl tightly with plastic wrap or close the bag and set the eggplants aside to steam for at least 15 minutes, until they are cool enough to touch.

Combine the vinegar, shallot, lemon juice, sugar, and 1 tablespoon of the salt in a small bowl. Using a fine Microplane, grate the garlic directly into the bowl. Add the olive oil in a slow, steady stream, whisking constantly to emulsify.

Remove the eggplants from the bowl and drain and discard any liquid in the bowl. Rip off and discard the stems and the charred skins from the eggplants and return the eggplants to the bowl. Season the eggplants with the remaining 1 tablespoon plus ¾ teaspoon salt and use a whisk as if you were making mashed potatoes to break apart the eggplants until they are mushy and stringy. Add the vinegar and oil a little at a time, whisking until the eggplants become mush.

Serve the eggplant purée or refrigerate, covered, for up to 2 days. Bring it to room temperature before serving. Just before serving, tear the mint leaves roughly, toss them into the eggplant purée, and gently fold them in. Transfer the eggplant purée to a deep serving bowl with a large spoon and serve with the garlic crostini, fett'unta, or toasted pita bread.

Fett'unta

4 (1½-inch-thick) slices from a large loaf of country bread

Extra-virgin olive oil for brushing the bread (if you are toasting the bread on a grill or grill pan)

1 medium or large garlic clove, peeled

¾ cup finishing-quality extra-virgin olive oil

Maldon sea salt (or another flaky sea salt such as fleur de sel)

Fett'unta, grilled olive-oiled bread, is a regular part of my entertaining repertoire. The word comes from the Italian *fetta*, or "slice" and *unta*, which means "oily." The way I make it, I slice country bread very thick, grill it until it's toasty and almost black in places, rub it with garlic, drown it with the best olive oil I have, and sprinkle it with sea salt. Although I make this olive oil–drenched bread year-round, I especially like to make it during late fall and early winter, just after the olive harvest, when *olio nuovo*, green, peppery "new olive oil," is available. A grill is my first choice for toasting the bread for fett'unta, but you can also toast the bread in a grill pan or on a baking sheet in the oven.

———

Preheat a grill pan or cast-iron skillet over high heat or adjust the oven racks so one is in the middle position and preheat the oven to 350°F.

If you are toasting the bread on a grill or grill pan, brush the bread slices on both sides with olive oil. Place the bread on the grill or in the grill pan and cook it until it's crispy and golden brown and even black in places, about 2 minutes per side. If you are making fett'unta in the oven, put the slices (without oil), on a baking sheet and cook for 30 minutes, turning the bread over halfway through that time, until it is golden brown and crispy on both sides.

Rub the garlic clove over both sides of each piece of toast and pour 3 tablespoons finishing-quality olive oil over each toast. Season the oiled side of the toasts generously with sea salt. Cut the bread on an angle into halves or thirds and serve with tongs.

Garlic Crostini

Garlic crostini, little bread toasts, are a staple of my entertaining repertoire both in Los Angeles and Italy. Crostini are a great use for day-old bread and a flavorful vehicle for spreads such as Chickpea Purée alla Massolino (page 30) and Labneh Toasts (page 123).

MAKES 8 CROSTINI

Adjust an oven rack to the middle position and preheat the oven to 350°F.

Place the bread slices on a baking sheet, brush the tops with olive oil, and bake the slices for 15 to 20 minutes, until they're golden brown and crispy, rotating the baking sheet from front to back halfway through the baking time so the bread browns evenly. Remove the crostini from the oven. Rub the oiled sides of the crostini with the garlic, sprinkle with salt, and serve.

8 (½-inch-thick) slices from a *bâtard* or fat baguette (or 4 slices from a large loaf of country bread), halved

Extra-virgin olive oil for brushing the bread

1 garlic clove, peeled

Kosher salt

Jalapeño Labneh

SERVES 6 TO 8

1 recipe Labneh (page 126 or store-bought)

3 Pickled Jalapeño Peppers (page 319 or store-bought), stems removed and discarded, and sliced into ¼-inch rings

Finishing-quality extra-virgin olive oil for drizzling (about 1 generous tablespoon)

Large pinch of sweet smoked paprika

When I serve labneh as part of my mezze-inspired spread, I scatter pickled jalapeño peppers over it because that's how they serve labneh at my favorite Middle Eastern restaurant, Carousel. I give a recipe for labneh on page 126, but if you want to skip that step you can also buy labneh at Middle Eastern stores and some supermarkets.

———

Spoon the labneh into a small shallow serving bowl. Use the back of a spoon to create a divot in the center of the labneh. Scatter the jalapeño slices over the labneh, drizzle the olive oil into the divot, sprinkle with the paprika, and serve.

Yogurt with Cucumbers

Yogurt with cucumbers, called *tzatziki* in Middle Eastern restaurants, is a classic combo: the Greeks make it, as do Indians, Lebanese, Armenians . . . When I make it, I use fresh mint in place of the more commonly used dill. I slice the cucumbers slightly thicker so they stay crunchy in the yogurt. One of the things I like best about this condiment is that crunch amid the creamy yogurt, which always seems like a surprise. I really can't think of any grilled meat or vegetable that this wouldn't go with, but it is a must if I'm serving lamb.

I like to use Persian or Japanese cucumbers whenever I can find them, and especially in this condiment. Both Persian and Japanese cucumbers are sweeter and more flavorful than conventional or English cucumber. And unlike conventional cucumbers, with Persian and Japanese cucumbers, neither the skins nor the seeds are bitter, so neither needs to be removed before adding the cucumbers to a dish.

To ensure crisp cucumbers, this condiment is best served just after it's been made. It's easy to make, but if you want something even easier, make Mint Yogurt Sauce (page 107) instead.

———

Put the cucumbers in a large strainer set over a bowl. Sprinkle with ½ teaspoon of the salt, toss to distribute the salt, and set aside for 1 hour to let the water drain out of the cucumbers. Press down on the cucumbers to release any excess water, then dry them with paper towels.

Put the yogurt, mint, lemon juice, and the remaining 1½ teaspoons salt in a medium bowl. Using a fine Microplane, grate the garlic into the bowl and stir to combine the ingredients. Just before serving, add the cucumbers and stir to distribute them. Transfer the cucumbers and yogurt to a deep serving bowl and serve with a spoon.

SERVES 8 TO 10

3 pounds Persian or Japanese cucumbers, sliced into ¼-inch-thick rounds

2 teaspoons kosher salt

2 cups Straus Family Creamery Organic Greek Yogurt (or another whole-milk plain, not overly thick, Greek-style yogurt)

3 tablespoons finely chopped fresh mint leaves (from about ½ cup packed whole leaves)

⅛ cup fresh lemon juice

4 to 5 medium or large garlic cloves, peeled

Marinated Radicchio and Beet Salad with Labneh Cheese Balls

Nearing the end of the process of writing this book, with room for only two or three more recipes, I took under serious consideration the idea that maybe I needed to offer a beet salad to my readers. I've always been pretty middle of the road in terms of my feelings about beet salad. If I was going to make a beet salad, I knew I had to venture far from the typical beet salad of mesclun, cooked beets, walnuts, and goat cheese, which is not an appealing salad to me on a number of levels. First off, because I have never liked red and green in combination when it comes to food, sticking with a color palette of red was the only way I could consider a beet salad. After much deliberation and experimentation, I created this, which consists of marinated radicchio and marinated roasted beets dotted with bite-size cheese balls that have been rolled, as if in an old-school cheese shop, in chopped walnuts. The cheese balls are such an un-Nancy thing to do, but I needed something to protect the white cheese from being stained by the beets, which always reminds me of an old lady's lipstick using the wrinkles on her upper lip to crawl up her face. The walnuts prevent that from happening. This salad is both visually pleasing and very tasty, if I do say so myself.

If you want to save the step of making labneh, use fresh goat cheese instead.

———

To make the vinaigrette, combine the shallot, vinegar, and salt in a small bowl. Add the olive oil in a slow, steady stream, whisking constantly to emulsify. Use the vinaigrette or refrigerate, covered, for up to 2 days. Bring the vinaigrette to room temperature and whisk to recombine the ingredients before using.

To prepare the beets, adjust an oven rack to the middle position and preheat the oven to 400°F.

Put the beets in a baking dish in a single layer, drizzle with the olive oil, season with 2 teaspoons of the salt, and toss to coat the beets. Cover the dish with aluminum foil and roast the beets for about 1 hour, until they are tender when pierced with a toothpick or fork. Remove the beets from the oven and remove the foil. Set the beets aside until they are cool enough to touch. Rub the beets with paper towels (or your least-favorite dish towel that you don't mind staining) to remove the skins; discard. (Use gloves if you have them to prevent staining your hands.) Cut the beets into halves or quarters, depending on their size.

SERVES 6 TO 8

———

FOR THE VINAIGRETTE

Heaping ¼ cup minced shallot (from about 1 medium or large peeled shallot)

½ cup balsamic vinegar

1 teaspoon kosher salt

½ cup extra-virgin olive oil

FOR THE BEETS

2 pounds small (but not baby) red beets, scrubbed thoroughly, tops trimmed and discarded

¼ cup extra-virgin olive oil

2¾ teaspoons kosher salt

1 teaspoon fresh lemon juice

FOR THE RADICCHIO

2 medium radicchio heads

2 teaspoons fresh lemon juice

¾ teaspoon kosher salt

FOR THE CHEESE BALLS

2 ounces walnut halves or pieces (about ½ cup)

2 teaspoons extra-virgin olive oil

½ teaspoon kosher salt

½ lemon

6 ounces Labneh (page 126 or store-bought, or goat cheese)

Put the beets in a medium bowl and drizzle with the lemon juice and half of the vinaigrette. Sprinkle with the remaining ¾ teaspoon salt and toss to coat the beets. Set the beets aside while you prepare the rest of the salad ingredients, or for at least 15 minutes.

Meanwhile, to prepare the radicchio, tear off and discard the outer wilted or unappealing leaves. Tear the remaining leaves from the cores and discard the cores. Tear the leaves into 3-inch pieces and put them in a medium bowl. Drizzle the remaining half of the vinaigrette and the lemon juice over the radicchio. Sprinkle the salt over the radicchio, toss gently, and massage the radicchio to coat it. Set the radicchio aside to marinate while you prepare the rest of the salad.

To prepare the cheese balls, adjust an oven rack to the middle position and preheat the oven to 325°F.

Spread the walnuts on a baking sheet and toast them in the oven for 10 to 12 minutes, until they're lightly browned and fragrant, shaking the baking sheet and rotating it from front to back halfway through the cooking time so the nuts brown evenly. Remove the walnuts from the oven and set them aside to cool to room temperature. Put the walnuts in a medium bowl, drizzle with the olive oil, sprinkle with the salt, and toss to coat the nuts evenly. Transfer the nuts to a cutting board, finely chop them, and return the chopped nuts to the bowl you tossed them in. Finely grate the zest of the lemon over the nuts and toss to distribute the zest.

Roll the cheese into 24 bite-size (¼-ounce) balls. Working with a few at a time, toss the cheese balls into the bowl with the walnuts and roll to coat the cheese on all sides. Transfer the walnut-covered cheese balls to a plate or a small baking sheet and continue coating the remaining cheese balls with the remaining nuts in the same way.

To serve, lift one-third of the radicchio leaves out of the bowl and scatter the leaves to cover the bottom of a large platter or sloping bowl. Scatter one-third of the marinated beets over the radicchio and nestle 8 of the cheese balls among the radicchio and beets. Repeat, building a second layer with another third of the radicchio, another third of the beets, and 8 more cheese balls. Build a final layer using the remaining radicchio and the remaining beets and nestling the remaining cheese balls among them. Serve with a large spoon.

Muhammara

For the longest time when I ordered side dishes from Carousel as part of the Middle Eastern–inspired spread that I serve at my house in Los Angeles, I referred to this condiment, made of roasted red bell peppers, walnuts, and pomegranate molasses, simply as "the red stuff." I could never remember the name or how to pronounce it, but I never forgot to order it, because it is just so delicious. I also never tried to make my own version because I was scared off by the thought of using pomegranate molasses, which is unfamiliar territory to me. Plus, Carousel's muhammara is so good, I figured, why bother? That changed one day when I was at the Osteria, stirring the romesco, a traditional Spanish condiment, behind the Mozzarella Bar. My version of romesco is made with roasted red peppers, garlic, bread, nuts, and olive oil, all ground together in a blender. That day, as I was stirring the romesco, as I have every day for the past eight years, it occurred to me how similar my romesco was to muhammara. With this familiar sauce as a jumping-off point, I bought a bottle of that mysterious ingredient, pomegranate molasses, and set about trying to make muhammara.

For some people, the model for the perfect muhammara might be their grandmother's, or something they remember having in Syria or Armenia. For me, it was without a doubt Carousel's. It's only fair for me to give credit where credit is due and to let you know that this condiment was made by committee. Because every one of my friends has been served Carousel's version at my house at one time or another, we all chimed in, while Liz or I stirred in a bit more of this or that, until we felt we'd gotten as close as we could to what we'd come to think of as The Original Muhammara.

Pomegranate molasses is pomegranate juice reduced with sugar. It's fairly common in Middle Eastern cooking, and you can find it at markets that specialize in the foods of that region. Look for a product that is thick and viscous and doesn't contain fructose or any other artificial ingredients.

I give you methods for charring the bell peppers on a grill, in a grill pan or cast-iron skillet, or roasting them in the oven. You can also char them directly over the flame of a gas stove.

SERVES 6 TO 8
MAKES ABOUT 1 CUP

5 red bell peppers

2 cups walnut halves or pieces (about 8 ounces)

½ small loaf of country bread (about 5 ounces)

3 tablespoons olive oil

¼ cup pomegranate molasses

2 tablespoons red wine vinegar

1 tablespoon plus 1 teaspoon kosher salt

1 tablespoon sweet smoked paprika

¾ teaspoon cayenne pepper

½ teaspoon ground cumin

2 to 3 medium or large garlic cloves, peeled

¼ cup plus 1 tablespoon finishing-quality extra-virgin olive oil, plus more for drizzling

To char the peppers on a grill or in a grill pan or cast-iron skillet, preheat the grill until it is very hot or preheat the grill pan or skillet over high heat. Place the peppers on the grill or in the grill pan or skillet, and cook, turning them frequently, until they are blackened all over and softened, 10 to 20 minutes.

To char the peppers over an open flame, turn the burner on a gas range to the highest flame. Put the peppers on the burner grate and cook, turning them frequently, until they are blackened all over and softened, 10 to 20 minutes.

To char the peppers in the oven, adjust the oven rack to the middle position and preheat the oven to 500°F. Place the peppers on a baking sheet and put them in the oven until they are charred on all sides, about 20 to 35 minutes, turning them once or twice with tongs during the cooking time so they char evenly. Remove the peppers from the oven.

Put the peppers in a plastic bag or a large bowl. Close the bag or seal the bowl tightly with plastic wrap and set the peppers aside to steam until they collapse and are cool enough to touch.

Reduce the oven temperature to 325°F.

Using a clean kitchen towel, remove and discard the charred skin from the peppers. (Do not rinse the peppers under water to remove the skins; you will rinse away the char flavor you just went to great effort to achieve.) Remove and discard the core and seeds. The peppers can be prepared to this point up to 2 days in advance. Refrigerate, covered, and drain the liquid released from the peppers before using them.

Spread the walnuts on a baking sheet and toast them in the oven for 10 to 12 minutes, until they're lightly browned and fragrant, shaking the baking sheet and rotating it from front to back halfway through the cooking time so the nuts brown evenly. Remove the walnuts from the oven and set them aside until they're cool enough to touch. Finely chop the walnuts to the size of the chunks in chunky peanut butter.

If the loaf of bread is whole, cut it crossways to reveal the inside of the loaf. Pull the bread out in 1-inch to 1½-inch chunks and put the chunks in a large bowl. Reserve the crumbs and crusts for another use, such as to make bread crumbs.

Prepare a bed of paper towels. Warm the olive oil in a small sauté pan over medium heat. Add the bread chunks and fry them until they are lightly browned and crunchy, about 5 minutes, turning them with tongs and shaking the pan so they brown evenly. Remove the bread to the paper towels to drain.

Put the peppers, including any juices that have released from them, in the bowl of a food processor fitted with a metal blade or in the jar of a blender. Add the bread and half of the walnuts and pulse until the bread and nuts are coarsely ground. Add the pomegranate molasses, vinegar, salt, paprika, cayenne, and cumin. Using a fine Microplane, grate the garlic into the bowl or jar and pulse until the muhammara is the consistency of wet, coarse meal. Transfer the muhammara to a bowl. Reserve 1 teaspoon of the remaining walnuts. Add the rest of the walnuts and the finishing-quality olive oil to the muhammara and stir to combine. Serve the muhammara or refrigerate, covered, until you're ready to serve it. Bring it to room temperature before serving.

To serve, transfer the muhammara to a small pretty bowl. Drizzle with finishing-quality olive oil and sprinkle the reserved walnuts over the top. Serve with a small spoon.

Kale Freekeh Tabbouleh

SERVES 6 TO 8

FOR THE FREEKEH

2 teaspoons kosher salt

1 cup freekeh (or cracked bulgur), rinsed under cold water until the water runs clear

2 tablespoons extra-virgin olive oil

FOR THE SALAD

2 bunches Tuscan kale
(also called cavolo nero, lacinato, or dinosaur kale; about 1 pound)

1 cup minced shallots
(from about 2 large peeled shallots)

½ cup fresh lemon juice

⅓ cup extra-virgin olive oil

1 tablespoon kosher salt

8 to 10 medium or large garlic cloves, peeled

1 pint small sweet tomatoes
(such as Sun Golds or Sweet 100s, or grape tomatoes), halved through the stems
(quartered if the tomatoes are larger than a marble)

No matter where you buy or order it, tabbouleh is almost always the same: bulgur wheat mixed with chopped curly parsley, lemon juice, garlic, oil, and chopped tomatoes. For this version, I use kale in place of curly parsley. I have an aversion to tomatoes concasse (finely chopped tomatoes), so I use small tomatoes, which add a burst of sweetness to the salad and also look pretty in it. I won't lie: cutting the kale for this recipe is time-consuming, but that's the bulk of the work involved in making the tabbouleh. You don't even make a vinaigrette; the oil and lemon juice it's dressed with are just tossed into the mix.

I gave a range for how much garlic to add because garlic cloves vary in size and in how pungent they are. Add some and then add more to taste until you have a tabbouleh that you love, not one that burns your mouth with the taste of raw garlic.

Freekeh, fire-roasted cracked wheat, is very popular in Middle Eastern cooking. It has a pretty, slightly green hue and is more flavorful than bulgur. I fell in love with it on a recent trip to Israel and am happy to see it gaining popularity here. You can find it in bags in specialty food stores and on the Internet. If you can't find it, use bulgur in its place.

To cook the freekeh, bring 1½ cups water to a boil in a medium saucepan. Add the salt and freekeh and return the water to a boil. Reduce the heat to medium-low and simmer the freekeh, uncovered, until all of the water has been absorbed and the freekeh is al dente, 8 to 15 minutes, depending on the freshness of the grains. Turn off the heat and fluff the freekeh with a fork. Spread the freekeh out on a baking sheet and put the baking sheet in the refrigerator to cool the freekeh to room temperature. (Refrigerating the hot freekeh stops it from continuing to cook.) Remove the freekeh from the refrigerator, drizzle with the olive oil, and toss with your hands to coat the grains.

To prepare the salad, cut or rip the leaves from the kale ribs and discard the ribs. If the leaves are large, you may need to cut them in half or thirds lengthwise to create 1-inch-wide strips. Stack 3 or 4 strips at a time on top of one another and slice the kale into ⅛-inch-wide chiffonade horizontally to create short ribbons. Add the freekeh, shallots, lemon juice, olive oil, and salt to the bowl with the kale. Using a fine Microplane, grate 8 garlic cloves directly into the bowl. Toss to combine the ingredients and distribute the seasonings. Taste and add more garlic if desired. Add the tomatoes and gently toss the salad, taking care not to smash them.

To serve, transfer the tabbouleh to a large platter or wide-mouthed bowl and serve with a large spoon.

17

Flattened Chicken Thighs with Charred Lemon Salsa Verde

SERVES 6 TO 9

FOR THE MARINADE

2 lemons, rinsed

¼ cup packed fresh oregano leaves, finely chopped

1½ tablespoons fresh thyme leaves, finely chopped

1½ tablespoons fresh Italian parsley leaves, finely chopped

10 to 12 medium or large garlic cloves, peeled and smashed with the flat side of a knife

1 teaspoon red chile flakes

3 tablespoons extra-virgin olive oil

FOR THE CHICKEN

9 bone-in, skin-on chicken thighs

4 tablespoons (½ stick) unsalted butter, cut into 9 equal slices

18 fresh sage leaves

4 large garlic cloves, peeled and sliced ¹⁄₁₆-inch thick lengthwise, preferably on a mandoline, to achieve 18 slices

1 tablespoon plus 1 teaspoon kosher salt

9 fresh bay leaves

Charred Lemon Salsa Verde (recipe follows)

While in Italy during the summer of 2014, I got a call from *Food & Wine* magazine asking me if I would develop several recipes for them for an upcoming "women's issue." They wanted recipes that were influenced by my favorite female chefs, specifically, the ladies who cook at Massolino, the white tablecloth restaurant in my town that the editor had heard me rave about in the past. I've already borrowed several recipes from Massolino, including a guinea fowl entrée, which I published in *The Mozza Cookbook*, and Chickpea Purée alla Massolino (page 30). For *Food & Wine*, I immediately thought of a special that the owner, Andrea's mother, Bruna, makes once in a while—chicken thighs braised with garlic, lemon, and capers. I used those flavors to create this dish, which consists of chicken thighs whose skin is stuffed with butter, garlic, and sage. The chicken thighs are weighed down and flattened while they're cooked, making the skin brown and crispy, and served with charred lemon salsa verde.

To flatten the chicken, you will need a cast-iron skillet that fits inside the sauté pan you are cooking the chicken in; or a lighter skillet weighed down with a brick or another heavy object, such as a large full can. You will also need a thin metal spatula, preferably a fish spatula, to turn the chicken thighs without ripping the skin. If you have a mandoline, use it to make easy work of slicing the garlic for this recipe.

———

To make the marinade, use a vegetable peeler to shave 9 strips of lemon peel from the lemons, taking care to cut into only the brightest yellow layer, and put the strips in a large bowl or baking dish. Add the oregano, thyme, parsley, garlic, and red chile flakes and stir in the olive oil.

To prepare the chicken, pat the chicken dry with paper towels. Working one at a time, gently lift up the skin of each chicken thigh with your fingers to create a deep pocket between the skin and the flesh, taking care to leave the skin attached to the thigh, and tuck 1 pat of the butter, 2 sage leaves, and 2 garlic slices under the skin. Put the chicken thigh in the bowl with the marinade and repeat, stuffing the remaining chicken thighs with the butter, sage, and garlic slices. When you have stuffed all the chicken thighs, toss them gently to coat with the marinade. Cover the bowl with plastic wrap and put the chicken in the refrigerator to marinate for at least 2 hours or as long as overnight.

Remove the chicken from the refrigerator. Remove the thighs from the marinade and put them, skin side up, on a baking sheet, reserving the marinade. Sprinkle 2 teaspoons of the salt on the skin side of the chicken. Turn the chicken thighs and sprinkle the flesh side with the remaining 2 teaspoons salt.

Transfer 5 chicken thighs, skin side down, to a large sauté pan. Put the sauté pan with the chicken over high heat and weigh down the chicken with the bottom of a clean cast-iron skillet (or a lighter skillet weighed down with a large full can, a brick, or another heavy object). Cook the chicken without moving it for 10 to 12 minutes, until the skin is brown and crispy. To check for doneness, gently lift the corner of a chicken thigh with a metal spatula. Remove the weight from the chicken and remove the thighs with the spatula, taking care to keep the skin attached to the thighs as you lift them. Transfer the thighs, cooked side up, to a clean baking sheet or plate. Cook the remaining 4 chicken thighs in the same way, this time turning off the heat and turning the thighs so they're cooked side up in the pan rather than removing them from the pan. Return the first batch of thighs to the pan, arranging them cooked side up in concentric circles in the pan with the second batch. (If you have a large enough sauté pan to fit the raw thighs, you can cook them in one batch.)

Fish the garlic cloves and lemon peels from the marinade and scatter the garlic around the chicken thighs. Put 1 lemon peel and 1 bay leaf between each chicken thigh. Put the chicken thighs in the oven to bake at 450° for 25 to 30 minutes, until the juices run clear when the chicken is pierced with a small knife. Remove the chicken from the oven and let it rest in the pan it was cooked in for 5 to 10 minutes. Gently lift the chicken thighs out of the pan with a spatula and place them, skin side up, on a large rimmed serving platter. Fish the garlic, lemon peels, and bay leaves out of the pan and scatter them over and around the chicken thighs. Serve the chicken with tongs, and the salsa verde in a small bowl with a spoon for guests to serve themselves.

Charred Lemon Salsa Verde

Makes about 2 cups

When I made the flattened chicken thighs for the first time, I remembered a party I'd had at my house the week before, where I met a young Angeleno chef named Ella Freyinger. Ella had made a lovely vinaigrette with oven-charred sliced lemons, so for a completely different dish, I borrowed her idea and added charred lemon to this otherwise traditional salsa verde—an addition for the ages.

2 lemons

1 cup plus 1 tablespoon extra-virgin olive oil, plus more as needed

1 cup packed fresh oregano leaves

1 cup packed fresh mint leaves

2 teaspoons kosher salt

2 anchovy fillets (preferably salt-packed; rinsed, backbones removed if salt-packed), finely chopped and smashed to a paste with the flat side of a knife

3 to 4 medium or large garlic cloves, peeled

2 teaspoons capers (preferably salt-packed; soaked for 15 minutes if salt-packed), rinsed, drained, and finely chopped

Adjust the oven racks so one is in the center of the oven and none are near the oven floor; you'll be putting the baking sheet directly on the oven floor. If you are using an electric oven or another oven where you can't put anything on the floor, adjust the oven racks so that one is in the center and the other is closest to the floor and put a pizza stone on it, if you have one. Preheat the oven to 500°F.

Slice the lemons into ½-inch rounds. Remove and discard the seeds from each slice and throw away the 2 end pieces from each lemon. Put the lemon slices on a baking sheet, drizzle with 1 tablespoon of the olive oil, and toss to coat the lemon slices. Scatter the lemon slices in a single layer on the baking sheet and put the baking sheet on the oven floor or the lowest rack to roast the lemons for 10 to 12 minutes, until the bottoms are caramelized and charred in places but still soft, not crispy and burned, shaking the baking sheet and rotating it from front to back halfway through the cooking time so the lemons color somewhat evenly. (When cooking vegetables or fruit on the oven floor, a lot of steam is produced from the water released, so just be careful of the steam that will arise when you open the oven door.) Remove the baking sheet from the oven. Using tongs, immediately turn each lemon slice so the colored side is facing up (if you don't do this just after the lemons come out of the oven, the lemons will stick to the baking sheet). Set the lemons aside until they are cool enough to touch.

Decrease the oven temperature to 450°F.

Roughly chop the lemons. Using the flat side of a knife, scoop all of the lemons off the cutting board, including all of the flesh stuck to the board, and transfer to a small bowl, discarding any blackened bits that were charred too much.

To make the salsa verde using a large mortar and a pestle, finely chop the oregano and mint leaves by hand and put the chopped herbs in the mortar. Add the salt and anchovies. Using a Microplane, grate the garlic directly into the mortar and pound with the pestle until the ingredients are mashed together and there are no visible chunks of any ingredients. Slowly stir in the remaining 1 cup olive oil, adding more if necessary to achieve a loose, spoonable salsa. Stir in the chopped lemons and capers.

To make the salsa verde using a mini food processor or blender, roughly chop the oregano and mint leaves by hand. Transfer the chopped herbs to the bowl of a mini food processor fitted with a metal blade or to the jar of a blender. Add the salt and anchovies. Using a fine Microplane, grate the garlic directly into the food processor or jar and pulse until the ingredients are finely chopped but not puréed. Scrape down the sides of the food processor or jar. With the motor running, gradually add the remaining olive oil through the feed tube, stopping after you've added half of the oil to scrape down the bowl of the food processor or jar again, then adding the rest of the oil. (Don't mix the salsa any longer than necessary as the blade heats up the garlic, turning it slightly bitter.) Transfer the salsa to a medium bowl. Stir in more oil if necessary to achieve a loose, spoonable salsa. Stir in the chopped lemons and capers.

The salsa can be made up to 1 day in advance; it discolors quickly, so I don't like to make it any further in advance of that. Refrigerate the salsa in a covered container until you're ready to use it. Bring it to room temperature and give it a stir to recombine the ingredients before using.

To serve, transfer the salsa verde to a small, deep, pretty bowl and serve it with a spoon for guests to help themselves.

Panicale Popcorn

SERVES 8 TO 10

¼ cup extra-virgin olive oil

6 to 8 medium or large garlic cloves, peeled and smashed with the flat side of a knife

2 (5-inch-long) fresh rosemary sprigs

8 fresh sage leaves

4 fresh bay leaves

2 árbol chile pods

1 tablespoon plus 1 teaspoon kosher salt, plus more to taste

½ teaspoon fresh coarsely ground black pepper, plus more to taste

1 cup popcorn kernels

¼ cup finishing-quality extra-virgin olive oil, plus more to taste

Wedge of Parmigiano-Reggiano for grating

Over the years that I've been going to Italy, I've started to see more and more American products available, and each time I find one, I get a little excited to know that a reminder of home is available to me if I want it. When my youngest son, Oliver, was little, for example, he got super excited when we found cornflakes at the market. Then, one year popcorn appeared on the shelves. Although I never make popcorn in Los Angeles, I bought a bag in Italy just because I could. And I found an occasion to make a batch for the kids one rainy day when they were watching a movie.

When I set out to make my popcorn that first time, I knew that because I was in Umbria, which is olive oil country, I wanted to make olive oil popcorn, not buttered popcorn. And when I think of cooking with olive oil, I think of Italian seasonings like garlic, rosemary, and bay leaves. I have a little potted herb garden, so I went out to my porch and started snipping away. I proceeded to make a seasoned oil for my popcorn. I've never had such flavorful popcorn. Now that popcorn has become a tradition.

When Americans think of popcorn, most of us think of the movies, but it's also nice to set out a big bowl of popcorn in place of a bowl of potato chips when guests arrive. If you want to serve this popcorn in paper bags, which I often do, you will need 8 to 10 small lunch-size paper bags.

Heat the olive oil in a large Dutch oven or another deep, heavy pot with a lid over medium-high heat until it slides easily in the pan and the oil around the edges of the pan begins to smoke, 2 to 3 minutes. Add the garlic, rosemary, sage, bay leaves, chile pods, and 1½ teaspoons of the salt and the pepper. Reduce the heat to low and cook for 5 minutes to infuse the oil with the flavors, stirring often so the garlic and herbs don't brown.

Add the popcorn and partially cover the pot with the lid. When you hear the first kernel pop, put the lid on to close the pot completely. Cook the popcorn, shaking the pan vigorously, until the popping slows from a constant *pop-pop-pop* to an occasional *pop*. Turn off the heat and continue shaking the pan to pop the last remaining kernels. Transfer the popcorn to a very large bowl. Drizzle with the finishing-quality olive oil and sprinkle with the remaining 2½ teaspoons salt and more pepper to taste. Using a fine Microplane, grate a generous amount of

Parmigiano over the top. Toss to coat the popcorn, and serve, leaving the herbs, chile pods, and bay leaves in the mix for color.

To serve, transfer the popcorn to several large serving bowls for guests to reach into and eat with their hands. Alternatively, scoop the popcorn into paper bags for each guest or pair of guests to take a bag for themselves, or serve the popcorn in an enormous bowl with a big scoop and the paper bags on the side for guests to fill themselves.

Pastrami Popcorn

FOR THE SPICES

¼ cup cumin seeds

¼ cup caraway seeds

¼ cup fennel seeds

¼ cup coriander seeds

2 tablespoons mustard seeds

2 tablespoons kosher salt

FOR THE POPCORN

8 tablespoons (1 stick)
unsalted butter

1 tablespoon orange zest
(zested with a Microplane)

½ cup canola oil

1 cup popcorn kernels

½ cup finely chopped fresh dill

Kosher salt

Every time I do a cookbook, just as the book is about to be finished, I think of one more recipe that I *must* include. That's what happened with this popcorn. The manuscript was finished and edited when I went to The Lark restaurant in Santa Barbara, where I was served Chef Jason Paluska's popcorn seasoned with pastrami spices. As much as I love my Panicale Popcorn (page 292), I was so excited by the idea of pastrami popcorn that I went to work creating this recipe for the book.

If you want to serve the popcorn in paper bags, which I often do, you will need 8 to 10 small lunch-size paper bags.

———

To prepare the spice blend, toast the cumin, caraway, fennel, and coriander seeds in a small sauté pan over medium heat for 1 to 2 minutes, until the seeds are fragrant and golden brown, shaking the pan often so they don't burn. Transfer the seeds, along with the mustard seeds, to a plate to cool to room temperature. Grind the seeds in a spice grinder or use a mortar and a pestle, transfer to a bowl, and stir in the salt.

To make the popcorn, combine the butter and orange zest in a small saucepan and heat to melt the butter. Turn off the heat.

Heat the canola oil with half of the spice mix in a large Dutch oven or another deep, heavy pot with a lid over medium-high heat until the oil slides easily in the pan and the oil around the edges of the pan begins to smoke, 2 to 3 minutes. Add the popcorn and partially cover the pot with the lid. When you hear the first kernel pop, put the lid on to close the pot completely. Cook the popcorn, shaking the pan vigorously, until the popping slows from a constant *pop-pop-pop* to an occasional *pop*. Turn off the heat and continue shaking the pan to pop the last remaining kernels. Uncover the pan. Drizzle the orange butter and sprinkle the dill and the remaining spices over the popcorn and toss to coat the popcorn and distribute the seasonings. Taste for salt and add more if desired.

To serve, transfer the popcorn to several large serving bowls for guests to reach into and eat with their hands. Alternatively, scoop the popcorn into the paper bags for each guest or pair of guests to take a bag for themselves, or serve the popcorn in an enormous bowl with a big scoop and the paper bags on the side for guests to fill themselves.

Pasta Salad with Bitter Greens, Parmigiano Cream, and Guanciale

I was in a little store in Venice, Italy, one year, where they had an entire wall display of tiny pasta shapes in cellophane bags. Looking at them next to one another made me think of how pretty it would look if you mixed the different shapes together. Although I'm not a fan of pasta salad in the old-school tradition of overcooked penne dressed with vinaigrette or pesto, when I saw these pretty shapes, I was intent on making the first pasta salad I would want to eat. I searched through the file in my brain where I store the recipe ideas that I've been intrigued with over the years, looking for the right sauce or dressing to bind the salad with. Eventually I thought of Parmigiano Cream, which I was introduced to in the 1990s, by the chef Todd English.

This pasta dish looks prettiest if you use three or four different pasta shapes. If the packages give the same cooking times, cook different shapes together. Otherwise, you need to cook them separately, because properly cooking the pasta is key to the success of this dish. If you want to make this salad using only one pasta shape, that would be fine, too, though it was all those pretty shapes that led me down the dark path of pasta salad to this unexpected victory in the first place. The guanciale in this recipe can be replaced with bacon, shredded prosciutto, or pancetta, or skip the meat altogether.

To prepare the greens, adjust the oven racks so none are near the oven floor; you'll be putting a baking sheet directly on the oven floor. If you are using an electric oven or another oven where you can't put anything on the floor, adjust the oven racks so that one is closest to the floor and put a pizza stone on it, if you have one. Preheat the oven to 500°F.

Put the arugula in a large bowl. Drizzle with 2 tablespoons of the olive oil, sprinkle with 1 teaspoon of the salt, and toss to coat the leaves. Spread the arugula out on a large baking sheet. Put the baking sheet on the oven floor or the lowest rack and roast the arugula until it's wilted and golden brown in places, about 4 minutes, shaking the baking sheet and rotating it from front to back halfway through the cooking time so the arugula browns evenly. (When cooking vegetables on the oven floor, a lot of steam is produced from the water released as a result of the vegetables cooking so quickly, so just be careful of the steam

SERVES 8 TO 10

FOR THE GREENS

8 cups lightly packed arugula (about 10 ounces)

¼ cup plus 2 tablespoons olive oil

3 teaspoons kosher salt

6 frisée heads (about 9 ounces), leaves torn from cores, cores discarded, and leaves torn into 2-inch pieces (about 6 lightly packed cups)

2 medium radicchio heads, outer leaves and cores removed and discarded, leaves torn into 2-inch pieces (about 8 lightly packed cups)

3 tablespoons sherry vinegar

FOR THE PASTA

1 teaspoon kosher salt, plus more for the pasta water

1 pound small pasta shapes (such as trofie, tubettini, farfalline, scuccuzzu, orzo, fregola, ditalini, anelli, tripolini, or conchigliette)

3 tablespoons olive oil

1¼ pounds guanciale, diced

Parmigiano Cream (recipe follows)

Freshly ground black pepper

that will arise when you open the oven door.) Remove the baking sheet from the oven and scrape the arugula into a large bowl separate from the one in which you originally tossed the arugula.

Put the frisée leaves in the first bowl in which you tossed the arugula with the oil. Drizzle with 2 tablespoons of the remaining olive oil, sprinkle with 1 teaspoon of the remaining salt, and toss to coat the leaves. Spread the frisée out on a large baking sheet. Put the baking sheet on the oven floor or the lowest rack and roast the frisée for about 5 minutes, until it is wilted and golden brown in places, shaking the baking sheet and rotating it from front to back halfway through the cooking time so the frisée browns evenly. Remove the baking sheet from the oven and scrape the frisée into the bowl with the arugula.

Put the radicchio in the original bowl in which you tossed the arugula and frisée with oil. Drizzle the radicchio with the remaining 2 tablespoons olive oil, sprinkle with the remaining 1 teaspoon salt, and toss to coat the leaves. Spread the radicchio out on a large baking sheet. Put the baking sheet on the oven floor or the lowest rack and roast the radicchio for about 6 minutes, until it's wilted and golden brown in places, rotating the baking sheet from front to back halfway through the cooking time so the radicchio browns evenly. Remove the baking sheet from the oven. Transfer the arugula and frisée to the baking sheet with the radicchio. Spread the greens out with tongs and drizzle them with the vinegar; it's important to do this while the baking sheet is still hot as you are essentially deglazing the baking sheet with the vinegar.

To prepare the pasta, for each shape of pasta you are cooking, combine 1 quart water with 1 tablespoon salt in a medium saucepan and bring the water to a boil over high heat. (If you are cooking only one type of pasta, use a larger pot, such as a pasta pot, and more water; add 1 tablespoon salt per quart of water.) Have a wire-mesh strainer handy to lift the pasta out of the water. Prepare an ice bath in a medium bowl.

Drop the pasta into the boiling water and stir to prevent it from sticking together. Boil the pasta, using the time indicated on the package instructions as a guide, until it's al dente. Lift the pasta out of the cooking water with the strainer and plunge it, still in the strainer, into the ice bath to cool completely. Lift the strainer out of the ice bath and shake it to drain as much water as possible. Transfer the pasta to a large bowl and drizzle with olive oil, using 1 tablespoon of the oil per ⅓ pound of pasta. If you are cooking multiple pasta shapes, cook each shape in the same way, adding more water to the pot if necessary. Add the pasta shapes to the bowl with the earlier cooked shapes after cooling them in the ice

bath and draining them thoroughly, drizzling and tossing them with more olive oil as you go.

Prepare a bed of paper towels. Cook the guanciale in a medium sauté pan over medium-low heat until the fat is rendered and the meat is crispy and browned, 7 to 8 minutes. Remove the guanciale from the pan with a slotted spoon or spatula and transfer it to the paper towels to drain.

Add the guanciale and ½ cup of the Parmigiano cream to the bowl with the pasta. Add the 1 teaspoon of salt and toss to coat the pasta with the cream and salt. Add one-third of the greens and gently fold them in with the pasta, distributing them evenly so they don't clump. Add another third of the greens, fold them in, and then add the last third of greens and fold them in.

To serve, transfer the pasta salad to a large wide-mouthed bowl or platter. Grind several turns of fresh pepper over the pasta, and serve with a big spoon.

Parmigiano Cream

Makes about 3 cups

I have been smitten with this cream sauce, made from the often-discarded rinds of Parmigiano, since the first time I tried it. It is rich, flavorful, and has an appealing, slightly grainy texture from the Parmigiano, and a lot of body as a result of the waxiness of the rinds. This recipe is the perfect excuse to save your Parmigiano rinds, and ask your friends to save theirs, or have your favorite Italian restaurant save them for you. If you don't have Parmigiano rinds on hand, you can buy them at many specialty stores, or just use the equivalent amount of Parmigiano cheese with rinds attached. It makes more than you'll need to toss with the pasta, but it's so delicious, I'm sure you will find ways to use it, including with Ella's Pinzimonio (page 20).

1 large yellow Spanish onion, peeled	1 tablespoon kosher salt
3 tablespoons olive oil	6 cups heavy cream
2 jalapeño peppers, stem ends cut off (to expose the seeds) and discarded	1¼ to 1½ pounds Parmigiano-Reggiano rinds
10 to 12 medium or large garlic cloves, peeled and smashed with the flat side of a knife	10 fresh thyme sprigs

Trim and discard the root end of the onion and cut the onion in half root to tip. Cut each half in half again root to tip so the onion is quartered. Separate the layers of the onion, stack 2 or 3 layers at a time on top of one another, and slice ¼ inch thick lengthwise.

Put the olive oil, onion, jalapeños, and garlic cloves in a large saucepan. Sprinkle with 1 teaspoon of the salt and cook over medium-low heat, stirring often so the vegetables don't brown, until the onion and garlic are soft, 10 to 12 minutes. Add the cream, Parmigiano rinds, and thyme sprigs and cook over high heat until the cream just starts to bubble around the edges. Reduce the heat to low, add the remaining 2 teaspoons salt, and simmer until the cream has reduced by half and the rinds look spongy, stirring and scraping the bottom and sides of the pan with a rubber spatula often so the cream doesn't scorch or discolor, 1 hour to 1 hour 15 minutes.

Meanwhile, prepare an ice bath in a large bowl. Put a smaller bowl in the ice bath and set a fine-mesh strainer in the smaller bowl.

Turn off the heat and pass the cream through the strainer into the bowl set over the ice. Set aside for the cream to cool to room temperature in the ice bath, stirring occasionally. Cover the bowl with plastic wrap and put the cream in the refrigerator to chill until it is set (it will be the consistency of crème fraîche), about 2 hours. The cream can be made up to 3 days in advance. Refrigerate, covered, until you're ready to use it.

Oily Garlicky Spinach

½ cup extra-virgin olive oil

½ cup large garlic cloves
(about 20 cloves), peeled and
sliced ⅛ inch thick

4 wide lemon zest strips
(peeled using a vegetable peeler)

2 teaspoons kosher salt,
plus more for the blanching water

3 árbol chile pods, broken in half

16 cups lightly packed spinach
(about 1 pound)

Italians are so great at cooking vegetables that I'm always surprised by how few *contorni*, or side dishes, are offered at restaurants in Italy. Generally speaking, in Umbria and Tuscany, where I eat most often, you'll see a simple green salad, roasted potatoes, beans (see White Beans, page 36), and sautéed spinach. Being a green vegetable fanatic, I'm "forced" into ordering a side dish of spinach pretty much every time I eat in a restaurant in the region. The way the Italians prepare spinach is so different from how we do. Here, sautéed spinach would be wilted in a light amount of oil, but in Italy, the spinach is cooked so slowly, and in so much oil, that it has the voluptuous texture of creamed spinach, but with olive oil in place of cream. At Massolino, when you order spinach, they give you the choice of having it cooked with red chile flakes, garlic, or lemon. When I make Italian-style spinach, I figure, what the heck? and season it with all three.

If you have a mandoline, use it to make easy work of slicing the garlic for this recipe.

———

Combine the olive oil, garlic, lemon strips, salt, and chile pods in a small saucepan over low heat and cook for 30 minutes to infuse the oil with the seasonings. The oil may occasionally bubble; reduce the heat if it is bubbling regularly or if the garlic or lemon is browning. Turn off the heat and set the oil aside until you're ready to use it. Before using the oil, remove the chile pods and lemon strips from the oil and discard them.

Meanwhile, fill a large saucepan with water, bring the water to a boil over high heat, and salt it to taste like the ocean, adding 1 tablespoon salt to each quart of water. Prepare an ice bath in a medium bowl and prepare a bed of paper towels.

Plunge the spinach into the boiling water to blanch for 1 minute, or until it is wilted. Drain the spinach in a colander and immediately plunge it into the ice water for 1 minute to cool. Lift the spinach out of the ice water with your hands and put it back in the colander. Push on the spinach to squeeze out as much water as possible. Put a weight on top of the spinach and leave the colander in the sink for at least 5 minutes to drain. Spread the spinach out on the paper towels or a clean dish towel to drain the spinach even more.

Put half of the seasoned oil, including half of the garlic slices, and a handful of the spinach in a large sauté pan over medium heat and cook the spinach for about 1 minute to begin to warm it through, gently folding the spinach leaves into the oil with tongs so the oil gets onto all of the leaves. (Take care not to wrinkle the spinach in the process of folding it; you don't want the finished product to look like frozen spinach.) If the spinach is crisping, reduce the heat; the idea is to steep the spinach in the oil, not to fry it. Add another handful of the spinach and fold it into the oil, adding another spoonful or two of the seasoned oil and garlic to the pan as the spinach wilts and the oil in the pan is absorbed into the spinach. Continue, adding the remaining spinach a handful at a time and folding it in with the oil until you've added all of the spinach and all of the oil. Continue cooking the spinach and oil together, folding the spinach gently, until there is no water in the pan, 5 to 10 minutes. Turn off the heat and transfer the contents of the pan to a large colander set over the sink to drain the excess oil.

Transfer the spinach and garlic from the colander to a medium dish. I use a white oval dish with 1-inch sides, because it looks Italian to me. Serve with tongs.

Kale Salad with Marinated White Anchovies and Ricotta Salata

It seems like just yesterday that kale was used almost exclusively to decorate salad bars and the vegetable section of supermarkets. Then, one day, somebody discovered that it was both healthy and delicious, and today, it's as if it's illegal to own a restaurant, at least in California, without a kale salad on the menu. Not being much of a health nut, I resisted the kale salad trend—both eating kale salads and making them—until, years into the movement, I discovered baby kale. I'd seen kale torn into pieces and cut into ribbons, but when I saw those small tender green leaves, I knew it was time to see if I had a kale salad in me. Because of the sturdiness of kale leaves (even baby kale leaves), I immediately turned my thinking to Caesar salad dressing. I took those flavors and made a dressing that could stand up to the pungent flavor and sturdy texture of the kale. I use ricotta salata, which is salted, aged ricotta cheese, in place of Parmigiano. And instead of putting anchovies in the dressing, as is done with Caesar salad, I tangle marinated white anchovies, a plump silver-skinned fish that you find sold in plastic trays at seafood stores or in the fish department of specialty food stores, in with the kale. If you think your guests might not be anchovy fans, lay the anchovies, including all of the marinating ingredients, on a small plate and serve them with small tongs or a small fork alongside the salad.

Much to my surprise, kale salad, done right, has won me over. And I no longer think it's a fad; I think the kale salad is here to stay.

———

To prepare the anchovies, lift them out of the brine they are packed in, discard the brine, and put the anchovies in a medium bowl. If the anchovies are butterflied (rather than separated into two fillets), tear each "butterfly" down the middle to create individual fillets. Add the olive oil, parsley, and red chile flakes. Using either a three-holed zester or a fine Microplane, grate the zest of the lemon directly into the bowl and gently toss to combine the ingredients, taking care not to tear the anchovies. Add more olive oil if necessary to cover the anchovies. Set aside the anchovies to marinate for at least 10 minutes, or cover the bowl and place the anchovies in the refrigerator to marinate for up to 3 days. Bring the anchovies to room temperature before serving.

SERVES 6 TO 8

FOR THE MARINATED ANCHOVIES

20 marinated white anchovy fillets

¼ cup extra-virgin olive oil, plus more as needed

1 tablespoon thinly sliced fresh Italian parsley leaves (from about 2 tablespoons packed whole leaves)

1 teaspoon red chile flakes

1 lemon

FOR THE DRESSING

2 tablespoons minced shallot (from about 1 peeled shallot)

2 tablespoons fresh lemon juice

1 tablespoon champagne vinegar (or white wine vinegar)

1 teaspoon kosher salt

¼ teaspoon freshly ground black pepper

¼ teaspoon red chile flakes

4 lemons

3 large garlic cloves, peeled

¼ cup extra-virgin olive oil

¼ cup finely grated ricotta salata (about 1 ounce; grated on a fine Microplane)

(continued)

¼ cup pine nuts, preferably Sicilian

6 lightly packed cups baby Tuscan kale (also called cavolo nero, lacinato, or dinosaur kale; or 2 bunches Tuscan kale), leaves torn from the stems, stems discarded, and leaves torn into 2-inch pieces)

1 tablespoon fresh lemon juice

½ teaspoon kosher salt

Wedge of ricotta salata for grating

To make the dressing, combine the shallot, lemon juice, vinegar, salt, pepper, and red chile flakes in a small bowl. Using a fine Microplane, grate the zest of the lemons and the garlic into the bowl. Add the olive oil and ricotta salata and whisk to combine the ingredients. (The dressing may separate but don't worry; that's just the nature of it.) Use the dressing or refrigerate, covered, for up to 2 days. Bring to room temperature and stir to recombine the ingredients before using it.

To make the salad, adjust an oven rack to the middle position and preheat the oven to 325°F.

Spread the pine nuts on a baking sheet and toast them in the oven for 8 to 10 minutes, until they are fragrant and golden brown, shaking the baking sheet and rotating it from front to back halfway through the cooking time so the nuts brown evenly. Remove the pine nuts from the oven and set them aside to cool to room temperature.

Put the kale in a large wide-mouthed mixing bowl, drizzle with the lemon juice, sprinkle with the salt, and toss gently to coat the leaves. Drizzle the dressing over the salad, toss, and massage the dressing into the leaves with your hands. You can do this somewhat aggressively because of the sturdy nature of kale; the important thing is to make sure each leaf is coated.

To build the salad, heap one-third of the dressed kale leaves in a separate large wide-mouthed serving bowl. Scatter one-third of the pine nuts and drape one-third of the anchovies over the kale, coiling the anchovies back over themselves in a way that looks organic and pretty. Using a fine Microplane, grate a generous blanket of ricotta salata over the first layer of salad. Build a second layer, adding another third of the kale leaves to the serving bowl. Scatter a third of the pine nuts, drape a third of the anchovies, and grate a generous blanket of ricotta salata over the second layer of salad. Build a third layer like the first two, using the remaining kale leaves, pine nuts, and anchovies. Grate a generous blanket of ricotta salata over the salad.

Serve with tongs and place the wedge of ricotta salata and the Microplane on a plate next to the salad for guests to grate more cheese on their portions and for you to freshen up the salad with a fresh snowdrift of cheese.

Roasted Onions with Crispy Bread Crumbs

One summer I was shopping for patio furniture and some other practical items for my house in Italy, which took me through the not-very-charming town of Magione more times than I'd been during the entire fifteen years I'd been visiting the area. Magione isn't a tourist town, but a busy little city in the countryside not far from where I live. As a tourist, you go there only when you need specific, functional things—like patio furniture. Every day as I drove to Magione and back, I passed a strip mall with a sign for a tiny food establishment that read *rosticceria*. I had seen the sign for years and I'd always thought, "I should stop in there sometime. . . ." I've been in these little rotisserie stores before, so I know that, in addition to roasted chicken, which I love, they invariably offer a few side dishes and other items. I was curious. That summer, passing by more often than usual, I finally stopped in.

What I found inside was a long, L-shaped glass counter with every vegetable *contorno* (side dish) imaginable behind it: marinated zucchini, fried potatoes, stuffed tomatoes, sautéed spinach, you name it—all of them dripping in oil and all of them, I have to say, looking really appetizing. The place, packed with locals who worked in the area taking their lunch breaks, was set up cafeteria style. You order from a woman behind the counter who puts what you want on a thin, plastic plate. You pay by weight and then you find a seat. I was with Carolynn and between the two of us we ordered just about everything they had, including a baked onion that sat lonely, with only two or three others, on a giant platter. Carolynn and I were pleasantly surprised at how tasty everything was, but the onions were clearly the standout. They were sweet and flavorful and practically melted in our mouths. This recipe was inspired by those onions. I braise the onions in chicken stock (vegetarians can use vegetable stock or water), which brings out the natural sweetness of the onions, and although they didn't do this at the shop in Magione, I top mine with bread crumbs because I like that crunchy texture with the soft onions.

For the sake of clarity, I wrote the recipe with the bread crumbs prepared before the onions go into the oven, but in reality, I make the bread crumbs during the two hours that the onions are in the oven. This recipe calls for sodium-free chicken stock. Use only 1 teaspoon of salt in the onion portion of this recipe if you are using chicken stock that contains salt. Panko are Japa-

SERVES 6 TO 12

FOR THE BREAD CRUMBS

1 teaspoon fennel seeds

¼ cup panko bread crumbs

2 tablespoons extra-virgin olive oil

1½ teaspoons chopped fresh sage leaves (about 5 large leaves)

1 teaspoon kosher salt

FOR THE ONIONS

6 small yellow Spanish onions, peeled

2 tablespoons extra-virgin olive oil

1½ teaspoons kosher salt

¾ cup Chicken Stock (page 59 or sodium-free store-bought chicken or vegetable stock or water), or as needed

12 bay leaves, preferably fresh

nese bread crumbs. They're larger than traditional bread crumbs and have a light, flaky texture that makes them really crunchy when fried or baked.

You can find fresh bay leaves packed in plastic clamshells, along with other fresh herbs, in most grocery stores.

You will need a large 12-inch round ovenproof sauté pan or baking dish to make these. Ideally, the onions are served in the same pan they're cooked in, so reach for something that you would feel good about putting on your table.

To make the bread crumbs, toast the fennel seeds in a small sauté pan over medium heat for 1 to 2 minutes, until they are fragrant and golden brown, shaking the pan often so they don't burn. Transfer the fennel seeds to a cutting board to cool slightly. Crush the fennel seeds with the underside of a heavy sauté pan or with a mortar and a pestle and put the crushed seeds in a small bowl. Add the panko bread crumbs, olive oil, sage, and salt and stir to combine.

To prepare the onions, adjust an oven rack to the middle position and preheat the oven to 425°F.

Trim off and discard the hairy ends of the onions, trimming only as much as necessary so the onion layers stay intact. Cut each onion in half root to tip. If your onions are too large, peel off 3 or 4 of the outer petals of each onion half so the half is about the width of three fingers. (Use the onion trimmings to make Chicken Stock, page 59, or chop them up and throw them in any dish that requires chopped yellow onion.)

Put the onions in a large bowl, drizzle them with the olive oil, sprinkle with the salt, and gently toss and massage the onions to coat them.

Put the onions, cut side down, in a 12-inch round sauté pan or baking dish, arranging them in a spiral pattern with one in the middle and the rest around it. Add enough chicken stock around the onions to come ¾ inch up the sides of the onion halves, pouring it around, not over the onions. Nestle the bay leaves between the onion halves. Put the lid on the pan, if it has one; otherwise, cover the pan tightly with heavy-duty aluminum foil.

Roast the onions for 1½ to 2 hours, until they're tender and almost translucent. To check for doneness, remove the pan from the oven and take off the lid or lift up one segment of the foil. Use a small sharp knife to check if the onions are tender. If they're not, replace the cover and return the onions to the oven until they're done. Remove the onions from the oven and remove the lid or remove and discard the foil.

Increase the oven temperature to 450°F.

Using a large spoon, gently turn the onions so they are cut side up, taking care not to tear them apart in the process. Remove the 2 innermost petals from each onion half, if necessary, to make room for the onions to be stuffed. (Drizzle them with olive oil, sprinkle them with sea salt, and offer them to lurkers in the kitchen to munch on.) Spoon a scant tablespoon of the bread crumbs into the cavity you created in each onion half, using all of the bread crumbs to stuff the onions. Return the onions to the oven, uncovered, to bake until the bread crumbs are golden brown and crunchy, about 15 minutes. Remove the onions from the oven.

Serve the onions in the dish you cooked them in, or transfer them to a medium round platter, arranging them in a spiral, flowerlike pattern on the platter and scattering the bay leaves around them. Serve with a flat spatula or large spoon.

18

Spicy Pork Stew with Butternut Squash and Roasted Tomatillo Salsa

Other Menu Options

Spicy Pork Stew with Butternut Squash and Roasted Tomatillo Salsa

SERVES 6 TO 8

MAKES ABOUT 3 QUARTS

FOR THE PORK

2 teaspoons coriander seeds

2 teaspoons fennel seeds

2 teaspoons cumin seeds

1 tablespoon plus 1 teaspoon kosher salt

1 teaspoon freshly ground black pepper

½ teaspoon cayenne pepper

3 pounds cubed boneless pork shoulder (from a 3½-pound pork shoulder, trimmed of the fat cap and cut into 1½- to 2-inch cubes)

FOR THE STEW

1¼ pounds butternut squash (or another winter squash, such as kabocha or acorn), peeled, seeds removed, and cut into 1½-inch cubes (about 3 cups)

2 bunches collard greens

6 tablespoons olive oil

1¾ teaspoons kosher salt

1 medium yellow Spanish onion, peeled, root end trimmed and discarded, and cut into ½-inch dice (about 2 cups)

I love a meal where guests gather in the kitchen eating and talking around the stove, and that's what this stew, and this meal, are all about. The inspiration for the meal came after a party I hosted in relation to Alex's Lemonade Stand Foundation, a charity devoted to raising money for children's cancer. Every year, the night before their annual fund-raiser in Los Angeles, I host the chefs who come from around the country to participate in the event. This year, about two hundred people showed up at my house, which was considerably more than expected. It was the first time I ever ran out of food. Or almost ran out. We were serving Sal's Roasted Pork Shoulder (page 48), along with all the fixings that go with that feast, and somehow managed to make sure every last guest had enough to make themselves a few tacos. But there wasn't a single bite of pork left for the staff and latecomers. Like any great party, it ended with close friends, family, and the occasional straggler standing around in the kitchen, emptying wine bottles and trying to make a meal of what was left. That moment of everyone picking at tortillas and cleaning the guacamole bowls really stuck in my mind, so for this, I planned the meal to *start* in the kitchen, not just end there.

The stew, minus the squash, can be made days ahead. This recipe calls for sodium-free chicken stock. Use half of the salt in the stew portion of this recipe if you are using chicken stock that contains salt.

———

To prepare the pork, toast the coriander, fennel, and cumin seeds in a small sauté pan over medium heat for 1 to 2 minutes, until the seeds are fragrant and golden brown, shaking the pan often so they don't burn. Transfer the seeds to a plate to cool to room temperature; grind the seeds in a spice grinder or use a mortar and a pestle and transfer to a small bowl. Add the salt, black pepper, and cayenne and stir to combine.

Put the pork in a large bowl. Sprinkle with the spice mixture, toss gently, and massage the spices into the pork with your hands to coat the pieces evenly. Set aside for the pork to come to room temperature while you prepare the rest of the ingredients, or for up to 2 hours.

To make the stew, adjust the oven racks so none are near the oven floor; you'll be putting the baking sheet directly on the oven floor. If you are using an electric oven or another oven where you can't put anything on the floor, adjust the oven racks so that one is closest to the floor and put a pizza stone on it, if you have one. Preheat the oven to 500°F.

Put the squash cubes on a large baking sheet. Drizzle with 2 tablespoons of the olive oil, sprinkle with ½ teaspoon of the salt, and toss to coat the squash. Spread the squash out into a single layer. Put the baking sheet on the oven floor or the lowest rack and roast the squash until it is fork-tender and caramelized around the edges, 18 to 22 minutes, rotating the baking sheet from front to back once and shaking it halfway through the cooking time so the squash browns evenly. (When cooking vegetables on the oven floor as you do in this recipe, a lot of steam is produced from the water released as a result of the vegetables cooking so quickly, so just be careful of the steam that will arise when you open the oven door.) Remove the squash from the oven. (If you are making the stew in advance, cook the squash the same day you are serving the stew.)

Decrease the oven temperature to 350°F.

Pull the collard leaves from the ribs. Trim and discard the very ends of the ribs and slice the ribs ½ inch thick on an extreme bias. Tear the collard leaves into 3-inch pieces.

Pour 2 tablespoons of the oil into a large Dutch oven or other high-sided heavy-bottomed pot, and heat the oil over medium-high heat until it slides easily in the pan and the oil around the edges of the pot just begins to smoke, 2 to 3 minutes. Add half of the pork, increase the heat to high, and sear the pork for 6 to 8 minutes, turning the pieces to brown all sides. Remove the pork chunks with tongs as they are done and put them on a baking sheet. When you've removed all of the pork, add the remaining 2 tablespoons oil and heat until it begins to smoke around the edges of the pan. Add the remaining pork and sear it in the same way as you did the first batch. Remove the second batch of pork from the pot and add it to the first batch.

Reduce the heat to medium-high and add the collard green stems, onion, and celery. Season the vegetables with 1 teaspoon of the remaining salt and cook them, stirring occasionally, for about 10 minutes, until the collard stems and onion are tender. Add the white wine and cook it over high heat until it has reduced by half, about 2 minutes. Add the collard leaves and the remaining ¼ teaspoon salt. Stir to combine the leaves with the rest of the ingredients and cook for about 2 minutes, until the leaves are wilted. Return the pork, including any juices that have collected on the baking sheet it was resting on, to the pot. Add the 3 cups chicken stock, or enough to come just to the top of the pork, with some of the top edges of pork peeking out of the stock. Add the cilantro bunch,

3 celery stalks, sliced ½ inch thick on an extreme bias (about 1 heaping cup)

1 cup dry white wine

3 cups Chicken Stock (page 59 or sodium-free store-bought stock), or as needed

1 bunch fresh cilantro

2 árbol chile pods

2 bay leaves (preferably fresh)

1 recipe Roasted Tomatillo Salsa (recipe follows)

chile pods, and bay leaves and bring the stock to a boil over high heat. Turn off the heat. Put the lid on the pot or cover the pot with heavy-duty aluminum foil and put the stew in the oven to cook until the pork is fall-apart tender, about 1½ hours. Remove the stew from the oven. (The stew can be made to this point up to 3 days in advance. Cool to room temperature and refrigerate, covered, until you're ready to finish and serve it.)

Increase the oven temperature to 500°F.

Remove the lid or foil from the pot, add the butternut squash, and gently stir to distribute the squash throughout the stew. Return the stew to the oven, uncovered, and cook for about 10 minutes, until the squash is warmed through and the stew has a slightly browned, glazed look. Remove the stew from the oven. Fish out and discard the chile pods, bay leaves, and cilantro. Set the stew aside to rest for at least 15 minutes and up to several hours before serving it.

Just before serving, bring the stew to a boil over high heat. Reduce the heat to medium, stir in the salsa, and simmer for 20 to 30 minutes, until the stew is a thick, saucy consistency.

Serve the stew on the stove top in the pot it was cooked in, with a long ladle and a stack of bowls so guests can gather in the kitchen and serve themselves. You know the kitchen is where they want to be anyway.

Roasted Tomatillo Salsa

Makes about 1¼ cups

We use this salsa to make the stew, but it also makes a delicious salsa on its own to serve with Sal's Roasted Pork Shoulder (page 48) or with tortilla chips for dipping. To serve as a condiment, double the recipe. This salsa can be made up to two days in advance.

1 pound tomatillos, husks removed, rinsed, and halved or quartered (depending on size)

½ large yellow Spanish onion, peeled, root end trimmed and discarded, and cut into ¾-inch dice

10 to 12 medium or large garlic cloves, peeled

½ lime, cut into 2 wedges

3 tablespoons olive oil

2 teaspoons kosher salt

¼ cup roughly chopped fresh cilantro leaves and stems

1½ tablespoons fresh lime juice

1 teaspoon champagne vinegar (or white wine vinegar)

Adjust the oven racks so none are near the oven floor; you'll be putting the baking sheet directly on the oven floor. If you are using an electric oven or another oven where you can't put anything on the floor, adjust the oven racks so that one is closest to the floor and put a pizza stone on it, if you have one. Unless the broiler is in a different section of the oven, put another rack closest to the broiler. Preheat the oven to 500°F.

Put the tomatillos, onion, garlic, and lime wedges on a large baking sheet. Drizzle with the olive oil, sprinkle with 1¼ teaspoons of the salt, and toss to coat the vegetables and lime wedges. Spread the vegetables and lime wedges and turn the tomatillos so the cut sides are facing up. Put the baking sheet on the oven floor or the lowest rack to roast for 10 minutes. When cooking vegetables on the oven floor, a lot of steam is produced from the water released as a result of the vegetables cooking so quickly, so just be careful of the steam that will arise when you open the oven door.

Change the oven setting to broil.

Move the baking sheet to the rack closest to the broiler or to the broiler section of the oven, rotating it from front to back when you move it. (There will be a lot of liquid on the baking sheet released from the tomatillos, so be careful when moving the baking sheet.) Broil the vegetables for 6 to 8 minutes, until the tomatillos have collapsed and the onion and garlic are soft, rotating the pan halfway through and stirring the vegetables so the onion and garlic don't burn. Remove the baking sheet from the oven or broiler and set aside for the vegetables to cool slightly.

Drain the contents of the baking sheet in a colander. Discard the liquids, and remove the lime wedges and set them aside. Transfer the contents of the colander to the bowl of a food processor fitted with a metal blade or to the jar of a blender. Squeeze the flesh from the roasted limes into the food processor or blender and discard the peels. Add the cilantro, lime juice, vinegar, and the remaining ¾ teaspoon salt and purée the salsa until it's smooth. Use the salsa or refrigerate, covered, for up to 2 days.

To serve, transfer the salsa to a small bowl and serve with a spoon, or alongside tortilla chips for dipping.

Spiced Rice with Pumpkin Seeds

When I serve stew or braised meats, I like to offer something such as this rice to soak up all the sauce that is invariably the best part of any dish. The pumpkin seeds add a nice crunchy element and are a reflection of the winter squash in the stew. In a perfect world, I would use the seeds that I scoop out of the squash for this rice, but even I have my limits, and I definitely stop short of shelling raw squash seeds.

This recipe calls for sodium-free chicken stock. Use half of the salt in this recipe if you are using chicken stock that contains salt.

———

Adjust an oven rack to the middle position and preheat the oven to 325°F.

Spread the pumpkin seeds on a baking sheet and toast them in the oven for 8 to 10 minutes, until they are fragrant and golden brown. Remove the pumpkin seeds from the oven, drizzle them with the olive oil, sprinkle with ½ teaspoon of the salt, and toss to coat the seeds.

Cut the shallot in half root to tip and trim and discard the root end. Separate the layers of the shallot, stack 2 or 3 layers at a time on top of one another, and slice 1⁄16 inch thick lengthwise.

Heat the butter in a medium sauté pan over medium heat until it melts, about 1 minute. Add the shallot, garlic, coriander seeds, cumin seeds, and ½ teaspoon of the remaining salt and cook for about 3 minutes, until the shallot and garlic are translucent, stirring often so they don't brown. Add the rice and cook for about 2 minutes, stirring constantly, until the rice is barely translucent and golden. Add the chicken stock and the remaining 1½ teaspoons salt. Increase the heat to high and bring the liquid to a boil. Reduce the heat, cover the pot, and cook the rice at a very low simmer for about 20 minutes (or according to the time indicated on the package), until all the liquid has been absorbed. Turn off the heat and let the rice rest, covered, for 10 minutes. Add the pumpkin seeds and use a fork to gently fluff up the rice and distribute the seeds. Just before serving, add the cilantro and gently fold it into the rice with a fork.

To serve, transfer the rice to a high-sided bowl and serve with a large spoon.

SERVES 8 TO 12
MAKES ABOUT 8 CUPS

¾ cup shelled raw pumpkin seeds

1 tablespoon extra-virgin olive oil

2½ teaspoons kosher salt

1 medium shallot, peeled

2 tablespoons unsalted butter

3 to 4 large garlic cloves, peeled and sliced ⅛ inch thick lengthwise

2 teaspoons coriander seeds, cracked with the bottom of a heavy pan or ground in a spice grinder, or use a mortar and a pestle, to one-quarter of their original size

2 teaspoons cumin seeds, cracked with the bottom of a heavy pan or ground in a spice grinder, or use a mortar and a pestle to one-quarter of their original size

2 cups basmati rice

2½ cups Chicken Stock (page 59 or sodium-free store-bought stock)

¼ cup thinly sliced fresh cilantro leaves (from about ½ cup packed whole leaves)

Quesadillas

The part I left out of the story in the headnote to the pork stew—when I was describing the party I had at my house that ended up, much to my delight, in the kitchen—was the point at which Carolynn, in a moment of genius, got the idea to order in twenty plain quesadillas and some guacamole from a local taco stand. When the food arrived, she put the tall stack of quesadillas, each on its own paper plate and wrapped in aluminum foil, in the center of my kitchen worktable. Those of us who had been eating plain tortillas now had quesadillas—which seemed so luxurious! We took the quesadillas apart, stuffed them with the pickled jalapeño peppers that came with the quesadillas in little Styrofoam containers, and dipped the quesadillas into the guacamole and salsas that were left from the party. It was such a fun, communal, and delicious conclusion to a great night, and in my opinion, it was the best part of a great party. Even the last remaining party guests who had eaten the main feast, as they came to say good night, were seduced by the quesadillas and tore into them also. These quesadillas are my attempt to re-create that special moment.

Plain cheese quesadillas are one of the rare foods, in my opinion, that do not benefit from being "upgraded" with fancy, artisanal ingredients. Supermarket flour tortillas, decent Jack cheese; toast them together until the cheese is melted . . . It just doesn't get any better than that. I serve these with Spicy Pork Stew with Butternut Squash and Roasted Tomatillo Salsa (page 310), but they would be equally good with Dean Fearing's Frito Pie (page 210) with or without the Fritos, or, for a humble weeknight meal, a pot of Refried White Beans (page 60) and a Caesar salad. I serve Pickled Jalapeño Peppers (page 319) alongside the quesadillas for those who want to tuck some inside, but I also give the option of making the quesadillas with the jalapeño peppers in them. Whether you put the peppers inside the quesadillas or serve the peppers on the side is strictly a matter of knowing your audience.

In this recipe, the quesadillas are toasted in a sauté pan without oil or butter, which I've been told is the traditional way to make quesadillas. I couldn't believe any quesadilla could be better than one grilled in butter, but I made them both ways, tasted them side by side, and was shocked to find that I preferred those toasted in a dry pan. The light char flavor that you get from toasting the tortillas in a dry pan is a delicious contrast to the mild cheese.

SERVES 6 TO 8

8 large flour tortillas

2 cups shredded Jack cheese (about 8 ounces)

Pickled Jalapeño Peppers (page 319 or store-bought; optional)

Seasoned Avocado Halves (page 321)

Adjust an oven rack to the middle position and preheat the oven to 200°F.

Put a tortilla in a large sauté pan over medium heat. Scatter ½ cup of the cheese on the tortilla, covering the surface and leaving a ½-inch border with no cheese. Lay as many jalapeño pepper rounds as you'd like over the surface of the cheese, if you're including them. Lay a second tortilla on top of the first one and cook the quesadilla until it is browned and slightly charred in places, about 3 minutes, pressing down on it gently with a spatula to help it brown. Flip the quesadilla and cook it on the second side until it is browned and crispy in places and the cheese is melted, about 3 minutes. Take the quesadilla out of the pan and put it on a baking sheet. Put the baking sheet in the oven to stay warm while you make the remaining quesadillas.

Repeat, cooking the remaining quesadillas using the remaining tortillas and cheese and when they are done, adding them to the baking sheet in the oven with the first batch. When you have made all the quesadillas, remove the baking sheet from the oven. One at a time, transfer the quesadillas to a cutting board and use a large knife or pizza cutter to cut each quesadilla into 6 or 8 wedges.

To serve, pile the wedges on a pretty, medium cutting board or platter and serve with the seasoned avocados (page 321) and the pickled jalapeño peppers (page 319) in small bowls alongside them.

Pickled Jalapeño Peppers

This is Liz's and my take on the pickled jalapeño peppers that are served in Mexican restaurants. My very favorite way to eat them is stuffed inside a plain cheese quesadilla; the burst of heat and acidity is the perfect complement to melted cheese. In this recipe, we call for you to cut sliced carrot rounds into flower shapes with a cookie cutter. You can skip this step, obviously. This was Liz's attempt to make them as authentic as possible.

———————

Slice the carrot into ¼-inch rounds. Use a 1-inch fluted cookie cutter to cut each slice into a flower shape. Discard the trimmed edges or save them for another use. Remove the papery skins from the cipollini. Trim and discard the dry root ends, trimming only as much as necessary so the onions stay intact. Cut each onion into quarters, through the root end.

Combine the vinegar, salt, sugar, and 2 cups water in a medium saucepan and bring the liquid to a boil over high heat. Add the jalapeños and return the water to a boil. Reduce the heat to low and simmer the jalapeños for about 6 minutes, until they're army green and tender, stirring occasionally to submerge the jalapeños in the liquid. Add the carrot slices and onions and return the water to a boil. Turn off the heat and set aside for the vegetables to cool to room temperature in the pickling liquid.

Serve, or transfer the vegetables to a 1-quart canning jar (or another container with a lid). Fill the jar with the pickling liquid and discard the remaining liquid. Close the jar and refrigerate the pickled vegetables until you're ready to serve them or for up to several months.

MAKES 1 QUART

———————

1 large carrot, trimmed and peeled

5 medium cipollini onions (about 3 ounces)

3½ cups apple cider vinegar

¾ cup kosher salt

2 tablespoons sugar

8 medium jalapeño peppers (about 12 ounces), stems left on, rinsed

Seasoned Avocado Halves

Not long ago, I did a cooking demonstration at Macy's; my presentation came after that of Mexican culinary authority Rick Bayless—a hard act to follow. Rick is such a wealth of information on every micro topic concerning Mexican food and the ingredients used to make it. I was fascinated by everything he said, but my takeaway from Rick's demo was his trick for keeping avocados from turning brown after they're cut: refrigerate them right up until serving them. The cool temperature keeps them from discoloring. I immediately put the trick to the test when I got back to Los Angeles and it worked. Nevertheless, I like to prepare the avocados as close to serving time as possible.

I season avocados before serving them to optimize their flavor, which is just as important whether someone is putting the avocado on a hamburger or quesadilla, or if someone wants to eat the avocado by itself. And I serve them in their skins, because I think they look pretty that way; it's also less messy and it's easier for guests to pick them up. When serving avocados as a burger condiment or alongside Dean Fearing's Frito Pie (page 210) or Spicy Pork Stew with Butternut Squash and Roasted Tomatillo Salsa (page 310), count on one-half of an avocado per person.

Large ripe avocados, such as Hass, Pinkerton, or fuerte

Lemons

Finishing-quality extra-virgin olive oil

Maldon sea salt (or another flaky sea salt such as fleur de sel)

Freshly ground black pepper

Cut the avocados in half lengthwise. Twist each half in opposite directions to separate them. Plunge the edge of a large knife into the pit and twist the knife to release the pit from the avocado. Remove and discard the pits. Using a large spoon, carefully scoop the avocado to separate it from the peel, but leave it in the peel. With the avocado still in the peel, slice each half lengthwise into 3 or 4 slices, depending on the size of the avocados. Squeeze the lemon juice and drizzle finishing-quality olive oil over the avocados. Sprinkle the avocados with sea salt and grind pepper over them. Refrigerate until ready to serve.

Serve the avocados, seasoned side up, on a small platter or cutting board with a small fork on the side to pierce and pick up the slice, stacking them if you wish.

19

**Southern-Style Korean Cut Short Ribs
with Vinegar Onions** 325

Other Menu Options

Southern-Style Korean Cut Short Ribs with Vinegar Onions

When we opened Chi Spacca, we were looking for unusual cuts of meat to offer, and Korean cut short ribs came to mind. *Korean cut* refers to short ribs that are thinly sliced against the grain. They cook quickly on the grill, and you pick them up and eat them with your hands, so they're a completely different eating experience from that of conventional short ribs, which are braised for hours until fork-tender. The problem was that we couldn't get the Korean cut short ribs to be tender like those we'd eaten in Korean restaurants in Los Angeles. We had several experienced cooks working on them, but nobody could crack the code.

Then Liz's mother, Jenee Kim, stepped in. Jenee owns Parks BBQ, a wonderful Korean restaurant in Los Angeles, and she told us that the secret to tender Korean-style short ribs is in the marinade, which traditionally contains pears, kiwi, or papaya, the acidity from which breaks down the meat, tenderizing the ribs. Ryan DeNicola, our chef at Chi Spacca, helped me take the short ribs in a southern direction as an excuse to serve southern-style side dishes that I love. These are ribs, after all. And making these is a lot easier than breaking out your smoker to make traditional Memphis- or Texas-style pork or beef ribs. The vinegar onions on top are a nod to the vinegary sauces that make those American ribs so irresistible.

These ribs are best cooked over a very hot charcoal or wood fire. The point is to char the outsides very quickly before you cook the meat so long that it becomes tough. Most gas grills don't get hot enough, and in the length of time it takes to char the outsides, the meat will toughen up. If your gas grill doesn't get super hot, you will need a square or rectangular grill pan, such as a 20-inch reversible grill/griddle to make these.

When ordering your short ribs, ask the butcher to remove the silver skin.

If you are using a spice grinder, you can grind all the spices at one time.

———

To prepare the ribs, trim and discard the root end of the red onion and cut the onion in half root to tip. Cut each half in half again root to tip so the onion is quartered. Separate the layers of the onion, stack 2 or 3 layers at a time on top of one another, and slice ¼ inch thick lengthwise.

SERVES 8 TO 10

FOR MARINATING THE RIBS

1 red onion, peeled

12 flanken-style short ribs, cut ½ to ¾ inch thick, silver skin removed

2 kiwi fruit, peeled

4 cups apple cider vinegar

1 quart olive oil

1 cup honey (preferably wildflower or another mild-flavored honey)

FOR THE RUB

¼ cup plus 2 tablespoons coffee grounds

¼ cup plus 2 tablespoons kosher salt

¼ cup dark or light brown sugar

3 tablespoons red chile flakes, ground in a spice grinder or use a mortar and a pestle

1 heaping tablespoon black peppercorns, cracked with the bottom of a heavy pan or ground in a spice grinder or use a mortar and a pestle to one-quarter of their original size

(continued)

1 heaping tablespoon coriander seeds, cracked with the bottom of a heavy pan or ground in a spice grinder or use a mortar and a pestle to one-quarter of their original size

1 heaping tablespoon cumin seeds, cracked with the bottom of a heavy pan or ground in a spice grinder or use a mortar and a pestle to one-quarter their original size

1 heaping teaspoon fennel seeds, cracked with the bottom of a heavy pan or ground in a spice grinder or use a mortar and a pestle to one-quarter their original size

1 heaping teaspoon yellow mustard seeds, cracked with the bottom of a heavy pan or ground to a powder in a spice grinder or use a mortar and a pestle

2 tablespoons sweet smoked paprika

1 tablespoon garlic powder

1 tablespoon onion powder

FOR THE VINEGAR ONION GARNISH AND SERVING THE RIBS

1 teaspoon coriander seeds

1 tablespoon fresh lime juice

1 teaspoon kosher salt

1 teaspoon fresh coarsely ground black pepper

6 tablespoons apple cider vinegar

1 small yellow Spanish onion, peeled

½ cup fresh Italian parsley leaves

¼ cup fresh cilantro leaves

¼ cup torn fresh mint leaves

Finishing-quality extra-virgin olive oil

Maldon sea salt (or another flaky sea salt such as fleur de sel)

Using a paring knife, score each rib on both sides in a ¼-inch diagonal cross-hatch pattern. Divide the ribs and onion slices evenly among three large sealable plastic bags and set aside while you make the marinade.

Put the kiwi and vinegar in the jar of a blender or the bowl of a mini food processor fitted with a metal blade and purée until the kiwi is liquefied. Transfer the contents of the blender or food processor to a medium bowl. Add the olive oil and honey and whisk to combine. Divide the marinade among the bags with the ribs and onion slices. Massage the marinade with your hands to coat the ribs all over. Close the bags and set aside to marinate the ribs for 2 hours. (Any longer and the acidity of the kiwi will cause the meat to break down to a fuzzy, unappealing texture.)

To make the rub, put the coffee grounds, salt, brown sugar, red chile flakes, peppercorns, coriander, cumin, fennel, mustard seeds, paprika, garlic powder, and onion powder in a medium bowl and stir to combine.

Working in batches that will fit on your work surface, remove the ribs from the marinade, scraping off the excess marinade and discarding the remaining marinade and onion slices. Pat the ribs on both sides using paper towels to remove any marinade and lay the ribs in a single layer on a flat work surface.

Sprinkle the ribs with the rub on both sides. Pat the rub into the meat to help it adhere and pat the meat onto any fallen rub to mop up the rub. Put the ribs on a baking sheet and continue, removing the remaining ribs from the marinade and coating them with the remaining rub in the same way. The ribs can be prepared to this point up to 3 hours in advance of grilling them. Cover the ribs and refrigerate. Bring the ribs to room temperature before grilling them.

To make the vinegar onions, toast the coriander seeds in a small sauté pan over medium heat for 1 to 2 minutes, until they are fragrant and golden brown, shaking the pan often so they don't burn. Transfer the seeds to a plate to cool to room temperature. Crush the seeds with the underside of a heavy sauté pan or use a mortar and a pestle and put the crushed seeds in a small bowl. Add the lime juice, kosher salt, pepper, and 2 tablespoons of the vinegar and set aside.

Trim and discard the root end of the onion and cut the onion in half root to tip. Cut each half in half again root to tip so the onion is quartered. Separate the layers of the onion, stack 2 or 3 layers at a time on top of one another, and slice ⅛ inch thick lengthwise. Put them in a medium bowl. Add the parsley, cilantro, and mint leaves and set aside while you grill the ribs.

Prepare a hot fire in a charcoal grill. Alternatively, to cook the chops indoors, preheat a square or rectangular grill pan over high heat. Cooking method and times will be the same as for grilling.

Pour the remaining ¼ cup of apple cider vinegar into a small bowl and put it near the grill, along with a basting brush.

Grill the ribs for 2 minutes per side, scraping them off the grill after the first minute to prevent the rub from sticking to the grill. Remove the ribs from the grill, brush both sides with the vinegar, and put the ribs on a baking sheet while you grill the remaining ribs.

Drizzle the vinegar mixture over the onions and herbs and toss to combine.

To serve, pile the ribs on a large platter or cutting board. Drizzle on finishing-quality olive oil and sprinkle with sea salt. Using your fingers, drop the vinegar onions on the ribs in clumps. Serve with tongs.

Pimento Cheese with Celery Sticks

SERVES 8 TO 10
MAKES ABOUT 2 CUPS

4 small Fresno chiles, halved (stems, seeds, and membranes removed and discarded) and sliced into threads ⅛ inch wide

1 cup plus 1 tablespoon extra-virgin olive oil

1¾ teaspoons kosher salt, plus more to taste

1 packed cup drained jarred roasted piquillo peppers (or other jarred roasted red peppers)

8 to 10 medium or large garlic cloves, peeled and smashed with the flat side of a knife, plus 3 to 4 medium or large garlic cloves, peeled

1½ cups shredded extra-sharp yellow Cheddar cheese (about 6 ounces), plus more as needed

½ cup smoked shredded Gouda cheese (about 2 ounces), plus more as needed

½ cup crème fraîche (or sour cream)

½ cup cream cheese, softened at room temperature

¼ teaspoon fresh coarsely ground black pepper

1 tablespoon grated yellow Spanish onion (grated on a medium-holed Microplane)

1 celery head

I first heard about pimento cheese through my friend Brad Springer. Brad was from Texas, and whenever he talked about how his family cooked back home, he would get very flamboyantly Texan and go on and on about deviled eggs, pimento cheese, and other regional specialties of his homeland. The way he talked about these foods, he was in part making fun of himself, because he worked in fine dining, but at the same time, he was obviously proud of where he came from, and these foods represented that for him. Brad described pimento cheese as a spread made with really cheap cheese, pimiento peppers, and mayonnaise. It couldn't have sounded worse, and needless to say, I never felt any great urge to eat it, much less to make it. That changed when I went to Sean Brock's restaurant Husk, in Charleston, South Carolina. I'm a big fan of Sean's cooking, so when I saw pimento cheese on his menu, I knew this was the time to try it. I did, and I loved it. Made with good cheese, Sean's cheese spread turned out to be a version that made me understand what pimento cheese could be, and that inspired me to try my hand at it.

Because I didn't grow up with pimento cheese, when I set out to make it for the first time, I wasn't trying to re-create a memory; I wasn't even trying to re-create Sean's. I just wanted to make a spreadable, spicy cheese dip using ingredients that I would feel good about serving to my family and friends. I bought more than a hundred dollars' worth of cheese—and that's a lot of money given that this wasn't fancy cheese—including many types of Cheddar, pepper Jack, and a couple of other whimsical choices. Liz and I had bowls of different cheeses and other ingredients set out like paints on a painter's palette. We played with different combinations, adding a bit of this or that, until we arrived at a mix of yellow Cheddar and smoked Gouda mixed with cream cheese and loosened with crème fraîche. Pimento cheese is typically served with crackers, but I prefer it with celery sticks. I like the pairing of the thick, creamy cheese and the crunchy, mineral-tasting celery: think old-school celery sticks with peanut butter. If you think all celery is created equal, think again. Good celery from a farmers' market is exceptionally crunchy and flavorful. I love the celery they grow at Chino Farm in San Diego, which is so mineral and salty it's hard to believe it's not seasoned.

For this recipe, I call for a combination of Fresno chiles, which we roast, and piquillo chile peppers, a special Spanish variety. If you can't find piquillo peppers, use another quality jarred roasted pepper and your spread will still be delicious. We cook the piquillos, which concentrates their flavor and also helps to break up the peppers so they are like delicate, scarlet ribbons laced throughout the spread.

Adjust the oven rack to the middle position and preheat the oven to 400°F.

Spread the Fresno chiles on a baking sheet, drizzle with 1 tablespoon of the olive oil, season with ¼ teaspoon of the salt, and toss to coat the chiles. Roast for 4 to 6 minutes, until they wilt slightly. Remove the chiles from the oven and set aside until they cool to room temperature.

Put the remaining 1 cup olive oil, the jarred peppers, smashed garlic cloves, and 1 teaspoon of the remaining salt in a small sauté pan. Cook over low heat, stirring often so the garlic doesn't burn, until the garlic cloves are soft and golden brown, and turning the peppers halfway through cooking time, about 20 minutes. Turn off the heat and allow the peppers to cool to room temperature in the pan. When they're cool enough to touch, remove the peppers from the oil, finely chop them, and set aside. Remove the garlic cloves from the oil to a small plate and smash them to a paste with a fork or the flat side of a knife; set aside. (Let the oil cool and reserve it to sauté anything you wouldn't mind the flavors of garlic and peppers with, which is just about anything I can think of to sauté.)

In the bowl of a standing mixer fitted with the paddle attachment mix the yellow Cheddar, Gouda, crème fraîche, cream cheese, black pepper, grated onion, Fresno chiles, and piquillo peppers. Using a fine Microplane, grate the raw whole garlic cloves directly into the bowl and mix on medium speed for 3 to 5 minutes to combine. Add more salt to taste and more grated cheese as needed to thicken the mixture to the consistency of creamy and dense cream cheese. The cheese spread can be made up to 1 day in advance. Refrigerate it, covered, until you're ready to serve it. Bring it to room temperature so it returns to a spreadable consistency before serving.

Separate the stalks from the celery head and reserve the largest stalks for another use. Peel the outer convex sides of the remaining celery stalks with a vegetable peeler and cut each stalk into 3- to 4-inch sticks on an extreme bias. Soak the celery stalks in a bowl of ice water for 20 minutes, to get them cold and crunchy. Drain and dry them well before serving.

Transfer the cheese spread to a small deep bowl and stick a cheese or butter knife into the cheese. Put the celery sticks upright in a glass or a small narrow-mouthed bowl and serve with the cheese spread.

Pickled Vegetables

When I entertain at home, whether I'm serving burgers, lamb, steak, or cured meats, I like to have some kind of pickle on the table to cut the fat in the meats I serve. The pickles listed on the following pages are what are referred to as "refrigerator pickles." They're not fermented and they're not canned, which means you have to keep them in the refrigerator, and they last, some for a week, others up to six months, instead of indefinitely, as canned pickles do. I store the pickles in canning jars, which I open up and plunk on the table come serving time. Like a nice dress that goes from day to evening, these pickled vegetables go from a starter for guests to munch on when they arrive to a vegetable side dish in the same meal. There are a lot of great, small-batch pickles of every type of vegetable and flavor combination imaginable available these days, but nothing tastes quite as good as it does when you make it yourself.

Husk-Style Pickled Green Beans

MAKES 1 QUART

5 large fresh dill sprigs, including stems (preferably those from a farmers' market, which are sold with longer stems than those from the supermarket)

3½ cups apple cider vinegar

¾ cup kosher salt

10 to 12 medium or large garlic cloves, peeled

3 jalapeño peppers, halved lengthwise

2 tablespoons sugar

1 teaspoon ground turmeric

1 pound green beans (preferably haricots verts), stem ends trimmed, tails left intact

At Husk, Sean Brock serves green beans, which he calls Dilly Beans, that have been pickled and then breaded in cornmeal and deep-fried. When we had dinner at the restaurant during a culinary event, Liz couldn't stop eating the beans, and Sean was nice enough to scribble a very basic recipe on a sheet of paper for her. Liz came home and played with the recipe until we got to what we think is a respectable version of Sean's—although we don't fry ours. The beans continue to absorb the salt that is in the pickling liquid, so if they're not used within a week of being made, they become too salty. If you want them to keep longer, cut the salt in this recipe in half.

Lay the dill sprigs in a large flat baking dish, such as a 13 x 9-inch baking dish.

Combine the vinegar, salt, garlic, jalapeños, sugar, turmeric, and 2 cups water in a medium saucepan and bring the liquid to a boil over high heat. Reduce the heat to low and simmer for 10 minutes to infuse the liquid with the seasonings. Increase the heat to high, add the beans, and return the liquid to a boil. Turn off the heat and immediately pour the contents of the saucepan into the dish with the dill. Set the dish aside for both the beans and the pickling liquid to cool to room temperature.

Transfer them, beans standing straight up, to a 1-quart canning jar (or another container with a lid). Strain the pickling liquid into a large bowl. Add the pickling spices that are in the strainer to the jar with the beans. Add enough of the pickling liquid to fill the jar and discard the remaining liquid. Close the jar and refrigerate the green beans for 1 to 2 days before serving them, or for up to 1 week.

To serve, if you stored the green beans in a cute jar, open the jar and lift up a few of the green beans so they're sticking out of the jar. Alternatively, remove the beans from the pickling liquid and stick them in a small narrow bowl. Serve with tongs.

Pickled Carrots

We use long, slender carrots to make these pickles. Those found at farmers' markets are ideal, but those sold in regular supermarkets in bunches with the tops on also work; choose carrots on the smaller side. The longer these carrots sit in the pickling liquid, the tastier they are.

MAKES 1 QUART

Combine the vinegar, salt, sugar, mustard seeds, coriander seeds, fennel seeds, peppercorns, chile pods, bay leaves, and 2 cups water in a medium saucepan and bring the liquid to a boil over high heat. Reduce the heat to low and simmer for 10 minutes to infuse the liquid with the seasonings. Increase the heat to high, add the carrots, and return the liquid to a boil. Reduce the heat to low and simmer the carrots for 2 minutes. Turn off the heat and let the carrots cool to room temperature in the cooking liquid.

Transfer them, tops facing up, to a 1-quart canning jar (or another container with a lid). Strain the pickling liquid into a large bowl. Add the pickling spices that are in the strainer to the jar with the carrots. Add enough of the pickling liquid to fill the jar and discard the remaining liquid. Close the jar and refrigerate the carrots for 1 to 2 days before serving them, or for up to 6 months.

To serve, if you stored the carrots in a cute jar, open the jar and lift up a few of the carrots so they're sticking out of the jar. Alternatively, remove the carrots from the pickling liquid and stick them straight up in a small narrow bowl. Serve with tongs.

2 cups champagne vinegar
(or white wine vinegar)

2 tablespoons kosher salt

1 tablespoon plus 1 teaspoon sugar

1 tablespoon plus 1 teaspoon
mustard seeds

1 tablespoon plus 1 teaspoon
coriander seeds

1 tablespoon plus 1 teaspoon
fennel seeds

1 tablespoon plus 1 teaspoon
black peppercorns

6 árbol chile pods

2 bay leaves

1 pound slender carrots
(about 1 large or 2 small bunches,
with the tops torn off)

Pickled Shallots

MAKES 1 QUART

1 pound medium shallots, peeled

2½ cups champagne vinegar
(or white wine vinegar)

1 cup sugar

3 tablespoons kosher salt

2 teaspoons mustard seeds

2 teaspoons coriander seeds

2 teaspoons fennel seeds

2 teaspoons red peppercorns

3 árbol chile pods

2 bay leaves

I'm not normally a fan of pickles on the sweet end of the spectrum, but pickled shallots are one exception. The extra sugar added to the pickling liquid really brings out the flavor of the shallots. These are a bit more labor intensive than other pickles, because the shallots are blanched and shocked in ice water three times before being pickled, a process that brings out the pretty pink hue of the shallots; not done this way, they turn an unappealing gray. These shallots are beautiful fanned out on a cutting board of sliced cured meats.

———

Using a small sharp knife, trim the roots off the shallots, leaving enough of the root end to keep the layers of the shallots intact. Cut the shallots in half root to tip. Peel the shallots and discard the peel and trimmed bits. Cut each shallot in half lengthwise again so you have equal-size wedges of shallot with the petals still attached by the root.

Prepare an ice bath in a large bowl and add the shallots to the bowl. Let the shallots sit, submerged in the ice water, for 30 minutes; this helps the shallots stay crunchy after being pickled. Prepare a bed of paper towels.

Combine the vinegar, sugar, salt, mustard seeds, coriander seeds, fennel seeds, peppercorns, chile pods, bay leaves, and 2½ cups water in a medium saucepan and bring the liquid to a boil over high heat. Reduce the heat to low and simmer for 5 minutes to infuse the liquid with the seasonings. Increase the heat to high. Using a strainer, fish the shallots out of the ice bath and remove any ice cubes that came along with them. Plunge the shallots, still in the strainer, into the saucepan with the pickling liquid. Return the pickling liquid to a boil and turn off the heat. Remove the strainer with the shallots from the pickling liquid and plunge the strainer into the ice bath to cool the shallots, adding more ice to the ice bath if necessary. Return the pickling liquid to a boil. Remove the strainer with the shallots from the ice bath, return it to the pickling liquid, bring the pickling liquid back to a boil, and immediately turn off the heat. Remove the shallots from the pickling liquid and return the strainer with the shallots to the ice bath to cool completely. Repeat, boiling and blanching the shallots one more time and adding more ice to the ice bath if necessary.

After you have cooled the shallots for the last time, remove them from the ice bath. Shake the strainer to remove the excess liquid and transfer the shallots to the paper towels to drain.

Transfer the shallots to a 1-quart canning jar (or another container with a lid). Strain the pickling liquid into a large bowl. Add the pickling spices that are in the strainer to the jar with the shallots. Add enough of the pickling liquid to fill the jar and discard the remaining liquid. Let the shallots cool to room temperature in the liquid then close the jar and refrigerate for 1 to 2 days before serving the pickles, or for up to 6 months.

To serve, if you stored the shallots in a cute jar, open the jar and lift up a few of the shallots so they're sticking out of the jar. Alternatively, remove the shallots from the pickling liquid and pile them in a small bowl. Or fan the shallots out on a pretty cutting board and serve them alongside cured meats. Serve with tongs.

Spicy Braised Greens with Vinegar and Ham Hock

SERVES 8 TO 10
MAKES ABOUT 6 CUPS

2 bunches mustard greens

2 bunches Tuscan kale
(also called cavolo nero, lacinato,
or dinosaur kale; about 1 pound)

2 heads escarole

2 small yellow Spanish onions,
peeled

¼ cup canola oil (or another
neutral-flavored oil)

1 cup large garlic cloves
(about 40 cloves), peeled and
sliced ⅛ inch thick lengthwise

3 to 5 árbol chile pods
(depending on how spicy you
want your greens)

2 tablespoons plus 2½ teaspoons
kosher salt, or to taste

1 smoked ham hock
(the bigger the better)

¾ cup apple cider vinegar

¼ cup finishing-quality extra-virgin
olive oil

Until recently, I'd always thought of braised greens as a southern thing. But in the last several years, with all the popularity of vegetables such as kale, mustard greens, chard, escarole, and beet greens that benefit from slow cooking, you're seeing slow-cooked greens served in all types of restaurants, including mine. When I first started preparing greens this way, I made rich greens that were braised in tons of olive oil. Now, I use a lot less oil and get the flavor instead by cooking the greens with a ham hock and vinegar. Also, where I used to braise only one type of greens, now I use a combination because I like the subtle taste variations and the less subtle differences in textures of the different vegetables. In this recipe I call for cavolo nero, Tuscan kale (also called black kale), which stays chewy, it seems, no matter how long you cook it; mustard greens, which have a spicy quality; and escarole, which is a cross between a sturdy lettuce and a braising green. If you want to use another combination, be my guest. Just consider how long each vegetable takes to cook and add the different varieties to the pot accordingly. Even though in Italy they throw them out, in the name of *cucina povera*, or "poor cuisine," I decided to try cooking the stems of the greens with the onions. I love the textural component they add as much as the idea of letting nothing go to waste.

If you have a mandoline, use it to make easy work of slicing the garlic for this recipe.

Trim and discard the tough ends of the mustard greens. Tear the leaves from the mustard green ribs. Slice the ribs into 2- to 3-inch segments on an extreme bias and put them in a bowl or pile. Tear the leaves into 2-inch pieces and put them in a separate bowl or pile. Prepare the kale in the same way: Trim off and discard the tough ends, rip the leaves from the ribs, slice the ribs into 2- to 3-inch segments on an extreme bias, and tear the leaves into 2-inch pieces. Put the kale leaves in one bowl and add the ribs to the bowl with the mustard ribs. Cut the escarole 2 inches from the cores to remove the cores and separate the leaves at the same time. Discard the cores, tear the leaves into 2-inch pieces, and put the leaves in a separate bowl or pile. Trim and discard the root end of the onions and cut the onions in half root to tip. Cut each half in half again root to tip so the onion is quartered. Separate the layers of the onion, stack 2 or 3 layers at a time on top of one another, and slice ¼ inch thick lengthwise.

Heat 3 tablespoons of the canola oil in a very large Dutch oven or another large pot over medium heat for about 1 minute to warm it slightly. Add the onions, garlic, and chile pods, and season with 1½ teaspoons of the salt. Cook the onions until they are slightly translucent, about 10 minutes, stirring often so they don't brown. Add the ham hock and the mustard ribs and kale ribs. Drizzle with the remaining 1 tablespoon oil and sprinkle with 1 teaspoon of the remaining salt. Stir to combine the ingredients, reduce the heat to low, cover the pot, and cook for about 20 minutes, until the ribs are tender.

Uncover the pot and add the kale leaves and 2 teaspoons of the remaining salt, adding the leaves a big handful at a time and folding them in with the cooked vegetables so they wilt slightly, making room in the pot for another big handful. Cover the pot with the lid (you may need to smash the greens down a bit to make them fit) and cook the greens for 30 minutes, uncovering the pot to stir and fold the greens and turn the ham hock from time to time, until the greens are tender but not mushy.

Fold in the escarole and 2 teaspoons of the remaining salt, adding the greens a handful at a time as you did the kale leaves and folding them in to wilt so they fit in the pot. Cover the pot and cook for 30 minutes, uncovering the pot to stir the greens and turn the ham hock from time to time, until the escarole is tender. Uncover the pot and fold in the mustard green leaves as you did the kale and escarole leaves. Cover and cook the greens for 30 minutes or more, uncovering the pot to stir the greens and turn the ham hock from time to time, until all of the greens and the ribs are tender. (By cooking the greens on low enough heat, they will release enough liquid to keep them from burning on the bottom of the pot. If the greens do appear to be scorching, add a splash of water and reduce the heat.) Taste for seasoning and add the remaining 2 teaspoons salt (or as much as you like), if you wish. Leave the greens on low heat.

Uncover the pot, remove the ham hock, and set it aside until it's cool enough to touch. Pull the meat off the bone and discard the bone. Finely chop the meat and return it to the pot with the greens.

Increase the heat to high and cook the greens, uncovered, until all of the liquid has cooked off, 5 to 10 minutes. Stir in the vinegar and continue to cook until all of the liquid has been cooked off, about 10 minutes. Turn off the heat and fish out and discard the chile pods. Drizzle in the olive oil and gently stir to combine it.

To serve, pile the greens in a medium deep bowl and serve with a big spoon or tongs.

Coleslaw with Green Goddess Dressing

FOR THE DRESSING

1½ teaspoons champagne vinegar
(or white wine vinegar)

1½ teaspoons fresh lemon juice

½ cup extra-virgin olive oil

½ cup canola oil (or another
neutral-flavored oil)

1 extra-large egg yolk

½ teaspoon kosher salt

1 tablespoon finely chopped
fresh sage leaves (from about
3 tablespoons whole leaves)

2 teaspoons finely chopped fresh
oregano leaves (from about
1 heaping tablespoon whole leaves)

2 teaspoons finely chopped
fresh thyme leaves (from about
3 tablespoons whole leaves)

2 tablespoons finely chopped fresh
Italian parsley leaves (from about
¼ cup whole leaves)

1½ tablespoons well-shaken
buttermilk

Coleslaw makes a great fresh, salad-y option for a buffet setting because the crunchy vegetables don't wilt with time the way lettuce does. Throughout the years, I have made every version of coleslaw imaginable, from traditional cabbage slaws to slaw made of celery and green apple. For this version, I pushed the coleslaw envelope even further by making it with thinly sliced bok choy, sugar snap peas, and fennel, in addition to the more predictable savoy cabbage. It's everything coleslaw should be—crunchy vegetables tossed in a rich, tangy dressing—but with much more flavor. All of the vegetables are on the pale green spectrum, and then tossed with a pale green, herb-flecked Green Goddess dressing, so it looks really bright and fresh and pretty.

My preferred way of making the dressing is to pound the herbs in a mortar, then make the dressing in a blender and combine the herbs at the end. Pounded in a mortar, the herbs release liquid, which stains the mayonnaise rather than the mayonnaise's just being dotted with the color of the herbs. If you don't mind the fifteen minutes or more of elbow grease required to pound the herbs, you'll be rewarded with a dressing vibrant in both color and flavor. If you don't use a mortar, chop the herbs as finely as you can.

You may not need all of the dressing for the salad; use the rest to dress another salad, or as an herb mayonnaise, within the next two days.

To make the dressing, combine the vinegar and lemon juice in a small bowl. Combine the olive oil and canola oil in a measuring cup with a spout.

Put the egg yolk and salt in the bowl of a mini food processor fitted with a metal blade and blend for about 30 seconds, until the yolk is pale yellow. Add a few drops of the combined oils and pulse to incorporate the oil into the egg. With the machine running, begin adding the remaining oil a few drops at a time until the egg and oil are emulsified; you will have added 2 or 3 tablespoons of oil. Turn off the machine, take off the lid, scrape down the sides of the bowl with a rubber spatula, and add the vinegar–lemon juice mixture. Continue adding the oil a few drops at a time with the machine running constantly until you've added about half of the oil and the dressing is very thick. Stop the machine again, take off the lid, scrape down the sides of the bowl, and add 1 tablespoon water. Return the lid and pulse to incorporate the water. Drizzle the remaining oil in a slow, steady stream until all of the oil has been added.

Spoon half of the dressing from the food processor into a medium bowl. Add half of the sage, oregano, thyme, and parsley to the food processor with the remaining dressing and pulse to incorporate the herbs. Turn the herb-flecked dressing out of the food processor into the bowl with the plain dressing and stir gently to combine. Stir in the remaining herbs and the buttermilk. Cover and refrigerate the dressing for at least 30 minutes and up to 2 days. Remove the dressing from the refrigerator just before using it and give it a gentle stir to recombine the ingredients.

To make the salad, remove and discard the outer leaves from the cabbage. Cut the cabbage in half through the core. Cut out and discard the core from each half. Lay the cabbage halves, cut side down, on a cutting board and cut them into ⅛-inch-thick pieces. Put the sliced cabbage in a large bowl.

Remove the bok choy leaves from the cores and discard the cores. Stack the leaves 3 or 4 at a time and slice ¼ inch thick lengthwise. Add the bok choy to the bowl with the cabbage.

Remove and discard the strings from the sugar snap peas and slice the peas ⅛ inch thick on such an extreme bias that you are almost slicing them lengthwise. Add the sliced sugar snap peas to the bowl with the cabbage and bok choy.

Cut off the fronds from the fennel bulb, if they are still attached, and discard them or reserve them for another use. Remove any brown or unappealing outer layers and cut the fennel in half lengthwise. Lay each half flat side down. Slice ¼ inch thin lengthwise. Trim the cut end of the fennel and discard all of the trimmed bits. Add the slices to the bowl with the cabbage, bok choy, and sugar snaps.

Trim and discard the root ends and any wilted greens from the scallions. Starting at the green ends and moving toward the white ends, slice the scallions ⅛ inch thick on an extreme bias. Add the scallions to the bowl with the other vegetables. Add the tarragon, drizzle with the lemon juice, and sprinkle with the salt. Toss gently to combine the vegetables and coat them with the lemon juice and salt. Spoon 1 cup of the dressing over the vegetables and massage to coat them with the dressing, adding the rest of the dressing as needed to coat the vegetables.

Pile the coleslaw on a platter and serve with tongs.

FOR THE SALAD

1 small savoy cabbage head (about 1 pound 5 ounces)

4 baby bok choy heads (about 8 ounces)

6 ounces sugar snap peas (about 1½ cups)

1 medium fennel bulb

1 bunch scallions (8 to 10)

½ cup fresh tarragon leaves

2 tablespoons fresh lemon juice

2½ teaspoons kosher salt

Erik Black's Potato Salad

SERVES 8 TO 10

2½ pounds small, thin-skinned waxy potatoes (such as small red rose, fingerlings, or Yukon gold), unpeeled

6 hard-cooked eggs (5 for the potato salad and 1 tester egg; see Perfect Hard-Cooked Eggs, page 82)

1½ cups Garlic Mayonnaise (page 84)

¼ cup apple cider vinegar

1 teaspoon freshly ground black pepper

1 tablespoon plus 2 teaspoons kosher salt

½ medium onion, peeled and cut into ¼-inch dice

1 celery stalk, peeled and cut into ¼-inch dice

½ cup ¼-inch diced sweet pickles

After leaving Mozza, one of our original sous-chefs, Erik Black, became obsessed with southern barbecue and began catering parties serving ribs, homemade sausage links, beans, and this potato salad. My sister, Gail, became a regular client of Erik's, so I ate that feast, and this potato salad, many times before I eventually asked Erik for his recipe. Erik is a traditionalist when it comes to all things barbecue, so naturally this is an old-school mayonnaise-based potato salad—complete with crunchy bits of celery and pickles—made with the talent and palate of a great chef. I had never made a potato salad in a mixer so I was surprised when I first saw his recipe, but it makes sense because what makes Erik's potato salad special, in an old-school way, is that it is creamy and homogeneous, all the ingredients are mixed together instead of being distinct.

Steam the potatoes until they are tender when pierced with a small sharp knife, about 20 minutes. Transfer the potatoes to a plate to cool to room temperature.

Peel the eggs under running water. Pat them dry with paper towels and separate the yolks and whites. Coarsely chop the yolks and set the yolks and whites aside.

Combine the mayonnaise, vinegar, pepper, and 1½ teaspoons of the salt in a medium bowl. Pass the egg yolks through a fine-mesh strainer into the bowl and whisk to combine the ingredients.

Put the potatoes in the bowl of a standing mixer fitted with the paddle attachment and mix at low or medium speed for about 1 minute, until the potatoes are broken up into large chunks but not mashed or puréed, stopping to scrape down the sides of the bowl two or three times and discarding any skins that collect on the paddles during that time.

Turn off the mixer. Add the onion, celery, pickles, egg whites, and the remaining 1 tablespoon plus ½ teaspoon salt and mix at medium-low speed to combine. Turn off the mixer, drizzle the mayonnaise mixture over the potatoes, and mix on medium-low speed to combine.

To serve, transfer the potato salad to a large deep bowl and serve with a big spoon.

Flaky Buttermilk Biscuits

I was recently at a South Carolina food festival where all sorts of chefs, bakers, and biscuit wholesalers were touting their biscuits. Although I have to assume that because these were food professionals from the South, where biscuits are traditional fare, they knew what they were doing, I came away thinking that I still hadn't seen biscuit perfection.

Being from Los Angeles, which isn't exactly biscuit territory, I'm hardly an expert. My biscuit memories are of those biscuits that my mother made by hitting a paper tube of dough on the corner of the counter. But I did have a biscuit ideal: one that was light, buttery, and salty, with just the right baking powder undertones, and I eventually found my perfect biscuit at a charity event in Philadelphia. The man responsible for these perfect biscuits was a chef from New Orleans, Alon Shaya. Knowing that I wanted to include a biscuit recipe in this book, Liz managed to track down Shaya, who was generous enough to share the secrets of his biscuit conquests with her, with me, and, thus, with you.

Shaya rolls the dough and then folds it and rolls it again: the same process used to give puff pastry its characteristic buttery layers. I had started folding biscuit dough this way a few years prior at the suggestion of a late Chi Spacca chef, Robert Shapiro. But Shaya's biscuits were still better than mine, and here, I learned, is why: He starts with frozen butter, which he grates into the flour. The little shards of butter melt in the oven, creating pockets of butter and air in the biscuits. So simple! So brilliant! It was a bittersweet, why-didn't-I-think-of-that moment for me, but at least I now had the secret to the perfect biscuit.

The generous amount of butter called for in this recipe is the result of a kitchen accident. The accident happened in Mozza's kitchen, when Sean Panzer, one of our pastry cooks, converted the amount of butter incorrectly. Shaya uses four sticks of butter. We, because of the error, used five when we tested it—and the recipe still worked!

My friend Ruth Reichl tested these when she was visiting Los Angeles last year. She agreed that they were the best biscuits she'd ever eaten—and the only biscuit she'd ever eaten that she didn't want to put butter on. Ruth prefers the four-stick version. After Ruth blogged about making these, *Saveur* magazine included them in its roundup of favorite recipes for 2015. And guess what? They use five sticks. Because, let's face it, when it comes to butter, I believe more is more.

MAKES 15 BISCUITS

5 cups unbleached all-purpose flour

2 tablespoons plus 2 teaspoons baking powder

1 teaspoon baking soda

1 tablespoon kosher salt

1 tablespoon sugar

1¼ pounds (5 sticks) unsalted butter, frozen for 2 hours (but not frozen solid), plus 8 tablespoons (1 stick) melted, to brush on the biscuits

2 cups well-shaken buttermilk, plus more as needed

Maldon sea salt (or another flaky sea salt such as fleur de sel)

Naturally, the biscuits are best right out of the oven. You can prepare them ahead of time and have them in the freezer, ready to bake, when you need them: even easier (and much tastier) than that tube of dough my mom cracked open on the counter.

With my last book, I started a tradition of having one recipe in every book that will cause the smoke alarm in your kitchen to go off. In *The Mozza Cookbook* it was the butterscotch *budino*. In this book, it's these biscuits. The combination of the high butter content and the high oven temperature may cause your oven to smoke so much that your smoke alarm goes off. When you taste the biscuits, you'll agree that a little smoke and noise are worth it.

——————

Put the flour, baking powder, baking soda, kosher salt, and sugar in a large bowl and stir to thoroughly combine.

Put a piece of parchment or waxed paper under a box grater and grate the butter on the large holes. Alternatively, grate the butter using the large-hole grater attachment of a food processor. Add the butter to the bowl with the dry ingredients and stir to combine the ingredients. Put the bowl in the freezer for at least 30 minutes to completely freeze the butter. Remove the bowl from the freezer. Add the buttermilk and gently work the dough together with your hands to create a shaggy mass that holds together only when pressed.

Dust a flat work surface and turn the dough out onto the flour-dusted surface. Using your hands, press the dough into a 10 x 7-inch rectangle with the long side parallel to the table's edge. Use a bench scraper (or your hands) to square the dough off as much as possible. Take the dough from your left side and fold the left third of the dough toward the middle. Repeat this process on the right side, folding the right side on top of the left side so the dough is now stacked three layers high. (Use your hands to keep the dough together because the dough will be a bit crumbly.) Rotate the folded dough a quarter turn clockwise so the long side again is parallel to your table's edge. This completes the first turn of three total turns.

Dust the dough with flour. Dust a rolling pin with flour and roll the dough out to a 10 x 7-inch rectangle with the long side parallel to your work surface. Repeat the folding process, folding the left side first, then the right side, and rotating the dough a quarter turn clockwise. This completes your second turn. Roll the dough out again to a 10 x 7-inch rectangle and fold it for the third and last time. After completing your third turn, roll out the dough to approximately 12 x 10 inches and ½ inch thick. Using a ruler or a very long knife, trim the edges so you have a nice clean rectangle. Use a knife to cut the dough into 2½-inch squares. Discard the end pieces or, better yet, bake them off and snack on them. Put the squares on a baking sheet and put them in the freezer until they are frozen solid, 1 to 2 hours.

Adjust an oven rack to the middle position and preheat the oven to 425°F. Line a large baking sheet with parchment paper.

Remove the biscuits from the freezer. Brush the tops with the melted butter and sprinkle them with sea salt. Bake the biscuits for 10 minutes. Rotate the pan from front to back.

Lower the oven temperature to 400°F.

Bake the biscuits for another 10 to 15 minutes, until the tops are golden brown and the biscuits are light and flaky. Remove the biscuits from the oven.

To serve, pile the biscuits in a towel-lined basket or bowl and flop the corners of the towel over the biscuits to help keep them warm.

20

Desserts

Spiced Carrot Cake with Molasses Cream Cheese Frosting (on the Side)

SERVES 10 TO 12

FOR THE CAKE

Nonstick cooking spray

1 cup walnut halves or pieces
(about 4 ounces)

1½ cups unbleached all-purpose
flour

1¾ teaspoons baking powder

1¼ teaspoons baking soda

1 teaspoon kosher salt

1 tablespoon ground cinnamon

1 teaspoon ground ginger

1 teaspoon ground allspice

½ teaspoon freshly grated nutmeg

¼ teaspoon ground cloves

1½ cups loosely packed light
brown sugar

3 extra-large eggs

1 tablespoon pure vanilla extract

2 ounces fresh ginger
(one 4-inch piece), peeled and
grated on a medium-holed
Microplane (about 1 scant
tablespoon)

¾ cup vegetable oil

2½ cups grated carrots
(grated on the largest holes of
a box grater; about 10 ounces
or 4 medium carrots)

I was a teen in the 1970s, when, fueled by the hippie movement, carrot cake was all the rage. I loved carrot cake then, and to this day, it's probably my favorite cake. Back then, my friend Wendy Mathews's mother, Marsha, had the coveted recipe for carrot cake. She used to bake and sell the cakes out of her house. Marsha gave me the recipe, and that cake, which was the first cake I learned to make myself, was my go-to potluck contribution for years. As time went by, poppy seed dressing and other icons of that era fell by the wayside, but carrot cake never did. I never got tired of eating it, and as a baker, I didn't tire of tinkering with it. This version, heavy on sweet spices and with bits of candied ginger in place of raisins, is like a hybrid between carrot cake and spice cake. I add molasses to the cream cheese frosting to reflect the molasses used to make spice cake.

I got the idea to serve the frosting on the side when Carolynn was planning the wedding of a friend. She and the bride-to-be had been to a tasting with a caterer who presented them with a sample of carrot cake. So they could focus on the cake and frosting separately, the caterer put the frosting on the side. Just when you'd swear you've seen it all, someone comes along with an idea that is so simple: frosting on the side! Who would have thought? It turns out to be a great idea for a buffet or family-style meal because instead of serving a frosted cake that starts to look messy after two or three people have helped themselves, the unfrosted cake stays nice and neat. It also means you can serve dessert with no forks, although you'd want to serve knives for people to slather the frosting on their slices.

Unlike many recipes for cream cheese icing, in this recipe, I didn't soften the cream cheese and butter before whipping them. They soften when they're whipped, and by starting with cold products, the finished frosting has the ideal consistency: spreadable, but with body. The frosting should be made no more than a couple of hours in advance of serving it. Refrigerated, it hardens, and it will soften unevenly at room temperature. You can make the cake 1 day in advance of serving it, but not sooner, and don't refrigerate it.

I serve this cake with egg pies (pages 131 to 135) for a retro 1970s California-themed meal. It also makes a nice end to a meal of Garlic-Rubbed Skirt Steak with Scallion Vinaigrette (page 194) and Staff Meal Oven-Roasted Chicken Thighs (page 162).

You will need a 6-cup Bundt or 10-inch angel food cake pan to make this.

To make the cake, adjust an oven rack to the middle position and preheat the oven to 350°F. Spray a 6-cup Bundt or 10-inch angel food cake pan generously with nonstick cooking spray and set it aside until you're ready for it. Set up a cooling rack.

Spread the walnuts on a baking sheet and toast them in the oven for 10 to 12 minutes, until they're lightly browned and fragrant, shaking the baking sheet and rotating it from front to back halfway through the cooking time so the nuts brown evenly. Remove the walnuts from the oven and set them aside until they're cool enough to touch. Break the walnuts into pieces with your hands or chop them coarsely.

Put the flour, baking powder, baking soda, salt, cinnamon, ground ginger, allspice, nutmeg, and cloves in a mixing bowl and stir to thoroughly combine the ingredients.

Combine the brown sugar and eggs in the bowl of a standing mixer fitted with the whisk attachment and mix at medium-high speed for about 10 minutes, until the mixture has lightened in color. Reduce the speed to medium, add the vanilla and fresh ginger, and mix to just combine. Lower the mixer speed to low. Add one-third of the dry ingredients and mix until there is no flour visible. Add one-third of the vegetable oil and mix until it is incorporated. Repeat, alternating between the dry ingredients and oil and mixing until each is incorporated before adding the other, until all of the dry ingredients and oil have been added. Turn off the mixer and remove the bowl from the stand. Add the carrots, candied ginger, walnuts, and pineapple and gently fold them in with a rubber spatula to combine the ingredients.

Pour the batter into the prepared pan and bake the cake for 30 to 35 minutes, until it is golden brown and springy to the touch, turning the pan halfway through the baking time so the cake browns evenly. Remove the cake from the oven and set aside to cool to room temperature.

To make the frosting, combine the cream cheese and butter in the bowl of a standing mixer fitted with the paddle attachment and mix on medium-high speed until they are combined and smooth, 3 to 5 minutes, scraping down the sides of the bowl with a rubber spatula two or three times in the process. Lower the speed to medium, add the confectioners' sugar and salt, and mix for 3 to 4 minutes, until there are no visible lumps. With the mixer running, gradually add the molasses and crème fraîche, and whip to just combine. Transfer the frosting to a medium serving bowl so that it is mounded high above the bowl like a snowy mountain.

1 cup chopped candied ginger (about 5 ounces)

¼ cup drained, canned crushed pineapple

FOR THE FROSTING

14 ounces cold cream cheese

8 tablespoons (1 stick) cold unsalted butter, cut into small cubes

¾ cup confectioners' sugar, sifted, plus ¼ cup for dusting

¼ teaspoon kosher salt

¼ cup blackstrap molasses

2 tablespoons crème fraîche (or sour cream)

To serve, if you used a Bundt pan, run a knife or offset spatula around the inside of the pan to release the cake from the pan and put a large plate on top of the pan. Swiftly flip the cake and plate to invert the cake onto the plate. Invert the cake again onto a large serving plate or cake stand. If you used an angel food cake pan, run a knife or offset spatula around the inside of the pan and lift out the bottom to release the pan. Place it on a large serving plate or cake stand with the uneven side of the cake (the side that faced up during baking) facing up.

Pour the confectioners' sugar for dusting into a fine-mesh strainer and tap the strainer over the cake to dust the cake lightly with the sugar. Serve the cake with a cake spatula or knife for guests to cut the size serving they want and serve themselves. Serve the frosting with small knives for guests to spread their frosting.

Polenta Cake with Brutti Ma Buoni Topping

This cake is the perfect union of two classic recipes: polenta cake and a traditional meringue-and-nut cookie called *brutti ma buoni,* which means "ugly but good." The cake portion of the recipe is a direct rip-off of the talented pastry chef Claudia Fleming's polenta cake, from her book *The Last Course.* I always gravitate to desserts made with brown butter, as this is, and when I made and tasted Claudia's polenta cake, I knew I had to bring it into my repertoire. (*Grazie,* Claudia!) I added the brutti ma buoni topping (which, incidentally, I don't think is ugly at all) to give a textural contrast to the dense, moist cake. I much prefer to embellish a dessert in this way, with something that adds to the story, rather than something purely decorative like, say, buttercream rosettes.

This is a dessert I would love to see on my Umbrian Tavola (page 18); although you don't see much polenta in my area, you will find brutti ma buoni cookies in every bakery. Likewise, you could serve this cake with any Italian-leaning meal, such as Saturday Night Chicken Thighs with Italian Sausage and Spicy Pickled Peppers (page 92), Eggplant Lasagne (page 249), Sicilian Swordfish Spiedini (page 181), or Braised Oxtails (page 220). It is best served the same day it is made.

You will need parchment paper and a 13¾ x 4¼-inch rectangular tart pan with a removable bottom to make this. I chose to make this tart in a rectangular shape because I liked the shape in contrast to the roundness of the nut clusters in the topping.

———

To make the topping, adjust an oven rack to the middle position and preheat the oven to 325°F.

Spread the almonds and hazelnuts in two distinct sections of the same large baking sheet and toast them in the oven until they are golden brown and fragrant, 12 to 15 minutes, gently shaking the baking sheet and rotating it from front to back halfway through the cooking time so the nuts brown evenly. Remove the baking sheet from the oven and set it aside until the nuts are cool enough to touch. Gather the hazelnuts into a clean dish towel and rub them together inside the towel to remove the skins. Discard the skins and transfer the almonds and hazelnuts to a bowl and set aside.

Increase the oven temperature to 350°F.

SERVES 8 TO 12

FOR THE TOPPING

1 cup slivered blanched, skinless almonds

1 cup hazelnuts

½ cup sugar

2 tablespoons plus 1 teaspoon honey (preferably wildflower, or another neutral-flavored honey)

1 teaspoon orange flower water

1 extra-large egg white

1 teaspoon pure vanilla extract

¼ teaspoon baking powder

¼ teaspoon kosher salt

FOR THE CAKE

Nonstick cooking spray

8 tablespoons (1 stick) unsalted butter

1⅓ cups confectioners' sugar, plus ¼ cup for dusting

¼ cup cake flour

¼ cup almond meal (also called almond flour)

2 tablespoons medium-ground cornmeal or polenta

4 extra-large egg whites

Put the sugar, honey, orange flower water, egg white, vanilla, baking powder, and salt in a medium bowl and stir with a rubber spatula to thoroughly combine the ingredients. Add the almonds and hazelnuts and stir to coat the nuts in the syrup. Set aside.

To make the cake, spray the inside of a 13¾ x 4¼-inch tart pan generously with nonstick cooking spray and place it on a baking sheet.

Warm the butter without stirring in a medium saucepan over medium-high heat for 3 to 5 minutes, until the bubbles subside and the butter is dark brown with a nutty, toasty smell, swirling the pan occasionally so the butter browns evenly and doesn't burn. Turn off the heat and set the butter aside to cool to room temperature.

Put the confectioners' sugar, cake flour, almond meal, and cornmeal in a large bowl and stir to combine the ingredients. Add the egg whites and stir with a spatula or wooden spoon to incorporate them. Stir in the brown butter.

Pour the batter into the prepared tart mold and bake it for 30 minutes, rotating the cake from front to back halfway through the baking time. Remove the cake from the oven. Using your fingers, quickly distribute the nut topping by crumbling it over the surface of the cake, allowing bits of cake to peek through lacy nut clusters. Return the cake to the oven for 20 minutes, until the nut topping is golden brown, rotating the cake halfway through the cooking time so the topping browns evenly. Remove the cake from the oven and set aside to cool to room temperature.

To serve, pour the remaining confectioners' sugar for dusting into a fine-mesh strainer and tap the strainer over the cake to dust it lightly. Gently push the removable bottom to lift the cake out of the pan and, using a long offset spatula, gently slide the cake from the metal bottom onto a long platter or pretty wooden cutting board (or you can simply put the cake, still on the metal bottom, on the platter or board). Serve the cake with a cake spatula or knife for guests to cut the size serving they want and serve themselves.

Torta di Riso

SERVES 8 TO 12

FOR THE CRUST

1½ cups unbleached pastry flour
(or unbleached all-purpose flour),
plus more for dusting

¾ cup confectioners' sugar

¼ teaspoon Italian leavening
(such as Benchmate or Paneangeli;
or ⅛ teaspoon baking soda plus
⅛ teaspoon baking powder)

Pinch of kosher salt

8 tablespoons (1 stick) cold
unsalted butter, cut into small
cubes, plus more for buttering
the flan ring

4 extra-large egg yolks

½ teaspoon pure vanilla extract

FOR THE PASTRY CREAM

12 extra-large egg yolks

¾ cup granulated sugar

3 tablespoons unbleached
all-purpose flour

3 tablespoons cornstarch

3 cups whole milk

1 teaspoon kosher salt

2 vanilla beans

2 teaspoons pure vanilla extract

In Italy this dessert is called *budino di riso,* or rice pudding. I call it *torta di riso,* which I think more aptly describes what it is: rice pudding baked in a tart shell. I first had torta di riso at the stunning Caffè Giacosa in the Roberto Cavalli store in Florence. What I love about this confection is that the flavor builds as you eat it; the tart somehow gets better and better with each bite, like a person who becomes more beautiful as you get to know him or her. As far as I've seen, in Italy, they make torta di riso only in individual portions, in deep oval molds, and I believe it is meant to be a morning treat because they bake enough to last just through the morning, not enough to last all day. I broke from the mold, as it were, and turned torta di riso into a large round tart—and I serve it as dessert. After sharing this tart with your guests, I hope you will have leftovers that you can enjoy the Italian way: with a morning coffee.

You can make the tart dough up to three days in advance and the filling up to two days in advance of serving it. Rice makes such a neutral dessert: you could serve this with Dave's Oven-Roasted Grouper with Spicy Tomato Marmalade and Tahini (page 232), Sicilian Swordfish Spiedini (page 181), or the Umbrian Tavola (page 18), with Braised Oxtails (page 220).

You will need an 11-inch flan ring (a straight-sided, bottomless tart ring) or an 11-inch fluted tart pan with a removable bottom, and parchment paper to make this. If you use a flan ring, you will need an 11-inch cake round to slide the tart onto after it's baked.

This recipe calls for Italian leavening, which you can find online and at well-stocked Italian specialty stores. In case you can't find it, I give an alternative using baking soda and baking powder.

———

To make the tart crust, combine the flour, confectioners' sugar, Italian leavening, and salt in the bowl of a standing mixer fitted with the paddle attachment and mix on low speed for a few seconds to thoroughly combine the ingredients. Add the butter and mix on low speed until the butter and the dry ingredients form a coarse cornmeal consistency with small chunks of butter visible, about 2 minutes. Add the egg yolks and vanilla and mix on medium speed until the dough is smooth, 2 to 3 minutes, being careful not to work the dough any more than necessary. Turn off the machine.

Dust a flat work surface with flour and turn the dough out onto the dusted surface. Knead the dough gently, just enough to bring it together into a ball. Pat the dough into a disk, wrap it in plastic wrap, and refrigerate it for at least 2 hours or up to 3 days; or freeze the dough for up to 2 months and defrost it overnight in the refrigerator.

If you are using an 11-inch flan ring, line a baking sheet with parchment paper, butter the inside of the ring and the parchment paper, and place the ring on the paper. If you are using an 11-inch fluted tart pan with a removable bottom, there is no need to put it on a baking sheet.

Remove the dough from the refrigerator. Reserve a third of the dough (about 6 ounces) for the top crust, wrap it in plastic, and return it to the refrigerator. Cut the remaining dough into 2 or 3 chunks. Dust a flat work surface with flour and knead each chunk until it is the texture of Play-Doh. Bring the dough together to form one ball, and pat the ball into a 1-inch-thick disk. Dust a rolling pin with flour and roll the dough out to a ⅛- to ¼-inch-thick circle large enough to line the bottom and sides of the flan ring or tart pan. Gently fold the dough into quarters and place it on top of the flan ring or tart pan, situating the point in the center of the pan and gently unfolding the dough so the edges of the dough flop over the edges of the ring. Gently push the dough down to fit snugly inside the ring or pan, lifting up the edges of the dough while pressing the dough into the crease on the inside circumference of the ring; dip the knuckle of your index finger in flour and press the dough into the crease with your knuckle to create straight rather than sloping sides. Don't stretch the dough to fit or it will shrink during baking. Roll the rolling pin over the top of the ring or pan to cut the dough, and pull off and discard the trimmed dough. Place the baking sheet with the flan ring or tart pan in the refrigerator to chill for at least 30 minutes or up to 1 day.

Remove the reserved dough from the refrigerator, unwrap it, and put it between two sheets of parchment paper slightly larger than the flan ring or tart pan. Roll the dough between the parchment into a circle 13 inches in diameter and 1/16 inch thick. Place the parchment paper with the dough sandwiched between it on a baking sheet and put it in the refrigerator to chill.

To make the pastry cream: beat the egg yolks and granulated sugar together in the bowl of a standing mixer fitted with a whisk attachment and mix on high speed, stopping once to scrape down the sides of the bowl, until the mixture is pale yellow and a ribbon forms when the beater is lifted from the bowl, 2 to 3 minutes. Turn off the mixer. Sift the flour and cornstarch together into a bowl to combine them. Add the flour mixture to the bowl with the eggs and mix on low speed to combine. Turn off the mixer, remove the bowl from the mixer, and set the mixture aside.

FOR THE RICE PUDDING

2 cups whole milk

½ cup Arborio rice

¼ cup granulated sugar

¼ teaspoon kosher salt

½ teaspoon freshly grated nutmeg

1 cinnamon stick

1 vanilla bean

FOR ASSEMBLING THE TART

½ cup pine nuts, preferably Sicilian

1 extra-large egg, lightly beaten

¼ cup confectioners' sugar
for dusting

Prepare an ice bath in a medium bowl. Set a bowl inside the ice bath and set a fine-mesh strainer in the smaller bowl.

Pour the milk and the salt into a large saucepan. Use a small paring knife to split the vanilla beans lengthwise. Use the back of the knife to scrape out the pulp and seeds and add the scrapings and the beans to the saucepan with the milk. Heat the milk over high heat until it begins to bubble around the edges, then immediately turn off the heat. Remove and discard the vanilla beans. Ladle out one-quarter of the hot milk and slowly pour it into the bowl with the eggs and flour mixture, whisking constantly to prevent the hot milk from cooking the eggs. Slowly pour the egg-milk mixture back into the saucepan with the milk, whisking constantly. Cook the pastry cream over medium heat, stirring constantly with the whisk, until it bubbles in the center and is the thickness of custard, about 3 minutes. Remove the pastry cream from the heat and pour it through the strainer into the bowl set in ice. Stir in the vanilla extract. Place a sheet of plastic wrap directly on top of the pastry cream and press it down to prevent a skin from forming. Set aside for the pastry cream to cool completely in the ice bath.

To make the rice pudding, combine the milk, rice, granulated sugar, salt, nutmeg, and cinnamon stick in a medium saucepan. Use a small paring knife to split the vanilla bean lengthwise. Use the back of the knife to scrape out the pulp and seeds and add the scrapings and the beans to the saucepan with the milk. Stir to combine the ingredients and cook over high heat until the liquid begins to bubble around the edges. Reduce the heat to low, cover the pot tightly with a lid or aluminum foil, and simmer the rice, without stirring, until it is cooked through and the pudding is thick and creamy, and all of the milk has been absorbed, about 40 minutes. Turn off the heat, uncover the pot, and set the rice aside to cool to room temperature.

Remove the pastry cream from the ice bath and fold the rice pudding into the bowl with the pastry cream. Use the filling or refrigerate, covered, for up to 2 days.

For the tart, adjust an oven rack to the bottom position and preheat the oven to 325°F.

Spread the pine nuts on a baking sheet and toast them in the oven for 8 to 10 minutes, until they are fragrant and golden brown, shaking the baking sheet and rotating it from front to back halfway through the cooking time so the nuts brown evenly. Remove the pine nuts from the oven and set them aside to cool to room temperature.

Increase the oven temperature to 350°F. Remove the tart shell from the refrigerator. If you are using a tart pan, put it on a baking sheet. Pour the filling into the shell and smooth to even with a spatula or the back of a spoon. Remove the thin sheet of dough from the refrigerator and peel off and discard the top sheet of parchment paper. Invert the dough onto the flan ring, centering it, and peel off and discard the remaining sheet of parchment. Gently run the rolling pin over the surface of the tart to seal the top sheet of dough to the sides of the dough. Trim and discard the crust that was hanging over the edges. Brush the top sheet of dough with the egg and scatter the pine nuts over it.

Bake the tart for 40 to 45 minutes, until golden brown, rotating the baking sheet from front to back halfway through baking time so the tart browns evenly. Remove the tart from the oven and set it aside to cool to room temperature. Pour the confectioners' sugar into a fine-mesh strainer and tap the strainer over the tart to dust the tart lightly with the sugar. If you are using a flan ring, slide the cake round underneath the tart and transfer it to a cake stand or a flat, unrimmed serving platter, and carefully remove the ring from the tart. If you are using a tart pan, gently push the bottom to remove the tart from the pan and place the tart, including the metal bottom, on a cake stand or platter. Serve the tart with a cake spatula or knife for guests to cut the size serving they want and serve themselves.

Dario's Olive Oil Cake with Rosemary and Pine Nuts

The brilliant butcher and my dear friend Dario Cecchini serves this at his restaurants in the town of Panzano, in Tuscany. After a seven-course fixed menu of meat dishes, Dario brings out this cake, cut into squares and stacked high on a plate. As he sets it down, he explains to guests that the reason he makes this cake after the animal-heavy feast is that it is the rare dessert that doesn't contain any dairy products—so it's a sort of nod to those who don't like to mix meat with dairy.

The olive oil cake I'd been making for years is made with equal parts olive oil and milk, so I was intrigued when I learned that Dario's cake doesn't contain milk. Dario's lovely wife, Kim Wicks, shared the recipe with me, and my pastry chefs worked to replicate the cake back in Los Angeles, which is always a challenge because of the difference in flours and leavenings used in Italy and here. After further experimentation by my friend Ruth Reichl, we determined what, deep down, I already knew: there is no substitute for Italian leavening. Alternatively, you can use equal parts baking powder and baking soda, and the cake will be delicious. But if you've ever had the pleasure of eating this cake in Dario's restaurant, perched as it is over the mountainside in his little village south of Chianti, you might notice that Dario's cake is ever-so-slightly airier.

As I said, I've made my own version of an olive oil cake for years, but where mine has a pretty straightforward, sponge cake–like texture, Dario's contains a lot of "goodies," including chopped oranges (including the peel), wine-soaked raisins, and pine nuts. But my favorite thing about Dario's cake is that it's so moist it lasts for days. Put it on a plate with a knife and leave it on the kitchen counter and I guarantee not a single individual will be able to walk by without taking a sliver.

I serve Dario's cake after the Panicale-inspired Flattened Chicken Thighs with Charred Lemon Salsa Verde (page 288). It would also be at home with Staff Meal Oven-Roasted Chicken Thighs (page 162), Saturday Night Chicken Thighs with Italian Sausage and Spicy Pickled Peppers (page 92), Eggplant Lasagne (page 249), Sicilian Swordfish Spiedini (page 181), and Lamb and Chicken Tikka Kebabs (page 270), and then hope there's some left so I can have a sliver with my morning coffee. It would also be great on a brunch table along with egg pies (pages 131 to 135). Really, this cake is so versatile that I

SERVES 10 TO 12

½ cup plump raisins
(preferably Flame raisins;
about 5 ounces)

¼ cup plus 2 tablespoons vin santo
(or another sweet dessert wine)

⅓ cup pine nuts, preferably Sicilian

Nonstick cooking spray

1½ navel oranges, halved through
the stems (unpeeled), seeds
removed and discarded

2 large eggs

2 teaspoons Italian leavening
(such as Benchmate or Paneangeli;
or 1 teaspoon baking soda plus
1 teaspoon baking powder)

¾ cup plus 2 tablespoons
granulated sugar

½ cup plus 1 tablespoon extra-
virgin olive oil

1¾ cups pastry flour
(or unbleached all-purpose flour)

Rosemary tufts pulled from 2 long
fresh rosemary sprigs

¼ cup confectioners' sugar for
dusting

could just say serve it with anything, at any time of day, although it may not be the best choice to serve with Mexican food.

You will need a 10-inch angel food cake pan to make this. Use a good extra-virgin olive oil, but not a drizzling quality oil, to make this ideally Italian.

Bring the raisins and vin santo to a simmer in a very small saucepan over high heat. Turn off the heat and set aside for the raisins to absorb the wine for at least 30 minutes or up to overnight.

Adjust an oven rack to the middle position and preheat the oven to 325°F.

Spread the pine nuts on a baking sheet and toast them in the oven for 8 to 10 minutes, until they are fragrant and golden brown, shaking the baking sheet and rotating it from front to back halfway through the cooking time so the nuts brown evenly. Remove the pine nuts from the oven and set them aside to cool to room temperature.

Increase the oven temperature to 400°F. Spray a 10-inch angel food pan generously with nonstick cooking spray and dust it lightly with flour.

Leaving the peels attached, lay the orange halves flat side down and cut into ¼-inch-thick slices. Chop the slices into ¼-inch-thick cubes.

Put the eggs, Italian leavening, and ½ cup plus 2 tablespoons of the granulated sugar in the bowl of a standing mixer fitted with the whisk attachment and mix on medium-high speed until the mixture thickens, 3 to 4 minutes. Gradually add the olive oil by pouring it down the side of the bowl in a slow, steady stream and mix until the batter is emulsified. Reduce the mixer speed to low. Add one-third of the flour and mix until it is no longer visible. Add one-third of the raisins and mix just to incorporate them. Stop the mixer and scrape down the sides of the bowl. Repeat two more times, mixing in one-third of the flour at a time, then one-third of the raisins at a time, and stopping to scrape down the sides of the bowl between additions, until all of the flour and all of the raisins have been incorporated.

Turn off the mixer and remove the bowl from the stand. Add the chopped oranges and use a rubber spatula to gently fold them into the batter. Set the batter aside to rest for 10 minutes. Scrape the batter into the prepared pan and scatter the pine nuts over the top. Sprinkle the cake with the remaining ¼ cup granulated sugar and stick the tufts of rosemary into the batter, distributing them over the surface of the cake in an attractive way.

Bake the cake for 10 minutes. Rotate the cake and lower the oven temperature to 325°F. Bake the cake for another 30 to 35 minutes, until the cake is golden brown and a toothpick inserted comes out clean, rotating the cake once during the baking time so it browns evenly. Remove the cake from the oven and set it aside to cool to room temperature.

To serve, run a knife or offset spatula around the inside of the pan to release the cake from the pan and put a large plate over the top of the pan. Swiftly flip the cake and the plate to invert the cake onto the plate. Invert the cake again onto a large serving plate or cake stand. Pour the confectioners' sugar into a fine-mesh strainer and tap the strainer over the cake to dust the cake lightly with the sugar. Serve the cake with a cake spatula or knife for guests to cut the size serving they want and serve themselves.

Mexican Wedding Cookies

MAKES 3 TO 4 DOZEN COOKIES

FOR THE COOKIES

2 cups pecan halves
(about 7 ounces)

12 ounces (3 sticks) unsalted butter

2 vanilla beans (or 2 teaspoons pure
vanilla extract)

¼ cup canola oil
(or another neutral-flavored oil),
plus more as needed

2 tablespoons dark rum

3½ cups unbleached all-purpose
flour

1 tablespoon baking powder

1 teaspoon kosher salt

FOR THE SUGAR COATINGS

1½ cups granulated sugar

1 tablespoon ground cinnamon

½ teaspoon ground ginger

¼ teaspoon freshly grated nutmeg

2 cups confectioners' sugar

My mother, Doris, was quite an accomplished and adventurous cook, but she made only two desserts, apple pie and Mexican wedding cookies, both of which she loved to eat as much as to bake. Mexican wedding cookies, also called Mexican wedding cakes, or, *polvorónes*, are Mexican shortbread made with ground nuts and rolled in confectioners' sugar. *Polvo* means "dust" in Spanish, and my mom used to tell me that the mark of a great Mexican wedding cookie was that it didn't just fall apart when you bit into it, but that the cookie exploded and made a mess of dust all over you. I like to think I would have made my mom proud with these cookies, which make a big mess indeed.

Mexican wedding cookies are traditionally made with pecans or walnuts, but I prefer them with pecans, which is what I call for in this recipe. To transform them into Italian Wedding Cookies, use hazelnuts, toasted and skins rubbed off, in place of the pecans in this recipe.

This version is unusual because the cookie dough doesn't contain sugar. Instead, the baked cookies are rolled in granulated sugar mixed with spices and then in a very heavy coating of confectioners' sugar. You must sift the confectioners' sugar that you're rolling the cookies in, otherwise, it won't be fine enough to sufficiently coat the cookies, and without that thick coating, the cookies aren't sweet enough.

I got the idea to wrap the cookies in tissue paper of various colors years ago, when I hosted a cookbook dinner for the Mexican cooking authority Diana Kennedy, who presented her *polvorónes* this way. It was just so festive and pretty that I have wrapped my Mexican wedding cookies ever since. I made that step optional, because I recognize that if you're hosting a big dinner and run out of time, the first thing you're going to have to sacrifice is the craft corner. But if you have the extra time or an extra pair of hands, the wrapped cookies sure are pretty. If they're wrapped, you can serve them piled up in a big bowl. If the cookies aren't wrapped, you don't want to stack them because they're very fragile.

These cookies are a must whenever I serve Sal's Roasted Pork Shoulder (page 48) and any other time I serve a meal that feels Mexican, such as Dean Fearing's Frito Pie (page 210) or Spicy Pork Stew with Butternut Squash and Roasted Tomatillo Salsa (page 310).

To wrap the cookies, you will need 3 to 4 dozen 6 x 6-inch square pieces of colored tissue paper.

To make the cookies, adjust the oven racks so one is in the top third of the oven and one is in the bottom third and preheat the oven to 325°F.

Spread the pecans on a baking sheet and toast them on the higher rack of the oven for 10 to 12 minutes, until they're lightly browned and fragrant, shaking the baking sheet and rotating it from front to back halfway through the cooking time so the nuts brown evenly. Remove the pecans from the oven and set them aside until they're cool enough to touch. Measure out ⅓ cup of the nuts and coarsely chop. Set the chopped pecans and the pecan halves aside separately.

Put the butter in a small heavy-bottomed saucepan. Using a small sharp knife, split the vanilla beans lengthwise. Use the back of the knife to scrape out the pulp and seeds and add the scrapings and the beans to the saucepan with the butter. (If you are using vanilla extract instead of the vanilla beans, add it when you add the rum, below.) Bring the butter to a simmer over medium-low heat. Reduce the heat to the lowest setting and warm the butter, undisturbed, until a layer of foam develops on top. Gently skim the foam and continue warming the butter and skimming the foam for about 5 minutes, until no foam is produced and the milk solids have sunk to the bottom so you see only clear yellow butter. Turn off the heat and gently pour the clarified butter through a fine-mesh strainer or cheesecloth into a liquid measuring cup, taking care not to agitate the solids at the bottom of the pot; discard the solids. Measure out 1 cup clarified butter and reserve the rest for another use; if you are short of 1 cup, add enough canola oil to bring it to 1 cup. Set the butter aside to cool to room temperature. Add ¼ cup of the canola oil and rum (and vanilla extract, if you are using it) and stir to combine.

Combine the flour, pecan halves, baking powder, and salt in the bowl of a food processor fitted with a metal blade and pulse until the mixture is the consistency of coarse meal. Add the butter-oil mixture in a slow, steady stream and mix until the dough is crumbly. Turn off the machine and turn the dough out into a mixing bowl. Stir in the chopped pecans.

Line two baking sheets with parchment paper.

Using a 1 tablespoon measuring spoon or a small scoop of a similar size, gather 1½ tablespoons of dough and roll it between your palms. Place the balls as you roll them on the prepared baking sheets, leaving 2 inches between each ball.

Put one baking sheet on each rack in the oven and bake the cookies for 10 minutes. Reduce the heat to 300°F. Rotate the baking sheets between the upper and lower racks and rotate them from front to back. Bake the cookies for another 20 minutes, until they are light golden brown. Remove the cookies from the oven and set aside until they're cool enough to touch.

While the cookies are baking, to prepare the sugar coatings, combine the granulated sugar, cinnamon, ginger, and nutmeg in a small bowl and stir to thoroughly combine. Sift the confectioners' sugar into a separate bowl.

When the cookies are cool enough to touch but still warm, carefully toss a few at a time in the spiced granulated sugar, turning them until they're completely coated. Transfer the cookies to the bowl with the confectioners' sugar and roll them around until you have a very thick coating of powdered sugar. Remove the cookies from the confectioners' sugar and line them up in a single layer on a baking sheet or plate. Set aside for the cookies to cool to room temperature.

If you are wrapping the cookies in colored paper, place one cookie in a piece of paper and twist each side of the paper to close the parcel like a candy. Repeat, wrapping the remaining cookies in the same way.

To serve, pile the wrapped cookies high on a platter or in a bowl. If you are not wrapping the cookies, stack them no more than two cookies high on a cake stand or platter.

Bittersweet Chocolate Tartufo with Olive Oil Croutons and Sea Salt

I've been making the tartufo portion of this dessert for special occasions for more than twenty years, but the recent addition of olive oil croutons and the drizzle of olive oil were the inspiration of Mozza pastry chef and my longtime partner in pastry crime Dahlia Narvaez. After a trip to New York, Dahlia came back raving about a dessert that combined dark chocolate and olive oil that she'd eaten at Casa Mono, a Spanish restaurant owned by my business partners Mario Batali and Joe Bastianich. *Tartufo* means "truffle" in Italian, and the texture of this tart is rich and dense, just like a chocolate truffle. The olive oil, surprisingly, lightens the dessert, and the crunchy croutons add a welcome textural contrast. If you want to skip the step of making the croutons, the olive oil and sea salt are enough to make this dessert a conversation piece.

I put the dessert on the table with the tiny croutons, olive oil, and sea salt on the side. Guests cut a slice for themselves and they have fun dressing it with these unexpected toppings. But eaters beware: it's the kind of dessert where you can just keep cutting a sliver, and then another, until you've eaten half the tartufo.

Because of the olive oil component, this is clearly a dessert to serve as part of an Italian meal, such as after Sicilian Swordfish Spiedini (page 181), Saturday Night Chicken Thighs with Italian Sausage and Spicy Pickled Peppers (page 92), Braised Oxtails (page 220), or on your Umbrian Tavola (page 18).

You can make the tartufo up to four days in advance and the glaze up to a week. The recipe for the glaze makes more than double what you'll need for this recipe. I don't like to make sauces in tiny amounts; more can go wrong, and I like having the leftovers. If you have a very small pan, you can cut the recipe in half. Better yet, make the whole recipe and drizzle the leftover sauce, which will last for weeks in the refrigerator, on ice cream.

The yield on this dessert varies greatly, depending on whether you're serving a group of chocoholics or a crowd of people who eat with some restraint.

You will need an 8-inch cake ring or flan ring to make this. If you use a flan ring, which has lower sides than a cake ring, all of the filling may not fit. Pour the excess in a bowl or ramekin, allow it to set, and then eat it.

SERVES 8 TO 20

FOR THE TARTUFO

10 ounces bittersweet chocolate (preferably 60% to 70% cacao), finely chopped (about 1¾ cups)

1 cup heavy cream

⅓ cup plus 1 tablespoon crème fraîche (or sour cream)

8 tablespoons (1 stick) unsalted butter, cut into small cubes and softened at room temperature

1 tablespoon plus ½ teaspoon light corn syrup

1 tablespoon whiskey

FOR THE CROUTONS

¼ pound bread, preferably Pullman, or any artisan sliced sandwich-style white bread

¾ cup extra-virgin olive oil

1 teaspoon kosher salt

FOR THE GLAZE

8 ounces (½ pound) bittersweet chocolate (preferably 60% to 70% cacao)

6 ounces (1½ sticks) unsalted butter

(continued)

3 tablespoons light corn syrup

3 tablespoons whiskey

Finishing-quality extra-virgin olive oil

Maldon sea salt (or another flaky sea salt such as fleur de sel)

To make the tartufo, line a baking sheet with parchment paper and put the cake or flan ring on the baking sheet.

Put the chocolate in a medium bowl. Heat the cream and crème fraîche in a medium heavy-bottomed saucepan over high heat until it just begins to bubble around the edges, but don't bring it to a boil. Pour the cream mixture over the chocolate and allow the hot cream to sit, without touching it, until the chocolate is melted, about 2 minutes. Add the butter and corn syrup and gently whisk to incorporate the additions into the chocolate mixture. Add the whiskey and gently stir it in with the whisk. Pour the tartufo mixture into the cake ring or flan ring. Refrigerate the tartufo, uncovered, until it is firm, at least 3 hours or up to 4 days.

To make the croutons, trim and discard the crusts from the bread and put the bread in the freezer for about 30 minutes, until it is slightly but not completely hardened. Cut the bread into ¼-inch cubes and set aside.

Heat the olive oil in a medium sauté pan over medium-high heat until it slides easily in the pan and it's almost smoking, about 3 minutes. Line a plate with paper towels. Add half of the bread cubes to the oil and cook them for 60 to 70 seconds, stirring once or twice, until they are golden brown all over. Use a slotted spoon to remove the croutons to the paper towels to drain and season them with the salt. Fry the remaining bread cubes in the same way. Transfer the croutons to a clean paper towel to drain further and cool to room temperature. Use the croutons or store them, covered, for up to 1 day.

To make the glaze, fill the bottom of a double boiler with water or set a stainless steel bowl over a pot of water; the bowl must be larger than the pot so that no steam gets in the bowl. In either case, make sure the water does not touch the bottom of the top vessel. Put the chocolate, butter, corn syrup, and whiskey in the top of a double boiler or the steel bowl. Heat the butter and chocolate, untouched, until they melt. Take the pan or bowl off the simmering water and whisk to combine the ingredients and cool them to room temperature. Pour ½ cup of the glaze over the cooled tartufo, tilting and swirling the baking sheet that the tartufo is on so the glaze covers the surface of the tartufo; the excess glaze will spill onto the baking sheet. Put the tartufo in the refrigerator to chill until the glaze is set, about 1 hour. Use the glaze or refrigerate, covered, for up to several weeks. Heat the glaze in the top of a double boiler set over gently simmering water (or in a bowl set over a pot of simmering water; note that the bowl must be larger than the pot so it doesn't fall into the pot), stirring constantly.

To serve, remove the tartufo from the refrigerator and lift it off the baking sheet. Carefully peel off and discard the parchment and transfer the tartufo to a cake stand or another flat serving platter. Wet two dish towels with very hot tap water. Wrap the towels around the cake ring and hold them there for about 30 seconds to help separate the tartufo from the ring. Carefully lift the ring off the tartufo and let the tartufo rest for 30 to 60 minutes, depending on the ambient temperature, to come to room temperature before serving. Just before serving, scatter a handful of the olive oil croutons around the tartufo and put the remaining croutons in a small bowl and serve with a spoon, letting guests put them on their own slices. Serve the tartufo with a cake spatula or knife for people to cut the size serving they want. Place a bottle (or another pretty vessel) of your best olive oil and the sea salt in a small bowl on the side for guests to drizzle and sprinkle on their servings. (Cover and refrigerate any leftovers. Bring leftovers to room temperature before serving again.)

Four-Layer Salted Chocolate Caramel Tart

When we opened Chi Spacca, our meat-centric, third restaurant on the Melrose-Highland corner, Dahlia wanted to have a chocolate dessert that was as bold and aggressive and unsubtle as the meat dishes on the menu. This four-layer chocolate and caramel tart was what we came up with. It consists of four separate components: a black chocolate crust; a rise-and-fall, chewy chocolate cookie filling; a salty caramel layer dotted with cocoa nibs (just to be sure to represent chocolate in all its forms); and a chocolate ganache topping. It's the richest dessert on earth, and it'll kill you if you eat too much of it, but if you're a chocolate lover and you can show restraint, it's one of the most satisfying desserts you'll ever eat. It's my friend Caryl Lee's favorite dessert at any of our restaurants, and Caryl is the opposite of a glutton; she doesn't even have a sweet tooth, and yet she loves this dessert.

It's definitely the most challenging dessert in the book to make, but because it is built of separate elements, all of which can be prepared in advance, it is very doable. That said, if you're just not up for a project, this isn't the dessert for you. Make the Bittersweet Chocolate Tartufo with Olive Oil Croutons and Sea Salt (page 365) instead. At the restaurant, we make individual round tarts, but for serving at home, we make the same dessert in the form of a long, slender rectangular tart, which guests can slice to whatever size they want.

This recipe calls for two types of unsweetened cocoa powder: Dutch process (also called black) cocoa powder and dark cocoa powder. Dutch process cocoa powder is black in color; I use it to give a deep, dark, very nearly black color to desserts. This type of cocoa powder is what I use to make my version of Oreo cookies. The problem with this cocoa powder is that if you use too much of it, your dessert will have a strange, almost mineral taste. My solution is to use a combination: dark cocoa powder for flavor and black Dutch process cocoa powder for color. If you can't find Dutch process cocoa powder, use all cocoa powder instead; the tart shell won't be as dark, but it will taste just as good.

This is such an elegant dessert, and because it takes some effort, I think of it as a bit of a special-occasion dessert. Serve it with Braised Oxtails (page 220), Saturday Night Chicken Thighs with Italian Sausage and Spicy Pickled Peppers (page 92), or Grilled Lamb Shoulder Chops with Mint Yogurt Sauce (page 104).

SERVES 8 TO 20

FOR THE TART SHELL

2 cups plus 1 tablespoon unbleached all-purpose flour, plus more for dusting

½ cup quality Dutch process (black) cocoa powder (such as Ghirardelli or another quality brand)

½ cup quality cocoa powder (preferably Valrhona or another quality brand; not Dutch process cocoa powder)

1 teaspoon kosher salt

8 ounces (2 sticks) unsalted butter, softened at room temperature, plus more for buttering the tart pan

½ cup plus 1 tablespoon granulated sugar

½ cup packed dark brown sugar

2 extra-large egg yolks

1 teaspoon pure vanilla extract

FOR THE FUDGE COOKIE

1½ cups confectioners' sugar

½ cup quality cocoa powder (preferably Valrhona or another quality brand; not Dutch process cocoa powder)

½ teaspoon kosher salt

1 extra-large egg

(continued)

1 extra-large egg white

2 ounces bittersweet chocolate (preferably 60% to 70% cacao), roughly chopped (about ⅓ cup)

1½ teaspoons cocoa nibs (about ¼ ounce)

⅓ cup light corn syrup

¼ cup granulated sugar

1½ tablespoons unsalted butter

¼ cup plus 3 tablespoons heavy cream, at room temperature

¼ cup plus 2 tablespoons cocoa nibs

1 tablespoon kosher salt

6 ounces bittersweet chocolate (preferably 60% to 70% cacao), roughly chopped (about 1 cup)

¾ cup heavy cream

1 teaspoon pure vanilla extract

½ teaspoon kosher salt

2 tablespoons quality cocoa powder (preferably Valrhona or another quality brand; not Dutch process cocoa powder)

The yield on this varies greatly depending on the degree of willpower of those you are serving.

You will need parchment paper or paper coffee filters, pie weights or rice, and a 13¾ x 4¼-inch rectangular tart pan with a removable bottom to make this.

———

To make the tart shell, pour the flour, Dutch process cocoa powder, cocoa powder, and salt into a fine-mesh strainer or sifter and sift the ingredients into a large bowl.

Combine the butter, granulated sugar, and brown sugar in the bowl of a standing mixer fitted with the paddle attachment and cream them together at medium-high speed until they're light and fluffy, about 5 minutes. Lower the mixer speed to medium, slowly add the egg yolks and vanilla, and mix until they are incorporated. Turn off the machine, add the dry ingredients, and mix at low speed until no flour is visible. Turn the dough out onto a lightly floured surface and knead it a few times to bring it together. Using your hands, shape the dough into a thick rectangle (about 9 x 5 inches) and wrap it in plastic. Refrigerate the dough for at least 2 hours or up to 3 days; or freeze the dough for up to 2 months and defrost it overnight in the refrigerator.

Line a baking sheet with parchment paper, butter the sides and bottom of a 13¾ x 4¼-inch tart pan, and place the pan on the baking sheet.

Remove the dough from the refrigerator and cut it into a few chunks. Dust a flat work surface with flour and knead each chunk until it is the texture of Play-Doh. Bring the dough together to form one ball and pat the ball into a 1-inch-thick disk. Roll the dough out to a 17 x 7-inch rectangle, ⅛ inch to ¼ inch thick, or large enough to line the bottom and sides of the tart pan. Fold the dough in half and carefully place it in the tart pan, centering it. Unfold the sheet of dough so the edges flop over the edges of the pan. Push the dough down to fit snugly inside the mold, lifting up the edges of the dough while pressing the dough into the crease on the inside perimeter of the pan. Dip the knuckle of your index finger in flour and press the dough into the crease with your knuckle to create straight rather than sloping sides. Don't stretch the dough to fit or it will shrink during baking. Roll the rolling pin over the top of the tart pan to cut the dough. Pull off and discard the trimmed dough. Place the tart shell in the refrigerator to chill for at least 30 minutes or up to 1 day.

Adjust an oven rack to the middle position and preheat the oven to 325°F.

Remove the tart shell from the refrigerator. Line the shell with parchment paper or coffee filters and weigh it down with pie weights or rice. Put the baking sheet in the oven to bake the shell until the edges of the shell look dry, about 18 minutes. Remove the tart shell from the oven and carefully remove and discard the parchment paper or coffee filters; reserve the pie weights or rice to use (as pie weights only) another time. Return the tart shell to the oven and bake until it is fully cooked, 8 to 10 minutes. Remove the tart shell from the oven and set aside to cool to room temperature.

Increase the oven temperature to 350°F.

To make the fudge cookie, pour the confectioners' sugar and cocoa powder into a fine-mesh strainer or sifter and sift them into a large bowl. Add the salt and stir to combine the ingredients. Make a well in the center. Add the egg and egg white to the well and whisk until the ingredients are combined. Add the chopped chocolate and cocoa nibs and use a rubber spatula to gently fold them into the batter. Pour the batter into the tart shell and use a small offset spatula to spread it evenly in the shell.

Bake the filled tart shell for about 25 minutes, until the fudge cookie cracks at the center, turning the tart halfway through the baking time so it bakes evenly. Remove the tart from the oven and cool to room temperature.

Meanwhile, to make the caramel, fasten a candy thermometer to the side of a medium deep saucepan (preferably one with a light-colored bottom). Put the corn syrup, granulated sugar, and 3½ tablespoons water in the saucepan and stir to combine. Cook the ingredients over high heat without stirring, tilting the pan so the sugar cooks evenly and brushing down the sides of the pan with a pastry brush dipped in water to remove the sugar crystals, until the caramel reaches 248°F. Add the butter and cream and stir to incorporate it, being careful because the caramel will splatter when you add the ingredients. Turn off the heat and stir in the cocoa nibs and salt. Set the caramel aside to cool slightly, but not so much that it is no longer a pourable consistency. Use the caramel or allow it to cool completely, then refrigerate, covered, for up to 3 days. Warm the caramel over low heat, stirring often, until it is a pourable consistency. Pour the caramel over the cooled fudge cookie layer of the tart. Put the tart in the refrigerator to cool the caramel completely, about 20 minutes.

To make the ganache, put the chocolate in a medium bowl. Heat the cream in a medium heavy-bottomed saucepan over high heat until it begins to bubble around the edges. Pour the cream over the chocolate and allow the hot cream to sit, without touching it, until the chocolate is melted, about 3 minutes. Add the vanilla and salt and whisk, working your way from the center of the bowl outward, until the ingredients are combined and the ganache is smooth. Set aside to cool until the ganache is the consistency of cake frosting, about 20 minutes. (If the chocolate cools too much and is stiffer than frosting, place it over gently simmering water and whisk it to loosen the consistency. Then set it aside again until it sets to frosting consistency.)

Spoon the ganache on the tart and use the back of the spoon to spread it to cover the surface, making peaks and valleys in the ganache to give the tart a pretty, textured surface. Place the tart in the refrigerator until the ganache is set (it will lose its shiny quality), about 1 hour. You can make the tart up to 1 day in advance of serving it.

To serve, pour the cocoa powder into a fine-mesh strainer and tap the strainer over the tart to dust it lightly. Gently push the removable bottom to lift the tart out of the pan and, using a long offset spatula, gently slide the tart from the metal bottom onto a long platter or pretty wooden cutting board. Serve the tart with a cake spatula for guests to cut the size they want and serve themselves.

Genevieve's Salted Walnut Shortbreads

These are the cookies that led to a baking career. Genevieve Gergis, then a home baker, brought these cookies to the memorial reception of a friend, Amy Pressman. Carolynn was so impressed that she asked me to taste the cookies. They were perfect: crumbly, not too sweet, and redolent of baked butter and walnuts. Genevieve's husband, Ori Menashe, was in the process of opening a restaurant in downtown Los Angeles, Bestia, slated for a year from that time. Based on that shortbread, Carolynn encouraged Genevieve to spend the next year learning as much as she could about pastry, and to become the pastry chef at Bestia. Genevieve took that advice and today Genevieve is a pastry chef at one of the most acclaimed restaurants in Los Angeles. This is the kind of cookie that I can't stop eating, because it's more buttery than sweet. Where one chocolate chip cookie is enough for me, I can just keep breaking off little pieces of these until I've eaten the whole panful. These shortbreads are topped with a sprinkling of Demerara sugar, unrefined brown sugar that is in a crystal-like form; it has a beautiful golden color and crunchy texture that make it ideal for decorating. You can find Demerara sugar at specialty food stores, or use turbinado (raw) sugar instead.

Cookies make a great dessert for entertaining because you don't need to serve plates or silverware with them. I like these with Lamb and Chicken Tikka Kebabs (page 270), Grilled Lamb Shoulder Chops with Mint Yogurt Sauce (page 104), and Dave's Oven-Roasted Grouper with Spicy Tomato Marmalade and Tahini (page 232).

You will need parchment paper and a 10 x 10-inch square cake pan to make this.

MAKES 12 COOKIES

Nonstick cooking spray

6 ounces walnut halves or pieces (about 2 cups)

12 ounces (3 sticks) unsalted butter, cut into small cubes

⅔ cup packed dark brown sugar

1 teaspoon kosher salt

1 tablespoon pure vanilla extract

2⅔ cups unbleached all-purpose flour

Demerara sugar (or turbinado or raw sugar) for sprinkling

Adjust an oven rack to the middle position and preheat the oven to 325°F. Line a 10 x 10-inch square cake pan with parchment paper and spray it with nonstick cooking spray.

Spread the walnuts on a baking sheet and toast them in the oven for 10 to 12 minutes, until they're lightly browned and fragrant, shaking the baking sheet and rotating it from front to back halfway through the cooking time so the nuts brown evenly. Remove the baking sheet from the oven and set aside to cool the walnuts to room temperature. Finely chop the walnuts and set aside.

Combine the butter, brown sugar, and salt in the bowl of a standing mixer fitted with the paddle attachment and mix at medium-high speed until the mixture is smooth, about 3 minutes. Reduce the mixer speed to low. Add the vanilla and mix to just combine. Add the chopped walnuts and mix on low speed until they are incorporated. Turn off the mixer, add the flour, and mix on low speed until no flour is visible. Turn the dough out of the bowl into the prepared baking pan and gently press it into an even layer with your hands.

Bake the shortbread until the top is golden brown and no longer doughy to the touch, about 1 hour 15 minutes, rotating the pan from front to back halfway through the baking time so the shortbread browns evenly. Remove the shortbread from the oven. Immediately sprinkle the surface of the shortbread with a generous covering of the Demerara sugar and set the shortbread aside to cool to room temperature.

Lift the corners of the parchment paper and slide the shortbread and parchment in one piece off the baking sheet and onto a large cutting board. Using a large sharp knife, cut the shortbread into 12 equal-size rectangles. (If, after the cookies have cooled and been cut, the shortbread seems doughy in the center, put the cookies on a baking sheet and return them to the oven at 325°F to bake for another 5 to 10 minutes, until they are no longer doughy.)

To serve, arrange the cookies in a single layer on a cake stand or a flat platter.

Chess Pie

When I walk into the businesses of colleagues who used to work for me, I always hope I'm going to love what they're doing. Sometimes I can actually see that a protégé has taken a dish or component of one that he or she learned with me and made it his or her own, which feels really rewarding. Other times, I'm pleased to experience something that is nothing at all like anything any one of them made with me but that nevertheless makes me feel as if they understood what I was trying to teach them. This chess pie, made by Margeaux Aragon, who worked with Dahlia Narvaez in the pastry kitchen at Mozza, fits into the latter category.

Chess pie, sometimes called vinegar pie because it contains vinegar, is a very simple custard pie, and a southern classic. When the pie bakes, a thin, sugary crust forms on top, which, as with crème brûlée, provides a lovely contrast to the creamy interior. After Margeaux left us, she went back to Atlanta, where she was from, to work in a restaurant there, and then she returned to Los Angeles and landed a job working with the very talented chef Josef Centeno at a new restaurant venture downtown. The version of chess pie she serves there is especially silky and luscious, and even better because she times the baking of it so that the pie comes to the table still warm.

Like Margeaux, I serve this pie still warm from the oven. There's something about the custard when it's warm that feels really great in your mouth. To serve, put it in the oven when you start serving your meal. Just remember to set a timer or, if you're anything like me, you'll forget it. I like to serve this pie with Southern-Style Korean Cut Short Ribs with Vinegar Onions (page 325) and the Backyard Peel 'n' Eat Shrimp Boil (page 258). Because it's served fresh from the oven, I also like to serve the dessert with what I think of as more indoor feasts, such as Braised Oxtails (page 220) and Staff Meal Oven-Roasted Chicken Thighs (page 162). It would also make a great alternative to the usual suspects on your Thanksgiving dessert table.

You will need a deep 9½-inch pie dish to make this.

—————

To make the crust, mix the flour, sugar, and salt in the bowl of a standing mixer fitted with a paddle attachment and mix on low speed for a few seconds to distribute the sugar and salt. Add the butter and mix on low speed until the mixture

SERVES 8 TO 10

FOR THE CRUST

1¼ cups unbleached all-purpose flour, plus more for dusting

1 teaspoon sugar

¾ teaspoon kosher salt

8 tablespoons (1 stick) unsalted butter, cut into small cubes and frozen

¼ cup ice-cold water, or as needed

FOR THE FILLING

¼ cup evaporated milk, plus more for brushing the crust

1 tablespoon distilled white vinegar

2 teaspoons pure vanilla extract

2 cups sugar, plus more for sprinkling on the crust

1 tablespoon medium-ground cornmeal or polenta

4 extra-large eggs

½ teaspoon kosher salt

8 tablespoons (1 stick) unsalted butter, melted and cooled

is the consistency of coarse meal with some dime-size chunks of butter visible. Add the ice water and mix for 2 to 3 minutes on medium speed until the dough just comes together—be careful not to mix it any more than necessary.

Dust a flat work surface with flour and turn the dough out onto the floured surface. Knead the dough gently, just enough to bring it together into a ball. Pat the dough into a disk, wrap it in plastic wrap, and refrigerate for at least 2 hours or up to 3 days; or freeze the dough for up to 2 months and defrost it overnight in the refrigerator.

Remove the dough from the refrigerator. Unwrap it and cut it into 3 or 4 chunks. Dust a flat work surface with flour and knead the chunks to soften them, until they are the texture of Play-Doh. Bring the dough together to form one ball and pat the ball into a 1-inch-thick disk. Dust a rolling pin with flour and roll the dough out to a 14-inch circle. Fold the dough in half and lift it into a 9½-inch pie dish. Using scissors, trim the dough, leaving 2 inches of dough hanging over the edges of the pie dish. Working your way around the pie, fold the dough at the edges under itself so that 1 inch of the dough is doubled. Use your thumb to crimp the edges of the pie into a scallop pattern. Refrigerate the pie shell for at least 30 minutes or up to overnight.

To make the filling, whisk the evaporated milk, vinegar, and vanilla together in a medium bowl to combine. In a separate bowl, whisk the sugar, cornmeal, eggs, and salt together until smooth. Add the evaporated milk mixture and whisk until the filling is smooth. Add the butter and whisk until it's combined. The filling can be made up to a day in advance; refrigerate, covered, until you're ready to use it.

Adjust an oven rack to the middle position and preheat the oven to 375°F.

Remove the pie shell from the refrigerator. Brush the edges with the evaporated milk and sprinkle liberally with sugar. Put the pie shell on a baking sheet and pour the filling into the shell.

Bake the pie for 10 minutes. Reduce the oven temperature to 325°F, rotate the pie from front to back, and bake the pie for another 30 to 35 minutes, until the crust is golden brown and the pie jiggles very slightly when you gently shake the pan, rotating the pie from front to back again halfway through the baking time so the pie browns evenly.

Remove the pie from the oven and allow it to cool slightly before serving. Serve the pie, still warm, with a knife and pie server for guests to cut the size they want and serve themselves.

Amy's Brunettes

These are my late friend Amy Pressman's version of the classic American blondie, which she developed to sell at her bakery, Short Cake, in the Farmers Market on Third and Fairfax in Los Angeles. Tragically, Amy died a few months before the bakery opened, so she was never able to see how well received both the bakery and her brunettes were. Blondies get their name from being a "blond" version of a brownie. Amy named hers brunettes because both she and her assistant, Hourie Sahakian, were brunettes, and also because she made the bars with muscovado, a very dark, molasses-y brown sugar. You can find muscovado sugar at specialty food stores, or use dark brown sugar instead. Amy said she borrowed the brunettes' recipe from a recipe of the great baker and cookbook author Dorie Greenspan, and then added the pine nuts and thyme. These make a neat and easy, grab-and-go dessert to serve with Garlic-Rubbed Skirt Steak with Scallion Vinaigrette (page 194), The Ultimate Hamburger (page 146), and Backyard Peel 'n' Eat Shrimp Boil (page 258). With the fresh herbs on top, they're pretty and unexpected and would also be a nice choice if you were asked to bring dessert to a picnic or party.

MAKES 24 BRUNETTES

14 ounces (3½ sticks) unsalted butter, cut into small cubes, plus more for greasing the pan and parchment

3 tablespoons pine nuts

3½ cups unbleached all-purpose flour

¾ teaspoon baking powder

½ teaspoon baking soda

1 teaspoon kosher salt

2 cups plus 2 tablespoons packed dark brown sugar

¾ cup plus 2 tablespoons granulated sugar

¼ cup plus 1 tablespoon dark muscovado sugar (or dark brown sugar)

3 extra-large eggs

1 teaspoon pure vanilla extract

1 heaping tablespoon fresh thyme leaves

Adjust an oven rack to the middle position and preheat the oven to 325°F. Butter a 9 x 13-inch baking dish. Line the bottom of the pan with parchment paper, butter the parchment, and set aside. Set up a cooling rack.

Spread the pine nuts on a baking sheet and toast them in the oven for 8 to 10 minutes, until they are fragrant and golden brown, shaking the baking sheet and rotating it from front to back halfway through the cooking time so the nuts brown evenly. Remove the pine nuts from the oven and set them aside to cool to room temperature.

Stir the flour, baking powder, baking soda, and salt together in a mixing bowl.

Beat the butter in the bowl of a standing mixer fitted with the paddle attachment on medium speed until it's smooth and creamy, about 2 minutes. Turn off the machine. Add the brown sugar, granulated sugar, and muscovado sugar and mix on medium speed until the sugars are incorporated into the butter, about 3 minutes. Add the eggs, one by one, mixing for about 1 minute to incorporate each egg before adding another one. When all of the eggs have been incorporated, add the vanilla and mix to combine. Reduce the mixer speed to low. Add the dry ingredients, mixing on low speed until no flour is visible. Transfer the batter to the prepared baking dish and use a rubber spatula to smooth the top. Sprinkle the pine nuts and thyme leaves over the surface.

Bake the brunettes for 1 hour 25 minutes to 1 hour 40 minutes, until golden brown on top and the brunettes have pulled away from the sides of the pan. Remove the pan from the oven and place it on the cooling rack to cool completely. Run a knife or offset spatula around the edges of the pan to release the brunettes from the pan. Put a baking sheet over the brunettes and swiftly flip the baking pan and baking sheet to invert the brunettes onto the baking sheet. Put a cutting board on top of the baking sheet to invert them again onto the cutting board so the decorated side is facing up. Cut the brunettes into 24 (3 x 1¼-inch) bars. Artfully stack the bars no more than two high on a cake stand, taking care not to knock off the thyme and pine nuts on top, and serve.

Dark Chocolate Pudding

When I think of a home-style dessert that you plop on the table, I think of two American dessert icons: apple pie and chocolate pudding. This chocolate pudding recipe is my "gift" to the home cook who wants to make a dessert that is as easy as picking one up at a bakery. It's ideal for those with a fear of baking. This version is made with dark chocolate and a splash of whiskey, so it's a grown-up or more sophisticated version of the American classic.

This old-school dessert goes with just about any meal but I especially like to serve it after The Ultimate Hamburger (page 146).

You will need a glass 9- or 10-inch pie dish, such as a Pyrex, to make this.

To make the pudding, combine the cornstarch, eggs, and ¼ cup of the milk in a mixing bowl. Whisk to combine and set aside.

Combine the remaining 4 cups milk, the sugar, cocoa powder, and salt in a large saucepan over medium heat and heat until the milk starts to bubble around the edges. Turn off the heat.

Gradually add 2 cups of the hot cocoa mixture to the bowl with the cornstarch and eggs, whisking constantly. Return this mixture to the saucepan. Cook the pudding over medium-low heat, whisking constantly until it thickens enough to leave a trail when you pass a whisk through it, about 5 minutes. Remove the pudding from the heat. Add the chocolate and whiskey and stir to combine until the chocolate melts. Pour the pudding into a glass 9- or 10-inch pie dish and chill until a skin develops and the pudding is set and cold, at least 3 hours or overnight.

To make the whipped cream, pour the cream into a chilled bowl and whip it with a chilled whisk until it thickens to soft peaks. Do not overwhip the cream because it will become curdled. Add the crème fraîche and gently beat until the whipped cream is thick and mousselike. Use the cream, or cover the bowl and refrigerate until you are ready to serve it; or for several hours. Before serving, whip gently to stiffen it if it separated.

To serve, using a large spoon, dollop the whipped cream side by side to cover the pudding in waves. Pour the cocoa powder for dusting into a fine-mesh strainer and tap the strainer over the pudding to dust it lightly. Serve with a big spoon and a stack of small bowls for guests to serve themselves.

SERVES 8 TO 10

FOR THE PUDDING

⅓ cup plus 2 tablespoons cornstarch

3 large egg yolks

4¼ cups whole milk

¾ cup plus 3 tablespoons sugar

1 cup plus 2 tablespoons cocoa powder (preferably Valrhona or another quality brand; not Dutch process cocoa powder), plus ¼ cup for dusting

¼ teaspoon kosher salt

2 ounces chopped bittersweet chocolate (preferably 60% to 70% cacao)

2 tablespoons whiskey

FOR THE WHIPPED CREAM

3 cups heavy cream

1 cup crème fraîche (or sour cream)

Devil's Food Rings with Spiced White Mountain Frosting

Every baker—or even just the occasional birthday cake maker—needs one classic chocolate cake recipe that he or she can't live without. For me, this devil's food cake is that recipe. It's everything I want a chocolate cake to be: moist, light, and so chocolaty it's almost black. For a long time I called it Michelle's Chocolate Cake, because I got the recipe from Michelle Wojtowicz, one of my pastry chefs, who went on to open the wonderful Big Sur Bakery. Just as they take a few ideas, recipes, or techniques with them, all the pastry chefs who spend some time in my kitchen have left their contributions with me; it's part of the evolution of our craft. I've used this recipe for years to make layered birthday cakes for my kids and for special orders at Mozza, sheet cakes for staff parties, and cupcakes for my nephew Nik's wedding. My latest thing is to bake the batter in metal doughnut molds. Dusted with confectioners' sugar and stacked up on a platter, the rings look really pretty and—although it may not be a very appetizing reference—they remind me of old-fashioned whitewall tires. The rings are a welcome alternative to cupcakes. I put the frosting on the side so guests can put as much or as little frosting as they wish on their cakes. It's also a unique and clever way to spare yourself the time and effort of frosting the cakes, and to get your guests to frost them for you.

White mountain is a classic fluffy meringue frosting that gets its name because of its white peaks, which hold up for hours after the frosting has been beaten. I love the contrast of the bright white frosting against this super-dark chocolate cake, but for this version, I spiced up the frosting with vanilla beans, cinnamon, and nutmeg, sacrificing the pure bright whiteness for the added flavors. Also, even though it's made with just egg whites and sugar, so it's definitely sweet, it's not as rich as, say, buttercream frosting. The frosting will hold up for two hours without issue, but any longer and you will want to stir it gently with a rubber spatula or a big spoon to recombine it.

This recipe makes a large portion, but because it calls for one egg, I decided not to cut the recipe in half. The cakes also stay moist and still good a day after they're baked, so leftovers shouldn't pose a problem.

Serve this all-American indulgence with Southern-Style Korean Cut Short Ribs with Vinegar Onions (page 325), The Ultimate Hamburger (page 146),

---

SERVES 12 TO 24
MAKES 48 LITTLE CAKES

FOR THE CAKE RINGS

Nonstick cooking spray

⅓ cup quality cocoa powder (preferably Valrhona or another quality brand; not Dutch process cocoa powder)

1⅓ cups granulated sugar

1⅓ cups unbleached all-purpose flour

1¼ teaspoons baking soda

¾ cup well-shaken buttermilk

½ cup plus 2 tablespoons canola oil (or another neutral-flavored oil)

1 extra-large egg

2 teaspoons pure vanilla extract

½ cup confectioners' sugar for dusting

FOR THE FROSTING

2 extra-large egg whites

½ teaspoon ground cinnamon

½ teaspoon freshly grated nutmeg

¼ cup light corn syrup

½ cup granulated sugar

1 vanilla bean
(or 2 teaspoons pure vanilla extract)

Garlic-Rubbed Skirt Steak with Scallion Vinaigrette (page 194), Dean Fearing's Frito Pie (page 210), or the Backyard Peel 'n' Eat Shrimp Boil (page 258).

You will need two full-size doughnut pans to make these. You could get away with using only one mold; it just means you'll have to bake the rings in more batches. Likewise, if you don't mind investing in doughnut ring molds, buy three or four to make the baking go even faster. Making the frosting requires a candy thermometer to cook the sugar to the accurate temperature. If the sugar is not cooked correctly, the frosting won't whip up properly and will be thin and shapeless rather than voluminous, which is one of its appeals. If you cook it too long, the syrup will harden into solid lollipop-textured strands.

———

To make the cake rings, adjust an oven rack to the middle position and preheat the oven to 350°F. Spray the doughnut mold pans liberally with nonstick cooking spray.

Prepare an ice bath in a large bowl and place a medium bowl in the ice bath. Mix the cocoa powder with ¾ cup water in a small saucepan and bring the water to a boil over high heat, whisking constantly, until smooth. Pour the cocoa syrup into the smaller bowl and let it chill completely in the ice bath.

Meanwhile, combine the granulated sugar, flour, and baking soda in a large bowl.

Once it is chilled, remove the bowl with the cocoa syrup from the ice bath and add the buttermilk, canola oil, egg, and vanilla and whisk to combine the ingredients. Add to the bowl with the dry ingredients and mix with a whisk or rubber spatula until the flour is no longer visible.

Ladle 2 tablespoons of batter into each mold and bake for 15 minutes, or until the cake pulls away from the sides of the mold, rotating the pan from front to back halfway through the baking time. Remove the pan from the oven and set it aside for about 15 minutes. Flip the cake rings out of the molds onto a baking sheet so the side that was facing down is facing up. Bake the remaining batter in the same way, spraying the molds before filling them between batches. You can bake the cake rings up to several hours in advance of serving them. Just before serving them, pour the confectioners' sugar into a fine-mesh strainer and lightly dust the cake rings with the sugar.

To make the frosting, put the egg whites, cinnamon, and nutmeg in the bowl of a standing mixer fitted with the whisk attachment and set aside.

Fasten a candy thermometer to the side of a small saucepan and add the corn syrup, ¼ cup plus 2 tablespoons of the granulated sugar, and 2 tablespoons water.

Using a small sharp knife, split the vanilla bean lengthwise. Use the back of the knife to scrape out the pulp and seeds and add the scrapings and the bean to the saucepan. Bring the liquid to a boil over high heat. Boil without stirring until the granulated sugar dissolves and the mixture registers 240°F ("soft ball stage") on the thermometer, about 5 minutes; dip a pastry brush in water and brush down the sides of the pan to clean off the sugar crystals that will form there as the sugar boils. Turn off the heat and remove and discard the vanilla bean.

About 2 minutes after the sugar mixture starts boiling, or when you begin to see bursting bubbles on the surface, begin whipping the egg whites and spices on low speed until they are frothy. Increase the speed to medium and continue to beat until soft peaks form. Increase the speed to high, add the remaining 2 tablespoons of granulated sugar, and gradually beat until stiff, glossy peaks form. When the sugar syrup has reached 240°F, pour it down the side of the bowl in a very thin, steady stream, beating at high speed until the meringue is shiny and stiff, 4 to 5 minutes. Add the vanilla, if you are using it, and reduce the speed to medium and beat until the outside of the bowl is cool to the touch. The meringue will be very smooth and stand in very stiff peaks.

To serve, use a rubber spatula to scoop the frosting into a medium serving bowl, using the spatula to create natural-looking peaks and swirls in the frosting, like a snow-covered mountain. Stack the cakes two or three high on a cake stand and serve with the frosting on the side and a large spoon for people to serve themselves.

Liz's Bird Food

MAKES 2 QUARTS

Nonstick cooking spray

8 tablespoons (1 stick) unsalted butter

⅓ cup honey (preferably wildflower or another mild-flavored honey)

1 vanilla bean (or 1 tablespoon pure vanilla extract)

1 tablespoon pure vanilla extract

1½ cups old-fashioned rolled oats

1 cup organic preservative-free, unsweetened cornflakes

½ cup organic preservative-free, unsweetened puffed rice cereal

½ cup hemp seeds

½ cup brown or golden flaxseeds

½ cup raw sunflower seeds

1 tablespoon poppy seeds

½ cup packed dark or light brown sugar

1 tablespoon ground cinnamon

2 teaspoons kosher salt

1 teaspoon freshly grated nutmeg

First, let me just say that this is not food for birds. It's granola. But it's such a departure from the granola I've been making and eating all my life that I felt I needed to come up with a new name for it. As much as I'd like to claim responsibility for this reinvention of granola, in fact, this version was inspired by a baking sheet of granola that I spotted cooling in the restaurant kitchen at The Modern Honolulu, where I was cooking for an event.

Just about every hotel kitchen and every small bakery in America makes its own granola, so seeing granola cooling in a hotel kitchen was, in itself, nothing remarkable. I know granola. I went to Sonoma State, which had the nickname Granola State, and I published my first granola recipe, in my second cookbook, more than twenty years ago, in 1994. And until I spotted the granola in that Honolulu kitchen, I would have said that all granola was pretty much the same. But not this one. Where most granola is made of oats and various combinations of dried fruits and nuts, and hardened into crunchy clusters, this granola was made in such a way that the individual oats stay loose and unattached. And there wasn't a dried fruit or nut in sight.

I started snacking on it, which I am wont to do whenever I see something like nuts, seeds, or granola cooling on a baking sheet. What I loved about this one and why I kept returning to that baking sheet for more, was that it was lighter and crunchier than any granola I'd seen or tasted. I must have eaten half a dozen servings straight off the tray.

Thankfully, the chef was kind enough to share his recipe with me. He starts with the usual suspects of rolled oats, butter, and brown sugar, but from there he goes rogue. He leaves the typical dried fruits and nuts behind and instead adds crunchy seeds and a variety of packaged cereals, which give the granola a light, airy feel. The result is a very delicate, and I must say, addictive granola. I like to serve little bowls of this for guests to munch on after dinner, like the dessert version of a bowl of salty cashews or chips. Of course, if you're more of a think-inside-the-box person, you could also serve it with yogurt or milk for breakfast.

When Liz was working on this recipe for the book, she tested it about a thousand times. She said it was because her boyfriend requested it, but for several weeks, Liz could be seen walking around the Mozza kitchens with a baggie of granola in her pocket, eating it all day long, which is how the recipe got its name.

Because of the old-school California vibe of granola, this granola is great alongside egg pies (pages 131 to 135), or Garlic-Rubbed Skirt Steak with Scallion Vinaigrette (page 194).

———————

Adjust an oven rack to the middle position and preheat the oven to 350°F. Line a large baking sheet or two smaller baking sheets with parchment paper. Spray the parchment lightly with nonstick cooking spray and set aside.

Put the butter and honey in a small saucepan over low heat. Using a small sharp knife split the vanilla bean lengthwise. Use the back of the knife to scrape out the pulp and seeds and add the scrapings and the bean to the saucepan. Cook to melt the butter and honey and to infuse them with the flavor of the vanilla bean for about 10 minutes. Turn off the heat and let the mixture cool slightly; you want the mixture to be liquid and pourable. Remove and discard the vanilla bean and stir in the vanilla extract.

Meanwhile, combine the oats, cornflakes, puffed rice, hemp seeds, flaxseeds, sunflower seeds, poppy seeds, brown sugar, cinnamon, salt, and nutmeg in a large bowl. Stir to combine the ingredients. Drizzle the butter and honey mixture over the cereal mixture and stir with a rubber spatula to coat the cereal.

Spread the granola mixture onto the prepared baking sheet or sheets in a thin, lacy layer; if the granola is too crowded, it won't brown and crisp up, and if there is too much space between the pieces, the granola will burn.

Bake the granola for 30 minutes without touching it. Stir the granola with a spoon or heat-proof rubber spatula and rotate the pans from front to back. Bake for another 40 minutes, until the entire tray of granola is an even shade of golden brown, stirring the granola from the edges inward and rotating the pan every 10 minutes so the granola browns evenly. Remove the granola from the oven and set it aside to cool to room temperature.

To serve, break the granola into large pieces and serve, or store, covered, at room temperature for up to 1 week. To serve, put the granola in pretty bowls as a dessert snack.

Deconstructed Stone Fruit Crisp with Sbrisolona and Mascarpone Cream

SERVES 6 TO 8

FOR THE SBRISOLONA

½ pound (about 1½ cups) whole almonds, with skins

12 ounces (3 sticks) unsalted butter

¼ cup plus 2 tablespoons granulated sugar

¾ cup confectioners' sugar

1¾ cup unbleached all-purpose flour

1¼ cups semolina flour

1 teaspoon kosher salt

2 extra-large egg yolks

3 tablespoons orange flower water

FOR THE MASCARPONE CREAM

¼ cup granulated sugar

4 extra-large egg yolks

4 cups mascarpone

2 tablespoons pure vanilla extract

FOR THE FRUIT

½ cup granulated sugar

2 tablespoons honey (preferably wildflower or another mild-flavored honey)

I love summer fruit desserts such as cobblers and crumbles, but because those are not remotely Italian, I couldn't justify putting such desserts on the menus at Mozza. But Dahlia Narvaez, my longtime pastry chef, found a way around that by using crumbled *sbrisolona*, a crunchy Italian cake made with almonds and scented with orange flower water as a crisp topping, thus Italianizing it. The resulting dessert is essentially a deconstructed fruit crisp. We stew the fruit in the oven, which makes a beautiful presentation on your buffet table. Put the sbrisolona and mascarpone cream on the side for people to construct their own crisps. It's the closest I'll ever get to a build-your-own sundae. Make this only if you have good, ripe, seasonal fruit, ideally from a farmers' market or a friend's backyard. If you use poor-quality or out-of-season fruit, you'll be disappointed in the results because the dessert is so simple, there is nothing for the fruit to hide behind. This recipe makes more sbrisolona than you need. Leftovers will keep, covered, at room temperature for up to three days, or bake off half of the crumbs and keep the other half in the freezer for up to several months.

This recipe calls for four types of stone fruit and three types of berries. If you can't find one or more of the fruits called for, just use the equivalent of another fruit so that the total number of stone fruits remains the same and the total amount of berries remains the same.

I like to serve the fruit in the pan I roast it in. If you want to serve it this way, reach for something you wouldn't mind putting out on your buffet. Alternatively, transfer the cooked fruit to a platter to serve.

Since this is without a doubt a summertime-only dessert, serve it to follow an outdoor meal, such as The Ultimate Hamburger (page 146), Garlic-Rubbed Skirt Steak with Scallion Vinaigrette (page 194), Umbrian Tavola (page 18), Niçoise Deconstructed: Olive Oil–Poached Albacore (page 69), Grilled Lamb Shoulder Chops with Mint Yogurt Sauce (page 104), Backyard Peel 'n' Eat Shrimp Boil (page 258), Lamb and Chicken Tikka Kebabs (page 270), and Southern-Style Korean Cut Short Ribs with Vinegar Onions (page 325).

To make the sbrisolona, adjust the oven racks so one is in the top third and one is in the bottom third, and preheat the oven to 325°F.

Spread the almonds on a baking sheet and toast them on the upper rack of the oven for 12 to 15 minutes, until they are fragrant and golden brown, shaking the baking sheet and rotating it from front to back halfway through the cooking time so the nuts brown evenly. Remove the almonds from the oven and increase the oven temperature to 350°F. Let the almonds cool to room temperature. Coarsely chop half of the almonds and leave the others whole. Set aside separately.

Warm the butter in a small saucepan over medium-high heat until it boils with large, loud, rapidly bursting bubbles. Reduce the heat to medium and continue cooking for another 5 to 7 minutes, without letting it brown, until the butter becomes foamy and the bubbles are fewer and quieter. Remove from the heat and transfer to a bowl to cool. Skim the foam off the top and measure out 1 cup of the clarified butter, leaving the milk solids at the bottom of the bowl. Discard the milk solids and refrigerate the excess clarified butter for another use.

Combine the whole almonds and granulated sugar in the bowl of a food processor fitted with a metal blade and pulse until the almonds are a sandy or mealy consistency but not ground to a paste. Transfer the contents of the food processor to a large mixing bowl. Add the confectioners' sugar, all-purpose flour, semolina flour, and salt to the bowl and toss with your hands to combine. Combine the egg yolk with the orange flower water. Create a well in the dry ingredients and pour the egg mixture and the clarified butter into the well. Scatter the almonds around the well. Work the dough together with your hands. Pick up the dough in handfuls and crumble it into streusel-like clumps on two baking sheets.

Bake for about 25 minutes, until the clumps are golden brown and crunchy and completely cooked, shaking the pan or stirring the clumps occasionally and rotating the baking sheets from front to back and from the upper to lower racks for even browning. Remove the baking sheet from the oven and set aside to cool to room temperature.

To make the mascarpone cream, combine the granulated sugar with ¼ cup water in a small saucepan over high heat. Bring the water to a boil and continue to boil until the sugar dissolves.

Set a stainless steel bowl over a pot of water. The bowl must be larger than the pot so that no steam gets into the bowl. Make sure the water does not touch the bowl. Remove the bowl. Bring the water to a simmer over medium heat. Reduce the heat to medium-low.

While the water is coming to a simmer, whisk the egg yolks in the bowl you chose to fit over the pot. Drizzle the hot simple syrup into the bowl, whisking

1 vanilla bean

3 peaches, halved, pits removed and discarded, and cut into quarters

3 nectarines, halved, pits removed and discarded, and cut into quarters

3 plums, halved, pits removed and discarded

3 apricots, halved, pits removed and discarded

½ cup blueberries

½ cup raspberries

½ cup blackberries

constantly to combine. Place the bowl over the pot of simmering water and cook, whisking constantly and scraping down the sides of the bowl frequently, until the eggs are pale yellow and thick enough to form a ribbon when you pass a whisk through them, about 5 minutes. Remove the eggs from the heat and whisk them for about 30 seconds; the eggs will keep cooking even when they're off the heat, so you whisk to prevent them from scrambling.

Transfer the eggs to the bowl of a standing mixer fitted with the whisk attachment and beat on medium speed until they cool to room temperature, about 2 minutes. Turn off the mixer, add the mascarpone, and beat on low speed to incorporate, stopping to wipe down the sides of the bowl occasionally. Increase the mixer speed to high and beat until the mascarpone cream is thick and mousselike, 1 to 2 minutes. Add the vanilla and beat to just incorporate. Use or refrigerate, covered, for up to 2 days.

To prepare the fruit, combine the granulated sugar, honey, and ¼ cup water in a small saucepan. Use a sharp paring knife to split the vanilla bean in half lengthwise. Scrape the pulp and seeds out of the bean with the back of the knife and add the scrapings and the bean to the saucepan. Place the saucepan over high heat and bring to a boil.

Lay the peaches, nectarines, plums, and apricots, cut side down, in a single layer in a large baking dish and pour the honey mixture over the fruit. Put the fruit in the oven for 10 minutes. Remove the dish from the oven and carefully turn each piece of fruit with tongs or a spatula. Return the fruit to the oven for 10 minutes, until it is spoon soft and the liquid is slightly syrupy. Remove the dish from the oven and sprinkle the blueberries, raspberries, and blackberries around the stone fruit. Return the dish to the oven for 5 minutes, or until the berries soften but still hold their shape. Remove the dish from the oven and set aside to cool slightly.

To serve, put the sbrisolona crumbs in a medium bowl and the mascarpone cream in a separate medium bowl. Serve the fruit in the dish you cooked it in or transfer it, including the sauce and vanilla bean, to a medium platter. Serve each component with a spoon and place a stack of bowls beside them so guests can build their own fruit crisps.

Robert Abele's White Chocolate Birthday Crunch

I am not a fan of white chocolate, so I was surprised at how much I liked the little white chocolate turndown candy that I found on my pillow at the Ace Hotel in Portland, Oregon. I recognized the treat as a version of a *rocher*, a traditional French white chocolate and slivered almond confection: the version at the Ace was laced with almonds and sunflower seeds, among other things. It was really crispy and delicate, and unexpectedly pleasing. The next day I saw the same little candies in the case of a bakery I was visiting. I asked if the bakery delivered to the Ace Hotel and they did. Seeing them in the case, I thought, "What a perfect little after-dinner treat." So I decided to make them myself, in large pieces that I or my guests would break up in a random way. I gave the project of developing such a treat to Sean Panzer, one of our former pastry cooks at Mozza, using different combinations of nuts, seeds, and other crunchy ingredients. The final recipe includes almonds, salty sunflower seeds, dried currants, and just a touch of anise. The "secret ingredient," if there is one, is *feuilletine*, which are half-bite-size flakes of very delicate French "cookies," used for baking; they are what gives this candy its characteristic crunch. I buy *feuilletine* at Surfas, a well-stocked cooking supply store in Los Angeles. I was convinced that there was no substitute until one day Sean and I looked at a handful of them and said in unison, "Cornflakes!" Indeed, cornflakes, crushed ever-so-slightly in your fists, are the perfect substitute if you can't find *feuilletine*.

Once Sean perfected these candies, I brought some to a dinner for my friend Robert Abele's birthday. After dinner, I put a platter that contained fairly large pieces of this "crunch" in the center of the table and let the guests pick away at it. Everyone loved the flavor and the experience of it, and the next day, Robert's wife, my friend Margy Rochlin, asked me for the recipe. Margy is a lifelong friend. (Our fathers were best friends before Margy and I were born.) Margy is mentioned in many, maybe all, of my books, including this one, but she has never had a recipe named for her. She reminded me of that when I gave this crunch its name. As much as she loves the crunch, I think she's a bit envious of my new name for it. Sorry, Margy, but the fact of the matter is, it wasn't your birthday!

I am a fan of the roasted, salted sunflower seeds they sell at Trader Joe's because they are both roasted and salted to perfection. If you don't have access

SERVES 10 TO 12

4 ounces slivered blanched, skinless almonds (about 1 cup)

4 ounces raw or roasted and salted shelled sunflower seeds (about ¾ cup)

1 teaspoon olive oil (if you are using raw sunflower seeds)

½ teaspoon kosher salt (if you are using raw sunflower seeds)

1 teaspoon aniseeds

2 ounces *feuilletine* (or organic preservative-free, unsweetened cornflakes), crushed with your fists (about 2 cups)

½ ounce (1 tablespoon) dried currants (or chopped black raisins)

6 ounces white chocolate

Confectioners' sugar for dusting

to those, start with raw sunflower seeds and roast and salt them according to the directions in this recipe.

Because of the French inspiration of these, I like to serve them after a lunch or dinner of Niçoise Deconstructed: Olive Oil–Poached Albacore (page 69). Serve it in big shards as a communal dessert in the center of the table of a sit-down dinner, or break it up into pieces, stack them on a platter, and put the platter on a buffet.

––––––––

Adjust an oven rack to the middle position and preheat the oven to 325°F. Line a large baking sheet or two smaller baking sheets with parchment paper.

Spread the almonds on a separate baking sheet and toast them in the oven for 12 to 15 minutes, until they are fragrant and golden brown, shaking the baking sheet and rotating it from front to back halfway through the cooking time so the nuts brown evenly. Remove the nuts from the oven and transfer them to a large bowl.

If you are using raw sunflower seeds, put them on a baking sheet and toast in the oven for 5 to 6 minutes, until they are fragrant and golden brown, shaking the baking sheet and rotating it from front to back halfway through the cooking time so the seeds brown evenly. Remove the seeds from the oven and set aside to cool to room temperature. Drizzle the seeds with the olive oil, sprinkle with the salt, and toss to coat the seeds.

Add the toasted sunflower seeds (whether you toasted them yourself or started with toasted seeds) to the bowl with the almonds.

Put the aniseeds in a small sauté pan and toast them over medium heat for 1 to 2 minutes, until the seeds are fragrant and golden brown, shaking the pan often so the seeds don't burn. Transfer the seeds to a plate to cool to room temperature.

Add the aniseeds, *feuilletine,* and currants to the bowl with the almonds and sunflower seeds and stir to combine.

Fill the bottom of a double boiler with water or set a metal bowl over a pot of water; the bowl must be larger than the pot so that no steam gets into the bowl. In either case make sure the water does not touch the bottom of the top vessel. Bring the water to a simmer over medium heat. Reduce the heat to medium-low so the water is simmering as gently as possible. Put the white chocolate in the top of the double boiler or the bowl to melt the white chocolate, scraping down the sides of the pot or bowl with a rubber spatula as the white chocolate melts. (White chocolate burns very easily so you want to make sure the water is simmering very gently.) Take the white chocolate off the simmering water and add it to the bowl with the nuts and seeds, or vice versa, if you melted the white chocolate in a large enough bowl. Stir with a rubber spatula to coat all the crunchy bits.

Dump the white chocolate mixture onto the prepared baking sheet or sheets and use your fingers to crumble and spread it out to the edges of the pan(s) so the mixture looks lacy, with bits of space between the crunchy ingredients.

Put the baking sheet(s) in the refrigerator until the white chocolate hardens, at least 30 minutes; the time will depend on how cold your refrigerator is. Remove the baking sheet(s) from the refrigerator and dust the "lace" lightly with confectioners' sugar.

To serve, break the lace into large sheets and transfer the sheets to a platter for guests to break off pieces for themselves.

Spiced Caramel Corn with Salty Peanuts

SERVES 8 TO 10
MAKES ABOUT 10 CUPS

1 cup Spanish peanuts, with skins

¼ cup peanut or canola oil
(or another neutral-flavored oil)

1 tablespoon plus 1½ teaspoons
kosher salt

⅓ cup unpopped popcorn kernels

2 cups sugar

2 tablespoons light corn syrup

¾ teaspoon ground cinnamon

1½ teaspoons freshly grated
nutmeg

⅛ teaspoon ground cloves

¼ teaspoon ground cardamom

1 vanilla bean

Think of these as homemade Cracker Jack, kicked up a bunch of notches with homemade caramel and super-salty peanuts. I am as guilty as can be of trying to make "upgraded" homemade versions of my packaged favorites, such as Oreos and Nutter Butters. As much as I loved the challenge, I was never quite sure if I loved the "gourmet" version better, or just felt better about eating it, knowing it was made with good ingredients and no preservatives. But this upscale version of the ball game snack is another story. Coated in a delicious, vanilla-and-spice-laced caramel and loaded with peanuts, you don't need to "guess what's inside"! It *is* the prize.

A version of this recipe is in my book *Pastries from the La Brea Bakery*. I decided to resurrect it here because it is such a crowd-pleaser. I like to set out a big bowlful along with small paper bags for guests to fill up and eat out of after a fun, casual meal, whether it's on movie night or at a pool party. I especially like it on occasions when I serve The Ultimate Hamburger (page 146), Garlic-Rubbed Skirt Steak with Scallion Vinaigrette (page 194), Dean Fearing's Frito Pie (page 210), and the Backyard Peel 'n' Eat Shrimp Boil (page 258). If you want to serve the popcorn in paper bags, you will need 8 to 10 small paper bags for serving this. Roll the bags so they are about 5 inches tall.

Adjust an oven rack to the middle position and preheat the oven to 325°F. Line a large baking sheet or two smaller baking sheets with parchment paper.

To toast the peanuts, put the peanuts in a medium bowl. Drizzle with 2 tablespoons of the oil, sprinkle with 1 tablespoon of the salt, and toss to coat the peanuts. Spread the peanuts in an even layer on a separate baking sheet and toast them in the oven until they are dark mahogany in color, 18 to 30 minutes, shaking the pan and rotating it from front to back halfway through the cooking time so the nuts brown evenly (the time varies greatly depending on the peanuts). Remove the peanuts from the oven and set aside to cool to room temperature.

Heat the remaining 2 tablespoons oil in a large deep heavy pot with a lid (preferably a pot with a light-colored bottom) over medium-high heat until it slides easily in the pot and the oil around the edges of the pot begins to smoke, 2 to 3 minutes. Add the popcorn and partially cover the pot with the lid. When you hear the first kernel pop, put the lid on to close the pot completely. Cook the popcorn, shaking the pan vigorously, until the popping slows from a constant *pop-pop-pop* to an occasional *pop*. Turn off the heat and continue shaking the pot to pop the last remaining kernels. Transfer the popcorn to a very large bowl. Wipe out the pot with a paper towel.

Line two baking sheets with a sheet of parchment paper.

Combine the sugar, corn syrup, and ¼ cup water in the pot you cooked the popcorn in. Stir in the cinnamon, nutmeg, cloves, cardamom, and the remaining 1½ teaspoons salt. Use a small paring knife to split the vanilla bean lengthwise. Use the back of the knife to scrape out the pulp and seeds and add the scrapings and the bean to the saucepan. Put the pot over medium-high heat and bring the mixture to a boil, without stirring. Dip a pastry brush in water and brush down the sides of the pot to clean off the sugar crystals that will form there as the sugar boils. Reduce the heat to low and continue cooking, swirling the pot and brushing down the sides, but not stirring, until the mixture just begins to smoke and is a deep brown caramel color, 4 to 5 minutes.

Add the popcorn and peanuts to the pot with the caramel and use a rubber spatula to coat the popcorn and peanuts with the caramel. Cook over medium heat until the caramel darkens to a deep mahogany color, about 5 minutes. Spread the popcorn out onto the parchment-lined baking sheets, dividing it evenly, and cool to room temperature. Remove and discard the vanilla bean.

To serve, scoop the popcorn into bags for each guest or pair of guests to take a bag for themselves. Alternatively, serve the caramel corn in an enormous bowl with a big scoop and the paper bags on the side for guests to fill themselves.

Chai Chocolate Chip Cookies

1 cup pecan (or walnut) halves
(about 3½ ounces)

1¾ cups plus 2 tablespoons cake
flour (or unbleached all-purpose
flour; 8½ ounces)

1⅔ cups plus 2 tablespoons bread
flour (or unbleached all-purpose
flour; 8½ ounces)

10 ounces (2½ sticks) unsalted
butter, softened at room
temperature

1¼ cups packed light brown sugar

1 cup plus 2 tablespoons granulated
sugar

1¼ teaspoons baking soda

1½ teaspoons baking powder

1½ teaspoons kosher salt

1 tablespoon ground cinnamon

1½ teaspoons ground cardamom

1½ whole nutmegs
(about 1½ tablespoons grated)

½ teaspoon freshly ground black
pepper

2 extra-large eggs

1 tablespoon plus 1 teaspoon pure
vanilla extract

1¼ pounds chocolate (preferably
60% to 70% cacao), roughly
chopped into ½- to ¾-inch chunks

For me, putting together a cookbook is a true collaborative process. For the year plus that I worked on this book, I worked with Liz and Carolynn to create a balance of dishes and meals, and to develop the recipes themselves that would add up to the book I wanted to present. Carolynn is a stickler for authenticity, and she wouldn't stop prodding me about including a chocolate chip cookie recipe in the book. "It's the dessert your guests are most likely to find when you entertain at home," she insisted. She was right. But I feel passionately that the recipes I include in my cookbooks offer combinations of ingredients or a way of doing things that readers haven't seen anywhere else, and I didn't have that to offer in a chocolate chip cookie.

The best chocolate chip cookie recipe in the world, I was convinced, is one by the pastry chef Jacques Torres. His recipe, which was first published in *The New York Times* about eight years ago, changed the chocolate chip cookie landscape, and raised the bar on chocolate chip cookies forever. In the years since it was published, it has been republished, blogged about, and copied more than any other recipe I can think of (other than maybe the Cronut). Bakeries across America use Jacques's base as a base to which they may (or may not) add their own twists, but twists or not, I can always tell a Jacques Torres cookie when I see or taste one.

His cookie is everything I want a chocolate chip cookie to be: moist and tender, with a beautiful cracked top that comes from a well-made rise-and-fall cookie, and loads of really dark, quality chocolate.

Those chocolate chip cookies became as much a part of my entertaining repertoire as red wine and Fett'unta (page 274). Wanting to include a chocolate chip cookie recipe in the book, but not wanting to steal Jacques's recipe verbatim, I tinkered with various elements. I browned the butter I used in the cookies. I played with the amounts and ratios of brown and white sugars. I added an egg yolk. I added oatmeal and seeds. But try as I did, none of these variations was as good as Jacques's cookie.

Despite Carolynn's disapproval, we were sending in the manuscript, sans chocolate chip cookie recipe, when I caught the tail end of a radio show in which they were discussing what was supposedly the best chocolate chip cookie in the world, from a café in Brooklyn called the Beaner Bar. My daughter, Vanessa, lived in Brooklyn, and knowing that she was coming out to L.A.

in a few days, I asked her to bring me one of these cookies. She did. I tasted it. The texture was similar to Jacques's cookies, and the flavor was redolent of cardamom and cayenne. With that, a lightbulb went off in my head. I decided, at the eleventh and a half hour, to try my hand at chocolate chip cookies one more time, this time playing with spices.

I gave the weighty challenge of improving upon the great Jacques Torres chocolate chip cookie to Sean Panzer, who worked in the Mozza pastry kitchen and had been helping me with dessert recipes throughout the process of writing the book. "Think chai spices," I told him. I threw out ideas for different combinations of spices and nuts that he might use. And—in an unprecedented move—I suggested he even try milk chocolate, which would mirror the milk in chai tea. After days of work and countless batches of cookies, Sean nailed it. He created a truly great, perfectly spiced chocolate chip cookie. Is it better than Jacques Torres's cookie? It's a different cookie experience. But in my humble opinion, it's every bit as good. (After all, it's still his base.) And that's saying a lot.

The cookies are best if the dough rests for twenty-four hours. This makes the recipe ideal for entertaining, because you can make the dough ahead of time and bake the cookies off a few hours before you want them.

I serve chocolate chip cookies more than any other dessert; there is not a single meal that these wouldn't be great with, and I wouldn't think of serving The Ultimate Hamburger (page 146) without them. After all, it's the ultimate American cookie.

––––––––––

Adjust an oven rack to the middle position and preheat the oven to 325°F. Set up a cooling rack.

Spread the pecans on a baking sheet and toast them in the oven for 10 to 12 minutes, until they're lightly browned and fragrant, shaking the baking sheet and rotating it from front to back halfway through the cooking time so the nuts brown evenly. Remove the pecans from the oven and turn off the oven. Set the nuts aside until they're cool enough to touch. Coarsely chop the nuts and set aside.

Combine the cake flour and bread flour in a large bowl and stir to combine.

Combine the butter, brown sugar, granulated sugar, baking soda, baking powder, salt, cinnamon, cardamom, nutmeg, and pepper in the bowl of a standing mixer fitted with the paddle attachment and cream at medium-high speed until the mixture is light in texture and color, about 5 minutes. Add the eggs, one at a time, mixing on medium speed until the egg is incorporated into the dough before adding the next egg. Add the vanilla and mix just to incorporate it. Reduce the speed to low. Add the flour mixture and mix until no flour is visible. Remove the bowl from the stand. Add the chocolate and pecans and mix to combine.

Cover and refrigerate the dough for at least 1 hour to chill it, or preferably overnight.

Adjust the oven racks so one is in the top third of the oven and one is in the bottom third and preheat the oven to 350°F. Set up two cooling racks.

Remove the dough from the refrigerator and roll it into 1¾-ounce balls (each will be a bit smaller than a Ping-Pong ball). Put 6 to 8 balls on each large baking sheet with at least 2 inches between each ball of dough. Put the remaining dough balls in the refrigerator until you are ready to bake them or for up to 2 days.

Put one baking sheet on each rack in the oven and bake the cookies for 12 to 14 minutes, until they are light golden, but still soft, and not wet looking in the middle, rotating the baking sheets between the upper and lower racks and from front to back halfway through the baking time so the cookies bake evenly. Remove the baking sheets from the oven and set them on the cooling racks to cool for about 5 minutes. Remove the cookies from the baking sheets and put them directly onto the cooling racks to cool completely. Repeat, baking the remaining dough in the same way.

To serve, stack the cookies no more than two high on a flat platter or cake stand.

Acknowledgments

This book could have been written without Carolynn Carreño. It wouldn't have been very good, but, it could have been done. From the tedious task of the actual writing of recipes to her talent of taking my thoughts and putting them on the page, Carolynn did a superb job. I've done three books with her and this is the first time we didn't have a yelling match. She's finally learning, when it comes to my cookbooks, I am always right.

For a week in the summer of 2015, I had two houseguests who could not have been more pleasant: photographer Christopher Hirsheimer and stylist Melissa Hamilton. I had long admired their work from the pages of *Saveur* magazine and The Canal House Cooking series of books and sought them out. They more than lived up to my lofty expectations.

Agent Janis Donnaud, the tough negotiator in my corner, came through again with her sharp ideas and a clear vision for this book. My editors, Peter Gethers and Christina Malach, helped clarify some text and caught the many mistakes in the drafts, which I think I'll blame on Carolynn. When Christina moved on to another career, Jenna Brickley stepped in seamlessly.

The book designers Kristen Bearse and Cassandra Pappas and jacket designers Abby Weintraub and Carol Devine Carson came through in outstanding fashion and I would gladly work with them again.

Now, a cook book is nothing without recipes testers, and I had a superb crew starting with Abigail Wolfe and Marcella Capasso, whose meticulous execution was vital.

Another team player who helped test a few recipes—including the already storied biscuits—was Ruth Reichl, an up-and-coming food writer who, if she sticks with it, has a promising future in this crazy business.

From the Mozza dugout, I wrangled several key players to help develop and test recipes. Among them were Dahlia Narvaez, Salvador Jaramillo, Tiffany Fox, Raul Ramirez, Ryan DeNicola, Chad Colby, Matt Molina, Carrie Whealy, Sean Panzer, and Hourie Sahakian; outside the box, my daughter, Vanessa.

My assistant, Kate Green—when not on Facebook or Instagram—was very helpful as the keeper of all things "techno" and arranging back-and-forth manu-script shipping.

Mozza's own personal Delta Force operator, Michael Krikorian, was great at keeping the madness away while this book marched forward.

Finally, last and probably not least, Elizabeth Hong, the laser-focused executive chef of Osteria Mozza, was truly instrumental in the creation of this book. She worked tirelessly—without complaint—countless hours in helping me develop the recipes, seeing them from conception to final photography. Thanks, Liz.

Index

pea(s):
   Fava, and Mint Salad with Fresh
      Pecorino, 143
   Spring Gem Salad with Soft Herbs and
      Labneh Toasts, 123–5
peaches, in Deconstructed Stone Fruit
      Crisp with Sbrisolona and Mascarpone
      Cream, 386–8
Peanuts, Salty, Spiced Caramel Corn with,
      392–3
pecans:
   Chai Chocolate Chip Cookies, 394–6
   Mexican Wedding Cookies, 362–4
pecorino, fresh:
   Fava, Pea, and Mint Salad with, 143
   Marinated Olives and, 95
peppers:
   Italian, Marinated Pickled, with
      Anchovies and Olives, 75–7
   Italian or Mexican, Charred, 62, 63
   red, in Muhammara, 281–3
   Sweet, Marinated Roasted, 24–5, 32
   see also chile(s)
Pesto, Celery Leaf, 34–5
Petit Trois, Los Angeles, 260
pickle(d)(s):
   Carrots, 331, 333
   Cucumber, Spicy, 159
   Green Beans, Husk-Style, 331, 332
   Italian Peppers, Marinated, 76–7
   Jalapeño Peppers, 319
   Mustard Seed Mayonnaise, 85, 153
   Mustard Seeds, 83
   Peppers, Spicy, 94
   Shallots, 331, 334–5, 335
   Vegetables, 330–5, 331
picnic food:
   Brunettes, Amy's, 377–8
   Farro Salad with Fresh Herbs and Feta,
      116–17
   Green Potato Leek Salad with Scallion
      Vinaigrette, 263–5, 264
   Marinated Summer Squash Salad,
      110–12, 111
   see also egg pies (quiches or torta rustica)

pie(s):
   Chess, 375–6
   Crust, 375–6
   Shell, All-Butter Par-Baked, 132–3
   see also egg pies (quiches or torta rustica)
The Pikey, Los Angeles, 203
Pimento Cheese with Celery Sticks, 328–9
pine nuts:
   Brunettes, Amy's, 377–8
   Olive Oil Cake with Rosemary and,
      Dario's, 358, 359–61
pinto beans, in Chris Feldmeier's Santa
      Maria–Style Beans, 200–1
Pinzimonio, Ella's, 19, 20–1
platters, 14
plums, in Deconstructed Stone Fruit Crisp
      with Sbrisolona and Mascarpone
      Cream, 386–8
Polenta Cake with Brutti Ma Buoni
      Topping, 351–2, 353
polvorónes (Mexican Wedding Cookies),
      362–4
pomegranate molasses, in Muhammara,
      281–3
popcorn:
   Panicale, 292–3
   Pastrami, 294
   Spiced Caramel, with Salty Peanuts,
      392–3
pork:
   Shoulder, Roasted, Sal's, 46, 48–9
   Stew, Spicy, with Butternut Squash and
      Roasted Tomatillo Salsa, 310–14
   see also bacon; ham
potato(es):
   chips, favorite supermarket brands, 155
   Chips with Atomic Horseradish Cream,
      155
   Egg Pie with Bacon, Caramelized Onion
      and, 128, 131–3
   Leek Salad, Green, with Scallion
      Vinaigrette, 263–5, 264
   Salad, Erik Black's, 340
   Twice-Roasted Smashed, with Rosemary
      and Sage, 97–8

presenting food, 13–15
Pressman, Amy, 377
Prosciutto Mozzarella Parcels, 253
puddings:
   Croissant Bread, with Creamed Spinach
      and Ham, 138–9
   Dark Chocolate, 379
puffed rice cereal, in Liz's Bird Food,
      384–5
Pumpkin Seeds, Spiced Rice with, 315

Q

Quesadillas, 316, 317–18
quinoa, in Mixed Grain and Seed Salad,
      239–41

R

radicchio:
   Marinated Beet and, Salad with Labneh
      Cheese Balls, 278, 279–80
   Pan-Roasted, with Balsamic Vinaigrette,
      33, 38–9
   Pasta Salad with Bitter Greens,
      Parmigiano Cream, and Guanciale,
      295–9, 297
   Salad with Bacon and Egg, 254–5
radishes:
   Roasted Turnips and, with Radish
      Sprouts and Dill, 234–5
   Spring Gem Salad with Soft Herbs and
      Labneh Toasts, 123–5
Refried White Beans, 60–1
Reichl, Ruth, 341, 359
Remoulade, 262
rice:
   and Carrot Salad with Ginger Sumac
      Dressing, 176–7
   puffed, cereal, in Liz's Bird Food,
      384–5
   Spiced, with Pumpkin Seeds, 315
   Staff Meal, 58–9
   Torta di Riso, 354–7
ricotta, in Eggplant Lasagne, 248, 249–52

A Note About the Authors

NANCY SILVERTON is the co-owner of Osteria Mozza, Pizzeria Mozza, Chi Spacca, and Mozza2Go, in Los Angeles, Singapore, and Newport Beach. She is the founder of the La Brea Bakery, and is the only chef ever to be awarded both the Outstanding Chef and Outstanding Pastry Chef awards from the James Beard Foundation. She is the author of nine cookbooks, including *The Mozza Cookbook, A Twist of the Wrist, Nancy Silverton's Sandwich Book, Nancy Silverton's Pastries from the La Brea Bakery* (recipient of a 2000 *Food & Wine* Best Cookbook Award), *Nancy Silverton's Breads from the La Brea Bakery,* and *Desserts.*

CAROLYNN CARREÑO is a James Beard Award–winning journalist and the coauthor of many cookbooks, including *Meat* (with Pat LaFrieda), *The Mozza Cookbook* and *A Twist of the Wrist* (with Nancy Silverton), *Eat Me* (with Kenny Shopsin), *Fresh Every Day* and *Sara Foster's Casual Cooking* (with Sara Foster), *100 Ways to Be Pasta* (with Wanda and Giovanna Tornabene) and the upcoming *Bowls of Plenty.* She lives in New York and San Diego.

A Note on the Type

The text of this book was set in Vendetta, a font designed for Emigre by John Downer and released in 1999. While inspired by fifteenth-century Venetian old-style types, Vendetta's character derives from a synthesis of old and new ideas, blending hallmarks of Roman type design with the contemporary concerns of type design in the digital era.

Composed by North Market Street Graphics,
Lancaster, Pennsylvania

Printed and bound by Toppan Leefung Pte. Ltd.,
Hong Kong

Designed by M. Kristen Bearse and Cassandra Pappas

11/4/16